WITHDRAWN

Ritual Matters

Dynamic Dimensions in Practice

EDITORS

Christiane Brosius and **Ute Hüsken**

Routledge
Taylor & Francis Group
LONDON NEW YORK NEW DELHI

First published 2010
by Routledge
912–915 Tolstoy House, 15–17 Tolstoy Marg, New Delhi 110 001

Simultaneously published in the UK
by Routledge
2 Park Square, Milton Park, Abingdon, OX14 4RN

Routledge is an imprint of the Taylor & Francis Group, an informa business

Typeset by
Star Compugraphics Private Limited
D–156, Second Floor
Sector 7, Noida 201 301

Printed and bound in India by
Baba Barkha Nath Printers
37, MIE, Bahadurgarh, Haryana – 124507

British Library Cataloguing-in-Publication Data
A catalogue record of this book is available from the British Library

ISBN 978-0-415-55378-0

Contents

Preface ix

Change and Stability of Rituals: An Introduction 1
Christiane Brosius and Ute Hüsken

Part I. Rituals on the Move

1. Staging Ritual Heritage: How Rituals Become Theatre in Uttarakhand, India 29
Karin Polit

2. Initiation, 'Re-birth' and the Emergent Congregation: An Analysis of the Svadhyaya Movement in Western India 49
Anindita Chakrabarti

3. Transferring and Re-transferring Religious Practice: ISKCON between 'East' and 'West' 76
Frank Neubert

4. 'Marginalised Islam': The Transfer of Rural Rituals into Urban and Pluralist Contexts and the Emergence of Transnational 'Communities of Practice' 88
Robert Langer

5. Sunni Concepts of Ritual Purity in a Contemporary Diaspora Context 124
Udo Simon

6. Old Rituals for New Threats: Possession and Healing in the Cult of Śītalā 144
Fabrizio M. Ferrari

7. Transfer of Ritual in a Local Tradition: Some Observations 172
Barbara Schuler

Part II. Psychological Aspects of Ritual

8. The Uses of Ritual 201
Sudhir Kakar

9. Dynamic of Emotions and Dynamic of Rituals: Do Emotions Change Ritual Norms? 210
Angelos Chaniotis

10. Rituals of Possession 236
William Sax and Jan Weinhold

11. Regarding Ritual Motivation Matters: Agency Concealed or Revealed 253
Fletcher DuBois, Rolf Verres and Jan Weinhold

Part III. Ritual Economy Beyond the Ritual Frame

12. The Power of Ritual in Marriage: A Daughter's Wedding in North-west India 271
Tulsi Patel

13. Ritual Economy and South Indian Ritual Practice 293
Ute Hüsken and K.K.A. Venkatachari

Part IV. Media and Sensual Dimensions of Ritual Action

14. Ritual Differs: Beyond Fixity and Flexibility in South Indian Hindu Ritual 311
Saskia Kersenboom

15. 'Wedding Design' Online: Transfer and Transformation of Ritual Elements in the Context of Wedding Rituals 330
Kerstin Radde-Antweiler

16. Gender, Generation and the Public Sphere: Islamic Values and Literary Response 356
Susanne Enderwitz

17. On the Representation of Presence: The Narrative of Devnārāyaṇ as a Multimedia Performance 369
Aditya Malik

About the Editors 386
Notes on the Contributors 388
Index 396

Preface

The present volume explores issues that generate change or stability in ritual performances in a range of different cultural, social, local and historical settings. The contributors to this volume, coming from scholarly disciplines in the Humanities, such as ancient history, anthropology, performance studies, Indology, sociology or psychology, approach these dynamics from the angle of their respective disciplines. We argue that rituals are a key domain of the inquiry and analysis of central human issues such as identity, culture, heritage, media and power. Instead of perceiving them as static instruments we consider them as overtly versatile, creative and thus persistent for many forms of cultural production.

This publication continues a sequence of monographs published in the context of the Collaborative Research Centre 'Dynamics of Ritual' and is a collection of contributions from a great diversity of research areas and methods. The Collaborative Research Centre is pursuing mainly three overlapping facets of ritual dynamics in diachronic and synchronic fashion: historical dynamics, social dynamics and structural dynamics.

Historical Dynamics

It is crucial to explore ritual dynamics by examining the development of a ritual in the *longue durée*. The historical dynamics of ritual studies relates us to concepts of agency (the competence to act upon and within the world) that change over time, and to the transfer of ritual performances, segments or scripts from one historical period to another. The fact that rituals are inscribed by and reflective of human agency is strongly related to the inventive power of rituals and the invention of rituals by a host of agents of collective and individual, human and even super-human kind. The question about the creators or authors of rituals has for long been neglected and avoided, even though it seems crucial to be able to distinguish whether a ritual is performed by and for a social elite, or subversively challenges the status of a particular group or ritual specialist at a particular time. The rituals discussed in the present volume show how the stability of rituals is impacted by various agents and agencies in different historical periods. The notion of 'ritual transfer' is also extremely important for a better understanding of ritual stability and change. One must pay attention to the subtle or obvious ways in which a ritual or a ritual element is transferred, or 'translated', from one context into another. 'Transfer' refers to the fluidity of time, space, and context. In the course of such transfers, rituals usually undergo significant changes and transformations.

Social Dynamics

The social dynamics of rituals are relevant to discussions of concepts such as identity, power, hierarchy, solidarity, control and efficacy. Rituals, like other modes of human action, are performed with a certain aim. It is frequently argued that rituals are performed intentionally in the sense that there is a certain motivation of a particular social agent behind the performance. Hence ritual efficacy is a matter of great concern; not only for participants in or observers of a ritual but also for scholars of ritual dynamics. However, if we talk about a ritual's 'efficacy', we may refer to the verifiable physical, psychological or social effects of a ritual, or we speak of the postulated effects of the ritual, action. What, then, constitutes the success of a ritual, and for whom? Rituals are tools for shaping social realities and identities. By reaching a host of audiences and publics they create different, sometimes overlapping spheres of action. But they are simultaneously shaped by their social context, an often heterogeneous context, by multiperspectivity that deserves our full attention and sharpening of interdisciplinary tools of evaluation. In what way can rituals be a form and a forum of today's social practice?

Structural Dynamics

The structural dynamics are caused by the change of media, the tension between structure and event, and the phasing of rituals. Rituals are produced, disseminated and 'handed over' to us by all kinds of media technologies, domains and social agents. The chosen method for communicating rituals strongly influences ways of participating in them, their perception, the retrospective control of the rituals and, consequently, their future performances. How is the reality of ritual mediated by technologies of media, performance, or power? To what extent are classical rituals changed by new forms, what elements are marginalised, enlarged, deleted or re-positioned? Such questions dominate with regard to the structural dynamics of rituals.

Given the multifaceted fields of historical, social and structural aspects that count for the dynamics of rituals, a notion of 'stability' of rituals is highly questionable. In the present volume, these issues are pursued through interdisciplinary collaboration and exchange with scholars of especially South Asian cultural phenomena. It comprises essays presented on two occasions organised by the editors of this volume. The first occasion was the panel 'Change and Stability in Ritual' held at the 19th European Conference on Modern South Asian Studies in Leiden from 27 to 30 June 2006. The second occasion was the International Symposium on the same topic held at Max Mueller Bhawan (Goethe Institute) in New Delhi from 11 to 14 October 2006. A selection of interdisciplinary and cross-regional essays from these occasions constitutes this volume. The contributions are divided into three sections: Part I looks at 'Rituals on the Move', Part II is dedicated to an exploration of 'Psychological Aspects of Ritual', Part III deals with 'Ritual Economy Beyond the Ritual Frame', and the essays in Part IV examine 'Media and Sensual Dimensions of Ritual Actions'.

The book would have not been possible without the Collaborative Research Centre of Ritual Dynamics at Heidelberg University, and the generous support of the German Research Foundation, in particular Susanne Anschütz and Brit Redöhl. We also want to thank the Delhi branch of the Goethe-Institute, Max Mueller Bhawan, where Stefan Dreyer, Heiko Sievers and their staff were of utmost support, as was Michael Köberlein from the Delhi branch of the South Asia Institute. Last but not least we are grateful to Nic Leonhardt for her supervision of the book proceedings in the final stage, to Omita Goyal and Nilanjan Sarkar and the anonymous readers.

Christiane Brosius and Ute Hüsken, Heidelberg and Oslo, November 2009.

Change and Stability of Rituals
An Introduction

Christiane Brosius and Ute Hüsken

Ritual activity is a genuine type of human action. It can and ought to be differentiated from other forms of action: Every known culture has rituals, and ritualising seems to be a fundamental human faculty. Even if denied or rejected, ritual survives and returns through the backdoor, possibly in disguise. With societies, cultures and contexts involved in ongoing processes of change, it is inevitable that rituals change, too. In fact, considering ritual as a cultural dynamic flow, despite its specific characteristics like formality, standardisation and repetition, is one of the key challenges in the Humanities today. Ritual is not only a central element of cultural practice, but also plays a crucial role in the shaping and change of socio-cultural order, in contemporary as well as in societies of the past and all over the globe.

Until recently, the history of the study of rituals in different disciplines has predominantly reduced rituals to genuinely religious, static, repetitive and formalistic action. Reflexivity, subversion and change were not seen as adequate tools to analyse ritual text and action. The present volume is a contribution to a change in perspectives, opening up new ways of understanding this essential way of human acting, in synchronic and diachronic ways. The Introduction to this volume aims at venturing into the relatively young domain of the study of ritual dynamics. First, we will take a look at the genesis of ritual studies. Following from there, we shall explore the complex — and impossible — undertaking of trying to define 'ritual'. The Introduction will then spread out the different levels of scholarly inquiry present in this volume. By no means are the approaches towards the study of rituals in Europe, the Middle East or India imbued by the desire to present a panoramic and encyclopaedic view of the 'phenomenon' ritual. For instance, political rituals (e.g., election campaigns) are missing from the edited volume. Yet, we are convinced that the four parts of this book open a wide enough field of debate and substantial ground for further ventures into the study and the understanding of rituals by students and scholars within the Humanities. With this book, we intend to stir a discussion away from the desire to diagnose a 'pure' ritual from a 'simple' ceremony, to categorise ritual action *in toto* according to 'meaningful' and 'empty'. Instead, the aim is to encourage fine tuning, a differentiated closeness and yet critical distance of readers to what has for long been oversimplified as 'ritual'. Several of the authors also point towards the fact that in many ways we cannot pin down ritual practice to particular regional sites. Instead, rituals move and thus make us reconsider categories of 'culture', 'community' and 'identity' according to geophysical territories and boundaries. With the changes of concepts and methods in the discussion on the study of ritual dynamics, we hope to contribute substantially to a more subtle engagement with processes of change and continuity, arguing that even what is perceived as continuity is part and parcel of ongoing negotiations and contestations, between structure and practice, turning alleged entities such as religious and political, private and public, 'high' and 'low' culture into fields of a fascinating discourse.

Considering Histories of Research on Ritual

The concept and understanding of ritual is always a child of its time, and of particular perspectives and modes of thinking about the self and others. A broader use of, and a strong interest in, defining the boundaries and the fabric of 'rituals' emerged only by the end of the nineteenth century. This was also due to an intensified academic interest in religious practices rather than 'just' religious ideas and texts. While disciplines such as sociology, anthropology, or religious studies were established at this time, the founding fathers and pioneers of these subjects — e.g., William Robertson Smith (1846–94), James George Frazer (1854–1941), Arnold van Gennep (1873–1951) or Émile Durkheim (1858–1917) — at the same time were the first theoreticians of the term 'ritual'. However, until the mid-sixties of the twentieth century, the term was imbued with stereotyping connotations referring to the odd, obsolete, primitive, timeless and thus unchanging, opposed to the notions of modern, civilised and progressive. Rituals were tied to religion and, according to a secular worldview, deemed an inappropriate form of action in a civilised, 'enlightened' society. However, this reduction of ritual to 'traditional' and 'religious' societies entirely ignored the blurring of boundaries between secular and religious, between elite and vernacular domains. Ritual, in this context, has clearly been used as a means of power and discourse, excluding certain groups from accessing a 'European modernity package'. Once stamped as 'ritual', a performative action was normally not investigated any further, and in particular not with respect to its dynamics for this would have also subverted scholarly logics of that time. Museumisation was one of the consequences, that is, the fixation and isolation of lived ritual in invisible, textual 'glass boxes' packaged for display to audiences who appreciated rituals in their exotic and aesthetic appearance.

New and different attention to the study of rituals emerged in the late 1970s when 'many established rites and ceremonies were questioned in Western societies, and when new rituals started to blossom' (Kreinath et al., 2006: XIV). So far, rituals of non-Western societies had predominantly been thought to inadequately represent the experience of modernity and globalisation.[1] This view then was challenged by new perspectives on rituals as adapting to new phenomena, such as secular and political rituals (see Moore and Myerhoff 1977; the first study on secular rituals). Ritual exotism — based on rendering and thus excluding traditional societies as 'timeless other' — was now increasingly challenged by findings that underlined how much even 'classical' or 'folk' rituals were impacted by innovation and change. Furthermore, the new perspectives revealed how globalised some of the performing societies had already been at the time of their 'discovery' by white scholars. The subversive and subaltern character of rituals practised by non-elite and marginalised groups came to the fore in such studies. It was through the works of scholars such as Victor Turner, Ronald Grimes, Richard Schechner, Stanley Tambiah, Irving Goffman and others that the transformative, performative, creative, subversive, communicative or experience-orientated aspects of rituals were recognised and emphasised.[2] Despite the ongoing usefulness of his concepts, the quasi-linear movement of liminality and communitas coined by Turner has by now been replaced by an understanding of the highly ambiguous character of rites of passage, which cannot be as strongly separated from the everyday as suggested by him. Evidently, the everyday and the transcendent are intertwined and impact each other in complicated ways, on different levels. Practice, process, multi-vocality and-perspectivity as well as multi-sensuality had moved centre-stage in the 1980s and with them, concerns with social agents, discursivity and symbolic capital. This was accompanied by a growing interest in new theories and methods, agents and topics, new fields and sites of data collection and different sets of data.

An even more critical stance of rituals and ritual studies as a discursive strategy was developed in the 1990s, on the grounds of Ronald Grimes's and Irving Goffman's earlier studies. It was then that the most comprehensive ritual theories were published, e.g., the monographs of Thomas E. Lawson and Robert N. McCauley (1990), Catherine Bell (1992), Caroline Humphrey and James Laidlaw (1994) and Roy Rappaport (1999).

Since the late 1990s, and in particular with the emergence of new sub-disciplines such as religious aesthetics (Münster 2001), media anthropology (Ginsburg et al. 2002) as well as the anthropology of the senses (Howes 2005), scholars started to take a different approach towards rituals in the light of paradigmatic shifts like the 'cultural turn', the 'performative turn' or the 'visual turn'. These new paradigmatic concepts strongly underlined the importance of practice, performance, and agency within cultural production. As a consequence, rituals too, could no longer be considered as homogenous entities, untouched by other media or performances. Instead, they are now approached as fields in and through which images, people and concepts move, rituals themselves having a 'biography' (Appadurai 1986), connecting different domains of publicity, governance and religious belief. Furthermore, ritual performances are distinguished as a means of visibility for social agents who claim access to and over this visibility. By now, ritual actions are understood as enabling us to explore how the future, or the past, of a group is imagined and interpreted, and as providing the symbolic as well as the sensual means for this.

A Uniform Definition of 'Ritual'?

In their introductory statement to 'Theorizing Rituals', Kreinath, Snoek and Stausberg propose that 'the rise of rituals in the cultural and academic domains […] indicates a fundamental change in the general perception of rituals. [...] rituals are nowadays generally held to be *the* master-keys to understanding cultures, including our own' (Kreinath et al. 2007: XV). However, what exactly are we talking about when we use the term 'ritual'? Perceiving ritual activity as a genuine type of action, as we do in this volume, requires to be specific about our notion of 'ritual', especially in relation to related terms such as 'ceremony', 'event', 'festival', 'play', 'theatre', 'custom' or 'routine'. However, neither in the performers' nor in the scholars' discourse is a standardisation of the use of these terms in sight (see Michaels 2003). We even propose here that a clear-cut definition of ritual is indeed neither possible nor desirable. Like other fuzzy concepts, 'ritual' seems to escape all attempts of essentialising. The term 'ritual' is used in a variety of ways, each embedded in specific discourses set in specific times and locations, defined by specific groups of people, for different reasons and with different intentions. In order to grasp the interplay of several levels in ritual action, 'framing' is one of several useful concepts. Both Irving Goffman and Richard Schechner have used this term to emphasise the dramaturgical display of human actions with clear and recognisable 'beginning' and 'ending' in between which a form of action takes place that is of different value than the action outside of the 'frame'. In their work, framing also refers to the fact that agents involved in ritual action are competent of shifting codes outside and within a frame of ritual performance, including the conscious play with different qualities of reality. Framing thus allows social agents to demarcate separate domains of practice/action from each other (see Köpping/Rao 2000: 6; Handelman 2006b). However, the codes of frames also have to be recognised both by performers and audiences, and this is where a lot of contestation takes place, in particular, as we show in the book, when rituals are 'on the move', transferred and adjusted to new contexts, be they of social, political or media-based kinds, or all in one. Another seemingly trivial but relevant new aspect of the study of ritual in this volume is the recognition of emic perspectives. The term 'ritual' is rather recent, but the phenomena covered by it are not. In the case of India what is called 'ritual' in English, is called by various other Sanskrit terms, such as *karma* or *kriyā* (action, domestic rituals), *sāṃskāra* (life-cycle rituals), *homa, yajña, yāga, iṣṭi* or *bali* (sacrifice), *utsava* (festival), *tīrthayātrā* (pilgrimage), *pūjā* or *sevā* (worship, service), *vrata* (vow), *yoga, dhyāna* (meditation) or *vīrya* (heroic deeds). Indian languages — like other languages — do not have a generic term for all these modes of action (see Kreinath et al. 2007: 37–50).

It is therefore tempting to deconstruct or even reject the term 'ritual' entirely. Jack Goody, for instance, objects to the use of 'ritual' in his much-quoted article 'Against Ritual: Loosely structured thoughts on a loosely defined topic' (1977), but does not offer an alternative. Don Handelman (1998) also opposes the inflationary, contradictory and monothetical use of 'ritual' and proposes the alternative term 'public events'. Both Bell (1992) and Humphrey and Laidlaw (1994) focus attention on individual social agents and groups. To them, ritual behaviour and ritualisation (the transformation of the everyday to ritual in Bell's terminology) implies that the action's quality differs from everyday behaviour. The agent succumbs to another order in which intentionality may remain but the agency is given up in favour of the ritualised act.

While some disciplines in the Humanities seem to have less trouble than others to define ritual, ethnographic empiricism of anthropology for instance, makes any such undertaking and comparison very difficult: 'Each ethnographic instance of "ritual" has validity in and of itself', writes Handelman (2006a: 37). Handelman even goes as far as to claim that 'there is no such phenomenon as RITUAL' (ibid.: 38), and that 'there is no meta-category of RITUAL' (ibid.: 39).[1] Rituals are what Jan Snoek has coined 'polythetic classes', that is, possessing 'a large but unspecific number of a set of characteristics' owned by a variety of members (Snoek 2006: 4–5). To conclude this section: we do not reject the importance of defining the concepts through which we aim to get a better insight into the human condition. But we argue that the possibility to capture something like 'ritual' at a glance must be rendered obsolete. The glance is multiplied, multi-facetted and caleidoscopic. Our sharpened tools, partly presented in this volume, ensure that we do not get lost in it.

About the Volume

The diverse contributions to this volume use the ambivalence of the term 'ritual' as a heuristic tool that enables them to remain aware of the ongoing negotiations and contestations within individual cases and for the general patterns of ritual action, capturing the ways in which rituals imbue and represent continuity and change, structure and practice. The concept of 'framing' has been elaborated above. However, diverse concepts and theoretical approaches have shaped the domain of the study of ritual besides this one: practice, aesthetics, performance, gender and relationality as well as complexity, efficacy, embodiment, formality, participation or reflexivity, to name only a few. Several of these concepts are elaborated upon in the diverse contributions to this volume.

We do not intend to explore rituals of a particular region in a comprehensive way. Instead, the essays highlight important concepts from different perspectives, in a diachronic and synchronic way. Scholars from diverse disciplines and regions, using various methodologies (from fieldwork to philology), focussing on different periods (from antiquity to modernity), and on a variety of geophysical arenas (India, Turkey, Egypt, Greece or the United States of America join in a discussion on the notion of ritual in the context of its relation to stability and change. The contributions to this volume, in their diversity of case studies and approaches, show that dynamics and change are the rule more than the exception within ritual practice, and that rituals have a remarkable transformative power (Turner 1967).

Part I: Rituals on the Move

The central recurring theme of the essays in 'Rituals on the Move' is the transfer and transformation, invention and re-invention of rituals. Even 'new' rituals have to use elements which have already appeared in other rituals. We argue that a particularly useful term to approach rituals with is that of the 'biography' or 'career' (see Appadurai 1986). This implies that a ritual must be seen in its genealogy, yet constantly progressing, through various and highly complex stages of life, thereby moving through different domains, connecting with and impacted by a host of factors and conditions. Some even argue that there exists a universal grammar (Michaels 2007) and morphology of ritual segments and action elements. These segments, like elements from a 'construction plan' (Oppitz 1999) are constantly borrowed, cited, or transferred from one ritual to another. The essays in this part of the volume draw upon various religious communities in different geographical regions. There are Muslim groups that migrated to Germany, bringing with them different notions of authenticity (Langer) and purity (Simon) which they attribute to rituals away from the homeland. Yet, a container theory of identity and thus ritual translation as happening in a neutral space would be far from adequate. The shaping of such rituals must be seen in relation to new social, economic and religious contexts of the hostland, and is often closely connected with the notion of integration — both into the dominant mainstream and the migrant subculture. Moreover, there are Hindu sects concerned with the translation and transfer of particular rituals between India and the USA, but also between 'biological' Hindus and converted or non-Hindus (Neubert), thus opening up a new discussion on ritual and identity by relating the experience of migration to that of religious conversion. Furthermore, there are particular ritual performances that migrate between a rural, more traditional and an urban, modernised milieu (Polit), and ritual performances as they shift meaning and value between a pantheon of regional deities in the course of inventing a completely new deity with similar rituals (Ferrari). It is evident that the rituals are part of a complex field of discourse, in which different social agents position themselves in relation to particular other groups, frames of meaning and status distinction. These examples highlight the dynamics of rituals by means of changing points of reference in relation to the construction of religious, cultural and civic identities. They also point towards taking seriously the ways in which a study of ritual may enable a better understanding of individual, community, network and institution.

To a large extent, the examination of ritual actions in this part of the volume is connected with the attempt of social groups to create, revitalise and affirm cultural heritage. Often, this agenda is placed in the context of migration, urbanisation, and globalisation. Rituals enable social agents to imagine historical and social continuity and rootedness while simultaneously responding to and legitimising change. Likewise, new ritual 'specialists' engage in staging rituals, new publics can be addressed and new means of performance are used to circulate and practice ritual. Anthropologist Karin Polit studies the transformation of a local ritual from a former kingdom in the Himalayas as it journeys from the marketplace in the village to a proscenium stage at a heritage festival in the region's capital.

In 'Staging Ritual Heritage: How Rituals Become Theatre in Uttarakhand, India', Polit explores a ritual performance around the trickster figure Burhdeva. She investigates how the notion of locality can be impacted by a range of interests and notions of authenticity, linking a variety of other social agents, such as families, migrant colleagues, politicians, or members of the same or another caste. The urbanised local elite, particularly, have come to emphasise ethnicity by means of cultural heritage, and ritual performance seems to be an ideal strategy to visualise status distinction, also in the context of local caste and party politics. As Polit argues, these rituals 'serve as an emblem of the new and alternative modernity of the state of Uttarakhand'. In some ways, such a ritual transformation also serves the needs of new social groups, and of horizontal groups whose members do not interact with each other on a daily and face-to-face basis, to imagine and render feasible the notion of a common heritage. In any case, the rituals help agents to strategically draw boundaries of inclusion and exclusion, often under the label of revitalising their 'lost' or 'threatened' traditions.

While Polit's focus is on a regional group that attempts to define a new sense of belonging through ritual as cultural heritage, anthropologist Anindita Chakrabarti studies rituals in the context of a particular enclosed, regional religious community in contemporary India. In her essay entitled 'Initiation, "Re-birth" and the Emergent Congregation: An Analysis of the Svadhyaya Movement in Western India', she examines this religious movement as a 'new association' at work, beyond constraints of traditional family and kinship setups in the context of modernisation and transnational migration. In this movement, she argues, the 'forming of the community' is achieved by means of weekly congregations during some of which video tapes of the spiritual leader Dadaji's speeches are circulated and consumed by followers. Consumption of these mass-reproduced media is restricted and coded. The emphasis on the moral community as site of practice and identity is crucial to understand the Svadhyāyis as an anti-ritualistic movement. Instead of performing rituals of initiation, individual membership in the community is achieved by a person's active participation, *bhaktipherī*. Therefore, Chakrabarti highlights the notion of a processual 'becoming', a 'process of initiation'. It is noteworthy that despite the proposed anti-ritualistic stance, many of the concepts on which the sect draws are appropriated from highly formalised Brahmanic ritual culture. While *bhaktipherī* can be interpreted as social spiritual work, the Svadhyāyis perceive it as a kind of temporary, inner-worldly asceticism. Underlining the dynamics of rituals in this field as constantly contested, the author concludes that the rituals of this moral community 'are not given but emergent and they operate in a field of experimentation and manipulation'. Frank Neubert, a scholar of religious studies, deals with processes of 'Transferring and Re-Transferring Religious Practice: ISKCON between "East" and "West".' He argues that the transfer processes related to the sects' rituals take place mainly on a discursive level. Diverse questions are contested in them, for instance, about what a ritual should stand for and how it can be practiced in a new context without stripping it off its efficacy and 'original meaning'. According to Neubert, these negotiations are an integral, communicative part of the transfer processes, as the rituals travel between the USA and India, between non-Indian Hindus and Indian Hindus. The author gives an account of the ISKCON founder's strategies of adapting 'Indian' rituals to the experiences and needs of his Western followers, sometimes because the disciples requested him to do so. Later on, negotiations on rituals and their proper performance took place on an even greater scale among ISKCON's members. In this process, several rituals or aspects of rituals were also newly invented, attesting to the ongoing surveillance and evaluation of rituals for particular needs. Yet another and different flow of rituals took place when predominantly white ISKCON members went to India and were not accepted by local Vaiṣṇava Brahmins, because ISKCON rituals were considered more 'authentic' when performed by 'ethnic Hindus'. Neubert concludes by coining the question of a ritual's 'identity', arguing that travel and transfer always involve adaptation and changes, and that the concrete mode of adaptation depends on the social context into which a ritual is transferred.

Travel, migration and transfer impact rituals on the move. This also becomes evident in Robert Langer's essay '"Marginalised Islam": The Transfer of Rural Rituals into Urban and Pluralist Contexts and the Emergence of Transnational "Communities of Practice"'. The scholar of Islamic studies deals with the migration of the ethnic group of the Alevis who migrated from Turkey to Germany in the late 1960s and 1970s. He examines the issues of ritual transfer and the participation of scholars therein, especially with respect to the positive effects of emigration on the self-perception and self-representation of this marginalised group. The newly acquired access to a public sphere made members and activities of this group more visible and, consequently, more self-confident — especially so, as they also came into the focus of Western media and scholarship. In this process of integrating into and negotiating a new position in a new place, the Alevis in Germany reinvented what they came to term as 'their' rituals. Langer introduces the distinction between a 'constellation of (resembling) practices' and a 'virtual community of practice', created by modern means of mobility and mediatisation. Udo Simon, a scholar of Islamic studies, discusses in 'Sunni Concepts of Ritual Purity in a Contemporary Diaspora Context', various negotiation processes involved in the reformulation of the notion of purity in rituals. The rituals examined were carried along and gained new relevance in the course of migration to Germany by groups of Muslims. Here, religious identity is generated into a resource for cultural heritage. Simon's central argument is that against the common stereotype of Islam as inflexible, the examination of purity rituals shows how much scope for negotiation and improvisation is available for the practitioners. The author traces various such transformations in different contexts. The last chapter in the section focusses on the persistence of the cult of Śītalā — the so-called smallpox goddess, worshipped mainly in Bengal. Centre-stage of Fabrizio M. Ferrari's chapter on 'Old Rituals for New Threats: Possession and Healing in the Cult of Śītalā' is the ongoing importance of the goddess in spite of the eradication of smallpox in 1977, and her ensuing additional 'responsibility' for HIV/AIDS. He does so by relating Śītalā to a recently 'invented' goddess and her cult in Karnataka, called HIV/AIDS-ammā. This is no exception, and Veena Das has examined the stunning re-invention of the goddess Santoshi Ma among middle class women by means of a film on the 'life' of the deity in the 1970s (Das 1981). In Ferrari's case study, the goddesses are interpreted as adaptations of South Asian 'plague goddesses' and as responses to new threats at the same time, even though in an entirely different manner. Ferrari contrasts a Western notion of organic dysfunction (disease) with local notions of functional dysfunction (possession). The essays in this section make clear that in a globalising world, with rapidly increasing means of transportation and communication, not only concepts and people circulate — rituals, as a subcategory of practice or quality of action, are also on the move. Tapping into James Clifford's seminal work on travel and translation (1997), the essays therefore show that it is important and revealing to trace the varied routes that rituals take, as well as the process of 'rooting' through which people tie ritual performances to particular meaningful sites and events, time and again. Rituals structure time and space, and relate them to our senses and everyday life. Thus, rituals are positioned in a space of betwixt and between, caught in a permanent paradoxical loop of temporary fixation and mobility, of structuring and being structured. Central for an exploration of ritual change and stability is the changing territorial, cultural and social reproduction of group identity, none of which can any longer be considered as homogenous entities with solid frames of reference. Instead, as evidenced in this section, rituals allow us to examine the slippages and interactions that occur when 'authenticity' of a group is sought to be given expression in a performance in contestation with another group. Barbara Schuler, in 'On the Transfer of Ritual in a Local Tradition: Some Observations', explores the design and transfer of a ritual performance for a Tamil goddess in South India from one to another context, shifting locality and social group but not tradition. She finds that the ritual's inner logic complexity changes in conspicuous agreement with each group's socio-cultural needs. Following Handelman, Schuler argues for a definition of ritual as a social field of discourse. Centre-stage of the ritual is the narrative and semiotic segment of the deity's flower-bed which is, in the course of the ritual transfer, underlined by different designs and imbued with different meaning, emic and etic, and in one case even completely eliminated. The meaning and power of the divine itself is thereby challenged and transformed. Evidently, the ritual space and performance allows for a participation of intimacy and positive emotionality, but also for acting out different gender roles and social realities.

Part II: Psychological Aspects of Ritual

Changes in the experiential dimensions of ritual can well hint towards shifts in the social and structural dynamics of ritual. The experience of ritual may be impacted by cultural and individual desires and expectations, patterns of interpretation, ritual techniques and design. The experiential and psychological dimension is crucial to many ritual actions, particularly invention and reinvention. How can we identify and analyse interpersonal and intra-personal differences and changes, diachronically and synchronically, when it comes to the experience of ritual (e.g., as efficient, inefficient, emotionally heightened or low)? Ritual action as a mode of social behaviour and personal experience is frequently explained in terms of psychology: the potential repeatability of ritual is said to give its participants a sense of security and stability in times of change. Furthermore, ritual is characterised as fundamental human need, which enables and channels emotions and thereby facilitates release or even healing, which offers a secure space for extreme or otherwise socially not approved emotions, a sounding board for various kinds of desires and fears. It seems that ritual allows for expressing desire and pleasure not accepted in 'everyday' behaviour, and effectively works on mind and consciousness. In short, this social behaviour is generally perceived as based on the human psychological condition. Four essays in this section deal with the psychological aspects involved in specific ritual action, and with their implications for the rituals' change or stability. The special value of Sudhir Kakar's partly autobiographical account 'The Uses of Ritual' is the balanced mixture of report and analysis in terms of psychology. The leading scholar of ritual studies, Ronald L. Grimes, repeatedly emphasised the importance of memories — along with text and performance — for the eventuation of rituals. We consider the scholarly, external as one of many positions taken. There is a long tradition of analysing rituals in terms of psychology, and, moreover, 'today it is remarkable how easily ritual is described in psychological terms or how matter-of-course the origin or ultimate function of ritual action is psychologically explained' (see Boudewijnse 2007: 123f.). This 'other' perspective is brought in by the psychoanalyst Kakar. He explicitly highlights the psychoanalyst's view on ritual — as an obsessive-compulsive disorder, a potential which he at least accepts as one of the dangerous sides of ritual. Especially his emphasis on the complementary functions of ritual as being protective and transformative at the same time is an important contribution to this volume and to ritual studies at large. In 'Dynamic of Emotions and Dynamic of Rituals: Do Emotions Change Ritual Norms?', ancient historian Angelos Chaniotis deals with the connection and interplay of ritual and emotions, based on ancient Greek material. He argues that norms, emotions and rituals have determined public life to a large extent. The scholar considers the general difference between ritual and emotions in that the former is more norm-driven, while identifying emotions as rather spontaneous (but nevertheless reflected) statements. Both, proposes Chaniotis, are ambivalent and frequently collide. Thus, ritual often serves as a means of establishing group identity. Simultaneously, it is a means of excluding others which can be accompanied by strong emotions on the side of the participants, be they within or outside the boundaries of membership. At times, ritual is also intentionally employed to insult people in public. Moreover, as 'emotionally laden activities' rituals often intensify already existing emotions. Chaniotis argues that 'both emotional experiences and the close observation of emotional responses to rituals were factors that could lead to the modification of preexisting rituals or even to the creation of new ones.' Through his source material, which contains ideal depictions or prescriptions rather than descriptions of actual events, the historian facilitates an innovative insight into the potential emotional backgrounds by literally reading between the text's lines. He presents several examples for specific means employed to strategically create, enhance or cover up a specific emotional atmosphere, all of which cause changes in ritual. However, some reflections on the 'cultural construction' of personal feelings are missing here — which would then 'tune in' with rituals as public events and cultural constructions again. This holds especially true for the instances of the 'prescription of emotions' during rituals which seems to be at odds with a Western notion of 'emotions as spontaneous outbreak of feelings'. In their inter-disciplinary inquiry 'Rituals of Possession', cultural anthropologist William Sax and psychologist Jan Weinhold, deal with the two explanatory frameworks of identical phenomena, labelled as 'dissociation' and 'spirit possession' respectively. The case study on which their essay is based is the North Indian healing and pilgrimage site of Balaji in Rajasthan. They observed phenomena that affect the entire body-mind system and are expressed with the body of the possessed. In their analysis, the authors therefore convincingly postulate a practice-approach to ritual (and cultural practices), which takes into account the particularity of practice in its specific social, local, and historical context. The essay by Fletcher DuBois, Rolf Verres and Jan Weinhold entitled 'Regarding Ritual Motivation Matters: Agency Concealed or Revealed' focuses on the individual and his modes of commencing upon, and maintaining, goal-oriented activity in rituals. It also addresses factors that influence those actions in order to develop a more inclusive notion of the complexities of ritual behaviour. Taking two scenarios involving adolescents in present day Germany as their examples (a ritualised setting of drug-consumption and the Christian religious ritual 'confirmation'), they ask for the motivations of the young people to participate or decline participation. In their interim conclusion they argue that the relationship between individual motives and the degree of participation is a promising research direction and should be, along with subjective experiences, more systematically included in ritual research. Looking at motivation and its role in ritual may help to move away from the over emphasis on individual processes cut off from their surroundings and cultural contexts. As the essays in this section show, the performative aspects of ritual are crucial. This emphasis shifts attention to intangible facts of cultural production and change: aesthetic dimension, the senses and emotions are taken seriously here as markers of ritual quality. In contrast to those scholars who assume the creation of consensus through and the formation of one message in ritual action (e.g., Victor Turner, Stanley Tambiah), the research presented here emphasises heterogeneous, multivalent ways of 'reading' a ritual 'message'. Transformation is not seen as a linear movement from A to B. Instead, it points towards multi-levelled changes of status, perception, reality or relation, to and fro.

Part III: Ritual Economy Beyond the Ritual Frame

Do rituals contain an open or implicit renunciation of everyday economic behaviour? Are forms of exchange (such as the gift) that are found in rituals simply another form of economising or opposed to it? The relatedness of ritual and economy is a domain that has hardly been explored so far. Especially when it comes to religious ritual, the interconnection of money and religion is often devaluated — not only in the Protestant context, but also in Indian traditions. Thus, since centuries Brahmanic temple priests face the accusation of 'serving the god for money', as a consequence of which they occupy a very low status among the diverse Brahmin subcastes. The two papers in this section on ritual economy, one by Tulsi Patel and the other by Ute Hüsken and K.K.A. Venkatachari, both raise the issue of to what extent the domain of ritual is influenced by economics, how economic conditions effect changes in the performance and perception of ritual, and in what ways ritual can be perceived as following the same logic as economics. While it has often been argued that ritual (especially sacrifice) is a 'waste' of resources, both contributions show clearly that rituals frequently involve contests for the control of 'high-status forms of property' (Harrison 1992) between actors competing for prestige: Rituals can be fruitfully interpreted as parts of elaborate processes of conspicuous consumption (Appadurai 1986). Writing about 'The Power of Ritual in Marriage: A Daughter's Wedding in Northwest India', Patel deals with the discourse on, and the practical economic implications of the duty to marry off one's daughter. The sociologist argues that the upwardly-mobile castes adopt the ritual of *kanya-daan* (the giving of a virgin), which in effect devaluates the wife-giving party as it places them on a socially lower plane than the wife-taking party. The implicit result is, she argues, increased female abortion following ultrasonography in upwardly-mobile caste groups in Northern India, who at the same time 'race for material prosperity'. Thus, the marriage ceremonies themselves are competitive events performed semi-publicly, and are the very *raison-d'être* for entire culture industries. Taking South Indian domestic and public rituals as an example, Ute Hüsken and K.K.A. Venkatachari argue in that ritual and economy must not be treated as entirely disconnected domains. Not only is ritual an occasion where major transactions and economic activities take place. Instead, participation in rituals, or the right to participate, is frequently also seen as a kind of property, and therefore as an extension of the personae involved. Contestation, conflicts about, criticism and the actual performance of ritual has therefore to be seen from the perspective of economics, too.

Part IV: Media and Sensual Dimensions of Ritual Action

Until now, the role of different media and sensories has not found much attention by scholars of ritual thought and action.[2] This seems almost paradoxical: not only are ritual and media similar because 'they both generate realities that are surprising, special, and outside everyday routines' and simultaneously impact everyday social life (Hughes-Freeland 2006: 595). Likewise, they also create domains of sensual experience and transgression in a way that other forms of action do not, shaping physical presence and participation that is considered as 'virtual' and 'inauthentic' by several critics. However, it should be examined, case by case, whether forms of participation in media rituals is genuinely less effective or unreal. For example, online rituals, in which people come to attend church services and become members of a virtual ecumenical community, are performed in 'places' like *Second Life* (see Radde-Antweiler, this volume). Moreover, the concept of the *darshanic gaze* (Babb 1981, Eck 1981) is a particular form of worshipping statues of deities (or politicians and filmstars) where the devotee 'milks' the eyes of the divine, experiencing a flow of sacred energy that also impacts the body. There are rituals of 'online *murti darshan*' too .[3] These mediated, immediate, intimate factors of ritual practice, and the ways in which they are constituted, circulate and reach different audiences, are centre-stage in this section. This requires that, on the one hand, we have to understand ritual in relation to general visual and media theories. On the other hand, we must acknowledge particular ways of seeing and media-usage that escape 'universal' concepts and demand understanding of emic categories (such as '*darshan*'). Ritual theory, like many other disciplines in the Humanities, has a relatively iconophobic attitude towards images and media, and the senses aligned to them: they are difficult to 'measure' and write about, they are genuinely resistant to plain interpretations and direct impact. Moreover, cultural pessimistic attitudes towards mass media technologies promulgate ideas of media rituals (such as Lady Diana's funeral broadcast on television) as diluted, disenchanted and inauthentic. The relatively negative and speechless attitude of social sciences towards media reflected in such a position is even more drastic today as more and more rituals are performed via highly flexible and long-distance networks, generating new and often temporary forms of social relations and religious practice. Rituals are enacted in mass media technologies such as television and hypermedia. But even 'traditional' rituals performed in local communities, face-to-face, require our attention and fine tuning of our terminology.

Rituals are produced, disseminated and communicated to us by diverse media technologies. These media are not ubiquitous but nest in particular historical and social contexts. The chosen means for ritual performances strongly influence ways of participating in them, their perception, the retrospective control of the rituals and, consequently, their future choreographies. This last section of the book deals with the questions of how rituals are a form and forum of today's social and religious practices, and how the reality of ritual is mediated by sensual means and mass technologies.

More often than we might be aware of a religious or a secular ritual that appeals to us as 'impressive' and 'convincing', 'new' or 'old-fashioned' because of the ways in which it is executed. The aesthetic dimensions of rituals have not yet been considered much by ritual studies scholars. This is also because the intangibility of rituals is considered to be difficult to 'measure' with conventional tools, and both media and aesthetics are often sidelined as marginal, trivial props or decorum. A shift of attention requires new theoretical and methodological approaches, and is, indeed, a very complex matter, located on many levels and at many sites, perceived by different social agents and at different moments in time. With the exception of art history most classical disciplines in the Humanities are rather text-focussed. This is why in ritual studies too, much scholarly focus has been on texts rather than other media. This included elite cultures, the doctrines, scriptures and handbooks of religious specialists, to mention only a few examples. As a consequence, many dimensions of ritual action were excluded from analysis. With the 'performative' and the 'cultural' turn, media, visuality and the senses became more centre-stage. If we consider the aesthetic and media dimensions of rituals we discover how heterogeneous approaches are; not only can the religious specialists be circumvented by new social groups and replaced by new media technologies, be it print or digital media, but the new media might also change our relationship *vis-à-vis* our sensories, and help us develop new approaches towards understanding them. The essays in this section address a variety of such cases from a multi-disciplinary and contemporary stance.

Spoken or written language can also be seen as a medium: it is habitus, metaphor and mimesis at work, a performative means to shape rituals not just in the Austinian way of doing and meaning by speaking, but more complex and holistic as a means of ritual embodiment. Verbal and non-verbal language as used in ritual recitations should be analysed as a force that navigates between formality and flexibility, connecting the divine and the mundane, the personal and the collective and non-human. According to anthropologist and performer Saskia Kersenboom, spoken language is at once performed and performative language, it is enacted and enacting upon, and to a large extent does so by playing with ambiguities that generate difference on different semantic levels. In this context, the body, too, becomes a ritual media embedded in 'linguistic, literary and aesthetic conventions of Sanskrit and Tamil' (Kersenboom, this volume). Language is essentially based on an embodied logic of practice in the Bourdieuian sense, and is both intuitive and rational knowledge. Taking the statement of a 'traditional performer' in a South Indian temple on the change of tradition as her starting point, Kersenboom's chapter 'Ritual Differs: Beyond Fixity and Flexibility in South Indian Hindu Ritual', emphasises oscillation between stability and change with respect to ritual. She argues for the capacity of 'tradition' to incorporate diverse perspectives: tradition is nothing that *is* or *should be*, but something that works with a great amount of inherent flexibility. Her emphasis is on the practice that constitutes ritual. While the 'closed rules' are the background for routine praxis, there is also a kind of 'development practice', the basis of which are 'open rules'. The latter is very context-sensitive and allows for a variety of meanings. Ritual actors are embodiments of the structuring structures of ongoing temple worship. Kersenboom examines the complexity of ritual language as it unfolds in social worlds and intermedial and intertextual contexts. Exploring rituals with a specific interest in media and aesthetics, we can then see how social agents try to shape reality through rituals, define and contest 'authenticity' and transcendence. What happens if new media technologies replace the religious specialist at the site? Can we still argue that the mass medium of the internet lacks the capacity to present the divine, transcendent? Furthermore, what do we conclude from the fact that people can get married online, that the witnessing of a funeral, or a wedding, on television can be as 'authentic' for a person as it can be a constitutive part of a brotherhood (Little 1995, Manuel 1993)? In her paper '"Wedding Design" online: Transfer and Transformation of Ritual Elements in the Context of Wedding

Rituals', religious studies scholar Kerstin Radde-Antweiler observes that online weddings are the most frequently performed rites of passage in virtual worlds. Assuming that the World Wide Web creates distinctly different worlds, it is surprising how much attention is placed on simulation of the 'real world'. The question of 'authenticity' and 'imitation' pops up in quite a drastic way here. In exploring the choreography of online weddings in the 3-D virtual world of *Second Life* and through ethnographic fieldwork, Radde-Antweiler is also concerned with questions about the kind of community that emerges in online worlds, notions of presence, but also with litigable ownership and claims over rights and relationships: 'Virtual Worlds offer a completely new field of research when it comes to studying culture, religion and especially ritual and their dynamic processes.' While investigating the transfer of wedding rituals into another media context, she focuses on the changes and transformations of actual 'real world' weddings that emerge. However, by no means does everything happen online that must not happen offline. Instead, Radde-Antweiler emphasises that ritual innovation is surprisingly rare. This new medium of representation also raises questions of authority and authenticity: Who renders the ritual effective and who ineffective? What must by any means be a part of the online wedding in order for it to be credible? What can be said about the ritual stance of the participants? The internet has increasingly been turned into a domain of ritual performance, challenging our understanding of reality and authenticity, participation and efficacy.

Media such as literature have also been turned into domains in which values linked to ritual could be contested in a larger public sphere, and by different, often subversive discourses and agents. Printed literature also opened access for groups who may have traditionally been excluded from ritual expertise and performance, such as the *dalit* ('Untouchables') in India who had to refrain from reading sacred literature or women who were often passive recipients of ritual rules, such as veiling, in Islam. The contestation of Islamic values and literary response in the context of gender-specific rituals such as veiling in twentieth century Egypt, Palestine and Lebanon are the core issues of Susanne Enderwitz's investigation 'Gender, Generation, and the Public Sphere: Islamic Values and Literary Response'. Enderwitz, scholar of Islamic studies and literature, explores how a new generation of women emerges and positions itself in the public domain, defining liberty, rights and duties of women. Both the descriptive genre of literature in and through which the stories unfold, and the embodiment of gender through ritualised behaviour, veiling, are centre-stage in this essay. She argues that the question of the 'right' Islamic dress has been linked to a dichotomisation of West and Islam, but also to the designation of and access to 'sacred' and 'secular' space, the ambivalent relationship of modernisation and emancipation by means of ritual dress and fashion. Veiling is embodiment, becoming a Muslima by putting on a dress; it is a rite of passage, relating the woman to various social roles such as motherhood, wife, but also working woman. The essay analyses the change of public space over time by following the discussions of the ritual of veiling and how it is contesting womanhood. Seemingly paradoxically, the veil unleashed itself from the religious sphere in the 1970s, becoming a marker of new confidence, worldliness and Islamic modernity for women. The essay focuses on stories by women, their testimonies of journeys to a new self, in highly politicised times, where the public sphere as a domain of civility and equality is highly contested.

In his essay 'On the Representation of Presence: The Narrative of Devnārāyaṇ as a Multimedia Performance', anthropologist Aditya Malik reflects upon the different modes of textual activity, spoken and written texts, in ritual performance and analysis. While the Western notion of text is often one of stasis, in India text frequently is organic, dynamic, performative, playing itself out in different dimensions. By analysing ritual from the perspective of Western textual traditions, we inevitably tend to reduce the meaning of text in a ritual in India. Malik explores this aesthetic dimension of generating and limiting ritual action and innovation by textual means in the case study of rituals related to the North Indian figure of Devnārāyaṇ. He argues that such a new approach to ritual studies opens up new dimensions for a better understanding of folk performance, divine presence and social meaning. This is a careful study of a particular performance in Rajasthan, where notions of time and of place evolve through the juxtaposition and choreography of various media (e.g., spoken text and image).

Concluding Thoughts

The increased scholarly interest in the term and concept 'ritual' goes hand in hand with the transformation of religious practice in the context of modernisation and secularisation of societies on a global scale. With the diagnosed disappearance of religious rituals from the public and secularised domain, it seems, the desire to hold on to its presence and to rationalise it by means of a common term increases. However, despite the often-purported 'disenchantment' of the modern world, rituals have by no means become extinct. Quite on the contrary, we can speak of a ubiquity of ritual practice in complex societies (for example in sports, education, politics, festivals and theatre). Accordingly, the contributions to the present volume, too, show in a variety of ways that rituals are not clearly separated from everyday life. They are therefore explored within their social, political, or historical context of production and enactment which account for transfers and transformations. Rituals take place in new media, and are not limited to the domain of past religious practice, but play an important role in new contexts within the public domain, civil society or secular nation-states.

The general perception still is that rituals follow strict rules and norms, that they are invariable, static, unchanging, and preserving the past in times of radical and rapid changes. The rituals' formality, a widespread characteristic of many rituals, contributes to this view. Bell (1997: 139), for instance, remarks: 'Formality is one of the most frequently cited characteristics of ritual, even though it is certainly not restricted to ritual *per se*. [...] In general, the more formal a series of movements and activities, the more ritual-like they are apt to seem to us.' She adds that '[o]ne of the most common characteristics of ritual-like behaviour is the quality of invariance, usually seen in a disciplined set of actions marked by precise repetition and physical control. For some big theorists, this feature is the prime characteristics of ritual behaviour' (ibid.: 150). Bell goes even further and states that despite evidence for change 'it is nonetheless quite true that ritual activities generally tend to resist change and often do so more effectively than other forms of social custom' (ibid.: 1997). On account of the case studies and their analyses presented here, we however argue that it is precisely the formality of rituals that provokes criticism and thus necessitates renewal. While rituals are often believed to preserve the old and sustainable, they are frequently criticised for precisely this factor. It is often the criticism that rituals have become stereotype and thus do not reflect the original intention anymore that makes people look for new, seemingly unfamiliar forms of rituals. Ritual criticism clearly is a constitutive part of most rituals that provokes permanent change (see Grimes 1990). Criticism through rituals or criticism of rituals helps to adjust rituals to the changing contexts and sometimes even creates new religious movements, as was the case with Buddhism or Protestantism.

This volume clearly shows that the study of ritual action enables us to better understand human action as constantly moving between stability and change. Both qualities, stability and change, must be understood in relation to and complementing each other. Obviously, rituals do not exclude alternatives, contingency or freedom but on the contrary include these aspects. They are not fixed and unchangeable but over and over again negotiated, contested, discussed and constantly adapted to new situations.

◈

Notes

1. Instead, Handelman prefers to use the term 'public event' and a multiplicity of terms that enforce each other (ibid.). This take, we propose, has its own difficulties because not every ritual act is taking place in public. There are private rituals as well which cannot be referred to as 'public event'.
2. By media, we mean both traditional media such as printed books and manuscripts, oral performance as well as television and cinema or new technologies such as the internet.
3. See, for instance, the service of BAPS on the homepage of the Swaminarayan Temple in London where daily online *murti darshan* is offered, (http://www.mandir.org/murtidarshan/index.php, accessed 13 January 2009).

References

Appadurai, A. 1986. 'Introduction: Commodities and the Politics of Value', in A. Appadurai (ed.) *The Social Life of Things: Commodities in Cultural Perspective*, pp. 3–63. Cambridge: Cambridge University Press.

Babb, L.A. 1981. 'Glancing. Visual Interaction in Hinduism', *Journal of Anthropological Research*, 37: 387–401.

Bell, C. 1992. *Ritual Theory, Ritual Practice*. New York, Oxford: Oxford University Press.

———. 1997. *Ritual: Perspectives and Dimensions*. New York, Oxford: Oxford University Press.

Boudewijnse, B. 2007. 'Ritual and Psyche', in J. Kreinath, *Theorising Rituals: Issues, Topics, Approaches, Concepts,* pp. 123–142. Leiden: Brill.

Clifford, J. 1997. *Routes. Travel and Translation in the Late Twentieth Century*. Cambridge: Harvard University Press.

Das, V. 1981. 'The Mythological Film and its Framework of Meaning: An Analysis of Jai Santoshi Ma.' *India International Centre Quarterly*, Special Issue, 8 (1): 43–56.

Eck, D. 1981. *Darshan: Seeing the Divine Image in India*. Chambersburg: Anima.

Ginsburg, F., Abu-Lughod, L., Larkin, B. 2002. *Media Worlds: Anthropology on a New Terrain*. Berkeley: University of California Press.

Goody, J. 1977. 'Against Ritual: Loosely structured thoughts on a loosely defined topic' in S.F. Moore and B.G. Myerhoff (eds) *Secular Ritual*. Assen und Amsterdam: Van Gorcum: 25–35.

Grimes, R. 1982. *Beginnings in Ritual Studies*. Washington, DC: University Press of America.

———. 1990. *Ritual Criticism: Case Studies in its Practice, Essays on its Theory* (Studies in Comparative Religion). Columbia, SC: University of Carolina Press.

Handelman, D. 1998. *Models and Mirrors: Towards an Anthropology of Public Events*. New York: Berghahn Books.

———. 2006a. 'Conceptual Alternatives to "Ritual" in Kreinath et al. (2007): 37–49.

———. 2006b. 'Framing' in Kreinath et al. (2007): 571–82.

Harrison, S. 1992. 'Ritual as Intellectual Property', *Man* (New Series) 27 (2): 225–44.

Howes, D. (ed.) 2005. *Empire of the Senses: The Sensual Culture Reader*, Oxford: Berg.

Hughes-Freeland, F. 2006. 'Media'. In Kreinath et al. 2007: 595–614.

Humphrey, C. and Laidlaw; J. 1994. *The Archetypal Actions of Ritual: A Theory of Ritual Illustrated by the Jain Rite of Worship*. Oxford: Oxford University Press.

Köpping, K.P., Rao U. (eds) 2000. *Im Rausch des Rituals: Gestaltung und Transformation der Werklichitke in körperlicher Performanz*. Münster: LIT.

Kreinath, J., Snoek J., Stausberg M. (eds) 2007. *Theorising Rituals: Issues, Topics, Approaches, Concepts*. Leiden: Brill.

Lawson, E.T. and McCauley, R.N. 1996. *Rethinking Religion: Connecting Cognition and Culture*. Cambridge: Cambridge University Press.

Little, J. 1995. 'Video Vacana. Swadhyaya and Sacred Tapes', In L.A. Bapp and S.S. Wadley (eds) *Media and the Transformation of Religion in South Asia*, pp. 254–84. Pennsylvania: University of Pennsylvania Press.

Manuel, P. 1993. *Cassette Culture: Popular Music and Technology in North India, Chicago Studies in Ethnomusicology*. Chicago: University of Chicago Press.

Michaels, A. 2007. '"How do you do?" — Vorüberlegungen zu einer Grammatik der Rituale', in H. Schmidinger and C. Sedmak (eds) *Der Mensch — ein "animal symbolicum"? Sprache — Dialog — Ritual*, pp. 239–58. Darmstadt: Wissenschaftliche Buchgesellschaft.

———. 2003. "Zur Dynamik von Ritualkomplexen". In *Forum Ritualdynamik* 3, December, http://archiv.ub.uni-heidel-berg.de/volltextserver/frontdoor.php?source_opus=4583 (accessed 2 January 2009).

Moore, S. F. And Myerhoff, B.G. (eds). 1977. *Secular Ritual.* Assen und Amsterdam: Van Gorcum.

Münster, D. 2001. *Religionsästhetik und Anthropologie der Sinne. Vorarbeiten zu einer Religionsethnologie der Produktion und Rezeption ritueller Medien*, München: Akademischer Verlag.

Oppitz, Michael. 1999. 'Montageplan von Ritualen'. In Corina Caduff and Joanna Pfaff-Czarnecka (eds.). *Rituale Heute: Theorien — Kontroversen — Entwürfe*, pp. 73–97. Berlin: Reimer Verlag.

Rappaport, R. 1999. *Ritual and Religion in the Making of Humanity*. Cambridge: Cambridge University Press.

Snoek, J. 2006. 'Defining "Ritual"'. In Kreinath et al. (eds.), *Theorising Rituals. Issues, Topics, Approaches, Concepts*, pp. 3–14. Leiden.

Tambiah, Stanley J. 1979. *A Performance Approach to Ritual, Radcliff-Brown Lecture*. London: British Academy.

Turner, V. 1967. *The Ritual Process: Structure and Anti-Structure*. Chicago: Aldine.

Part I
Rituals on the Move

1

Staging Ritual Heritage

How Rituals Become Theatre in Uttarakhand, India

Karin Polit

The idea that rituals are dynamic and ever-changing is not new in anthropological discourses. In fact, the insight that rituals create and sustain solidarity as well as a sense of a common past, present and future through ever-changing ritualised actions was first proposed more than a century ago by William Robertson Smith (1894). These original ideas had to be rediscovered recently as thinking about ritual and ritual actions had since become more or less a thinking about so-called primitive cultures and their presumed irrational traditions. The idea that modernity and ritualised performances could go hand-in-hand had long been rejected in ritual studies.[1] However, as I will show in the course of this essay, rituals are not only an integral part of modern society but can also be a means to construct alternative modernities. It is the sense of a common past, present and future that is created in ritualised performances that makes rituals so well-suited to unite people and to project a modern, yet traditional character onto communities. Rituals produce the illusion of tradition, as Barbara Myerhoff (1984) has rightly pointed out. Ritual performances thus produce political, social and individual bodies of tradition.

The question central to the analysis of this essay is what happens when such 'traditional' rituals are intentionally changed into a performance at a different place, with different people, different costumes and different audiences? Is a ritual still a ritual when it is performed on a theatrical stage or does it become something else? When is the thin line between ritual and theatrical performance crossed? The relationship between ritual and performance has been a major concern in anthropology for the last three decades[2]. This essay addresses some of the leading discussions of ritual as performance and deals with the question of what distinguishes a ritual performance from a theatrical performance. It becomes central in the case study where local people from the Himalayan state of Uttarakhand in India perform 'traditional' rituals rooted in their villages on theatre stages in Delhi or the regional capital of Dehra Dun. What is understood in the local discourse as the preservation of heritage and authentic performances may be interpreted by the outsider as the creation of a common heritage and the performance of a common identity.

Uttarakhand is a new Indian state, carved out of Uttar Pradesh in November 2000. Located in the central Himalayas with international borders with Nepal and Tibet and home to many important pilgrimage sites, it is *Dev Bhumi*, the land of the gods. The majority of the population is Hindu and daily life in the mountain villages of Uttarakhand is influenced heavily by religious and ritual practices. Every valley has a prevailing ritual tradition. As a consequence, the state's performative traditions are rich, various and diverse. Usually these performative ritual traditions are identified with a specific region in Uttarakhand and while the people to whom these traditions belong cherish their customs they are mostly understood as part of the various ritual obligations people of a certain place, caste and family have. Rituals are 'work'. Generally, such performative rituals are repeated regularly to ensure the prosperity of the land and people of a certain area (see e.g., Sax 2002, Polit 2006). During such performances the divine presence is called through music and drumming. When the deity arrives he or she dances, blesses the land and the people of the land and is appeased and re-energised by the gifts and the enactment done in the deity's name. Therefore, many villagers understand these performative ritual traditions as part of their 'work', and duty, as villagers and householders of a particular caste and village.

Of late, however, a different understanding about these village traditions has emerged throughout the region. In combination with the movement for an independent state that started to gather momentum in the mid-1970s, Uttarakhand's political and intellectual elite has increasingly started looking at Uttarakhand's rich ritual traditions as valuable in their own right. Today, in some people's eyes, the folk traditions are important pieces of culture worthy of protection and promotion, pieces of culture that Uttarakhand's people can be proud of.

Different from the formation of many other states in India, Uttarakhand was separated from Uttar Pradesh not on the basis of ethnic divides but political differences. One of the reasons was the increase in the number of reserved seats for low castes and Other Backward Castes (OBCs) in the state of Uttarakhand in the years before the formation of the state. But there were also many other political and economic reasons. It is important to note that the reasons for forming a new state did not emerge out of a feeling of unity among Uttarakhandis who wanted to distinguish themselves as a group from the rest of Uttar Pradesh's population. Uttarakhand has as yet no common 'imagined community'. It is, in fact, divided into several parts and spread across several societal levels. A popular saying in the local vernacular, Garhwali, exemplifies this immense diversity: 'When you walk through Garhwaḷ, always remember; every two miles the water changes, while the dialect changes after every mile.'

However, ever since the movement for a separate state gained social and political pace, various groups and people have attempted to strengthen the sense of community, common history and heritage of the people of Uttarakhand in different ways. In this context efforts have also been initiated to promote different traditions within Uttarakhand as the common heritage of the new state. Performative and ritual traditions have been drawn into the internal politics of power and dominance in the process of the new state's formation. I argue that the ritual background of these performative traditions seems to have played a major role in the choice of certain traditions over others. Furthermore, I suggest that they have been chosen by the intellectual and political elite of Uttarakhand because they are ritually identified with the land of the gods, on the one hand, to serve as the link to a mythical past of all people of Uttarakhand but are sufficiently theatrical on the other hand to serve as an emblem of the new and alternative modernity of the state of Uttarakhand. In this process, certain traditions have been uprooted from the village or region of origin and at the same time been newly emplaced across the whole of Uttarakhand. As such, the performance of ritual traditions on regional and national stages are part of a process to construct a useable past (Lowenthal 1985, Utz 2005), that is thought to strengthen people's sense of identity with Uttarakhand as a whole through performative traditions. In this sense, the ritual traditions of Uttarakhand have become pieces of heritage, a concept that is itself closely linked to 'modern' understandings of community, nationhood and past (see e.g., Ashworth 2005). On the following pages I will deal with this transformative and complex relationship of 'traditional' ritual to cultural heritage and folklore. I understand heritage in this context not as an object but as a process of discourse, a process of finding and defining a useable past for a particular group of people at a particular point in time.

My central argument here follows Benedict Anderson's concept of the nation as an 'imagined community', that refers to communities in which most members do not 'know most of their fellow members, meet them, or even hear of them, yet in the minds of each lives the image of their communion' (1983: 6), and the concept central to that of the imagined community, the creation of a common history, a usable past. Following Utz (2005), the creation of a useable past, the selective and interpretive use of past events, mythology and imagination, however, is not accidental nor is it a process that can be individually manipulated. Utz shows that 'creating a useable past for a large community requires some sort of social consensus about the historical experience' (2005: 628). As such the shaping of a 'usable past' must also be understood as part of an ongoing public discourse about belonging, power and historical experience. I argue that ritual traditions are particularly suited to serve the purpose of building a useable past for the citizens of the new state of Uttarakhand because they are central to an embodied form of social experience that can create a notion of collective memory for both the urban as well as the rural population. In this sense I further take up Taylor's (2003: 3) argument that performances should also be understood as a kind of cultural archive that carries and transmits cultural knowledge in a deeply-embodied way. I argue that the intellectual and political elite of Uttarakhand, while creatively transforming Uttarakhand's ritual traditions into new, more aesthetic and modern traditions for the purpose of preserving the region's cultural heritage, contribute at the same time to the construction of an alternative modernity for themselves and Uttarakhand. While cultural knowledge and tradition are highly valued in the sense that this is what modern nations do, traditional performances become folkloristic emblems for this modern society that are particularly well-suited to fuse the rural and the urban populations, new and old values and as such become vehicles for the dream to be true to the place's spiritual, deeply Indian heritage and still become a thriving, modern place of business, education and sophistication.

Ritual and State Formation

Most ritual systems are also systems of control and hierarchy as they confirm and reconstitute human relationships and provide an arena where different identities are negotiated (Bell 1992: 130). In many performative ritual traditions social positions, of individual people as well as of groups of people, are performatively negotiated, defined and redefined (Sax 2002: 5–10). As Bell has pointed out, ritual activities can therefore not be understood as acting upon or reflecting the social system. Instead, 'these loosely coordinated activities are constantly differentiating and integrating, establishing and subverting the field of social relations' (1992: 130). In the same line of argument I understand the performative rituals of Uttarakhand as important instances of political and religious identity formation. In the newly-formed state, the heterogeneity of social actors and internal tensions among different actors also led to processes of invention and reinvention of ritual traditions, accumulating in the attempt to produce a unified heritage of the region. In this sense, the rituals looked at in this essay can clearly be understood as having a homogenising effect by bridging the gaps and inner tensions between different political fractions. At the same time, ritual traditions have served as vehicles for Uttarakhand to become visible as a collective and active agent in the national context of India. Here, the performative ritual traditions, as many rituals all over the world, can be understood as having power, an agency of their own. As Sax has argued, public ritual performances are an especially powerful means for creating (and sometimes undermining) selves, relationships and communities, precisely because they inscribe cultural concepts on the whole person, the body as well as the mind, and they do so by requiring of their participants a public, embodied assent to those concepts (2002: 12).

This special form of human practice, the practice of rituals, enables people in a very special way to reinvent themselves and to differentiate a people as a group from the 'other'. The reinvention of the ritual traditions of Uttarakhand is a crucial aspect of the creation of an identity for the people of Uttarakhand, with their new state as a community, on the one hand, as well as the differentiation of this community against the homogenising efforts of the Indian nation state as well as similarly homogenising influence of a global scale, on the other. Here I am concerned with the production of 'intangible cultural heritage' of a region in India, which, in my view, stands exemplary for similar processes all over India and in fact represents a global process of 'heritagisation'. I am interested in both the power and the dynamics of ritual and also in people's fear of losing what they perceive as their own, original and regional identity. This essay is therefore also about ritual as part of dominant discourses of, for example, aesthetics, caste, political power and modernity.

For several reasons, the performative ritual traditions of Uttarakhand are particularly suited to become part of the 'heritage' of Uttarakhand. First, the rituals are appropriate for such an endeavour because they usually give people the illusion that what is performed, presented or constructed in front of them is part of a larger, legitimate and important cultural framework. They create the impression that these ritual actions have always been an element of people's lives and that of their ancestors before them. Myerhoff argued as early as 1984 that rituals are paradoxical, precisely because they are conspicuously artificial and theatrical yet designed to suggest the inevitability and absolute truth of their messages. Ritual is a form by which culture presents itself to itself. In ritual, not only are particular messages delivered, but the ritual also creates a world in which culture can appear. Further, rituals create a setting in which persons can appear, by appearing in their culture, by devising a reality in which they may stand as part (1984: 56).

Rituals and ritually-informed performances represent themselves as cultural truths. However, as I have argued earlier, rituals are fields of discourse, where social positions are negotiated. Therefore, acts of ritualisation, deritualisation or even heritagisation of rituals are always also acts that strategically distinguish one group of people from the other. When ritual traditions come to be conceived as heritage; that is, as iconic of certain ethnic groups, regions, or nationalities, processes of selection, change and reinvention are always involved, and therefore 'heritage' is nothing other than part of a public discourse. This has similarly been argued by Singer five decades ago. In his concern about the power of ritual and cultural performances, he argued that people seem to see their culture as encapsulated in discrete performances, which can be exhibited to outsiders as well as to their own people. Quite often, according to Singer, these cultural performances are performative rituals (Singer 1959: xii). And while Singer's formulations have been criticised by many anthropologists since, especially arguing that there exits neither a cultural essence nor is this essence forever fixed in rituals, the people in the region of Uttarakhand unknowingly share his view that their culture has an essence and that this essence needs to be preserved and saved — not only from the influences of globalisation or the Western world, but also from forces within India, as e.g., the Hindutva movement that argues for a single Hindu tradition of India, wanting to wipe out local particularities.

The Heritage Industry of Uttarakhand

The data I present in this essay has been gathered during my postdoctoral research in Uttarakhand over several months-long visits to the region during 2005–2007. I have worked with and observed the work of non-governmental organizations (NGOs) and different groups constituted by the small elite of the region, such as teachers at the regional University of Srinagar in Uttarakhand, at high schools and inter-colleges of the region, as well as by young students. Several groups have formed over the past two decades that concern themselves with the re-representation of rituals as well as musical, oral and performative folk traditions during events that celebrate culture, local or national, such as local heritage festivals, fairs in market places and on the occasion of religious gatherings. The self-stated interest of these groups lies in the preservation and promotion of the region's oral and ritual traditions. As will become clear in the course of this essay, however, and as is clear from the anthropological literature (see, e.g., Van der Veer 1996, McCauley 1996, Scheer 2002) processes of preservation and representation always involve selection and exclusion. It is as important to understand who makes decisions about what is to be staged as Uttarakhand's heritage and why, as what kind of views on aesthetics are involved in the decision-making process and to understand the economic benefits of such events and who is the beneficiary. Here, I am especially interested in the ways in which different groups of local people assume responsibility and sometimes ownership over certain ritual traditions through the process of changing and staging them.

As a case study I choose to present the work of one theatre group based in Srinagar, Garhwal. While they also stage older pieces of classical stage theatre written in Garhwali dialect, their main focus lies in writing and staging performances based on village ritual traditions. The process of producing a new play involves research in the villages and analysis of data and only then does the creative writing and production of the stage performance take place. The motivation for the people involved in the various projects is, as they say, the preservation and promotion of what they call 'the cultural heritage of Uttarakhand'. Therefore, at the beginning of each project, they visit the villages where the performances take place and record the songs, take videos of all aspects of the performance and conduct interviews with the village people involved in the performance. Then they use this data as a basis for their stage performances. They look at the dances and the costumes and base their choreography as well as the costumes on the village style. They listen to the music, write down the texts sung and base their own music and texts on the data gathered. However, they also make aesthetic changes to the movements, the costumes, the language and the music in order to make the performance more appealing to the different audiences. When the group started their work, this process used to take years, but as they have found out more and more about the regional traditions, less and less time is put into the research. With time, the ritual traditions still performed in the villages have lost their importance while the actual plays have moved into the focus of people's attention and gained attention as something curiously 'different' and at the same time familiar. Some of the plays have been very successful on stages in Uttarakhand as well as in Indian national theatres, such as the play 'Burhdeva' that is based on a theatrical tradition performed during certain deities' processions in Chamoli district, Uttarakhand.

Jakh's Procession and Narad's Performance

This tradition is strongly connected with the religious landscape of the region and one of many yearly processions between October and May in Uttarakhand. Many local deities in Uttarakhand regularly go on a procession, to visit their home area, their so-called in-law communities in the case of a male deity (*devta*), or the villages that are thought of as their parental home in the case of a female deity (*devi*). Most deities are on the road for six months or longer. They travel from village to village and rarely spend more than one night in a single village. During this time of pilgrimage they are usually accompanied by a group of men from different castes. There are priests who are responsible for the regular worship of the deity; there are men from Rajput *jatis* (subcaste) who carry the deity; and there are low-caste men who are responsible for the music and sometimes for the performances. Few *devis* and *devtas* today require regular, nightly performances in the different villages. However, the Jakh *devtas* of the region, between Gopeshwar and Urgam valley, who reside as kings over this area demand an entourage of entertainers to travel with them during the six months of their procession. This entourage usually consists of a group of low-caste drummers and bards as well as of dancers and performers from a Rajput *jati*. Between September 2006 and February 2007, I witnessed the Jakh *devta* of Kujaum, a village about 15 kilometres from Gopeshwar, come out of his temple after seventy-five years. The villagers said that there was fighting between the three responsible villages, the fields had become dry and infertile and there was a general feeling of misfortune among the devotees of the deity. All these were reasons to devote the time and money involved in a six-month-long procession of the deity to renew the bond between the deity and its devotees, recharge the deity's powers and give the deity the opportunity to bless the land and people. A committee of Rajput men from the three villages got together with the deity's oracle. In an oracular session, the deity announced that the men should do their religious duty (their work) and organise a procession through the 'kingdom' (Sax 2002: 192–210). As soon as the decision was made, people started to collect money and rations for the journey, called the ritual specialist, the drummers and the bards to train three young men of the village, the *daris*, to carry the deity in the right manner, to sing and dance for and with the deity. The *daris* were also trained to perform the role of Narad, or Burhdeva. Narad is the most important character of the performances that take place every night during the six-month-long procession through the different villages of Jakh *devta*'s kingdom. During the day, the deity's entourage, consisting of a Brahmin priest, a Rajput priest, the oracle of the deity and oracles of other deities, an accountant and other helpers travel barefoot from one village to the other. During the night all these people dance the *pattars*, the masks of different deities who accompany them on their journey.

Before a procession starts, the three *daris* have to undergo purifying rituals. They and the priest will be the only ones allowed to touch the deity during the procession. They will carry the deity from one village to the other; the deity will direct them how to dance; they will establish the temporary shrine for the deity in every new village at the time of arrival; they will wake the deity through ritual singing in the morning and put it to rest in the evenings. During the six months of the procession they will bathe twice a day, they will not cut their hair or their nails, nor shave, eat food made by a woman's hand or do anything else considered polluting, lest they anger the deity.

But there are more demands on the three *daris*, still. Each night after dinner, around ten o'clock at night, Burhdeva, or Narad, makes his appearance. When the drummers start playing, the villagers appear in the courtyard of the house where the deity chose to reside for the night, and settle to watch Narad and thirteen to eighteen ancient deities appear before their eyes. It's a peculiar performance — both ritual in the sense that it is dangerous and efficacious and theatre in the sense that it is entertaining and educating. From the moment the *dari* puts on Narad's mask and costume, the half-deity's divine power is with him. For the time of the performance he will not feel tired, hungry, thirsty or the need to relieve himself. However, while Narad's divine power is thought to be present all night, the person impersonating him is not thought of nor thinks himself to be possessed by the deity. One of the *daris* of the 2006–2007 procession described his role and his relationship to the deity to me as follows.

> It is like this, we have to look around all day in the village to prepare for the evening's performance. You know, it is Narad's role to make

> fun about what's special in this village. So we look around all day and think about what we can mention during the night's performance. So if I see something that I find funny or noteworthy I won't talk about this to anyone all day but at night in the court I will make jokes about it. For example, there was a village that seemed full of cats and at night I said: There are so many cats, I could not sleep, because the little bells around their necks chimed so loudly! It's different things we make fun about, in one village it's the food, in the other the fat wife of the village master, in the next village it will be the water and so on. I am able to make up these jokes during the performance because Narad gives me his powers, he makes my brain work faster. He makes me strong so I don't get tired, so that I do not need to pee all night. I do not have to make up my jokes beforehand, I just have to observe during the day and he will give me the words to make a strong performance at night. It is all because of his divine powers.

The figure of Narad, while believed to embody a divine presence, is also dependent on the man behind his mask and what is being said is based on this man's observances. Narad's role during the nights' performance is that of a trickster figure. He is a deity born as a human being and doomed to endure all a human has to suffer and as such he is the link between the other deities and the village audience. He is the trickster figure who can joke with the deities and the village audience alike. Narad makes teasing remarks on people, politicians, places and recent events in the region or the village. He can make jokes about local politicians, recent scandals, or simply report on what happened in the last village the night before. In a conversation with the bard and drummer, he walks up and down among the people, constantly uttering jokes about the people in the last villages, he recites the funny things that happened, and then goes on to make fun of village life. In the performances I witnessed, he joked about the close-fistedness of one village chief, the ugliness of the women in another village, the food they were served in yet another place and so on. He told the story of the procession's journey, and among the jokes included the information about who sacrificed a goat and when and who was particularly devoted to the deity. His performance is also a satire of village life in general. As a human being, he has to find a wife, deal with the priest and the wedding party, who both want nothing but money and alcohol; he gets possessed and meditates;

he ploughs the fields and becomes a father. At the same time, Narad serves as a sort of director of the performance. His own story frames the rest of the performance. While he is the deity who gets born on earth as a human being and has to undergo all stages of a human life, his rather comical, but still divine, story is interrupted by appearances of different deities in the village courtyard. They appear in the form of masks, worn by men from Jakh *devta*'s entourage and are accompanied by songs in an old Garhwali dialect that tell the stories of the deities. The masks are said to be the deities in the sense that they are the vessels of divine power. Their dance at night is not only meant to entertain Jakh and the villagers but is itself understood as a form of worship. The villagers insist that the masks need to be danced, the masks demand to be danced. If they are not danced for one night during the procession, the power in the masks will make them dance by themselves and their human devotees will lose control over the deities' powers. Losing control over divine power is dangerous as only in the controlled form can it be benevolent. If uncontrolled, such a deity does not know the difference between good and bad and things can go terribly wrong.

Therefore, during the deity's procession, there will be a performance every night. But not all performances last all night. Depending on the date, the number of goats offered by villagers and devotees to be sacrificed, such a performance can last from two hours on a regular night to up to eight or ten hours on a full night's performance. There are deities that can only appear if there are sacrificial animals as blood is needed to control their divine power and appease their anger. If all eighteen masks are danced, it is required of Narad as well as the audience to stay in the arena of performance from the time the sun sets until it rises again. From a certain point onwards, nobody is allowed to leave the space of performance for there are dangerous beings lurking in the dark. Attracted by the drums and the beauty of the singing voices all sorts of divine and superhuman creatures gather around. The divine power of the gods protects everybody inside an invisible circle around the performance ground, but whoever leaves the place, even to relieve her/himself, is at risk of getting attacked by one of those beings and thus in mortal danger. When all the gods have danced, when the goats have been sacrificed and when the sun rises announcing the beginning of a new day, the dangerous superhuman beings leave the place together with the night's darkness. Narad and all the other deities leave the village and finally, audience as well as performers can rest before the duties of Jakh's worship start once again.

Acts of Worship, Acts of Play

The night performances, while clearly very entertaining at times, are evidently also acts of worship that have an efficacy beyond the moment of performance. There is danger in not performing and the performance promotes the well-being of the performers as well as the welfare of land and people of the host village. The longer the performance's duration, the greater is the benefit and prestige for the hosting village. The performance is clearly framed as a religious and ritualistic event. In other words, the performance is part of the Jakh tradition's ritual repertoire. However, when the tradition came to the attention of Srinagar's theatre group, and got reframed as Uttarakhandi Heritage and a local folk theatre tradition, the theatrical aspects were underlined while the ritualistic aspects were sidelined. A play was written that takes this village tradition as a starting point, but is adapted to the requirements of modern theatre. One of the main creators of the play, D.R. Purohit, argues that the tradition has always been more theatrical than ritualistic. He bases that on the use of the term *Pattar* for the masks. 'The term "Pattar" is a corruption of the Sanskrit word 'paatra' meaning 'role performer' or actor. The *Pattar* performances, therefore, can be taken as mimetic action at their very roots, and "pattar" would clearly mean play' (Purohit 1993: 126).

According to Purohit, the Narad performances are first and foremost a tradition of folk theatre and should be preserved and promoted as such. On the basis of audio and video recordings, a team of people developed a play that was suited for a modern stage in terms of aesthetics and length, but which employs what they understood as the essence of the village performances — the figure of Narad, the other funny characters, and a considerably shortened version of the deities' dances and songs. In the stage performance, the story of Narad, as exemplary of every Uttarakhandi villager's story, in other words, as exemplary of the folk, is in focus, whereas the mask dances of the deities as well as their songs are sidelined.

The context, a deity's procession, is hinted upon by an image of the deity made out of paper that is carried on the stage before the beginning of the main performance. While the masks in the village tradition are made by ritual specialists and are thought of as vessels of divine power, the masks of the new theatre tradition are made of carton and are thought of as pure requisites that vanish into a suitcase after the performance. But does that mean that the performance is inauthentic or that the producers of such displays of tradition are distorting the ritual traditions? I think not. Neither the main bearers of the local ritual tradition, the low-caste bards, nor the authors, directors and performers of the play understand their performance in this context. To them, both the theatrical performance on stage as well as the ritual performance in a village square are authentic in the sense that both produce, reproduce and display Uttarakhandi heritage. Of course, they do make a difference between the efficaciousness of the village ritual and the effect of the stage performance. The authors and directors of the Burhdeva play do not want to stage a ritual, but a contemporary Uttarakhandi tradition. As I mentioned earlier, it is the elite of Uttarakhand who is interested in the creation of Uttarkhandi heritage. And, as Utz points out, while ideas of modernity and regionalism may derive from the elite of a region for different reasons, they would never be able to advance these interests without 'referring to a larger collective body' (2005: 635). Typically this is done by referring to the folk, the countryside and its ritual traditions. On the one hand, it is the region's ritual traditions that make Uttarakhand special as a place on the other it is the same ritual traditions that make the people backward and superstitious in the eyes of the modern, educated Uttarakhandi. Therefore, the pieces of theatre re-representing the ritual traditions, be it Narad, the Chakravyuh (an episode from the local Mahabharata, the great Indian epic), Kumaoni Holi or the Hill Yatra of Pithoragarh, are not intended as rituals on a modern stage but as images of rituals. This serves two purposes. The first is to actually preserve what the elite has identified as old traditions worthy of preservation. Here, the Uttarakhandis have understood that it is not enough to record a tradition on paper, on video or audio tape to preserve the knowledge connected with such a tradition but that it is only the actual performance that can transmit this cultural knowledge in the most effective way. The second purpose is a speculative. It seems that the elite want to avoid or even get rid of an image of backwardness and superstition but do not want to drop the religious and ritual annotations of their performative traditions altogether. The redefinition of certain ritual traditions as theatrical spectacles and the resulting performative dialogue between traditional and modern aesthetics, between rural and urban population, I argue, is heavily influenced by national sentiments about the state of Uttarakhand. Clearly, the performance changed considerably through the adaptation on a modern Indian stage. It is no longer possible to call this stage adaptation a ritual, nor would it be useful to try to define it as such. However, it is important to keep in mind the ritual background of the stage adaptation to understand the effects it has on Uttarakhand as a state and its people as a community.

Building an Alternative Modernity

These adaptations of ritual performative traditions are presented mostly on stages that have to do with the representation of Indian regional traditions or with the promotion of Uttarakhandi heritage. The Burhdeva play has been invited to New Delhi's National School of Drama's 'Indian Folk Theatre Festival' several times. It has been on the stage of the 'Virasat' heritage festival in Dehra Dun, and is staged several times a year as cultural programme in fairs and festivals held on different religious occasions throughout the state of Uttarakhand. Of course, the play 'Burhdeva' is not the only play based on a ritual tradition; there are several ritual traditions that have been adapted in a very similar way by different groups. The Burhdeva play is but one example of the processes that transfer ritual to pieces of heritage in the region. But it is a good example to help me understand how people engage with such ritual performances. In my opinion it exemplifies how the educated elite of Uttarakhand are engaged in building an alternative modernity for their new state. I argue that the very engagement with ritual traditions and their transformation is a practice of discourse and a negotiation among different understandings of aesthetics, performance and tradition. In this context, the theatre stage is the frame that de-ritualises the tradition on the one hand, but gives it a sophistication and sense of informed modernity that the village tradition lacks on the other. In a way, the framing of a performance as a ritual in the village connects it to the land and the well-being of the region, while the framing of the same tradition as a sophisticated and modern stage performance connects it to the prosperity and welfare of the state of Uttarakhand. If we understand these different performances and their different contexts in the sense of Baumann (1977) — which means not only as a form of communication that can only be understood in an embodied way by insiders, but also as containing in them the power to transform social structures — then it becomes clear that the effects created on these stages of cultural production is much more than a simple struggle for recognition and preservation of dying traditions. It might rather be interpreted as the attempt of certain people to create their own modernity.

While I was initially somewhat intrigued by the question of how people distinguish between the ritual and the theatrical performance, I soon discovered that the much more interesting questions here circled around local and regional discourses of political power, caste and modernity. And that it was these discourses and the fact that they all somehow seemed to be embedded in the local ritual traditions that was fascinating and special for the region I studied and shed the most light on the power and the dynamics of ritual performances. In order to understand these processes, we have to do away with the Western concept of authenticity. I admit that I, as many other anthropologists, tended to think of the stage performance as a mere copy, an inauthentic one at that, of the village rituals. To me, the stage performance was thus less powerful, less authentic and less romantic. And even though there have been quite a few publications on this problematic lately (see e.g., Bendix 1997, Köpping 1998), this is a view many anthropologists still seem to share. However, the people engaged in the production of the stage plays that are based on ritual traditions as well as those responsible for the village tradition do not see their work in the same way. This is so because the lines between ritual and theatrical traditions have always been fuzzy. While the village performances are always connected to real and specific deities, who can either bless or curse the people responsible for the ritual, the stage performance represents the traditions of all these regional deities. While the ritual performance in the villages is thought of as efficacious and thus also potentially dangerous in the sense that it is part of people's direct engagement with their deities, the stage performance cannot offend any deity nor satisfy a deity in the same sense. It is, however, thought of as efficacious in the way that it represents the engagement of the people of Uttarakhand with their deities and thus creates a sense of community amongst the people of different traditions of Uttarakhand. It is clear why rituals so often play an important role in these discourses of knowledge transfer. As I have elaborated earlier, it is a feature of rituals to create and recreate the social worlds. They give the audience the impression that what they are seeing has not only always been done this way, but that it also belongs to them in a very peculiar and embodied manner. Ritual actions are not connected to order, stability and continuity alone. Even when dealing with changes, the new is embedded in an established framework, connecting new events to old ones, so that they can be recognised as standing in an old line of tradition. It thus creates a basis to be proud of a common ritual tradition and as such a sense of community among the Uttarakhandis in the audience and on stage. Current understandings of the representation of a mythical past of Uttarakhand lead to costume designs, the use of language, performative and musical styles that any person who has seen some sort of village performance once in any region of Uttarakhand will be able to recognise. Most of the costumes are based on the village performance of the tradition that is represented. However, the aesthetic changes are informed by knowledge of other regions' traditions and historical documents. The same is true for performative styles and the use of language. The musical style is heavily influenced by classical and popular Indian music and link Uttarakhandi musical traditions to the highly-valued Indian artistic traditions and as such add to the feeling of pride and identity produced by the performance as a whole. In this sense, I understand performative rituals and the theatrical engagement with performative rituals much in the sense that Taylor understands performance in general. Ritual performances and performances are vital acts of transmitting social and cultural knowledge, memory, as well as a sense of identity. The embodied practices I have presented here help to produce a new tradition that is based on something that inherently pretends to be timelessly old — the ritual traditions. As I mentioned earlier, one of the motives for Uttarakhand's heritage groups to create 'modern' stage performances is to engage young Uttarakhandis in the practice of their local language and to awaken an interest in the old traditions of their homeland in them through the use of their performative archive — the dances, plays and costumes that are recognised by most villagers of Uttarakhand. People in Garhwal seem to have recognised that it is only the embodied practice that offers this unique way of knowing. It is not important that the performance itself is not done in a ritualistic framework. It is, however, important that the performance is based on the village tradition, that, what the people understand to be the 'essence' of the stories and the songs as well as that of the dances and other movements are transmitted in this embodied way. It seems that the people of Uttarakhand have realised that it is impossible to transmit cultural knowledge about ritual traditions simply by writing them down, by taking pictures of them, or even by video- or audio-taping them. It is therefore important to the groups involved in the theatrical representation of their ritual traditions that the young and educated people of Uttarakhand should know about the embodied heritage of their home. The only way to transmit this knowledge, in their opinion, is to engage people physically and mentally in the performative traditions.

◈

Notes

1. For further discussions on the development of ritual studies, see Bell (1992).
2. See, for example, Beeman (1993), Köpping (1998), Schechner (1985), Schechner (1990), Turner (1986).

References

Anderson, B. 1983. *Imagined Communities: Reflections on the Origin and Spread of Nationalism*. New York: Verso.

Ashworth. G.J. 2005. 'The commodification of the past as an instrument for local development. Don't Count on it', in J. Kaminski (ed.) *Heritage Impact*, pp. 133–40. Brighton: EPOCH.

Bauman, Richard. 1977. *Verbal Art as Performance.* Rowley, MA: Newbury House.

Beeman, W.O. 1993. 'The Anthropology of Theater and Spectacle', *Annual Review of Anthropology*, 22: 369–93.

Bell, C. 1992. *Ritual Theory, Ritual Practice.* New York: Oxford University Press.

Bendix, R. 1997. *In Search of Authenticity: The Formation of Folklore Studies.* Madison: University of Wisconsin Press.

Köpping, K.P. 1998. 'Inszenierung und Transgression in Ritual und Theater', in B.E. Schmidt and M. Münzel (eds) *Ethnologie und Inszenierung: Ansätze zur Theaterethnologie*, pp. 45–86. Marburg: Curupia.

Lowenthal, D. 1985. *The Past Is a Foreign Country.* Cambridge: Cambridge University Press.

McCauley, R.N. and Lawson, E.T. 1996. 'Who Owns "Culture"?', *Method and Theory in the Study of Religion*, 8: 171–90.

Myerhoff, B. 1984. 'A Death in Due Time: Construction of Self and Culture in Ritual Drama', in J. MacAloon (ed.) *Rite, Drama, Festival, Spectacle: Rehearsals Toward a Theory of Cultural Performance.* Philadelphia: Institute for the Study of Human Issues.

Polit, K. 2006. 'Keep My Share of Rice in the Cupboard: Ethnographic Reflections on Practices of Gender and Agency among Dalit Women in the Central Himalayas', PhD Thesis, University of Heidelberg.

Purohit, D.R. 1993. 'Medieval English Folk Drama and Garhwali Folk Theatre: A Comparative Study', PhD Thesis, H.N.B. Garhwal University.

Sax, W.S. 2002. *Dancing the Self: Personhood and Performance in the Pandav Lila of Garhwal.* Oxford: Oxford University Press.

Schechner, R. 1985. *Between Theater and Anthropology.* Philadelphia: University of Pennsylvania Press.

———. 1990. *Theater-Anthropologie: Spiel und Ritual im Kulturvergleich.* Reinbek bei Hamburg: Rowohlt.

Scheer, P. 2002. 'Copyright Heritage: Preservation, Carnival and the State in Trinidad', *Anthropological Quarterly* 75 (3): 453–84.

Singer, Milton. 1959. Preface, in Milton Singer (ed.) *Traditional India: Structure and Change*, pp. ix–xviii. Philadelphia: American Philosophical Society.

Taylor, D. 2003. *The Archive and the Repertoire: Performing Cultural Memory in the Americas.* Durham and London: Duke University Press.

Turner, V. 1986. *The Anthropology of Performance.* New York: PAJ Publications.

Utz, R. 2005. 'Nations, Nation-Building, and Cultural Intervention: A Social Science Perspective', in A. von Bogdandy and R. Wolfrum (eds) *Max Planck Yearbook of United Nations Law*, 9: 615–47.

Van der Veer, P. 1996. 'Authenticity and Authority in Surinamese Hindu Ritual', in D. Dabyden (ed.) *Across the Dark Waters*, pp. 131–46. London: Macmillan.

Robertson Smith, W. 1894. *Lectures on the Religion of the Semites*. London: Adam and Charles Black.

2

Initiation, 'Re-birth' and the Emergent Congregation

An Analysis of the Svadhyaya Movement in Western India

Anindita Chakrabarti

At the Delhi railway station, as I sat in Ashram Express on my way to Gujarat for fieldwork, I watched a middle-aged woman and a man on the platform. They were bidding goodbye and there was an air of intensity between them. Before she boarded the train, with tearful eyes, she bent down and touched his feet. I tried hard but could not figure out their relationship. She sat down opposite me and we began to chat. She told me that the man on the platform and she were disciples of the same guru. She smiled and added, 'We are *satsangis*.'[1]

The incident recounted above, captures in an allegorical sense the theme of the essay. I had failed to guess the relationship between the man and the woman because all my guesses were within the fold of the social structure of kinship and family whereas the relation of '*satsangis*' lies precisely outside its pale. The rituals I describe in this essay are rituals of forming this new association and not rituals of sacrament that confirm one's caste and kinship status. The relation of sectarian association is based not on ascription but on the basis of voluntary initiation (*dīkṣā*). Beyond the rituals of sacraments that make the individual a member of the social structure, there are rituals that initiate the individual as a member of a sect. It has been pointed out by scholars of Hinduism and Buddhism that it is this initiation rather than the initiatory rites of passage that is viewed as soteriologically relevant. Moreover, unlike the initiatory rites of *upanayana* they are not only accessible to upper-caste men but to all irrespective of gender (Rospatt 2005:221). This essay traces the process of initiation in Svdhyaya, a Hindu sectarian movement in Western India. It describes the rituals of self-transformation that the followers of Svadhyaya—known as Svadhyayīs—undergo to be 'born' in the Svadhyaya 'family'. Citing their lack of emphasis on traditional modes of worship, Svadhyaya is avowedly 'anti-ritualistic'. Yet, a closer scrutiny reveals how Svadhyaya creates its own ritual field by imbuing the traditional religious calendar with new meaning and introducing new rituals/rites of worshipping the 'sacred'. In the essay I shall approach the rituals of the emergent congregation as a dynamic process through which a new identity is constituted, experienced and articulated by the practitioners.

Saving the Self by Saving the Other: Svadhyaya's Theology of Reform

The Svadhyaya sectarian movement was founded by Pandurang Shastri Athavale (1920–2003) who claimed that reforming Hinduism was not possible without reforming Hindu society. Dadaji—as Athavale is addressed by his disciples—based his teachings on the soteriological premise that saving the self is unattainable without saving the other. The Svadhyaya reform is strongly reminiscent of a protest against what Louis Dumont had described as the 'asocial' nature of renunciation in Hinduism. Dumont had pointed out that the conscience of Hindu society, beyond the hierarchical opposition of purity/impurity, is embodied in the person of the *sannyāsī* who is an individual outside society and powerless against it. By renouncing caste, the renouncer becomes asocial—an individual outside society. Therefore, the developments of renunciation, with all their riches, are contained after all within narrow limits, which they were unable to go beyond (Dumont 1999). Svadhyayīs describe their reform as a protest against this individualistic soteriology. They articulate as Svadhyaya's 'origin myth' how Dadaji took up the challenge of 'bringing back the conscience of Hindu society' which has been lost in the wilderness of world-renouncing asceticism.

According to the historical narrative of the movement, it was the participation at a Conference of World Religions in Japan in

1954 that made Dadaji take up the task of bridging the gap between Hinduism as a 'discipline of salvation' and as a 'way of life'. The Svadhyaya initiative was the outcome of this reform agenda. At the Conference, Dadaji had spoken on the importance of religion in human life, the dangers of the machine-centric worldview and the great teachings of the Gītā, one of the key texts of Hindu religion (Athavale: 1954). It is said that the participants at the conference said that they were convinced of the greatness of the message of the Gītā, but asked him if he could show a single village in India where life was based on its principles. Dadaji could not answer in the affirmative and it made him take up the challenge that it was possible to bridge the gap between the theory and practice of the teachings of Hinduism.

Dadaji began his reform by pointing out that *sannyās* never meant renunciation. It did so as a result of serious misinterpretation of the Vedant.[2] In his discourses he reinterpreted *sannyās* as '*saṃyak nyās*', which signified keeping things in a perfect manner and not reclusive existence away from society. The Svadhyaya concept of 'non-renunciation' is based on the idea that salvation is not possible outside society. On the contrary, it entails performing one's tasks without attachment (*niṣkām karma*). According to Dadaji, *mokṣ* should be sought in *gṛhasthāśram*. But *gṛhasthāśram* in itself does not automatically lead to *mokṣ*. In many of his discourses Dadaji recites the following English nursery rhyme, which is about the brevity, monotony and finite nature of human life.

Solomon Grundy,
Born on Monday,
Christened on Tuesday,
Married on Wednesday,
Took ill on Thursday,
Worse on Friday,
Died on Saturday,
Buried on Sunday:
This is the end
Of Solomon Grundy.

In Hindu society the sacraments of birth, marriage and death are fulfilled within the parameters of caste and kinship rules. But this does not lead to *mokṣ* but its opposite, i.e., to be trapped by the dictates of the Lower Self. In order to attain salvation one needs to do more than what Solomon Grundy did in his life. Leading such a life and seeking salvation in reclusive renunciation would not yield any results. Thus, declaring renunciation of renunciation as the real Hinduism, Dadaji urges his audience to realise that questioning our everyday life is the beginning of the journey towards *mokṣ*. Arjun's remorse (*viṣād*) in the field of Kurukṣetra is the beginning of his search for God (Athavale 1998).[3]

Dadaji taught in his discourses that salvation was as important as the other three *puruṣārtha* and could not be pursued either within the parameters of sacraments of caste and kinship or in asceticism, instead it called for an engagement with society.[4] Dadaji used the concepts of *karmayoga*, *yajña* and *lokasaṃgraha*[5] to illustrate that engagement with society was indeed a religiously sanctioned way of seeking *mokṣ*. Dadaji explained to his disciples that *karma* had nothing to do with *karmakānd*, i.e., 'ritual action', but meant active engagement with society. The task of *lokasaṃgraha* was to inspire people to achieve their own *puruṣārtha* and that was the vocation of the sages in the ancient times. A real guru is considered as an extraordinary being (*mahāpuruṣ*) because he/she performs this task.[6] Doing *lokasaṃgraha* is, therefore, doing God's work. Dadaji inspired those who came to listen to him to seek their salvation not in meditative yogic practices but by going to society and helping the people address their own spiritual and social problems. *Lokasaṃgraha* can be performed only in a collective which is a sacred association based on the concept of sacrifice (*yajña*). *Yajña* symbolises 'sacrifice for the sake of the larger good' Dadaji told his audience. Svadhyayīs believe that Dadaji's sacrifice has shown them the correct path and has led to the formation of the Svadhyaya family (*parivār*). It is pointed out at a number of Svadhyaya discussions that we should not forget Dadaji's sacrifice for the sake of our culture and religion.[7] To be a Svadhyayī, in turn, means that one is willing to make sacrifices for the sake of collective well-being.

Being a member of this family involves a process of rebirth, i.e., to be born into a new association. Unlike other sects, in Svadhyaya there is no formal *dīkṣā* or any gradation of *dīkṣā* like that of the Mata Amritanandamayi Mission or the Svaminarayan Sampraday. The Svadhyaya activists themselves spread the message of Svadhyaya going to different localities and communities. There are Svadhyayīs in remote villages of Gujarat who have been practising Svadhyaya for many years but have never met Dadaji in person. Yet Svadhyayīs speak of a *process* of initiation. A Svadhyayī woman had once told me as we travelled in a bus from Surat to Amereli district of Gujarat that she is a *dvija* or 'twice born'[8], just like an egg! She was born to her parents but her real birth was in a family of Svadhyayīs from whom she had learnt Svadhyaya. How and when does the process of 'conversion' begin as one undergoes transformation and becomes a 'Svadhyayī'? It could be said that the process of 'rebirth' begins with a congregational act of listening to Dadaji's sermons on video tapes or delivered by Svadhyayīs who travel and communicate the Svadhyaya theology through exegesis. By regularly listening to these discourses one begins to understand Svadhyaya theology but it remains incomplete without 'doing' Svadhyaya, that is, going to others as one's religious duty. In the following sections, I will describe how the process of initiation begins as the congregation of listeners take up the task of 'doing God's work' by becoming itinerant messengers.

The Sangha of Listeners

In this section I will describe the event of 'sacred listening' in/as a congregation which constitutes the first step towards becoming a Svadhyayī. In Svadhyaya, the most important sacred event is Dadaji's sermon that takes place every Sunday at the Pāṭhśālā in Mumbai. The Pāṭhśālā has two floors and Dadaji sits on the first floor. The Svadhyayīs who sit on the ground floor watch him on television screens. The devotees who work as volunteers set the stage for the performance of the sermon. Couple of hours prior to Dadaji's arrival, audio tapes of Svadhyaya devotional songs are played at the premises of the Pāṭhśālā. But just before Dadaji arrives, the congregation begins to sing. Next, the congregation chants *Isa Upanishad,*[9] along with Dadaji and then he begins the sermon. These sermons are video taped and then played every week at the Svadhyaya Video Kendra 'sermon centres'. For Svadhyayīs attending these 'video sermons' constitutes the most important weekly ritual.[10] Apart form these Video Kendras there are *kendra*s where the Svadhyayī leaders themselves deliver sermons.

In order to bring out the congregational aspect of sacred listening in Svadhyaya I will contrast it with *darśan* or the 'visual perception of the sacred' (Eck 1998: 3). *Darśan,* which forms the core of bhakti worship, is never a simple, passive sight of the deity. The deity also gazes on the devotee and it is a moment of consecration (Gonda 1969, Fuller 1992, Morgan 2005). Lawrence Babb has described *darśan* in sectarian Hinduism as a special intimacy, a 'closure' between the guru and the devotee where the latter is uplifted through a superior visual transaction (Babb 1981: 391, 396; see also Eck 1998). *Darśan,* therefore, is often an *individual* act of worship where the congregation does not have any role to play. In contrast, the sacred event of listening is not even possible without a congregation. The act of sacred listening, unlike *darśan,* is dependent on the presence of a collective. This aspect of Svadhyaya is captured by the restrictions on the distribution of the Svadhyaya video cassettes. The Svadhyaya Parivar owns them and they are circulated by activists who undertake the responsibility of running the video discourse centres. The idea behind this is that these discourses are not for individual viewing. They have to be watched only in/as a congregation.[11] This aspect has been noted by John T. Little when he wrote that not only were the video cassettes not to be sold, borrowed or rented out but even when the activist possessed the tape but missed the Video Kendra, s/he would not watch the tape at home (Little 1995: 273). The taboo against private viewing of the video tapes is significant because it reveals that it is the congregation that constitutes the sacred event and not just the presence of the video tapes.

This is also evident from the fact that even when Dadaji's video cassettes are not present, the Svadhyaya Kendras are sacred events from the participants' point of view. Each Svadhyaya Kendra begins with a prayer, which is an invocation of Lord Kṛṣṇa. The moment of collective chanting invokes the presence of God, and therefore everything that happens till the valedictory prayer takes place with God as witness. This was pointed out to me by a Svadhyayī activist when she complained against those who came late at the Svadhyaya Kendras. She said, 'Once we chant the prayer *Vasudevasutam devam* [...] we are actually invoking God to be present. How could someone arrive late for such a gathering?' The underlying idea is that in the presence of God (invoked by collective chanting of *mantra*) individuals form a congregation. Therefore, more than a satsang between Svadhyayīs through 'video-*vacana*', as suggested by Little, a triadic relationship is established between the Self, God and the Other in this context. And it is the presence of the three that turns the group into a congregation—equally accessible to all those who partake in the performance of collective listening and sermonising.

By participating in this congregation, the individual begins a journey of entering into a 'divine relation' with others—from those they had so far remained estranged due to the lack of recognition of this sacred bond. Thus begins a process of 'conversion' whereby the self undergoes transformation by way of reaching out to others. This transformative journey is called *bhaktipherī* or the 'devotional sojourn'. It is the beginning of 'rebirth' into the Svadhyaya Parivar where individuals go to others as messengers of the movement. In the following section I will discuss the process of *bhaktipherī* which signifies a process through which the one who walks on the path of Svadhyaya forms a new congregation by communicating Dadaji's message to the uninitiated.

The Itinerant Messenger: Becoming a Svadhyayī Through *Bhaktipherī*

'You are studying Svadhyaya but are you a Svadhyayī?' — I have very often encountered this question during my fieldwork. It is an ineffable experience and one truly understands Svadhyaya only by practising it. Therefore, to experience and participate in Svadhyaya and yet to describe oneself as a non-Svadhyayī, as I did, was an oxymoron. For Svadhyayīs, only by way of practice could one experience Svadhyaya and become a Svadhyayī. They often pointed out that even in the Gītā, it was said that the knowledge described was not to be talked about and discussed academically but that it must become an inward experience. N.R. Sheth, a scholar who was closely associated with Svadhyaya for several years, was struck by the zeal with which the Svadhyayīs inquired from each other whether they were going to the villages or not. If a person was not going for *bhaktipherī* to the villages, it was seen as a compromise on one's religious merit. Apart from spreading the message of Svadhyaya during *bhaktipherī*, the activists initiate a range of activities akin to development projects which the communities are supposed to continue and manage.[12]

I shall describe the method of *bhaktipherī* which was undertaken for the first time in 1958. Ileshbhai was one of those nineteen persons who went for the first *bhaktipherī* in Amreli district in Gujarat from Mumbai. He pointed out in an interview:

> We were city-bred people and it was an experience for us to live without electricity, newspaper or radio. Dadaji had asked us to just interact with the people. At that time we did not know that such a thing would happen. We were very young and we were unhappy with the way religion was practised. We also wanted to do something for society and did not know how. The nineteen of us split into three groups. We spend three days in each village and we covered five villages in a span of fifteen days.[13]

During *bhaktipherī*, one is supposed to spend at least one night outside home and it is never undertaken as an individual. This practice stands in contrast with the lone figure of the *sannyāsī*. Svadhyayīs point out that *bhaktipherī* is collective work. It is desirable that husband and wife go together for these visits. Men go in small groups and stay overnight but when women travel in groups they are supposed to return on the same day. This is, however, a rule for the volunteers and not applicable to the leaders. When travel does not involve an overnight stay and consists of visits in the neighbourhood or village, it is called *bhāvpherī* or 'goodwill visit' in Svadhyaya terminology. Another mode of travel is undertaken by the women on the ritually significant day of *ekādaśī* (the eleventh day of a lunar fortnight) when they go to another village in a group and meet with the people there. They go and come back on the same day. When I travelled with the women on an *ekādaśī* day, we walked about six kilometres to reach a neighbouring village. We carried our own food, and on reaching the village, we went to different neighbourhoods (*faḷia*, literally 'lanes') of the village. We had been to the Harijan quarter, as well as to a Muslim house. The topics of discussion varied from listening to an elderly woman's woe regarding her husband's extramarital affair to a religious discussion on the oneness of God with a Muslim woman. In this case, the common practice of observing *ekādaśī* was imbued with a new significance and incorporated into the praxis of *bhāvpherī*.

During these *bhaktipherīs*, Svadhyayīs often say that they do not accept anything else apart from water, mat and light. Gujaratis' fondness for hyperbole is reflected in another statement that is popular, that Svadhyayīs do not ask for *lot* (food, lit. flour), vote (meaning electoral support) or note (money). In a context where the main purpose behind visits from religious groups is the collection of donations, this non-acceptance of even a cup of tea brings a refreshing change. In the villages, I have often heard villagers contrasting between the Svaminarayan sect[14] and Svadhyaya, pointing out that whereas the Svaminarayan sadhus collected money from the devotees and the devotees, in turn, asked for money from the villagers, Svadhyayīs never collected money from others. In fact, during the first few visits, Svadhyayīs tell the people that they have come just to meet them. For a period of time, they might not mention anything about Svadhyaya. *Bhaktipherī* is periodically undertaken to other parts of India and sometimes abroad. For the last few years, a *bhaktipherī* team has been coming to Delhi from Ahmedabad. They meet with the people, contact the youth, hold programmes for children and perform street plays for the community. Those who work in the slums live with the people under considerable discomfort. The work they initiate is meant to be carried on by the local leaders.

It is very often repeated by the Svadhyayīs that they do not go to teach or help the people. It is for the purpose of self-development and learning about oneself (which is the literal meaning of Svadhyaya) that such journeys are undertaken. Since one is related to all other human beings by virtue of being the children of the same Supreme God, it is one's religious duty to develop relations with others. The individual is supposed to undergo changes as a result of this relationship-building process. During *bhaktipherī*, one is required to step outside one's social position like the *sannyāsī*. It is during this itinerant state that the self is made to undergo a status-less existence. The hardship and humiliation that one suffers during *bhaktipherī* are constitutive of the new self that the one who walks on the path of Svadhyaya aspires for. As mentioned earlier, this reaching out to others through *bhaktipherī* is the most important aspect of being a Svadhyayī. One cannot be a Svadhyayī without doing *bhaktipherī*. The homeless, ascetic state is what Svadhyayīs have to embrace temporarily and periodically but not permanently. It is through these practices that the Svadhyayī develops a new *sanskār*,[15] i.e., a refinement of the self.

Bhaktipherī is the most crucial metaphysical as well as organisational aspect of Svadhyaya which is carried out by Svadhyayīs themselves without any administrative structure or expenditure. Once *bhaktipherī* has been successful in an area, the local Svadhyayīs begin to celebrate a number of festivals centred around the religious calendar. These festivals involve both reinterpreting the popular religious calendar as well as including a range of new Svadhyaya rituals. In the next section, I shall describe some of these religious festivals and rituals focusing particularly on the ritual of *bhūmipūjan*. This re-interpretation of traditional religious festivals and incorporation of new rituals demonstrate the nature of innovation that constructs the core of Svadhyaya sociation.

Reinterpreting the Ritual Calendar

Whereas *bhaktipherī* is not dependent on any fixed ritual calendar there is an emergent calendar of religious festivals/rituals that Svadhyayīs perform. First, traditional religious events such as *rāmnavamī, janmāṣtamī* are celebrated with Svadhyaya re-interpretation and second, new religious festivals and rituals have been introduced over the years. Some of these new festivals are Manusya Gaurav Din, Yogeśvar Day, Madhavrund, Gitajayanti. In order to highlight the innovations in the Svadhyaya festivals/rituals I will describe how the religious calendar is a dynamic process of negotiation between what is given and the emergent. From the practitioners' point of view old religious festivals acquire new significance and at the same time new rituals are performed for new sacred events.

I will describe in some detail how two popular traditional religious festivals — *rāmnavamī* and *janmaṣtamī* — are celebrated by the Svadhyayīs in Gujarat. On *rāmnavamī,* the birthday of Lord Rama, I attended two Svadhyaya celebrations. In the morning I attended the *pāṭhotsav*[16] of a Yogeśvar temple at a village where most of the households belonged to Kanbi Patel caste. The village was celebrating the twenty-fifth anniversary of its Yogeśvar temple.[17] Ajitbhai, a senior Svadhyayī from Vapi, a neighboring town, was invited to deliver a speech at the *pāthotsav*. A bright-coloured canopy (*mandap*) was put up at the temple. After reciting the *stotrās,* Ajitbhai delivered a discourse focusing on Dadaji's life and personal qualities. I was told that the married women of the village had written letters to their natal homes inviting their families to come and attend the function. Likewise, parents with married daughters had invited their daughters. The guests who came to attend the festival were taken to different homes for lunch. After the lunch, the Svadhyayīs had a leisurely chat with the villagers on a range of topics including Svadhyaya activities in the area. In the evening, I went to another village which was celebrating *rāmnavamī* by performing Matru-Pitru Pūjan, 'saluting the parents'. At the programme, some Svadhyaya devotional songs (*bhāvgīt*) were sung and the village Svadhyayī leader delivered a sermon. After that, all the parents of the village were made to sit on chairs and their children greeted them by touching their feet. Svadhyayīs explained to me that such a festival strengthened the bond between generations. The *rāmnavamī* festival was organised by Svadhyayīs, but non-Svadhyayī villagers also participated in this festival. The birthday of Lord Kṛṣṇa is celebrated as *janmaṣtamī* or *gokul āṭham* in Gujarat. I participated in this event in 2001. Singing joyous songs men, women and children went to different spots in the neighbourhood where earthen pots containing curd were tied on poles or trees. The young men in the group formed a human pyramid. A toddler or a boy, dressed up as Kṛṣṇa, stood on their shoulders, broke the pot and distributed the curd. Unlike *rāmnavamī* which was celebrated in a novel way, the *janmāṣtamī* function did not deviate from its traditional format. Both these events were celebrated as village festivals and those who were not Svadhyayīs also participated. But *for* Svadhyayīs they were Svadhyaya celebrations.

Apart from reinterpreting the religious calendar, a number of religious events and rituals have been introduced by Svadhyayīs. Though some of them are not completely new, such as celebrating Dadaji's birthday or performing the re-consecration ceremony (*pāṭhotsav*) of temple, they are performed with unique Svadhyaya 'understanding/meaning'. Gītājayantī, which Svadhyayīs believe was the day when Kṛṣṇa had recited the Gītā to Arjuna, is one such event. It is celebrated by Svadhyayīs by holding elocution competition on concepts from the Gītā. Men and women participate in this competition in large numbers and the final event takes place at the Pāṭhśālā where Dadaji declares the name of the winner. Dadaji's birthday on 19 October is celebrated as Manuṣya Gaurav Din. At the Manuṣya Gaurav Din function that I attended in Surat city in 2001, a special video-discourse was delivered by Dadaji on the topic of humanity, and then a dance performance was put up by the young Svadhyayī women. Dadaji's wife Tai's birthday on 3 August is celebrated as Varṣāmilan, a special programme for the fishing community — one of the marginalised communities who have embraced Svadhyaya in large numbers. Dadaji explained to his disciples that one should offer one's labour as worship. On the basis of this principle, Svadhyayīs work on orchards and undertake construction of water tanks and check dams. Dadaji's daughter who is currently heading the movement is addressed as Didiji. The Svadhyayīs celebrate her birthday on 12 July by planting saplings and also doing *pūjā* at the Vṛkṣmandir — the 'temple orchards'. It should be noted that according to the *dharmasāstras* constructing orchards come under *pūrta dāna* and they are considered as extremely meritorious acts of religious charity.[18]

For the followers of different sects it is a common practice in Gujarat to offer worship to their religious heads on *gurupurṇimā*.'[19] On this day, a large number of Svadhyayīs visit the Tatvajñāna Vidyāpīth at Thane, Maharashtra and they take out their '*bhagvān kā bhāg*', i.e., a portion of their earning as a token of their gratitude to God, and offer this money to Dadaji. Dadaji explained that in ancient India Brahmin was not a caste but people who worked selflessly for the welfare of all. Brahmins reminded the people of their moral duty to others and even reprimanded the king when he failed to fulfil his royal obligations. As a token of gratitude the people gave a portion of their earnings to Brahmins so that they could continue being the 'conscience-keepers' of society. This idea is operative in all Svadhyaya projects and resources for the movement are generated on this basis. I shall describe in some detail the ritual of *bhūmipūjan* that is performed when Svadhyayīs undertake Yogeśvar Kṛuṣi — a Svadhyaya 'experiment' (*prayog*) where farmers work on a piece of land as a way of worshipping God. According to Svadhyayīs by making material contribution to the movement they 'adopt a Brahmin', in this case Dadaji, who has shown them the path. Two-third of the earnings from the Yogeśvar Kṛuṣi is contributed to the movement and one-third is spent on the local community. These contributions through voluntary labour make the movement financially self-sufficient. No donation is accepted from those who are not Svadhyayīs. The details of the ritual performed by a Svadhyayī leader belonging to Koli Patel — a backward caste — capture the innovation of ritual in Svadhyaya.

The ritual of *bhūmipūjan* is conducted like a sacrifice but without lighting the sacrificial fire. During this ritual a group of Svadhyayīs — *jajmāns*[20] in this context — take a religious vow to 'adopt' a Brahmin. The ceremony, as innovative as the purpose itself, is informative of ritual innovation in Svadhyaya. The *bhūmipūjan* ritual that I attended in 2001 took place on the day of *akhā trīj* — a special day for the peasant (*kheḍut*) which signified the beginning of a new agricultural cycle. At Umbhel, a village in Surat district, where the Yogeśvar Kṛuṣi was to start *bhūmipūjan* began with a procession (*śobhāyātrā*) through the village. One of the Svdhyayīs from the village sat on a decorated bullock cart with the images of Kṛṣṇa (worshipped as Yogeśvar by Svdhyayīs), Shiva and Parvati with baby Ganesh. The girls were dressed up in their ethnic costumes and carried a coconut on a *kalaś,* pot, on their heads. Singing devotional songs, we reached the Yogeśvar Kruṣi ground and the *pūjā* began. On the ground, *patli*s or small wooden seats were placed and covered with red cloth. On one *patli* rice was kept and on the other one, wheat. Dadaji's and Yogeśvar's photographs were kept next to them. Maheshbhai, a Svadhyayī leader, was the officiating priest. There were about twelve couples who were the *jajmān*s and about twenty-odd Svadhyayī spectators. The ritual went on under the blazing April sun. First devotional songs were sung, followed by the Svadhyaya prayer. In order to capture the innovative aspect of this ritual I describe it from my field notes:

> Maheshbhai drinks water by cupping his palm, says, '*svāhā*'. He does a few *prāṇāyām* 'breath-exercise', and tells the others that since they do not know *prāṇāyām,* there is no need for them to do it. He asks the couples to tie threads around each other's wrists. *Abil-gulāl* (coloured powders) and areca nuts are kept on a plate in front of them. Then Maheshbhai recites *śloks* from the Prarthana Prīti, the Svadhyaya prayer book, and the others repeat after him. He tells them:
>
> Take water in your right hand and take the vow to 'reconsecrate' our culture (*sanskṛuti*). From the left side the demonic forces (*piśāc*) enter, let us pray that whatever is inauspicious is purged out of our body. East is *Ṛg Veda,* west is *Sām,* south is *Yajur* and north is *Atharva.* Sprinkle water on yourself. Take water in your left palm and sprinkle it with your right hand on the items kept on the plate. When Arjun goes to the battle ground, Indra, the King of gods, sends Urvashi, the celestial courtesan, in order to lure him

with her charm. Arjun touches her feet. Likewise, when a woman asked Vivekananda to marry her so that she can have sons like him, Vivekananda touched her feet and told her that she should consider him as her son.

Then everyone takes rice in right hand and goes round in a circle. They tap their right heel on the ground three times. They take marigold flower, *gulāl*, pray and put them on the *kalaś*. As the ritual proceeds, Maheshbhai gives a commentary on the qualities of the different ingredients used in the ritual. A homology is imputed between them and the personal qualities that Svadhyayis need to develop. He says:

The purpose is to build one's character, it should be white and pure (*śubhra*) like milk. Why is curd considered as auspicious (*śagun*)? Because it has power. A little bit of curd can turn 20 lt. of milk into curd. If one person from India goes with Indian culture to the West he is like curd and the Western culture that 20 lt. of milk. *Ghi,* clarified butter, is the symbol of *sneha*. From *ghi* emanates holiness in the environment. There could be darkness under the lamp but not around it. You can make others your own when you take a good proposition/idea (*vicār*) in society. *Madhu,* honey, has a special quality; just like sugar it dissolves and gives sweetness. The unique quality they have is the capacity for sacrifice. Women also have this quality. They sacrifice their own identity. It is said that behind every successful man there is a woman. We celebrate Dadaji's birthday as Manuṣya Gaurav Day because he has sacrificed his own existence for this work. When we are doing Svadhyaya the exemplary life of this *mahāpuruṣ* should be in front of us. Now let us bathe the Gods with aromatic water (that is, water mixed with camphor). Bathe the two areca nuts that symbolise Gaṇapati and Yogeśvar.

At this point, the water is taken from everybody's plate into a bigger vessel. 'Now it is time to do *abhiṣek* on Yogeśvar', saying this, Maheshbhai recites Narayanamantra. They put areca nut on the rice in front of Yogeśvar. Maheshbhai continues, illustrating with examples that it is possible for Brahmins to work as 'conscience keepers' only when the society takes care of their material needs:

There are two Brahmins in front of us: Vashistha and Dronacarya. Dronacarya was dependent on royal power for his livelihood, whereas Vashistha was not. Vashistha could tell Rama what he should do. But Dronacarya could not say anything to the Kauravas. We should adopt a Brahmin. We should make financial contribution for the Brahmin (Dadaji) who has sacrificed his own life. This will be done through Yogeśvar Kṛuṣi. What is the significance of the sacred thread (*yajñapavit*)? It is a reminder that God is with us 24 hours. Demons and spirits (*bhūt, piśāc*) leave when *yajñapavit* is present. It is also to remind us that we are the soldiers of God for 24 hours.

Maheshbhai asks for sandalwood paste (*candan*), but it was not on their plates. He continues:

Well, turmeric and vermillion would do. Turmeric (*haḷdar*) is *ayurvedic*. It is a medicine. It is used during weddings. It brings glow to the skin. *Kumkum* is the symbol of good fortune. Putting *kumkum* on forehead signifies the worship of intellect. There is no time to go into detail. You please offer them to God. Take rice, *kumkum, abil* and *gulāl*. God has given us flowers. What is the credit in giving it back to God? You should dedicate your life as a flower (*jivanpuṣpa*). You have to turn five people into active Svadhyayīs. That is the real offering to God.

He asks for tender grass blades (*dūrbā*) but there was none and he gives an alternative. Saying, *'Om'*, they move the incense in a circular motion. Maheshbhai continues:

God has to be shown the oil lamp (*dībā*). Fennel, which is offered to God as a mouth-freshener, has bile-reducing (*pittanāśak*) quality. You should always sit in consultation with God. The one who gives credit (*yaś*) to others is Yasoda. The one who always says, *'mai, mai'* becomes a goat. All these are the fruits of *karma* of several rebirths. *Dakṣiṇā* has to be given with a big heart along with intellect.

Ārti is done. The *jajmāns* go in circle and take the vow to do *bhaktipherī*. Husband and wife swap places. They salute the gods and make an offering of flowers. Everybody together recites Gayatri Mantra. A plow is brought and it is worshipped as the instrument of *bhakti*. *Srisuktam* is recited. Two persons dig on the ground with the plow. At the end of this rather spontaneous ritual Maheshbhai begs the gods for forgiveness if there had been any mistake in the *pūjā*. Then they recite some *stotras*. *Lapsī*, a sweet made out of broken wheat and molasses, is distributed at the end of the ceremony. It is a traditional sweet eaten by peasants on the day of *akhā trīj*.[21]

The *bhūmipūjan* ceremony describes a novel ritual that Svadhyayīs undertake in order to 'offer their efficiency' for the Svadhyaya movement. Throughout the *bhūmipūjan* ceremony the emphasis has been on the 'meaning' of each and every ritual action. In this schema things have inherent meaning and the purpose of the ritual is to communicate them to the congregation. The aim of the ritual is not system-maintenance but to create a new congregation through innovative interference of everyday symbols. Thus, in the place of 'empty ritualism' objects are infused with qualities, and the activists are urged to acquire those qualities. The virtues extolled are those which lead to the formation of a collective and individuals are urged to give up their egos for the sake of larger good. A.M. Hocart had noted this dynamic role of rituals in the context of ethical religions where this-worldly bounty was no longer the aim of rituals but goodness and spiritual elevation were. In this context, everything needed to be reinterpreted to fit the changed point of view; everything became edifying symbolism. Thus, the lamp no longer symbolised the sun but the saviour who lighted the way to salvation. In this ritual field good conduct is regarded as higher offering and the word is no longer the compelling force (Hocart 1970: 77–78). Thus in Svadhyaya terminology it is not the ritual flower but *'jivanpuspa'* or the 'gift of life' that is to be offered to God. The *bhūmipūjan* ritual emphasised that this could be achieved by emulating the exemplary life of Dadaji who has sacrificed his life for the greater good.

So far I have described the rituals through which an emergent congregation is formed, beginning with the act of collective listening to Dadaji's interpretation of Svadhyaya theology and then going to others as messengers of *bhakti*. I have also shown how a new semantic field is created in Svadhyaya rituals through reinterpreting the religious calendar and by introducing innovative rituals such as *bhūmipūjan*. In the following section I shall describe the rituals that Svadhyayīs observe in private, at an individual level. If for Svadhyayīs the way of acting upon oneself is by acting on the world, there is also a process of self-purification that is personal and intimate. These ritual actions are supposed to help in acquiring a new *sanskār* which is necessary for the process of self-development.

'In Consultation with God': Acquiring a New *Sanskār*

When I tried to find out whether there is some sort of *dīkṣā* in Svadhyaya, I was always told that there was none. Svadhyayīs pointed out that there is no secret *gurumantra* that the disciples received from Dadaji. But like in all sectarian movements it is not on the ethical doctrine but on the ethical conduct that premium is placed by the group. Though there was no formal *dīkṣā,* over a period of time, I noted several practices that are to be observed if one is walking on the path of Svadhyaya. One 'becomes' a Svadhyayī not through *dīkṣā* but by acquiring *sanskār*. In this section I will dwell on the multivocal nature of the concept of *sanskār* and show how it captures the process of moral self-development in the context of Svadhyaya. It clearly illustrates that sectarian identity is a status that is 'achieved' as opposed to the 'ascribed' caste identity.

Reciting the *trikāl sandhyā* — a set of prayers — signifies the act of remembering God three times in a day and it is mandatory for all Svadhyayīs. One must recite these three set of prayers in the morning, before taking a meal, and at night, before going to bed. Apart from reciting *trikāl sandhyā,* Svadhyayī activists perform daily worship at home. I have heard activists discuss the importance of sitting in 'consultation' with God everyday so that they do not deviate from the work they set out to do. They pray to God to give them the courage and strength to do the work they have taken up. Once I overheard an activist telling a junior Svadhayayī, 'Whenever I am hurt by a co-worker's behaviour or upset with anybody in Svadhyaya, I sit in consultation with God and remind myself that I am doing God's work and therefore nothing else matters.' Apart from daily worship, family prayers are recited every evening by the head of the family and the others repeat after him/her. Messages from Dadaji's office are circulated among active Svadhyayīs. These are read out after the family prayer. These messages are called *sûkti* (good sayings).[22] The content of the Svadhyaya *sûkti* is based on a range of ethical and moral sayings such as, 'One should be satisfied with the food one eats and with one's own wife.' Or, 'Whoever (and whatever) is a hindrance on the path of God's work (*prabhukārya*) should be immediately discarded.' The *sûkti* changes every two weeks, and the paper on which it is written is either burnt or put in flowing water. These are sent by post to the district headquarters and the leaders from different *taluka*s come and copy them out by hand for the Svadhyayīs of his/her locality. These and most other Svadhyaya material are never photocopied.

The food taboos that Svadhyayīs observe also subtly capture this transformative process. Though food taboos are not as aggressively prescribed as in the case of the strictly vegetarian Vaiṣnavites such as the Vallabhacaryas or Svaminarayan sects, they are very much present. Food is necessary for survival but it can also be a source of attachment. Therefore, prescriptions/proscriptions regarding food are important not only in the context of caste but also for renouncers. Patrick Olivelle points out that love of food results in greed, a vice that the renouncers must constantly guard against (Olivelle 1992: 105). The most important taboo is *vis-à-vis* non-vegetarian food and alcohol. At a fishing village in Valsad, I had a meal at the home of a Svadhyayī fisherman who served me fish curries but did not eat any. Later I found out that while he had given up non-vegetarian food, the other members of his family had not. I noticed that certain food taboos are observed only by those committed Svadhyayīs who have been given the sacred-thread (*yajñapavit*) by Dadaji. They would not accept food at a pregnancy ritual (*sīmant*), *vāstu pūjan* (ceremony performed when a house is built) or a funeral (*śrāddh*). When I asked one of them why he would not accept food at these rituals he pointed out that at these ceremonies, the unfulfilled desires of the spirits who were either coming into or departing from the world would get transferred through the food served at these occasions. Like all food taboos these also communicate the knowledge that something might be eaten and others can eat it but not the excluded individuals because they are who they are at the moment (Lewis 2004: 161). Here the underlying implication is that one who is walking on the path of salvation cannot put oneself at the risk of incurring more worldly desires.

It is interesting to note that Svadhyaya food taboo is obverse of the concept of purity/pollution as practised in the context of caste. The following incidence captures this aspect of Svadhyaya commensality. While doing fieldwork in Saurashtra, in Gujarat, I heard Svadhyayīs asking their local leader — Khyatiben, a woman in her early-thirties — in an informal meeting what they should do when they are offered water by the Harijans during *bhaktipherī*. The Svadhyayīs belonging to the Patidar community did not have any problem in drinking the water but what kind of repercussion would it have on Svadhyaya work in the village, they wondered. The rules of commensality *vis-à-vis* the Harijans were very rigid and there was the danger that the Svadhayayīs could be boycotted by their caste members if they came to know that Svadhyayīs were drinking water at Harijan homes. Khyatiben advised them that they should drink the water which would signify commensality across rigid caste barrier, without worrying about its effect on the Svadhyaya work in the village.[23] Through one's engagement with Svadhyaya one is supposed to acquire *sanskār* which refers to a self-purificatory process acquired through right action and it does not follow the caste-based notion of purity/pollution.

During fieldwork, I noticed that in everyday conversations people — both Svadhyayī and non-Svadhyayīs — often use the word *sanskār* and *sanskārī*. Observing this concept, I realised a two-fold play in the word *sanskār*. While one meaning of *sanskār* is life-cycle rituals, the other refers to a propensity towards correct moral action. Every Hindu, no matter what caste or community he/she belongs to, is the subject of rituals at birth, marriage and death. Such rituals are intended for the moral refinement of the individual. Life-cycle rituals constitute *sanskār*, i.e., the process whereby one is 'made complete or perfect' and after death, transformed into an ancestor. As an ancestor, one is in contact with one's descendents through the rituals of feeding that the latter performs. By passing through the sixteen *sanskār*, one is also rendered fit for performing the task of discharging the debt to the gods, sages, ancestors. At Harshupur, a village in Surat district where I stayed during fieldwork, I noticed an interest in performing *sanskār* rituals among the Svadhyayīs, some of which were not done a generation ago. Every now and then I was told how a Svadhyayī woman had performed all the *sanskār* when she was pregnant. A prominent activist from a village in Bharuch district who belonged to the Koḷi Patel caste organised *muṇḍan* ceremony for his sons which, I was told, went on for hours. During my stay at Harshupur, a number of Svadhyayī activists in the village performed the *sanskār*s when they had children, starting with *garbhādhān*. When I quizzed Maheshbhai, my Svadhayayī host, about why *sanskār*s should be performed, he was reticent. He only pointed out that they made the child *tejasvī* (brilliant).[24] But these life-cycle sacraments constituted only one aspect of what the concept of *sanskār* means in the everyday context.

The word *sanskār,* common to a number of Indian languages, very broadly refers to correct or good behaviour. In this context, *sanskār* is not the ritual that produces the desired result but the result itself. A close look at the concept of *sanskār* as described in different contexts by the Svadhyayīs would make this clearer.

Gobardhanbhai, a Svadhyayī in a Saurashtra village, narrated the following to make me understand what real *sanskār* was.

> A Svadhyayī woman who was busy with her household duties could not do much of Dadaji's work. But she wanted to give good *sanskār* to her two sons so that they followed Dadaji's path. She made them memorise the entire Gītā. And she gave them remarkable *sanskār*. I would not have believed it if I had not met the boys myself. I would have thought that people were exaggerating. But the boys are remarkable. Suppose a guest comes to their house to meet their mother and she is not at home; the boys would ask the guest to sit and offer a glass of water. Then they would make some tea and after offering the tea, would inform that their mother had gone out. Such was their *sanskār*!

The illustration of *sanskār* revolves around action: how one should receive and treat guests. It was applauded as correct mode of action and exemplary behaviour. Very often when a girl behaves well, it is said that she is *sanskārī*. In the context of the village, a person with good *sanskār* is the one who is judicious and uncorrupt, captured in the expressions such as, '*dudh kā dudh, pānī kā pānī*.' Likewise, undesirable action is explained in terms of lack of *sanskār*. Once in Harshupur, a daughter-in-law pointed out to me that her mother-in-law's bad nature was due to deficiency in *sanskār*. She asked me in exasperation, 'Who knows from where she has got such *sanskār*?' *Sanskār* is, therefore, not something esoteric but manifested in the concreteness of everyday action.

Explaining the concept of *sanskār* to me, a Svadhyayī woman pointed out that *sanskār* should be distinguished from *śiks□ā* or instructions. While *śikṣā* referred to formal, goal-oriented education, something imposed from outside, *sanskār* was something that the mind picked up on its own. This view of *sanskār* is closely related to the theory of *karma*. It solves the mystery of individual responsibility and self-effort in Hinduism. The problem with the theory of *karma* is that if everything we do is the inevitable consequence of what we did in the past, all moral responsibility should become meaningless. In response to this question, it is important to remember that every deed that we do, leads to a double result. It not only produces a direct result but it also establishes in us a tendency to repeat the same action in future. This tendency is termed *sanskār*; whereas the direct fruit of the *karma* is known as its *phala*. Every action yields *phala* but at the same time, the *sanskārs* are within one's control. As a result, self-exertion becomes congruent with the theory of *karma* (Hiriyanna 1993: 129–130). One's birth might be determined according to one's *karma* but one is born with one's *sanskār* and subsequent self-development depends on this. Dadaji used to say that how far one would take up Svadhyaya depends on the *sanskār* one is born with. *Sanskār* in this context explains self-effort expressed through exemplary/ethical conduct which follows the principle of transmigration.

This new identity cannot be kept a secret and it has to be publicly acknowledged. The narratives of public confession, known as *bhāvprasang* (which could be roughly translated as emotional vignettes) have an important effect on the construction of the Svadhyaya identity. These public confessions become morally and socially binding on those who continuously preach them. Especially when they are not passive listeners of virtues but regularly go to others to talk about them (at the time of *bhaktipherī* and other visits). It could be a spiritually significant life-experience or a narrative of a bad past and the process of transformation through Svadhyaya. The worse the past, the greater the moral appeal. The narrator in this context becomes an exemplar who bears testimony of the *sanksār* that he has acquired through his engagement with Svadhyaya and invites others to partake in the same. The invitation to membership outside one's family, caste group and region gives rise to a new community marked by conviviality, commensality and common faith in the path shown by Dadaji. In the concluding section I shall highlight that religious movements such as Svadhyaya bring to the fore the often overlooked truism that for a religion to be alive it has to be reinvented by the practitioners.

Conclusions

In Svadhyaya a new congregation is formed as individuals seek salvation through *karmayoga*. The new identity that the disciples develop is 'achieved' as opposed to the 'ascribed' status of caste. Paying attention to the concept of *prasād* (propitious offerings to the deity) in the Svadhyaya context would help us to appreciate that the notion of election is very much present in Svadhyaya membership. Svadhyayīs point out as an example of Svadhyaya's 'anti-ritualism' that no *prasād* is distributed at Svadhyaya temples. This was a true statement but when I heard the expression *'prasād'*, it was not in the context of a temple but that of a Svadhyaya training camp meant for committed activists. At the end of the day-long training programme, the organisers served food to those who attended the programme. It was unusual since Svadhyayīs carry their own food on such occasions. As we were eating, a Svadhyayī leader sitting next to me exclaimed that the food that we were eating was *prasād* since Dadaji had sent the money for the food from Mumbai. I was surprised to hear the word *prasād* in Svadhyaya for the first time and realised that an ordinary meal had become *prasād* since it was seen as a symbol of Dadaji's blessings towards those committed on the path of Svadhyaya. Only those who had worked towards it were eligible for this magical meal. Mary Douglas articulated this paradox of anti-ritualism by pointing out that after the protest stage once the need for organisation is recognised, the negative attitude to rituals conflicts with the need for a coherent system of expression. Thus, fundamentalists, who are not magical in their attitude to the Eucharist, become magical in their attitude to the Bible (Douglas 1973: 40). While the traditional *prasād* distributed at the temples is bereft of any religious significance for Svadhyayīs, an ordinary meal becomes *prasād* in this special context.

Becoming a Svadhyayī is a process through which the self is re-constituted through the congregational acts of speaking and listening, reaching out to others through the process of *bhaktipherī* and imbibing the qualities of an exemplar, in this case, Dadaji. From this perspective, ritual is understood as an active process that reorganises lived experience. In Svadhyaya, the age-old rituals acquire new significance and new rituals are introduced to communicate Svadhyaya reform. How would a new church, school, kingdom, nation, party come into being except through its own characteristic rituals? Asked John D. Kelly and Martha Kaplan as they pointed out that the rituals in ongoing practice are a principal site of new history being made, and the study of the plural formal potentialities of rituals could be basic to efforts to imagine possibilities for real political change (Kelly and Kaplan 1990: 141). For Svadhyayīs, the task is to reform Hinduism by renouncing renunciation, and they need to develop a soteriology for doing so. In the place of flight to the wilderness of asceticism, the seeker of salvation engages with the world of work and labour. Thus, God is worshipped through tilling the soil and the plough becomes an instrument of worship. Communities undertake Svadhyaya projects as 'experiments' in the sphere of religious reform and their rituals capture the theological innovation.

Finally, it could said that the Svadhyaya rituals of the sacred congregation are not given but emergent and that they operate in a field of experimentation and manipulation. During fieldwork, I have often heard Svadhyayīs debating over what is the correct *ācārsanhitā* or code of conduct that they should follow or discussing how a particular ritual such as the *bhūmipūjan* should be conducted. S.J. Tambiah noted this dynamic aspect of rituals by pointing out that ritual oscillates in historical time between the poles of ossification and revivalism. All the substantive features which nourish the formalism of ritual also conspire to empty it of meaning over time. And it is in periods of religious revivalism or when new cults are initiated by charismatic leaders that there is a deliberate attempt to coin new doctrinal concepts and mold new rituals bursting with meaning attached to contents of the acts *per se* (Tambiah 1985: 165–166). An anthropological enquiry into the semantics of rituals of religious movements like Svadhyaya from the practitioners' point of view helps us to better appreciate the dynamic nature of rituals and how they are imbued with new possibilities in each act of congregational worship.

◈

Notes

1. *Satsangī* refers to those who share the divine/sacred relation that binds the followers of a guru.
2. Vedant refers to one of the six classical philosophical systems that are based on the Vedas.
3. The remorse that is alluded to constitute the backdrop of the teachings of the Gītā — the religious classic of the Hindus. It is a set of teaching uttered by Lord Kṛṣṇa to Arjuna on the eve of the fratricidal war at the fateful field of Kurukshetra. The text raises the question of the problem of human action. In S. Radhakrishnan's words the central question that Gītā addresses is, 'How can we live in the Highest Self and yet continue to work in the world?' (Radhakrishnan 1993: 13).

4. *puruṣārtha* refers to any one of the four objects or aim of existence in Hindu theology. It has been pointed out by the scholars of Hinduism that the 'ordinary' *puruṣārtha* of *dharma*, *artha* and *kāma* that the caste system is based on, and the 'extraordinary' *puruṣārtha* of *mokṣ* 'salvation', the basis of sectarian Hinduism, are necessarily opposed (Larson 1972: 149).
5. *Lokasaṃgraha* means welfare of the world or world-solidarity. It also refers to the experience gained from having intercourse with other human beings. The concept of *yajña* refers to worship, consecration and sacrifice. *Karmayoga* refers to the way of salvation through action.
6. Jan Gonda points out that the basis of the peculiar veneration of the guru lies in the conviction that he is a link in a long chain of transcendental beginnings, a mediator able to bring his disciple and God together, or a medium through whom God is willing to reveal Himself (Gonda 1965). The Svadhyayīs perceive Dadaji fulfilling this role in their lives.
7. At the reconsecration ceremony of the Bhavnīrjhar temple at Ahmadabad in 2001, when Dadaji entered the temple on his wheelchair in the midst of devotional songs and clapping, it was a poignant moment. The woman sitting next to me sighed and said that Dadaji had sacrificed his body for the sake of our culture. The expression she used was that Dadaji had turned his body into manure (*khātar*).
8. 'Twice born' refers to upper-caste Hindu males who at the time of their initiation (*upanayana*) ceremony are considered to be re-born as full members of their caste group. In this context, the Svadhyayī woman uses the same expression for explaining her 'rebirth' in the Svadhyaya 'family'.
9. The Upanishads form part of the tradition of religious literature that is known as the Veda. The *Isa Upanishad* belongs to the white *Yajurveda* and is traditionally placed first in collections of Upanishads.
10. I was told earlier that audio tapes of the same used to be played at the 'discourse centres'. After Dadaji passed away in October 2003, his video taped discourses are played at the Pāṭhśālā.
11. One can contrast this with the cassette sermon in Egypt, studied by Charles Hirschkind, which are meant for individual listening (Hirschkind 2001).
12. For details of these projects undertaken by Svadhyaya, see Dharampal-Frick (2001), Giri (2005), Roy (1993), Shah, et al. (1998), Sheth (2002), Srivastava (1998).
13. The interview took place at his office in Mumbai, November 2000.
14. The Svaminarayan sect is a popular Vaishnavite sect that has its origin in nineteenth century Gujarat. At present, several denominations

exist, and the one that is referred to is headed by Hariprasadsvami and their main temple is at Sokhda, Gujarat.

15. The Sanskrit word *sanskār* has two meanings. First it refers to life-cycle rituals or sacraments. The usual number of *sanskār* rituals is considered to be sixteen — *garbhādhān* being the first and *antyeṣti* being the last *sanskār*. The other meaning of *sanskār* is not sacrament but a process of refinement, cultivation and training.
16. *Pāṭhotsav* refers to the commemoration ceremony of the consecration (*prāṇpratiṣṭhā*) day of a temple.
17. I was told that in 1976 on *rāmnavamī* day, Dadaji himself had performed the consecration ceremony of the temple.
18. In his essay on charity in Hinduism, B.K. Mukherjea has pointed out that *pūrta* work which is not connected to Vedic sacrifice covers a range of philanthropic acts ranging from constructing temples, water tanks, rest houses as well as organising relief for the sick. They are open to all and have been extolled by later Smriti writers as the means of securing salvation (Mukherjea 1952: 12).
19. It falls on *āṣāṛ* sud 15 and in the absence of the guru, disciples worship her/his image or photograph.
20. *Jajmān* refers to one who requests and pays for the performance of a sacrifice.
21. Field Diary, 26 April 2001, Surat district (Gujarat).
22. It is interesting to note that *sûkta* means something that is well-said, and in the early history of Indian literature the term was used to refer to the inspired hymns of the Vedic seers that make up the collection of the *Ṛg Veda*.
23. It should be mentioned here that the rejection of caste does not necessarily mean that the caste rule of commensality is not observed by the renunciate. The Ramanandis believe that one's mind and body are formed of one's caste and Ramanandi renouncers observe caste rules of commensality among themselves and while accepting food from others (Burghart 1983: 644).
24. My friends in the village showed me a couple of books on *sanskār* rituals, with titles such as *Daivi Santān* written in Gujarati.

References

Athavale, P.V. 1954. *Lectures Delivered at the Second World Religious Congress: Shimizu City, Japan*. Bombay: Shrimad Bhagwad Geeta Pathshala.

———. 1998. *Gītāmritam*. Bombay: Sat Vichar Darshan Trust.

Babb, L.A. 1981. 'Glancing: Visual Interaction in Hinduism', *Journal of Anthropological Research* 37 (4): 387–401.

Burghart, R. 1983. 'Renunciation in the Religious Tradition of South Asia', *Man* 18 (4): 635–53.

Dharampal-Frick, G. 2001. 'Swadhyaya and the "Stream" of Religious Revitalization', in V. Dalmia et al. (eds) *Charisma and Canon: Essays on the Religious History of the Indian Subcontinent*. New Delhi: Oxford University Press.

Douglas, M. 1973 [1970]. *Natural Symbols: Explorations in Cosmology*. Harmondsworth: Penguin Books.

Dumont, L. 1999 [1970]. *Homo Hierarchicus: The Caste System and its Implications*. New Delhi: Oxford University Press.

Eck, D. 1998 [1981]. *Darśan: Seeing the Divine Image in India*. New York: Columbia University Press.

Fuller, Ch. 1992. *The Camphor Flame: Popular Hinduism and Society in India*. New Jersey: Princeton University Press.

Giri, A.K. 2005. 'Globalization of Hinduism: Swadhyaya in England and Sai Baba in Bali', in *Reflections and Mobilizations: Dialogues with Movements and Voluntary Organizations*. New Delhi: Sage Publications.

Gonda, J. 1965. *Continuity and Change in Indian Religion*. The Hague: Mouton.

———. 1969. *Eye and Gaze in the Veda*. Amsterdam: North-Holland Publishing Company.

Hocart, A.M. 1970 [1936]. *Kings and Councillors: An Essay in the Comparative Anatomy of Human Society*. Chicago: The Chicago University Press.

Hiriyanna, M. 1993 [1932]. *Outlines of Indian Philosophy*. Delhi: Motilal Banarasidass Publishers.

Hirschkind, Ch. 2001. 'The Ethics of Listening: Cassette-sermon Audition in Contemporary Egypt', *American Ethnologist* 28 (3): 623–49.

Kelly, John D. and Kaplan, Martha. 1990. 'History, Structure and Ritual', *Annual Review of Anthropology* 19: 119–50.

Larson, Gerald James. 1972. 'The Trimurti of Dharma in Indian Thought: Paradox or Contradiction?', *Philosophy East and West* 22 (2): 145–53.

Lewis, G. 2004. 'Religious Doctrine or Experience: A Matter of Seeing, Learning or Doing' in H. Whitehouse and J. Laidlaw (eds) *Ritual and Memory: Toward a Comparative Anthropology of Religion*. Walnut Creek: Altamira Press.

Little, J.T. 1995. 'Video Vacana: Swadhyaya and Sacred Tapes', in L.A. Babb and S.S. Wadley (eds) *Media and the Transformation of Religion in South Asia*. Philadelphia: University of Pennsylvania.

Morgan, D. 2005. *The Sacred Gaze: Religious Visual Culture in Theory and Practice*. Berkeley: University of California Press.

Mukherjea, B.K. 1952. *The Hindu Law of Religious and Charitable Trusts*. Kolkata: Eastern Law House.

Olivelle, P. 1992. *Samnyasa Upanisads: Hindu Scriptures on Asceticism and Renunciation.* New York: Oxford University Press.

Radhakrishnan, S. 1993 [1948]. *The Bhagavatgita.* New Delhi: Harper Collins.

Rospatt, A. von 2005. 'The Transformation of the Monastic Ordination (*pravrajya*): Into a Rite of Passage in Newar Buddhism', in J. Gengnagel et al. (eds) *Words and Deeds: Hindu and Buddhist Ritual in South Asia.* Wiesbaden: Harrassowitz.

Roy, R. 1993. 'Swadhyaya: Values and Message', in P. Wignaraja (ed.) *New Social Movements in the South: Empowering the People.* New Delhi: Vistaar Publications.

Shah, V. et al. 1998. 'Swadhyaya: Social Change through Spirituality' in M.L. Dantwala et al. (eds) *Social Change through Voluntary Action.* New Delhi: Sage Publications.

Sheth, N.R. 2002. 'A Spiritual Approach to Social Transformation', in T. Shinoda (ed.) *The Other Gujarat: Social Transformation among Weaker Sections.* Mumbai: Popular Prakashan.

Srivastava, R.K. 1998. *Vital Connections: Self, Society, God: Perspective on Swadhyaya,* New York: Weatherhill.

Tambiah, S.J. 1985. *Culture, Thought and Social Action: An Anthropological Perspective.* Cambridge, Mass: Harvard University Press.

3

Transferring and Re-transferring Religious Practice

ISKCON between 'East' and 'West'

Frank Neubert

In this essay, I deal with the history of cultural transfer processes connected to the International Society for Krishna Consciousness (ISKCON), mainly with the transfer of so-called Kṛṣṇa-conscious practice to the West, and back to India from there. In short, I deal with the transfer of religious practice (see Neubert 2006) in the history of ISKCON.

After a short introduction to the history of the movement, I present a few examples of transfer of religious practice from India to the West. One focus will be on the processes of negotiation between devotees, the Founder and Indian Vaiṣṇavas about the performance and significance of these practices that took place in the course of the transmission. Further, I suggest some readings of the 're-transfer' of ISKCON's religious practice to India, especially by considering the pilgrimage town of Vrindavan. Finally, I present some preliminary conclusions and hypotheses that will have to be subjected to further research. I argue (*i*) that the transfer processes are mainly (though not merely) taking place on an ideal, 'discursive' level; (*ii*) that different adaptations and changes in the practices have to be negotiated between members, leaders and outsiders of the movement in such processes; and (*iii*) that these negotiations are an integral part of the transfer processes.

ISKCON[1] was founded in New York in 1966 under the guidance of a 70-years-old guru who had come to the United States of America (USA) from India just a year earlier. His Divine Grace A.C. Bhaktivedānta Svāmī Prabhupāda[2] attracted a number of disciples from the so-called counter-culture of New York's Lower Eastside. They had been attracted by his ongoing and sincere chanting of what they perceived to be sacred Indian hymns, his lectures on the philosophy and religion of Vaiṣṇavism and 'Vedic culture',[3] and by the fact that he offered them food and a place to stay in the small 'matchless gifts' storefront that served as ISKCON's first temple-room in New York. Most of the visitors to this new site remained outsiders, but some became serious disciples of Prabhupāda and helped to establish and spread the Hare Kṛṣṇa Movement in America, and later in Europe and in branches all over the world. Thereby, they consciously helped to fulfil Caitanya's[4] prediction that one day Kṛṣṇa's name will be heard and worshipped 'in every town and village'. Even though the first temple was established in New York, others were to follow soon (in Boston, Chicago, San Francisco and Los Angeles). In 1968, an ISKCON temple was founded in London. From there, the movement spread to Germany (see Dāsa 1996), France, and other European countries (see the accounts in T.K. Goswami 1984) by the early 1970s. At the same time, Prabhupāda had already sent some of his disciples to India to establish ISKCON temples. Based on the movement's success among Indian immigrants in the West, India became a new centre of ISKCON's proselytising activities. Nowadays, India hosts the fastest growing ISKCON community in the world.

The global spread of Kṛṣṇa consciousness has been the most important purpose of Prabhupāda's journey to the US, and of the movement's activities immediately after its foundation. As Kṛṣṇa consciousness shows mainly in the performance of specific rites and in the adherence to a particular lifestyle, it is especially these practices that had to be preached and transmitted to other people. Examples of these processes of a transfer of religious practice form the main part of this essay.

I want to start with accounting several episodes about Śrīla Prabhupāda's teachings about religious practice, about the process of teaching and learning it, and about the negotiations evolving around proper Kṛṣṇa conscious 'etiquette'. The material I present here is taken mainly from Tamāl Kṛṣṇa Goswami's[5] autobiographical work *Servant of the Servant* (1984). In this book, he describes his first years in the movement, and his relationship with the Founder, and cites from many of Prabhupāda's letters.[6]

First, the religious practices referred to led young people from New York and San Francisco searching for alternative ways of life away from 'materialist notions of well-being', and into closer contact with the movement. The feasts, chanting, lectures, dancing, *saṅkīrtan* (public chanting of Kṛṣṇa's names) — all attracted newcomers to the temples. According to a number of psychological and sociological studies, people for whom sensations play a predominant role in reception and decision-making processes have joined the movement as the religious practice performed in the temples serves such aesthetic needs very well.[7] One of the people responding to the aesthetic appeal of the movement and the rituals is Thomas Herzig, (initiation name Tamāl Kṛṣṇa Dāsa), later on known as Tamāl Kṛṣṇa Goswami. From his autobiographical work and from a number of other sources, one can see how Prabhupāda introduced religious practices like chanting rather slowly, step by step. Prabhupāda had started with the chanting and the lectures in New York as early as 1965. He then introduced feasts, then First Initiation, a reduced form of temple worship, Second Initiation to 'make Brahmins',[8] full temple service, the rites of renunciation. And, most importantly, many of the practices that he taught were adapted to the assumed or real needs of his Western disciples. At times he decided to make such adaptive changes from the very beginning; sometimes, his Western disciples asked him to do so, or made suggestions as to what might have to be adjusted. Tamāl Kṛṣṇa reports:

> Prabhupāda knew that it would not be possible to immediately introduce the complicated system of *pūjā* followed in the strict Vaiṣṇava temples in India — it was all his American disciples could do to make a few offerings […] and to chant Hare Kṛṣṇa — but he had every intention of elevating disciples to the proper platform. (Goswami 1984: 56)

Here Tamāl Kṛṣṇa makes explicit reference to the fact that most American disciples did not have any experience of performing or understanding Vaiṣṇava religious practice. Based on a limited knowledge of chanting and making offerings, Prabhupāda nevertheless taught them how to be Vaiṣṇava in order to be able to make them into Brahmins through the rite of Second Initiation, i.e., to enable these 'new' Brahmins to perform 'proper' deity worship in the temples. Adjustment and change occurred within the framework of transfer of religious practice in ISKCON. The examples below enumerate these changes.

The first example concerns chanting which is the most important religious practice in the Gauḍīya Vaiṣṇava religious tradition, as chanting the names of Kṛṣṇa is considered to be the only way to salvation in the Dark Age of Kali in which we all live.[9] From the very beginning, Prabhupāda asked his disciples to chant the *mahāmantra* ('Hare Kṛṣṇa, Hare Kṛṣṇa, Kṛṣṇa Kṛṣṇa, Hare Hare. Hare Rāma, Hare Rāma, Rāma Rāma, Hare Hare.') sixteen rounds a day.[10] In the writings of his predecessors Bhaktivinoda Ṭhākur and Bhaktisiddhānta Sarasvatī, as well as in the *Haribhaktivilāsa*, a sixteenth- or seventeenth-century ritual text of the Gauḍīya Vaiṣṇava, a number of sixty-four rounds of the *japamālā* for people following the path of *vaidhi bhakti* (the *bhakti* of prescribed rules and regulations) had been prescribed. Prabhupāda wrote about his reasons for reducing the number to sixteen in his *Upadeśāmrita: The Nectar of Instruction* (1971):

> Everyone begins his devotional life from the neophyte stage, but if one properly finishes chanting the prescribed number of rounds of hari-nāma, he is elevated step by step to the highest platform, uttama-adhikārī. *The Kṛṣṇa consciousness movement prescribes sixteen rounds daily because people in the Western countries cannot concentrate for long periods while chanting on beads.* Therefore the minimum number of rounds is prescribed. However, Śrīla Bhaktisiddhānta Sarasvatī Thākura used to say that unless one chants at least sixty-four rounds of japa (one hundred thousand names[11] he is considered fallen (*patita*). According to his calculation, practically every one of us is fallen, but because we are trying to serve the Supreme Lord with all seriousness and without duplicity, we can expect the mercy of Lord Śrī Caitanya Mahāprabhu, who is famous as patita-pāvana, the deliverer of the fallen. (Prabhupāda in Vedabase 2003: 5.3.6.4; emphasis added).

Prabhupāda here makes use of a *topos* in the interpretation of Indian-Western relations that dates back to the mid-nineteenth century which describes India as the homeland of spirituality that 'the West' had completely lost, and this spirituality is what India can and must convey to 'the West'. The often-raised statement that Westerners are equipped with a deficit by birth, that is, they could not properly perform Hindu religious practice because they were not born Hindu, fits into this scheme as well as the intention to modify the practices to fit their abilities and limitations. Thus, chanting 'a minimum number' of rounds was what Prabhupāda considered practicable for his followers, and necessary for their 'spiritual advancement'. However, this was not a decision put into practice at once but rather a matter of negotiation, as a report in the *Back to Godhead* magazine indicates. The devotees were themselves not sure about the prescribed number, and only after some uncertainties was the matter resolved by a decision made by Prabhupāda, as Satsvarūpa Dāsa Goswami describes:

> Prabhupāda said that devotees in India chanted at least sixty-four rounds of beads a day. Saying the Hare Kṛṣṇa mantra on each of the 108 beads constituted one round. His spiritual master had said that anyone who didn't chant sixty-four rounds a day was fallen. At first some of the boys thought that they would also have to chant sixty-four rounds, and they became perplexed: that would take all day! How could you go to a job if you had to chant sixty-four rounds? How could anyone chant sixty-four rounds? Then someone said Swamiji had told him that thirty-two rounds a day would be a sufficient minimum for the West. Wally said he had heard Swamiji say twenty-five-but even that seemed impossible. Then Prabhupāda offered the rock-bottom minimum: sixteen rounds a day, without fail. Whoever got initiated would have to promise. (Goswami 1980)

In his *Japa Reform Notebook* (1982), Satsvarūpa Dāsa Goswami, one of the earliest followers of ISKCON, wrote in detail about his problems in chanting the sixteen rounds properly. The book was intended to be a kind of additional instruction and edification of how he solved this issue.

As with chanting, Prabhupāda adjusted and simplified other practices to make them understandable and practicable for his followers. Not only did he take up an active part in the adaptation processes, but on some occasions, the disciples themselves asked for certain changes to be implemented. Tamāl Kṛṣṇa, for example, describes how certain logistical problems with the distribution of *prasādam*, sacred food that is offered to Kṛṣṇa before being consumed by the devotees, were sought to be solved. Normally, during a Sunday Feast, the food for the devotees would be prepared and a portion of it offered to Kṛṣṇa during the worship. Thus, all the prepared food would take up the purified essence left over by Kṛṣṇa. Distribution of the thus sanctified food usually started only after the lecture and worship. However, there were too many guests present at the Sunday Feasts, and it was not possible to serve them in a reasonable period of time. Thus, the disciples suggested preparing the plates of *prasādam* even before the worship would start. Prabhupāda replied positively, but with some precautions. Again, Tamāl Kṛṣṇa writes:

> In the course of preaching, some rules may be modified, as is evidenced in Prabhupāda's advice regarding the distribution of feast *prasādam*. Prabhupāda gave permission that all of the plates could be made up even before the offering was made, as long as the Lord's plate was made up first and kept in a special high place until the offering. (Goswami 1984: 153)

Changes in the concrete practice were thus negotiated between Prabhupāda and his followers. And, as the foregoing quotation shows, they were very consciously reflected by Prabhupāda as well as his devotees. In this process, he turned them into ritual specialists as he permitted them to perform increasingly complex rituals. For the purpose of performing *pūjā,* he made them Brahmins and therefore introduced 'second initiation' as an important rite of passage in the group. As more temples were founded and had to be maintained, the devotees took responsibility of the deity worship and became *pūjārī*s, an office that has earned a lot of respect within the community. Of course, the negotiations on religious practices and their proper performance also involved severe debates among ISKCON's members. Thus, for example, in the late 1990s the Governing Body Commission installed a Deity Worship Research Group which included a number of swamis, *pūjārī*s and scholar-members of the movement. This group's intention was to create a standard for deity worship in ISKCON, and thus solve some internal disputes about its performance.

My final example highlights yet another form of dynamics of religious practice: the invention of new forms of practice that were modelled after an image the disciples had in mind. This form arose when traditional Vaiṣṇava festivals started to be celebrated in the temples. The temple residents then came up with ideas, asked Prabhupāda for his permission, organised everything and then performed. Their ideas were modelled after the knowledge they had gained from reading Prabhupāda's texts and translations, and from listening to his lectures. Tamāl Kṛṣṇa, again, describes such an event:

> The many Vaishnava festivals described by Śrīla Prabhupāda were opportunities to attract the local population by introducing them to the Vedic culture in a very pleasant way. To celebrate Dadhibhānda, we recreated the pastime of the *gopīs* churning butter by fashioning a large churning pot out of a ten-gallon steel milk container. Each guest took turns working the churning rod, and at the end we all enjoyed eating the fresh butter after it was offered to Kṛṣṇa. (Goswami 1984: 139)

Field studies show that this practice can still be observed on the occasion of Dadhibhānda festivals in the Western temples of the movement. In addition, studies in older texts from the tradition of Bengali Vaiṣṇavism show that there were no proto-types for this festival, and no rules that would prescribe when and how to celebrate it. Similarly, the individual temples are very creative in fashioning festivals and celebrations. The ISKCON temple authorities in Heidelberg, for example, are regularly sending e-mail invitations for such events and announcing the performance of 'new', 'fashionable' or 'surprising' rites and celebrations.

I now want to add some thoughts on 'the other direction of transfer'. In the early years of the Hare Kṛṣṇa movement, this mainly meant the establishment of a Centre in Vrindavan, a town in north India which has been the sacred centre of Kṛṣṇa devotion in India since at least the time of Caitanya and his successors, the six goswamis (see Brooks 1989: ch. 2). Prabhupāda himself had lived there for about ten years before he went to New York in 1965. His plan had been not only to bring Kṛṣṇa consciousness to the Western 'spiritually depraved' world but also to revive it in its own 'homeland' where it had degraded rapidly over the last centuries, as he and many other orthodox Vaiṣṇavas perceived the situation. In the early 1970s, he started sending his Western followers to Vrindavan to establish an ISKCON temple there. As new and — according to their self-perception — very traditional devotees of Kṛṣṇa, they wanted to help in the revival of Kṛṣṇa consciousness in its homeland India. They came to Vrindavan and started to work for the construction of an ISKCON temple. Charles Brooks, in *The Hare Krishnas in India* (1989), describes in detail the problems the disciples had to face, especially in relation to the customs of bureaucratic negotiation and communication with the town and temple authorities in Vrindavan. His book is an excellent analysis of the relations of Western Hare Kṛṣṇas with the people residing in or travelling on pilgrimage to Vrindavan, which is situated only two-and-a-half hours south of Delhi. After having overcome many difficulties often based on cultural misunderstandings or prejudice, ISKCON constructed a temple that became a major pilgrimage centre not only for members of ISKCON, but also for Indian Vaiṣṇava who visit Vrindavan. Many of them visit the Kṛṣṇa-Balarāma Mandir during their short stay in the town just before leaving, as the temple is situated right on the way out of town. The main reason to visit the temple for many is to experience a very clean, orderly and well-managed temple. But as many visitors told me during my field research in 2006, they are also driven by the curiosity to see a temple that was established and is managed by Western devotees, who are still perceived as 'foreigners', yet 'gone native'. The strong stress on proper religious practice, cleanliness and orderly management within the discursive space of ISKCON has thus become a means for distinction as an accepted temple in Vrindavan, and at the same time for gaining acceptance among the traditional temples. Of course, all Indian visitors worshipped Kṛṣṇa during the ceremonies, but only a few of them told me that they had come especially to do so. They had already fulfilled their 'pilgrimage duties' in the old, traditional temples of Vrindavan. It seems, however, that this situation has been changing recently. One indication for this is the fact that native Indian ISKCON members (so-called 'ethnic Hindus') are performing as *pūjārī*s in the temple in Vrindavan now, whereas only about a decade ago this role was mainly played by Europeans or Americans. This may have to do with the fact that ISKCON's membership in India itself is growing rapidly. It seems, however, that there is an awareness among the temple's management that ethnic Hindus are more apt to accept the temple's deity worship as authentic when there are Indian *pūjārī*s. Western devotees, even the high-ranking ones, mostly occupy the role of temple officials, speakers in the Bhagavatam and Bhagavad Gita classes and leaders of the permanently performing *saṅkīrtan* group.

Prabhupāda had very early predicted the difficulties the devotees would face in gaining acceptance among the orthodox Vaiṣṇavas in Vrindavan. Brooks writes:

> [...] Bhaktivedanta knew that not everyone in Vrindavan would automatically accept his disciples as legitimate. The caste goswamis especially, he felt, feared ISKCON because it threatened their hereditary social pre-eminence [...] Thus he communicated an admonition to his followers that whenever they were in Vrindavan

> they had to be on their best behaviour, emphasizing the proper etiquette for living there. He emphasized, 'In the holy *dhāma*, if one of my disciples drinks from a jug incorrectly and he contaminates that jug, everyone will notice it. Don't be criticized for uncleanliness, or I will be criticized. It is the duty of the disciple to follow these etiquette habits very austerely. […]' ISKCON's acceptance and integration in Vrindavan, Bhaktivedanta was keenly aware, depended on the devotees' proper presentation of self in public. (Brooks 1989: 90)

Prabhupāda's instructions to his devotees in India eventually materialised into long 'etiquette' instructions that can be found on many ISKCON homepages and in guide books, and they concern nearly every section of daily life. The most recent version of the ISKCON Vrindavan Information Guide contains five pages of instructions, ranging from 'Offenses to be avoided in the Holy Dham (the sacred area of Vrindavan)' to 'Safety Tips' and 'Etiquette to be observed'. The tips include hints for avoiding the usual trapdoors for visitors to India (e.g., 'Always fix the fare in advance.'), but also many clues that remind the devotees of their status (e.g., 'Remember, you are representing Śrīla Prabhupāda.').

In conclusion, three relevant points seem to emerge from the foregoing exemplification of the transfer processes in ISKCON's history.

First, the transfer processes are mainly ideal processes that take place at a discursive level. That is, what is transferred is only ideally 'a thing'. Of course, ISKCON devotees perform 'real Vedic, Gauḍīya Vaiṣṇava practices'. And of course, in the eyes of the followers and of many other Gauḍīya Vaiṣṇavas, Prabhupāda did transmit 'real Vaiṣṇava practices' to the West. Viewed in a positivist manner, however, there are huge differences between 'a transferred practice' in its original and in its new social context. The question that arises is one of identity: what constitutes the identity of a (transferred) religious practice? It seems that for answering this question it is necessary, instead of looking at the performances and techniques, to consider discursive structures as more relevant: why is a certain performance practised in the USA considered as identical with a practice performed regularly in Vrindavan, India? Under what conditions does such identification gain and retain validity? How can such discursive identity be maintained even though changes are explicitly acknowledged, e.g., in the sense of purer and stricter performance?

Second, I have tried to show that for such transfer processes different kinds of adaptations have to take place. They concern changes in the practical performance of the practices as well as adaptations to the necessities of the new context. These adaptations differ according to the character of the new context. While transferring Vaiṣṇavism to the West mainly meant simplifications and structural changes so that 'inexperienced' Western devotees could follow the instructions, re-transferring religious practice to India meant a new stress on rigidity and formal correctness. The reasons for these changes were rather different, according to the direction of the transfer process — Western lifestyle and the envisioned attraction of youths from New York's counter-culture of the 1960s on the one hand, the struggle for acceptance as true Vaiṣṇavas and even as Brahmins in India, on the other.

Third, the negotiations playing a role here are an integral part of the transfer processes. They take place on different epistemological and social levels. Of course, in the eyes of the actors involved, the practices help them negotiate and communicate with Kṛṣṇa. Of course also, for the analyst from outside, the practices negotiate the relationships among the participants. But in addition, the performance itself is permanently being negotiated among participants, ritual specialists and the wider public. And finally, the negotiations are socially structured. It makes a difference if a devotee discusses procedures or features of religious practice such as chanting with Prabhupāda, or with a fellow disciple, or even with an outsider to the movement. It also makes a difference whether he explains Vaiṣṇava religious practice to new devotees or to the public during a *Ratha Yātrā* (Cart Festival). All these kinds of negotiations have an influence on how the practices change in the course of the transfer processes.

◈

Notes

1. For a more detailed introduction, see Squarcini and Fizzotti (2004) and Knott (1988). Shorter ISKCON-biographies of the founder, Srila Prabhupāda, are Goswami (1983) and Rosen (1992). Shinn (1989) analyses ISKCON's negative image as a 'dangerous cult' in the debates about new religious movements during the 1980s and 90s.
2. This is the official title and name of ISKCON's spiritual leader.

3. On the use of the term 'vedic' in ISKCON's publications, see Das (1996).
4. Caitanya is the sixteenth-century founder of the Bengali religious tradition from which ISKCON descended.
5. On Tamāl Kṛṣna Goswami, see for example the special volume 11/2 (2003) of the *Journal of Vaishnava Studies*.
6. All material is to be found on a most helpful digital documentation, namely the Vedabase 2003 CD-Rom, edited by ISKCON.
7. See Poling and Kenney (1986) as an example of a psychological study concerning the characteristic features of ISKCON-personalities.
8. Second Initiation refers to the rite of passage similar to traditional Hindu *upanayana*, when a devotee receives the *Gāyatrī-mantra* and a sacred thread from his spiritual master (*guru*) and is from then on considered to be a Brahmin. At the basis of this ritual in ISKCON lies the assumption that *varṇa* (class) is not a matter of birth but of personal qualification.
9. On the usage and meaning of the *mahāmantra*, see Beck (2004).
10. 'Chanting one round' refers to a procedure during which a devotee chants the *mahāmantra* on every pearl of a kind of rosary consisting of 108 pearls. For a well-versed devotee, it takes about five to eight minutes to chant one round.
11. 64 rounds of 108 *mantra*s is 6,912 mantras, each one containing 16 names of Kṛṣṇa (8 Hari, 4 Kṛṣṇa, 4 Rāma), which totals 110,592 names.

References

Beck, G.L. 2004. 'Hare Krishna *Mahamantra*: Gaudiya Vaishnava Practice and the Hindu Tradition of Sacred Sound', in E.F. Bryant and M.L. Ekstrand (eds) *The Hare Kṛishṇa Movement: The Postcharismatic Fate of a Religious Transplant*, pp. 35–44. New York: Columbia University Press.

Brooks, C. 1989. *The Hare Kṛishṇas in India*. Princeton: Princeton University Press.

Das, R.P. 1996. "Vedic" in the Terminology of Prabhupāda and His Followers', *ISKCON Communications Journal* 4(2): 23–38.

Dāsa, V. 1996. *Śrīla Prabhupāda and His Disciples in Germany*. Jalon: Mandir Media Group.

Goswami, S.D. 1980. 'The Biography of a Pure Devotee', in *Back to Godhead*: vol. 15 (11), electronically edited on Vedabase 2003.

———. 1982. *Japa Reform Notebook*. La Crosse: Gita Nagari Press, electronically edited on Vedabase 2003

———. 1983. *Prabhupada: Your Ever Well-Wisher*. Los Angeles et al.: Bhaktivedanta Book Trust.

Goswami, T.K. 1984. *Servant of the Servant.* Los Angeles et al.: Bhaktivedanta Book Trust, electronically edited on Vedabase 2003.

Knott, K. 1988. *My Sweet Lord: The Hare Kṛṣṇa Movement.* San Bernardino: Borgo.

Neubert, F. 2006. Ritualtransfer: Eine projektbezogene Präzisierung. *Forum Ritualdynamik* 15.

Poling, T.H. and Kenney, J.F. 1986. *The Hare Kṛṣṇa Character Type: A Study of the Sensate Personality.* Lewiston: Edwin Mellen.

Prabhupāda. 1971. *Upadeśāmṛta: The Nectar of Instruction.* Los Angeles et al.: Bhaktivedanta Book Trust, electronically edited on Vedabase 2003.

Rosen, S. 1992. *Passage from India. The Life and Times of His Divine Grace A.C. Bhaktivedanta Swami Prabhupāda. A Summary Study of Satsvarūpa Dāsa Goswami's Śrīla Prabhupāda Līlāmṛta.* New Delhi: Munshiram Manoharlal.

Shinn, L.D. 1989. *The Dark Lord: Cult Images and the Hare Krishṇas in America.* Philadelphia: The Westminster Press.

Squarcini, F. and Fizzotti, E. 2004. *Hare Krishna.* Salt Lake City, Utah: Signature Books. (Studies in Contemporary Religions, 6.)

Vedabase 2003. *His Divine Grace A.C. Bhaktivedanta Swami Prabhupāda: The Complete Teachings.* Published by the Bhaktivedanta Archives, Bhaktivedanta Book Trust.

4

'Marginalised Islam'

The Transfer of Rural Rituals into Urban and Pluralist Contexts and the Emergence of Transnational 'Communities of Practice'

Robert Langer

The Islamic Studies/Ottoman Studies sub-project of the Collaborative Research Center 'Dynamics of Ritual' at Heidelberg University focuses on formerly so-called 'heterodox' groups of Islamic origin. These groups emerged in the late middle ages and early modern times in the region around Upper Mesopotamia, reaching out into Southern Caucasia and Western Iran. Upper Mesopotamia was from the sixteenth century onwards part of the Ottoman Empire.[1] The region nowadays comprises Central and Eastern Anatolia, Northern Syria and Iraqi Kurdistan. Modern migrations brought the ritual practice of heterodox Muslim groups form the rural Near East into its urban centres — such as İstanbul or Ankara — and even further to Western Europe. In the course of this development and in connection with high degrees of mobility, communication and media representation (especially the medialisation of rituals), diaspora groups of Islamic origin developed transnational 'communities of practice'[2] comprising the diaspora communities, the groups in urban centres of the Near East, as well as the remaining village communities in the regions of origin. This essay deals mainly with the Alevis from Turkey and aims to exemplify some aspects of the concept of 'transfer of ritual', which was developed at Heidelberg as an analytical means to analyse the relation between transformations of rituals and changing contexts of cultural performances.

A classical Islamic studies' perspective defined the historical starting point of many 'heterodox' Muslim groups as an extremist, radical ideology (*ghulûw*, 'exaggerating' — in this context: exaggerating the role of the Imams, worshipping them as emanations of God). This ideology developed out of the schism of the early Muslim community after the death of Muhammad, at that time mainly a conflict over how succession in the leadership of the Muslim community should be realised: electoral or hereditary ('the imams'). Taking up the viewpoint of Muslim orthodoxy (Sunni as well as Shii), non-conformist groups were qualified as 'sectarian' (*firaq*, 'sects', singular: *firqa*). In fact, they were a reservoir for (economically, politically or religiously) discontent parts of the population as their ideology to 'liberate the downtrodden' in connection with millenarian expectations was very attractive to them. This ideology of redemption was appealing to socio-economically marginalised groups such as the non-Arabs in the first centuries of Islamic history. The reason for this was the identification with the suppressed and murdered, but highly-revered leaders of the Shiite branch of Islam, the so-called imams. The most important incident in this history of suppression was the Karbalâ` incident, when Husayn, the grandson of Muhammad and son of his cousin and son-in-law, ´Alî, was murdered by soldiers of the Sunni dynasty of the Banû Umayya (Omayyads) in the Iraqi desert. The ideology of the so-called *ghulât* or 'exaggerators',[3] who themselves were Shiite, but 'exaggerated' the veneration of ´Alî, Husayn and other imams, was in the middle ages accommodated by tribal groups, mostly speakers of Iranian and Turkic languages and partly tribal Arabs. The adherents of several *ghulûw* traditions were mainly Turkmen and Kurdish tribesmen. In the course of history, ethno-religious groups emerged, triggered by social uprisings of rural populations (nomadic as well as sedentary) against state authority.

In order to take up a perspective independent of orthodox Islam, instead of 'heterodox Muslim sects', at least in a modern context, Islamic studies should rather refer to such traditions as 'marginalised ethno-religious groups of Islamic origin', as they were marginalised by an 'orthodoxisation' of mainstream Muslim teaching and practice through central state authorities. Their beliefs and practices are 'heterodox' from a theological position that defines orthodoxy, a distinction that has not to be decided for by an academic discipline.[4] To name some of the groups still existing: Arab Nusayri (´Alawiyyûn), Kurdish Yezidi/Yazîdî (Êzdî) and Ahl-e Haqq (Yârsân),[5] and Turkic as well as Kurdish Alevi, also called Kızılbaş with many subgroups from the Balkans to Northern Iraq and North-western Iran. Many of these groups — although not all of them — share a strong veneration of ´Alî and his descendants, e.g., the name Alevi, i.e., 'pertaining to ´Alî (cousin and son-in-law of Muhammad)', underlines.[6]

The Alevis especially were successfully pacified, put under indirect state control or marginalised in remote areas during Ottoman times; and even today — under republican rule — they still have restricted access to political power and economic wealth in Turkey. Nevertheless, they constitute a strong demographic force in modern Turkey, as reasonable estimates hold 10 to 20 per cent of the actual Turkish population — both Turkish and Kurdish — as Alevi.[7] The Arab Nusayris (´Alawiyyûn), on the other hand, are part of the ruling Syrian elite, represented by the Asad family.[8] The Yezidi — never completely subdued by Ottoman authority — still practice their military tradition, either as part of Kurdish movements that fought against the regime of Saddâm Husayn or as activists in the 'Kurdish Workers Party' in Turkey, also known as PKK (*Partiyê Kârkerân-ê Kordestân*).[9]

Because of the above-mentioned political and economical marginalisation, members of these groups participated over-proportionally in the migrations of the twentieth century, to the mega-cities of the region or to Western Europe, either as labour migrants or as political refugees. More than ever before, this brought them into contact with mainstream Islam, with secularised movements as well as with Orientalist scholarship. Nationalists interpreted their religious traditions as the 'true' religion of the respective ethnicity ('nation') in opposition to orthodox Islam. This way, Kurdish intellectuals presented Kurdish forms of Alevism or Yezidism as the 'true' Kurdish religion (belonging to the Iranian-Zoroastrian tradition), depending on their respective ethno-religious background. Turkish Alevism on the other hand was described as continuing the religion of the pre-Islamic 'shamanistic' Turks or at least as the original Turkic kind of Islam by Turkish scholars, as opposed to the Arab Islam, but equally opposed to the orthodox Shia of the Persians. Movements from within the communities, on the other hand, willingly took over the promises of nationalist or socialist ideologies after World War II, secularising their specific identities in terms of these ideologies. The migration processes generated urban and diasporic communities[10] of these non-orthodox, non-Sunni Muslims who, formerly, had been entirely semi-nomadic or sedentary rural populations within a semi-autonomous tribal system, hidden away from the perception of urban orthodox religious authorities as well as from Western scholarship.[11]

Starting in the 1980s, Alevi activists took up religious elements of their cultural tradition and re-invented religious ritual practice after having migrated away from the rural areas. Consequently, they transferred their ritual into large near eastern cities and into pluralist Western societies. This transfer of rituals into new contexts altered the ritual practice according to the new context factors.[12] This is especially evident in the case of the Alevi *cem*-ritual, a congregational gathering with communal prayers, singing and ritual dancing, usually framed by animal sacrifice before, and a communal meal at its end (see Langer 2006). In the so-called *ayin-i cem* (from Persian *â'în*, 'rule, regulation', and Arabic *djam´*, 'collecting, assembling'), an Alevi local community congregates from time to time to conduct a service under the leadership of members of their priestly caste, the so-called *dede*s (Turkic, literally 'grandfathers', i.e., 'elders').

In traditional contexts such as the village community, this ritual also fulfilled the important task of a local law court, presided over by the *dede*s, as members of 'heretic' groups avoided the official *qâdî* courts, which applied orthodox Sunni law until the end of the Ottoman Empire. In Europe as well as in the Turkish cities such as İstanbul or Ankara, their congregational *cem*-ritual, formerly practised only in secret seclusion within the village community, became more public, and was partly even used in secular demonstrations and festivals.[13] This had a reverse impact on the remaining village culture, where the traditional *cem*-ritual was no longer practised regularly since the 1970s, due to (self-) secularisation of the younger generation and harsh suppression of non-Sunni religious practices by state authorities following the re-Islamisation of Turkey during the rule of the conservative 'Democratic Party' in the 1950s.

As far as pre-modern contexts up to the end of the nineteenth century are concerned, we are not able to recognise — out of contemporary sources — an Alevi identity that comprised all such groups, which can be considered as proto-Alevi. Even the designation 'Alevi' was not used in the modern sense as a term for a distinct Muslim group of 'confession', but only in its narrower meaning as 'pertaining to ʿAlî' or 'stemming from ʿAlî'. The 'Sunnification' of the Muslim population of the Ottoman Empire since the sixteenth century (after the victory of the Ottomans over Safavid Iran) led to a retreat of 'heterodox' groups into the geographical periphery of the empire (rural and especially mountainous areas).

Although we can find networks of religious specialists and their lay-people, attached to each other over generations, stretching across wide ranges of Anatolia and Upper Mesopotamia, and although the groups in question indisputably shared several beliefs and practices that are common to modern Alevism, we can only speak of a 'constellation of (resembling) practices'.[14] This fact can be proven by means of ethnographical material describing different forms of religious practice (although we have no complete description of a pre-modern ritual), and by the fact that contemporary Alevis complain about the different local traditions on how to conduct a 'proper' *cem*-ritual. Alevis usually see this local differentiation of practice as a direct result of Sunni oppression. Activists want to overcome this heterogeneity of ritual forms by a 'unified' *cem*. In fact, a survey of ethnographic material shows a set (or rather *continuum*) of many different (though resembling each other) 'communities of practice' from different areas stretching from the Balkans across Anatolia up to Caucasia, Western Iran and Upper Mesopotamia (Northern Iraq). This differing 'communities of practice' during the last decades came into contact in urban and diaspora contexts due to migration and urbanisation of rural Alevis. As the migrated Alevis hold or have re-established contact with their rural regions of origin, and the diaspora communities have strong ties with the urban communities in Istanbul or Ankara, we can speak of a triangular village–city–Western diaspora, which now forms the transnational field of discourse and practice.[15] This has developed only recently through the relatively cheap access to modern transportation and information technologies. As a result, modern means of mobility and medialisation (of rituals) have made possible the creation of a virtual 'community of practice', out of what formerly could only be referred to as a 'constellation of (resembling) practices': the modern *Alevìlik* ('Alevism').

The contemporary situation concerning the *cem*-ritual can be described as follows. The ritual is most regularly practised in the city *cemevi*s ('assembly houses'), in many cases on a weekly basis, taking place usually on Thursday evening (which is called the 'Friday evening', according to the traditional Near Eastern concept of time measuring where the day starts with sunset). This weekly *cem*-rituals, performed in a distinct Alevi architectural environment attended by urban Alevis, are the most likely forms of ritual that modern Alevis have the chance to participate in. In many villages, such modernised forms of congregational ritual organised to last only one or two hours according to modern concepts of daily working routine are present either through television broadcast from the cities' *cemevi*s or as actually practiced rituals led by urban *dede*s in newly-built village *cemevi*s. In spite of the ubiquity of this modernised ritual, most Alevis still refer to the pre-modern village *cem*s that functioned as a legal court and lasted many hours, as the 'real' or 'ideal' *cem*, although in reality these forms of *cem* have no longer been regularly performed for decades. It has to take place in the village community, which is no longer functioning as the sole entity of religious, social and economic life due to migration. Some communities tried to re-establish this pre-modern form by bringing together all families from the same village in an urban *cemevi*.

When we analyse recent performances of *cem*-rituals, we can distinguish different transmission or reception lines: continuing traditions from regional contexts, and modern *cem*s or parts of the *cem*. These modern *cem*s are perceived by Alevis either as live performances (in *cemevi*s, at festivals, etc.) or through television broadcasts. Both, the recollections of village religious culture as well as patterns of recent *cem* performances were transferred to Western Europe through migration. Alevis in the diaspora perceive their modern *cem*-rituals, which are conducted in the communities in Europe only irregularly once or twice a year, as 'not being the proper ritual'. Instead, they tend to imagine the 'authentic' *cem* to take place in a pre-modern setting, i.e., the village community. In certain cases, people who plan to migrate back to their village of origin (and set the ground for these plans by building modern houses in the villages) have a special interest in re-establishing religious live 'back home'. This is a counter-movement towards standardised forms of the ritual as well as against the political organisations that are responsible for such attempts at standardisation and centralisation and are attempting to monopolise the representation of 'Alevism'. However, contemporary urban Alevis naturally have become acquainted with Alevi ritual only in the migrational contexts, through its discourse, way of thinking and modernised practice.

In the course of my research, I encountered an example of this temporary bringing back of Alevi congregational ritual practice to the village in one East-Central Anatolian village. In 2006, a *cem*-ritual was organised by a German Alevi who went to his village of origin for a short visit to his old mother. Although he encouraged the elderly villagers to practise the ritual as they remembered it from their childhood, it had a modern structure, as there was no one left who dared to lead the ritual in its entirety as it was practised in the past and only some sequences were re-enacted in the traditional way. In order to lead the ritual, an urban *dede* from the city was brought, who practised it in a more standardised form. In addition to such direct influences, the omnipresence of television, including private stations run by Alevi entrepreneurs and organisations, which regularly broadcast weekly *cem*-rituals from urban *cemevis*, transports several modern forms of ritual practice from the cities into the village houses. Most striking examples for that are staged rituals such as the *semah* dance, performed by dancing groups in designed costumes, professional, amplified music performances by professional musicians, especially designed and decorated rooms for the ritual (*cem salonları*), et cetera. It has to be kept in mind that the transmission of ritual knowledge is nowadays occupied by such medialised forms of rituals (television, books, magazines), and not by the practise of ritual itself (mimetics), nor by traditional learning from generation to generation by oral transmission. The influence of these virtual, medial forms can be detected in their modern religious practice as they exercise elements from broadcasted rituals in their actual ritual performances. This complex network of mutual influences is a basis for the establishment of a 'virtual community of practice', replacing the former, pre-modern field of a constellation of related, but autonomous practices. This realisation of standardised ritual elements nowadays characterises the field of Alevi ritual in as far a geographical range as from England to Eastern Anatolia, and from Sweden to Australia.

In this essay, I am focussing on the Alevis from Turkey in order to exemplify some aspects of the concept of transfer of ritual.[16] Moreover, I show how easily scholars can be involved in identity politics, not only at the group but also at a national or even transnational level. This happens when the researcher is dealing with processes of transfer and transference of ritual, e.g., from Turkey to Germany or from Turkish to German language, which can be interpreted as acculturation or — worse — as assimilation processes. It has to be taken into account that nationalistic ideology has recently gained much importance and broad acceptance in Turkey. The so-called 'moderate Islamicists' of the ruling 'AK Party' (*Adalet ve Kalkınma Partisi*) and their prime minister Recep Tayyip Erdoğan are struggling for Turkey's European Union membership, trying to fulfil certain requirements set by European politicians, e.g., in respect of minority rights. Thus, opposition towards the 'Islamic' politicians as well as towards the European Union — an attitude that gained ground with the Turkish public in recent times — is formulated along nationalistic lines.

In order to exemplify my points I will quote from a Turkish newspaper. I use citations from this article later on as a means to exemplify aspects of the transfer of Alevi ritual from Turkey to Germany as well as dynamic transferences between Alevi religious life and the surrounding German culture. Several statements by the author of the article, which was a reaction to a lecture I gave at a congress on Alevi culture in Şanlıurfa (Turkey), should serve to highlight some aspects of the transfer of ritual processes. This concerns particularly the dynamical alterations rituals go through when their contexts are changed as well as the effects transformations of rituals can have on social actors confronted with such processes (here, first of all, the author of the article). The text in its English translation[17] runs as follows:

> A lecture about 'South-Eastern Anatolian Religious Culture in the Life of Alevis in Germany and the Role of Their Rituals' was given by the German scholar Dr. Robert Langer [at a congress in Şanlıurfa, Turkey]. The lecture given by Langer displayed pretty well the Germans' point of view concerning the Turks and how they wish

> to destroy the values of the Turks by means of an official [German] state policy. Langer, in his presentation, spoke about an Alevi *dede* [a religious specialist] from Tunceli [formerly Dersim, in Eastern Turkey] performing [the Alevi congregational] *cem*-ritual in Germany in German language instead of Turkish and at the same time he showed this ceremony to the audience on the screen. The German scholar was absolutely content, satisfied and happy that an Alevi *dede* had performed *cem* in German language. In his presentation, he pushed it even further when he mentioned with tears in his eyes and sadness in his voice that the Zazas and Kurmancis [two Kurdish groups in Turkey] have lost their languages. Because of that, [Professor] Arslanoğlu jumped up from his chair and gave an amazing speech [...]: 'I congratulate the Germans, for they are assimilating Turkish children and even Alevi *dedes*. Dr. Langer mentions with sadness that Kurmancis and Zazas have lost their languages. However, I guess he does not at all regret that Turkish children forget their language; he is even contented. Not too long ago a German person in charge suggested that Turkish children who speak Turkish on the schoolyard should be sentenced to clean the school's yard. As you know, the German minister of interior has said that assimilation is the best way to adjust Turkish children to Germany.' While receiving vows of applause, the hall screaming for more, Arslanoğlu continued his speech. 'By accepting Alevism as a religious minority, the European Union wants to use it against Turkey. However, the patriotic Alevis do not approve of that. Westerners do not research just for the research. The research done by them has to serve their purposes and their advantage. Well, for our entry to the European Union they want us to give up Cyprus, accept the Armenian genocide and give away the straits and the waters of Tigris and Euphrates to an international foundation. That makes their aims more than clear.' [...] I congratulate Arslanoğlu with all my heart, who gave a pretty nice lesson for the other speakers, who stayed silent and just supported the German scholar who spoke at an international academic congress like someone officially in charge of assimilation.[18]

This article appeared in the newspaper of a Turkish nationalistic party.[19] Professor Arslanoğlu, a friend of the party leader, is employed at a state-sponsored institute for research on Anatolian 'folk Islam' in Ankara. The article uses a propagandistic style and is manipulative, as its author, in line with the cited professor, equals the presentation of empirical data, which I presented at the mentioned congress, with influencing processes of acculturation through migration in general and transfer of ritual especially in a political way with the aim of assimilation. This is not so astonishing if we reconsider the mechanisms of Turkish politics towards the cultural, linguistic and ethnic heterogeneity of Turkey. In a quasi-magical fashion, facts that would destroy the picture of an ethnically and culturally homogenous country were not to be spoken of. In order to reach the general aim of Turkish cultural politics since the foundation of the Republic, namely to create a homogenous culture of 'Turkishness', ethnic and cultural differences have officially been neglected.

The cited article gives a good starting point in order to demonstrate how considerable parts of the Turkish public, who were socialised for generations in a framework of Turkish nationalism, receive cultural transformations, such as transfer of ritual between Turkey and Germany, within ethno-religious groups from Turkey as well as research on that process. Besides, it gives a clear-cut example of how easily and quickly the scholar and his — from his own point of view impartial — research can be utilised for political propaganda. He is then perceived as part of an official German state policy, unfortunately not only by political extremists. It is not conceivable for most people socialised in the thoroughly centralised Turkish Republic, that there is no central, well-planned policy behind processes of acculturation. Moreover, anyone who is familiar with the political system of Federal Germany is aware that, even if there would be attempts for such a policy at a central level of the Federal state, the governments of the German member countries would not accept interference of Federal authorities in cultural-educational politics. The reason for that is that they are in charge of cultural and educational politics guaranteed to them by the Constitution and do not allow the interference of Federal authorities in their genuine fields of competence. Therefore, at best, one could inquire for planned cultural politics towards migrant communities in the respective member countries of the Federal state. However, this is most often not the case. While talking to some members of German Federal state ministries of culture on the topic of Turkish Alevis, it became clear to me that state officials dealing with the question of Muslim religious education at state schools (which involves the Alevi wish of separate lessons for their children) were generally not familiar with the religio-cultural tradition and practices of the groups in question. Other ministries are not involved in issues touching on Alevi religious practice. In short, there is no German official capable of such an assimilation mission, as was stated in the article, even if the German politicians wished to assimilate Alevis and their religious and cultural traditions.

However, the article highlights points of cultural transformations, although they are not engineered by a sinister state policy of assimilation. They are part of a process of cultural transfer processes and transferences of certain elements (such as language or dates of festival calendars of the society where the migrants have settled), which have been formulated theoretically for the context of ritual (Langer, Lüddeckens, Radde, Snoek 2006). Instead of repeating here the theory as a closed concept, I will use the case of the Turkish Alevis in connection with points made (and omitted) in the Turkish article quoted above in order to illustrate the analytical, heuristic potential of the theoretical concept of 'transfer of ritual'.

Cultural performances such as rituals materialise within certain contexts, which are formed by nature, society and respective sociocultural, political and economical processes, as well as historical correlations. The contexts change in the course of time, maybe faster when change of place is involved like in the case of recent migrations during the twentieth century, when modern means of transportation and communication enabled more rapid and larger exchanges of population, material culture and ideas. These contextual aspects, such as media, space, ecosystem, culture, religion, politics, economy, society, gender and social groups, influence rituals or elements of ritual. In such cases, the function of the ritual may change, its script may be adjusted, the performance adapted to the new contexts, and so on. On the other hand, such 'internal dimensions' of rituals can be altered deliberately or unconsciously. Consequently, this has an effect on the contexts surrounding the 'ritual'.

Such is the case with the Alevi *cem*-ritual, which Alevi functionaries intentionally instrumentalised and used strategically in an accordingly modified popularised form, especially in the large Turkish cities, where the '*cem*-houses' serve also as a political and cultural centre, where functionaries can reach a large public, attending the congregational ritual on a weekly basis. Functionaries and intellectual leaders of the Alevi communities had an interest in establishing such facilities and organisations in order to mobilise Alevi masses, on the one hand, and to generate political awareness of their identity politics in the society and political class, on the other. Functionaries and intellectuals were experienced in organising the masses from their previous activities in (mostly leftist) political organisations in which they were active before the *coup d'état* in Turkey of 1980. (At that time, religious affiliation was not on the agenda as a marker of identity.) Consequently, they were able to organise and publicise Alevism in a professional manner. This newly-gained publicity of Alevism, besides mobilising Alevis, also had an impact on the non-Alevis who either opposed and even attacked the Alevis physically as 'heretics' or accepted them as harmless fellow citizens. The last point illustrates the two sides of the coin of the emancipation processes of marginalised communities. They gain a modernised identity and establish organisations to serve their interests, which were earlier occupied by (mostly socialist and communist) political organisations. On the other hand, they become visible and therefore open to criticism or even attack, whereas before the migration in their rural regions of origin they held a low profile, practising *taqîya* (the Qur'ânic concept of dissimulating one's belief to safeguard oneself in a hostile surrounding) whenever they were outside of their communities. Some points concerning contextual aspects of transfer processes of Alevi ritual shall be elaborated in the following paragraphs.

The Historical Context

The historical perspective is deliberately not presented explicitly in the Turkish article, as it is part of an ongoing struggle within and beyond the community over the 'essence' of Alevism: namely, whether it supports the state or, to the contrary, is a danger to the state. The groups under investigation in our research project were traditionally called Muslim 'sects', attributed as 'syncretistic' and 'heterodox' by Western scholarship and simply as 'heretic' by orthodox Muslim sources.[20] They formed under the influence of different extremist Shiite and mystical ideologies of economically marginalised groups, which often were part of tribal systems and of specific ethnic backgrounds such as Kurdish, other Iranian people (like Zazas) or Turkmen. Those ideologies were used by folk religious leaders (who later came to be considered as 'holy men') — in the tradition of Shiism as the ideology of the downtrodden — as a means to stimulate socio-political uprisings against established orthodox dynasties and the economical oppression enforced by state structures. This formative phase stretches from the emergence of Turkic dynasties in the core region of those groups (i.e., Anatolia, Upper Mesopotamia, South Caucasia and Western Iran) in the eleventh century to the consolidation of an Ottoman-Iranian dualism in the sixteenth century. From sixteenth to nineteenth centuries, both states — the Ottoman and Iranian empires — conducted a two-fold policy of extermination and integration towards heretic groups, with the support of Muslim orthodoxy, Sunni in the case of the Ottomans, Twelver Shii in the case of Iran. One instance of attempts to integrate 'heterodox' Muslims into state structures can be seen in the attitude of the Ottoman Empire towards the adherence of the 'holy man' (*velî*) Hacı Bektaş, the eponymous founder of the Bektashi order. This order of dervishes (the *Bektaşiyye*), which was already in charge of taking care of the spiritual needs of the elite infantry corps of the Janissaries, was restructured as an order bound to the state by means of 'pious foundations' (*evkâf*, singular: *vakıf*). These *evkâf* were established by sultans and state officials, in order to control and 'pacify' (proto-)Alevis in West and Central Anatolia. This control was established when Alevi groups accepted the 'monastery' (*tekke*) of Hacıbektaş as their spiritual centre. In late Ottoman times (nineteenth to twentieth century), Hacı Bektaş Velî was increasingly seen as a kind of 'national' Turkish saint, in the context of the development of Turkish nationalism (out of an 'Ottoman' patriotism) at the turn from the nineteenth century. The Bektashi order — after a phase of suppression as a result of the extermination of the Janissary troops in 1826 until the end of the nineteenth century, when it had recovered again — gained even more influence over Turkish Alevis during World War I and the independence wars of the Turkish Republic. At that time, the leadership of the Bektashi order mobilized people to take part in the wars against the Western allies occupying Anatolia and against the Greek invasion troops. Consequently, many Turkish Alevi *dede* lineages (*ocak*, Turkic, literally 'hearth', hence 'family, clan, lineage') which received diploma from the seat of the order[21] came to be indirectly linked to state authority. The establishment of modern state structures in the region from the nineteenth century onwards and especially the economically caused migrations after World War II brought the heterogeneity of the Near Eastern Muslim population again to the surface.

As this historical context can be interpreted either as a tradition of resistance to states perceived as 'Turkish', or, to the contrary, as a 'patriotic' Turkish folk Islam, which is a source of national pride, the author of the cited article is omitting to refer to the tricky problem of contextualising 'Alevism' historically. This is of special importance to the contextualisation of the 'heterodox' ritual forms of Alevism, in comparison to orthodox Sunni Islam; namely the gender equality within the participating congregation, the leading of the ritual by 'holy men' stemming from the family of the prophet, singing and dancing during the ritual. These constitutive elements of Alevi ritual can, by means of historical and ethnographical data, be interpreted either as an 'Old Turkic', 'shamanistic' tradition (a positive interpretation by Turkish nationalists, especially from an anti-Islamic tradition), or alternatively as a special form of 'Turkish Islam' (supreme to the Arabic 'Wahhabism') or as a heretical Shiite influence.

The Geographical and Spatial Context Aspect

As far as the contextual aspect of geography/space is concerned, in the cited article, the major geographical regions of settlements of Alevis and other marginalised ethno-religious minorities are mentioned as the core region of Turkish national interests, which are threatened by Western interests, such as in Iraqi Kurdistan, which borders the Turkish regions settled mainly by Kurds. The geographical-spatial description of the region in the article corresponds to the actual settlement area of the Alevi population: Anatolia from Greater İstanbul ('the straits') to Upper Mesopotamia, i.e., the upper flows of Tigris and Euphrates and its tributaries. This rather detailed description of geography is in opposition to the simple use of 'Germany' referring to the (West-European) Alevi diaspora. 'Germany' here stands as a symbol of

Turkish life outside Turkey; its diversity in different European countries, cities and regions is normally not available to Turks living in Turkey. The author of the article, according to his political aim (i.e., to describe the Turks in Germany as victims of an assimilation policy), is clearly not willing to take into account that the geographical and cultural change through migration from Turkey to Germany influences the Alevi *cem*-ritual, even without a 'German state policy'. He, therefore, blames an assimilation policy by the German state to force Alevi religious leaders to conduct their rituals in German and generally to force the Turks in Germany to abandon their language in favour of the German language. The language question was recently raised again within a congress of the 'Alliance of the Alevi Youth in Germany' (*Bund der Alevitischen Jugendlichen in Deutschland e. V.* / AAGB = *Almanya Alevi Gençler Birliği*) at Heidelberg (23 November 2007). Many delegates stated that rituals had to be conducted or at least 'explained' in German, as the younger generation is not able to understand Turkish, especially that of the rituals, properly. As this problem is not adequately answered by the organisations and especially not by the practising older *dede*s, the youth organisation takes the responsibility of organising '*cem*-rituals for the young generation' (*gençlik cemleri*). How controversial and explosive the situation is, is shown by the fact that, for the first time during the last years of my research, I was not allowed to film the ritual.

The Contextual Aspect of the Carrier-Group of the Ritual

One important contextual aspect is the group bearing the ritual tradition in question: The 'Alevis' are not defined explicitly in the cited article. However, they are presented as being — at least partly — 'patriotic Turks'. The non-Turkic groups, which are mentioned in the article, 'Zazas' and 'Kurmancis', on the other hand, are referred to as if having nothing to do with Alevism. However, a considerable percentage of the so-called 'Kurmancis' (i.e., Northern Kurds) and many of the speakers of the West-Iranian Zaza language (living in Eastern Anatolia) are in fact Alevi themselves. This point has been omitted in the article, although I had highlighted this fact in the lecture in Turkey because the German-speaking *dede* I had presented is himself a Zaza-speaker from Tunceli (formerly Dersim), one of the main centres of the Zaza language. Nevertheless, he is a very active *dede* in the German Alevi community. As he said in a meeting witnessed by me some years ago, 'Our children will lose the ability to speak Turkish, and even Zaza and Kurdish, but what they will definitely know to speak in the future will be German. That's why we need to conduct the *cem*-ritual also in German.' He is referring to the emergence of a group of 'German Alevis', the children of the first and second generations, who have grown up in Germany and consequently speak and understand better German than Turkish. With this we see how a new group carrying the ritual tradition can emerge even after shifting to the language of the country to which their parents or grandparents had migrated. At the same time, one can observe the emergence of a group of 'patriotic Alevis' in Turkey subscribing to a chauvinist, sometimes even racist nationalism. The reason for this last point is the strong link between Turkish-speaking Alevis (mainly with traditional ties to the Bektashi order) and the Turkish republican state. These Alevis supported Mustafa Kemal (Atatürk) in the 'war of independence' (following World War I in Anatolia). At that time, they saw the establishment of a secular, laical republic (laicism is one of the 'Six Principles' of the republic, protected against abrogation by the Constitution) as a chance to get rid of the Sunni control of the Ottoman Empire ruled by the sultan-caliph. The recent re-emergence of an ultra-nationalist Turkish attitude has to be seen in the context of the emergence of political Sunni Islam since the 1980s, to which nationalism is perceived as the only effective counter-ideology (after the downfall of socialist ideologies finally symbolised in the dissolution of the Soviet Union). Another factor is Kurdish nationalism, which is supported by some 'Kurdish' Alevis (speakers of Kurmâncî and Zaza). The aim of this ideology, namely to emancipate Kurdish language and culture from historical suppression within the Turkish republic, which is seen as a major threat to the political system of the republic by the majority, gives the 'language question' even in contexts such as Germany a special notion.

In terms of ritual, we can ascertain the language shift from Turkish to German in Germany on the one hand, and — in Turkey—the presentation of Turkish national symbols within the public *cem*-rituals, on the other. These national symbols usually are the national anthem (*İstiklal Marşı*) played at the beginning of community gatherings, Turkish flags and the portrait of Atatürk that are displayed during mass *cem*-rituals, blessings spoken by the *dedes* for state authorities, the military and the police forces. The last example is obviously a parallel to the old Sunni tradition of referring to the ruling authority in the Friday sermon (*hutbe*), as the modern weekly *cem*-ritual invented in the cities was interpreted sometimes as a reaction to the orthodox Friday prayer (*cuma namazı*).

The Context of Material Culture and Aesthetisation

Generally, in modern *cemevis* we can find an increasing aesthetisation of ritual spaces within urban contexts. This leads to a permanent demarcation of ritual space. I observed in most of the Alevi *cem*-halls portraits of saintly figures such as the Twelve Imams (Oniki İmam), Hacı Bektaş Velî, Ahmed Yesevî, Pîr Sultân Abdâl, or Mustafa Kemal Atatürk, wall paintings, carpets, special wooden floor on the place (*meydân*) for the ritual dance (*semah*) in the form of a twelve-pointed star, symbolising the Twelve Imams, et cetera. In the village, any room could serve for the ritual and there were no material symbols or pictures on display, because of fear of being labelled by the authorities as 'heretic'. Additionally, in Turkey I also found that some Alevi organisations or individual *dedes* try to Islamicise the *cem*-ritual by adding Qur`ân recitations and prayers in Arabic to the ritual. Contrary to that, leading functionaries of the official Alevi Community Organisation in Germany (*Alevitische Gemeinde Deutschland e. V.*) sometimes entirely reject the notion of Alevism being a part of 'Islam'. Both the nationalisation as well as the Islamisation of the ritual script and *decorum* is due to the different strains of Turkish politics, Nationalism and (political) Islam. It is interesting to note, that in Alevi contexts (such as the *CEM Vakfı* organisation) as well as in Turkish politics these ideologies formerly perceived as mutually exclusive coexist side by side, even within the mindsets of acting individuals as well as within the same organisation. This coexistence of Turkism and Islam was even institutionalised in the 1980s by state officials by means of the semi-official so-called 'Türk-Islam Synthesis' (*Türk İslam Sentezi*), that has been made the official basis of the centralised education system since then.

The Change of the 'Dimensions of Ritual' Through 'Transfer of Ritual'

'Dimensions of ritual' is a concept introduced by Jan G. Platvoet (1995) to describe elements of ritual (such as function, aesthetics, communication, etc.) derived from the different perspectives taken by several academic approaches to the phenomenon of human ritual(ised) modes of action. These 'dimensions' were integrated into the analytical concept of 'transfer of ritual' in order to specify the transformations within rituals that occur when their contexts change. Only some dimensions, those most relevant in connection with the Alevi *cem*-ritual, will be taken up in the following paragraph.

Once again, the above-cited article can serve as a medium to elucidate aspects of 'transfer of ritual'. In the Turkish article, the 'Germans' are simply the 'others' trying to 'destroy the values of the Turks' which are deliberately not specified. There is only the reference to language. In this ideology, the preserving of the Turkish language and the use of 'pure' Turkish is a value in itself. The change of the language is seen as the main attack on 'Turkish values', a deliberately unclear concept strongly linked to language and 'race' (*ırk*). The (partial) language change is mainly a transformation of the medium of the prescriptive instructions within the ritual, which are given by the specialist to the congregation, such as sermons at the beginning and instructions and advices during the ritual. Prayers and hymns tend to stay in the 'spiritual language' Turkish, as they are not easy to translate. Even modern Turks do not fully understand these, as these texts were mainly composed in fifteenth–seventeenth century in an old form of Anatolian Turkish not entirely comprehensible to modern Turkish-speakers. However, I took part in events where ritual hymns especially composed in German were performed. To 'keep clean Turkish language and race' may well be understood as the 'Turkish value' *per se* by the propagandists and supporters of such an ideology. In their perspective other 'Turkish values' often referred to, such as 'piety', 'cleanliness', 'braveness', et cetera, directly result from 'racial purity'.[22]

Interestingly, the article did not mention how the dimension of the performance also changed, most strikingly in that the

German Alevis sit on chairs during the ritual, whereas in Turkey all participants would sit on the floor. In praxis, this can lead to very emotional discussions, when Alevis from Germany attend *cem*-rituals in Turkey and want to sit on chairs there too, as they are no longer accustomed to the bodily practice of sitting on the floor (which then can be quite painful). Normally, *dede*s will most probably reject such attempts, as chairs within the ritual are only accepted for sick people in Turkey. In Germany on the other hand, in some communities (though certainly not in the majority of them) a ritual event cannot take place if not enough chairs can be provided. On such occasions, the sitting on chairs can be considered as part of the ritual prescription. However, even in those cases *dede*s would prefer to sit on the floor, which leads to spatial incongruities, the ritual leader sitting on a lower level than the congregation.

It is noteworthy that the article misses another aspect of 'transfer of ritual' that could have been extracted from my lecture. It concerns the context of Christianity as the denomination (at least nominally) of the majority of the population. Turkish radical nationalism, the context of the author of the article and the publishing newspaper (published by a right-wing political party), is generally obsessed with the fear of Christian missionaries, a *topos* widely shared by the Turkish public opinion. The dangerous impact of this ideology on Turks of the younger generation resulted in the murder of members of a Christian publishing house in Malatya city this year and of Christian priests earlier. Consequently, in Turkey we do not encounter transferences from other religious traditions apart from other Islamic ones (namely Sunni, partly also Shii from Iran). This is different in Germany: the mentioned Alevi ritual leader in the German case sings his prayers in a rather 'Christian' melody and not in the traditional Anatolian way. He learned these melodies during his inter-religious practice, such as jointly marrying mixed Christian-Alevi couples in a church together with a Christian priest. As he is quite a young person who admitted that he did not learn the practice of a *dede* (*dedelik*) in the traditional way from an elder person, we can presume that he adopted Christian melodies in a mimetic process from Christian priests. Such a transfer of a Christian ritual element could only occur — out of reasons described above — within a mainly Christian milieu such as in Germany, where inter-religious meetings and seminars are quite common and some Alevi *dede*s and community activists participate regularly in such occasions. It is also quite significant that several of the first performed public *cem*s in Europe were conducted in Christian churches (see Sökefeld 2005: 218, 223); and even now Alevi communities without their own premises conduct rituals in church buildings given to them by Christian communities for rent or for free.[23] A reason for that is the generally friendly attitude of Alevis towards Christians whom they perceive as their natural allies towards radical orthodox Islam. (It is unheard, and for most Alevis I asked inconceivable, that a *cem* could be performed in a mosque.) As demographically significant Christian groups no longer exist within Turkey, this can naturally only occur within diaspora communities. They are sometimes eager to differentiate themselves from non-Alevi Muslim migrants from Turkey. As far as historical Anatolia — until the extermination of the Armenian population by the Young Turk regime in 1915 — is concerned, we know of the sometimes symbiotic relation between these two minority groups, which at times even shared the same building for their religious services in mixed villages in the Eastern parts of Anatolia.[24]

However, in contemporary Turkey, I observed the integration of typical orthodox, 'Sunni' ritual elements into Alevi ritual, especially in İstanbul. This must be interpreted as a kind of mimicry in urban contexts (and is criticised as such by some Alevi intellectuals) and, at the same time, as an attempt to reclaim certain elements generally perceived as typically Muslim by outsiders as well as insiders. This is namely the figure of the prophet Muhammad and the Qur`ân. Besides an increased mention of Islamic personae, such as Muhammad, there is the tendency to integrate Qur`ânic formulae into the *cem*-ritual in practice, in one case even a classical Qur`ân recitation as an opening ceremony for a *cem*-ritual I observed at the end of the Alevi *Muharrem* fast in 2005 at the *Gazi Cemevi* in İstanbul. Both the German case (Christian melodies) as well as the cases observed in İstanbul (Qur`ân verses) are examples of the changed religious context — a predominantly Christian milieu in Germany and a mainly Muslim-Sunni environment in Turkish cities — and the impact of this changed context of the elements of the ritual. An enhancement of traditionalism within the Alevi communities was not possible in both cases, as the traditional structures of the 'caste' of the religious specialists, namely the transmission of their knowledge, the reproduction of their authority and economical power, broke down in the secularisation processes the young Alevi generation went through in the 1960s and 70s. The only potential for a revival of Alevism in the 1980s was in the hands of intellectuals and functionaries socialised in secular movements, who had no possibility of recourse to special traditions but only to general notions of Alevism. They needed the help of the remaining religious specialists. Nevertheless, until today, the *dede* caste has not re-established the level of intellectual and practical knowledge, which they once had as the main carriers of ritual tradition in former times. Moreover, they are not able to regain the economical power over their flock, which they exercised in 'pre-modern' times taking contribution called *hakkullâh* ('God's right') from them. Because of that loss of structural and economical power, the practicing *dede*s nowadays serve as employees of the communities, not as their leaders.

If we consider the agency concerning the modern Alevi *cem*-rituals, we can observe a switch from traditional *dede*s towards modern functionaries, most of them of lay origin (*tâlib*). Traditional authority remains partly with the *dede*s born from a 'holy lineage' (*ocak*). Still, the congregational ritual (including the animal sacrifice connected to it)[25] is considered valid in most of the cases only if it is conducted by a *dede* from a 'holy lineage' (*ocakzade* = 'born from an *ocak*', Turkic *odjaq* plus Persian–*zâde*, 'stemming from'). We can find some (over-)traditionalising elements here, in that this requirement ignores the fact that in the past *dede*-helpers appointed by *ocakzade-dede*s to conduct rituals in their absence, e.g., in far away villages, were quite common, and even today in the villages we find lay people conducting life-cycle rituals such as burials. Although I encountered some people practising *dedelik* without being *ocakzade* (legitimised by their charisma, knowledge and ability to perform songs, music and prayers), such cases are the exception. An important point is the overall authority. In traditional contexts, *dede*s made their decision on where, when and how to conduct the ritual gatherings on their own. In interviews conducted by me in villages in the Malatya province in 2006 among people between the ages of sixty and over ninety, I was told that these traditional *dede*s held complete authority in such questions, enforced by harsh penalties imposed by them on misbehaving group members. The agency of 'traditional' *dede*s concerning ritual practice was additionally enforced by the fact that they in most cases were not living in the villages of their direct followers, but visited them only once or twice a year. Therefore, their followers were dependent on their visits, during which the *dedes* held court over community quarrels, if they did not want to lose their 'judges' and spiritual guides.

In fact, the decisive authority on how and when to conduct the ritual in migration contexts such as cities and diaspora communities nowadays is taken over by functionaries who are in most of the cases laymen. Moreover, in many cases they do have a past as functionaries of leftist organisations and parties. Some of them are also Alevi intellectuals, bearing the 'title' *araştırmacı-yazar*, 'researcher-writer', who are the main proponents of the 'Alevi revival' of the 1980s. These 'researcher-writers' gained their authority in the fields of history and ethnography of Alevism. They published extensively on such topics in the many magazines and book series that were published by Alevi publishing houses mainly during the 1980s and 1990s. Since the establishment of Alevi media in the 1990s, daily newspapers, radio and television stations, many of them work as journalists. Besides the agency of such socio-political functionaries and professionals, the actively or passively participating community gained a partial agency through the discursive field that evolved around Alevi religious identity and practice. As one main topic in the indigenous Alevi publications and media is the *cem*-ritual, many people participated in the discourse that evolved around 'the ritual' (Paul/Zimmermann 2005). They did so as writers of 'letters to the editor', as discussants at modern symposia (basically on topics of Alevi identity) that are regularly held by Alevi associations, and as group members actively participating in the congregational rituals. The last point is enabled through the traditional inclusion of lay people into the ritual as officiants (the so-called 'twelve duties', *oniki hizmet*, analogous to the Twelve Imams, 'Oniki İmam'). These duties were professionalised in courses for the *oniki hizmet* that are organised by almost every Alevi community in Turkey and Europe. With this professionalisation of religious duties, lay people could gain a considerable agency in the ritual, for example by excluding 'normal' (especially elderly) lay people from the ritual dance *semah*, performed during the *cem*. This dance, which has the potential to induce altered states of consciousness, was in former times conducted by experienced (oftentimes older) people, who could step to the dancing floor (*meydan*) if they wanted to. Nowadays it is in most of the cases occupied by 'official' dance groups, generally young people, and performance is considered more valid if rehearsed figures are performed and the participants wear especially designed costumes. In this context, not only lay people, but also the younger generations — the main clientele of dance and music courses — emancipated themselves from traditional roles and gained agency in the field of modern ritual practice.

The role of 'the ritual' as a discursive *topos* in printed and electronic publications and broadcasts is worthy of consideration. As this *topos* gained so much importance, it might not be exaggerated to speak of a kind of 'agency of the ritual' itself, as the very presence of *ayin-i cem*, 'the ceremony of the *cem*', (and core elements of it in secular festivals) as the main performative marker of Alevi identity, developed a dynamic of itself. The acting human agents of these processes are no longer clearly identifiable, and the presence of the imagined as well as the actually practiced Alevi *cem* in medialised formats can be considered as one 'actor' in the described cultural processes. At least, we can state that many more people are talking about and publishing on the *cem*-ritual, than actually participating in it — a process which was described as the 'virtualisation of ritual' (Motika/Langer 2005: 95–100). When we calculate around 150 *cem*-houses in İstanbul, which contain space for up to 300 persons, only 45,000 people could participate regularly. If we roughly estimate the Alevi population of İstanbul as amounting to three million people, only 1.5 per cent of this population is in fact able to practice the *cem*. The participation in it, on the other hand, is considered as constitutive for every Alevi. This explains why it is extremely important for many Alevis to have the ritual being broadcasted via television every week into the Alevi households of the city. Another reason for the loss of agency of the traditional *dede*s was their lower rate of migration. Those *dede*s, who still were into the tradition of practising the ritual, obviously did not participate at the same rate as the lay people or non-practising *ocakzade* in the migrations of the past decades. At the same time, consequently, they did not participate in modern education as the other group members. Even if they did, usually they abandoned the traditional education in favour of a modern one, which led to the loss of ritual knowledge. In a kind of conversion of roles, traditional rural *dede*s started to visit urban Alevi centres in order to get 'work' (not necessarily official employment) as religious specialists, or at least to find modern 'knowledge' (such as the access to economic resources) there. They visited such modern centres (which themselves sometimes gained their legitimation and authority by the fact, that they were historical lodges of the Bektashi order) to establish new networks and regain their lost legitimation in their village communities. This somehow parallels the visits of the traditional *dede* to the central Bektashi lodge of Hacıbektaş in order to get 'allowance' (*icazet*) (to lead his community) and knowledge (by serving there for some time and taking back handwritten ritual handbooks) from the main seat of the order. This attraction of modern urban centres for traditional religious leaders is proven by the success of three 'Meetings of Religious Leaders of Anatolia' until now, organised by the Alevi organisation *CEM Vakfı* at Istanbul during the last years, where hundreds of Alevi *dede*s attended (Aydın 2000, [2003?], n.d.). Moreover, the Alevi researcher Ali Yaman documented the endless visits of Anatolian *dede*s to the old Bektashi lodge and modern Alevi Centre of Şahkulu Sultan in İstanbul (Göztepe), where he worked as an employee in the 1990s. For his work on the system of 'holy lineages' (*ocak*) in Anatolia, he made use of this fact by interviewing many *dede*s at Şahkulu (Yaman 2006). This shows that the authority of the formerly powerful *dede*s has diminished significantly in the process of migration and urbanisation (Dressler 2006), as the traditional *dede*s lost their powerful role as spiritual, juridical and sometimes even political leaders of their rural followers. With the emergence of urban Alevism, an unprecedented fact in the history of 'heterodox Islam' (which was predominantly rural or nomadic), only a minority could regain partial authority as employees of modern cultural centres, which are managed by secular functionaries.

Simultaneously, another political decision of one influential Alevi organisation in Turkey brings about modifications of the ritual structure and its symbolism. This is the inclusion of other Sufi groups into the domain of Alevism. Last year the İstanbul-based *CEM Vakfı* started to conduct large public *cem*-rituals in sport arenas, together with one branch of the İstanbul Mevlevî dervish order. With this collaborative exercise, the political leaders of the *CEM Vakfı* try to find new allies and position themselves in a broader Islamic context. It is important to note that Mevlevî Sufism is considered as the intellectual and aesthetic high peak of Turko-Islamic mysticism, both within Turkey as well as in the West. Consequently, *Mevlevîlik* (the tradition and practice of the *Mevleviyye*-order) is a potential partner against political Islam of a 'Wahhabist' type, which in turn is a declared enemy of *tasavvuf* (Sufism). As *Mevlevîlik* is accepted by official Sunni state Islam, an alliance with or even incorporation of at least a considerable part of the Mevlevîs would serve as an entry card into state sponsored official religion. (The 'Directorate of Religious Affairs' finances all officially recognised mosques all over the county together with thousands of employed imams, preachers, müèzzins, et cetera, whereas Alevis are struggling for at least a legalisation of their *cemevis* as places of worship.) On the other hand, a step towards more Sunni forms of Islam, such as Mevlevî *tasavvuf*, is strongly rejected by anti-Sunni Alevis from a leftist tradition, especially those in Germany. A reason for this is the perception of the Mevlevî order as a rather 'Sunni' form of Sufism, as Mevlevîs were well integrated into the leading elite of the Ottoman Empire, which excluded non-Sunnis from its ranks. The public rituals performed by *CEM Vakfı* Alevis together with Mevlevî dervishes are broadcasted by the television channel of the *CEM Vakfı* and other Alevi-run stations in Turkey and via satellite to Europe. This ritual transfer from Sufi orders into Alevism is consequently made visible by medialising the *cem*-ritual via television. Television broadcast for migrants in transnational, diasporic contexts is a very important and effective means to gain access to cultural resources, such as knowledge about rituals (see Vertovec/Cohen 1999: xxiii). Moreover, political orientations are communicated to the public by the modern media. Discussions on identity, history, daily politics and, not least, ritual fill the discussion boards and guest books of Alevi Internet sites (Zimmermann [forthc. 2010]).

The dissemination of identity debates and debates on cultural practice connected to specific organisations that in turn are identified with certain political orientations (from more 'Islamic' to rather 'leftist') via modern mass media owned by these organisations in turn contributes to the differentiation of places of worship and religious practice. This situation has led to the fact that nowadays in most Turkish cities where Alevis have settled during the last decades there exist at least two places of worship (cultural centres/*cemevis*). For instance, one is run by a local branch of the rather state-conform *CEM Vakfı* and one by another, competing organisation, either an association affiliated with the Turkish *Alevi-Bektaşi Federasyonu* ('Alevi-Bektaşi Federation') or one local branch of the *Pir Sultan Abdal Dernekleri*, which are considered to maintain the leftist spirit of the early Alevi movement. The Turkish *Alevi-Bektaşi Federasyonu* is supported by the main diaspora organisation, the *Avrupa Alevi Birlikleri Konfederasyonu*. This 'Confederation of Alevi Unions of Europe', which is the umbrella organisation for the Alevi federations of Germany, The Netherlands, Denmark, et cetera, supplies considerable amounts of money to built *cemevis*, collected among the European Alevis during many festivals, which in turn also show elements of religious ritual within a framework of a ritualised secular event. Obviously, the competition of several Alevi organisations over resources, places and ritual forms is also linked to the inner-Turkish struggle for or against European Union membership. This development is also visible in the villages where the people try to re-establish their religious lives according to patterns picked up from television broadcasts or brought back directly by (part- or full-time) re-migrants from Europe. This can result in the construction of rather oversized *cem*-houses within the villages (some of them never finished because of the lack of money) and in congregational *cem*-rituals modelled according to modern medialised standards (amplified music, electric illumination, dance groups, special dresses, shortened ritual sequences, movements and song texts learned from television, etc.).

Conclusion

The aim of this eassy was to show how contextual aspects and ritual dimensions are interlinked with each other. My main task was to illustrate how the concept of 'transfer of ritual' can be used as an analytical instrument in order to make changes both within the ritual itself and in its surrounding contexts visible by naming the interdependencies of contexts and cultural performances (such as ritual). The case of formerly isolated marginalised groups, which develop a trans-regional identity through urbanisation and then a diaspora culture through transnational migration, was taken as an example. This case is highly significant, as together with the people cultural resources such as rituals travel, are transferred, transformed, medialised, virtualised and re-transferred. These groups, in their traditional contexts different communities of practice, became a constellation of resembling practices through developing an identity transcending the formerly localised contexts, being aware of each other. Parallel to that, ritual was transferred into new contexts (urban and diaspora), and as far as into media and Internet representations. Considering the fact that ritual practice is present in modern media that are available to most of the group members, we might even dare to speak of virtualised ritual forms. These in turn contribute to the emergence of a transnational (virtual) community of practice, including diaspora and urban groups as well as the members left behind in the rural regions of origin. Remembering crucial points of Alevi history, one is reminded of somehow similar events that have taken place in early modern times, in one of the formative phases of Alevism. The fifteenth and sixteenth centuries have been a time of extensive migrations during upheavals of large parts of the Eastern Anatolian, West Iranian and Upper Mesopotamian populations. Envoys of the Safavî order who carried 'commandments' of the order's Sheikhs, including descriptions of rituals, travelled the wider region to their followers, the *Kızılbaş*. During the wars between the Ottoman and Iranian empires, the system of 'holy lineages' (*ocak*) must have shaped from such religio-political-*cum*-tribal structures, a system that was functioning until the Twentieth century.[26] Members of *dede* families, bound by spiritual-hereditary ties to their followers, who often finally settled in far away regions spread over the whole of Anatolia, started their yearly travels, transferring 'the ritual' over the region, a task taken over nowadays by modern associations and their television channels.[27] These historic, itinerary religious specialists would be an example of a pre-modern, 'traditional' form of 'transfer of ritual', which can also be analysed using the transfer paradigm, as far as historical documentation allows.

Further research has to be done especially on the grades of reflection and reflectiveness concerning ritual practice and identity in the described processes. It can be expected to see further changes triggered by the developing self-reflective attitude of modern, economically developing Alevi communities, especially in cities and the diaspora, but also in villages, which partly prosper from re-transferred economic wealth, while some on the other hand will probably not recover from the depopulation through migration. Much discussion is going on within the emerged transnational Alevi 'community of practice' over contents of the faith and meanings of rituals, up to the point that some interviewed highly successful Alevi businessmen consider the *cem*-ritual as a psycho-social therapy or 'esoteric' practice for themselves. But as we enter more deeply into the oral history of Alevi communities going back into the village histories before the migrations set in (i.e., before approximately 1960), we also encounter a highly discursive culture with a certain level of discussion over faith and practice, even with arguments against religious authorities [see Langer (forthc. 2010)].

Moreover, to overcome traditional gender roles is a very important issue in the inner-Alevi discussion on (religious) authority. Traditionally, all religious specialists presiding over a *cem*-ritual were male *dede*s, although their wives, the so-called *ana*s, in the village context had a special but rather informal role, too, especially as healers. As modern Alevism has developed an explicitly formulated ideology of gender equality and more women take over functions in the organisations, especially in Europe, the male domination of Alevi religious leadership may change within a short time. The newly-elected German Alevi council of *dede*s already includes one *ana*. The same woman has previously led one *cem*, although so far only in a private context. We can expect this to happen in a more public context in the future, as several Alevi women utter the wish to become practicing ritual specialists, too. The German *Alevitische Gemeinde e. V.* consequently refers to 'alevitische Geistliche' ('Alevi priests') practicing a gender-equal language during the last years always as 'Dede/Ana'. It would be instructive, then, to investigate how a development to also appoint female ritual leaders may transform the performativity of the ritual across gender lines. We need to compare this further development, then, to the change in the ritual structure, which came along with the change of the ritual from a secret meeting of a community (functioning to establish, reproduce and maintain group solidarity in closed tribal groups) to a large, public, though shortened ceremony, which serves to mobilise masses in an industrial, modern society. However, we have to bear in mind that a major change concerning the ritual is the degree of participation: in pre-modern times, it was obligatory for every group member to participate in the yearly *cem*-rituals, with non-participation meaning social death. (The heaviest punishment for an Alevi at that time was *düşkünlük*, exclusion from the community, symbolised in preventing the person from participating in the ritual.) Nowadays in the cities and in the diaspora, just as in industrialised societies in general, only a small proportion of the population practices religious rituals at all on a regular basis. Thus, actual ritual practice is delegated to a minority, whereas media representation and virtualisation of ritual has given the majority another channel to access cultural resources such as religious performances, which are needed in order to reproduce a specific Alevi identity.

◈

Notes

1. For an outline of Ottoman history, see Ursinus (2003).
2. For an innovative use of this primarily sociological concept in the field of religious studies, see Stausberg (2001).
3. See Hodgson (1965).
4. See Langer and Simon (2008).
5. The preferred self-designations of the groups are given in brackets. As they are not commonly used in the academic literature, the traditional names, which are nowadays perceived as designations given to them by outsiders such as Nusayri and Yezidi, are used in this paper.
6. See as an overview: Moosa (1988).
7. For the Alevis see Shankland (2003).
8. Conf.: Halm (1982).
9. On the Yezidi religion, see Kreyenbroek (1995).
10. For a convincing argumentation for the use of 'diaspora' as an abstract concept in recent migration studies, emancipated from its former use restricted to classical 'diaspora groups' with a long history of migration such as Jews and Armenians, see Ackermann (2003). See also in more detail and with another case study Baumann (2003). For an overview on migration studies in this context see Ackermann (1997).
11. Reliable demographic data on Anatolia concerning religious affiliation and ethnicity is not available because of political reasons. A survey done by the Turkish state in the 1960s in connection with the so-called 'village inventories' was only published partly. For a short period, a Western geographer, Luise Nestmann, had access to the data. Today it is said the archives have been destroyed by floods.

See Nestmann (2002). I am grateful to Prof. em. Klaus Kreiser for his reference to this important data material and to the work of Nestmann, which was unfortunately never published as a larger study.

12. For an overview on the transfer processes under consideration, see the contributions in: Langer/Motika/Ursinus (eds) (2005).
13. For several aspects of this modern form of the *cem* ritual conf.: Motika/Langer (2005).
14. For the concepts of 'community of practice' and 'constellation of practices' in the context of religion, see Stausberg (2001).
15. David Shankland (Anthropology, University of Bristol, UK) has worked in an Alevi village in Central Anatolia and subsequently has done work on the Alevi people, who have migrated from that village to Germany. His work on the German part of the community is not yet published. For the village part, see Shankland (2003). For the German part, see Shankland and Çetin (forthc. 2010). For a Turkish Sunni community a comparable work has been done by Schiffauer. See Schiffauer (1987 and 1991).
16. For the concept see Langer/Lüddeckens/Radde/Snoek (2006).
17. Translation by Janina Karolewski and Robert Langer.
18. Bayraktar (2006). Conf. the original Turkish text:
    Profesör Dr. İbrahim Arslanoğlu, Gazi Üniversitesi'nde görev yapan çok değerli bir bilim adamı. Alevilik konusunda Türkiye'nin sayılı uzmanlarından. Kendisini Milli Ekonomi Modeli kongrelerinde, İstanbul ve Bakü'de sunduğu tebliğlerden, gazetemizde yazdığı çok değerli araştırma yazılarından da tanıyorsunuz. İbrahim Arslanoğlu, soyadı gibi tam bir "arslan oğlu" olduğunu ortaya koyan bir hadise yaşadı geçtiğimiz günlerde. Önce olayı kısaca nakledelim: Cem Vakfı tarafından Urfa'da 24–28 Mayıs tarihleri arasında "GAP Bölgesi Alevi Bektaşi Yerleşimleri ve Şanlıurfa Kültür Mozaiğinde Kısas" konulu bir uluslararası bir sempozyum düzenlenir. Prof. Arslanoğlu da katılımcılardan biridir. Alman bilim adamı Dr. Robert Langer tarafından "Almanya'da Alevilerin Yaşamında Güneydoğu Anadolu İnanç Yaşamı ve Ritüellerinin Rolü" konulu bir tebliğ sundu. Langer'in sunduğu tebliğ, Almanların Türklere bakış açısını, bir devlet politikası olarak Türklerle ait değerleri nasıl yok etmek istedikleri çok güzel ortaya koyuyordu. Langer konuşmasında Almanya'da Tunceli asıllı bir Alevi dedesinin Türkçe yerine Almanca cem yaptığını anlattı ve bu ayini aynı zamanda perdeye de yansıtarak tüm izleyenlere gösterdi. Alman bilim adamı bir Alevi dedesinin Almanca cem ayini yapmasından son derece memnun ve keyifliydi. Konuşmasında daha da ileri giderek Zazaların ve Kurmancıların dillerini kaybettiğinden üzüntü ile bahsetti. Bunun üzerine Arslanoğlu kürsüye çıktı ve çok enfes bir konuşma yaptı. Arslanoğlu özetle şunları dedi: "Almanları

tebrik ederim, bırakın Türk çocuklarını Alevi dedesini bile asimile etmiş durumdalar. Dr. Langer, Kurmancıların ve Zazaların dillerini kaybettiklerinden üzüntü ile bahsediyor. Fakat Türk çocuklarının dillerini unutmaları sanırım onu hiç üzmüyor, hatta memnun da ediyor. Zaten bir Alman yetkili yakın bir geçmişte okul bahçesinde Türkçe konuşan Türk çocuklarına ceza olarak, okul bahçesini süpürmeyi önermişti. Bildiğiniz gibi Alman İçişleri Bakanı, Türk çocuklarının Almanya'ya en iyi uyumunun asimilasyon olduğunu söylemişti." Salondan büyük alkış alarak konuşmasına devam eden Arslanoğlu, sözlerine şöyle devam etti: "AB, Aleviliği dinsel bir azınlık olarak görerek Türkiye aleyhine kullanmak istiyor. Ancak vatansever Aleviler buna itibar etmiyorlar. Batılılar bilimi sadece bilim için yapmıyorlar. Yaptıkları araştırmalar mutlaka kendi çıkarlarına ve stratejilerine hizmet eder. Nitekim AB'ye girmemiz için Kıbrıs'ı vermemizi, Ermeni soykırımını tanımamızı, Boğazlar ile Dicle ve Fırat'ın sularını uluslararası bir kuruluşa vermemizi istiyorlar. Bu da niyetlerini apaçık ortaya koyuyor." Uluslararası bir bilimsel toplantıda, bir asimilasyon valisi gibi konuşan Alman bilim adamına ve bu konuşmaya sessiz kalıp adeta destek veren diğer konuşmacılara çok güzel bir ders veren Arslanoğlu'nu yürekten kutluyorum. Kendisiyle son olarak Azerbaycan'da, Milli Ekonomi Modeli Kongresi dolayısı ile çok keyifli günler geçirdik. İbrahim Hoca'nın Urfa'daki bu kükreyişini duyunca daha bir keyiflendim. "Bravo Arslanoğlu!" dedim. Her bilim adamı bu uluslararası kongrelerde senin gibi isyanını ortaya koyup, küresel sömürü odaklarına dersini verse her şey çok güzel olacak, ama neyleyelim ki ülkede arslan sıkıntısı var.

19. It is the "Independent Turkey Party" [*Bağımsız Türkiye Partisi*] led by a Turkish Professor of, interestingly, Oriental studies, employed at the State University of Baku in Azerbaijan, a Turkish nationalistic Islamist with a tendency to Sufism.
20. The traditional terms in orthodox Muslim texts are *râfidî*, i.e., 'those who reject [the truth]' or *ghulât*, i.e., 'those who exaggerate'.
21. In order to legitimise their role as religious leaders, *dede*-lineages (*ocak*) either received diploma stating their *seyyid*-status, i.e. descendants of the family of the prophet Muhammad, or as qualified spiritual leaders following the advice of the descendants of the saint Hacı Bektaş, the so called Çelebis or *Dedegân*-wing of the Bektaşiyye. As the Bektaşiyye was connected to the state structures since Ottoman times, the former *seyyid-ocaks* rather stayed independent from official institutions.
22. A good example for the involvement of Turkish academia in processes of the reproduction of 'Turkish values' is the recently held "Symposium on Cleanliness in Turkish Culture". This was held to celebrate the 75th year of the foundation of the state sponsored 'Academy for Turkish Language' (*Türk Dil Kurumu*, founded by an order of Atatürk)

at the Marmara University, İstanbul, 21–22 November 2007. For the programme of the conference see http://www.tdtkb.org/index2.php?option=com_content&do_pdf=1&id=254 . I am grateful to my colleague Paula Schrode, who participated in the conference, for an account on the presentations given there and on the general 'spirit' of the conference as well as on the attitude of its organisers.

23. In Berlin, one of the Alevi communities there has bought an old church building to be used as their cultural centre and *cemevi* (see Kulturzentrum Anatolischer Aleviten e. V. / Anadolu Alevileri Kültür Merkezi — Cemevi Berlin e. V. http://aakm-cemevi.de/), a striking parallel to a Hindu temple in North London, documented by Waghorne (2004: 196–203).
24. For a concrete, biographical case study, see Kieser 2005. For a detailed study of 'Eastern Alevi'-Armenian relations, see Kieser (2000: 69–81, 167–70, 182–412). 'Eastern Alevis', as Kieser calls the ('Kurdish') Kızılbaş-Alevis, oftentimes saved their Armenian neighbours during the massacres of 1915–1916. This historical relationship was only recently turned against the Alevis by a member of the Turkish Prime Minister's 'Directorate for Religious Affairs' (*Diyanet İşleri Başkanlığı*), who 'defamed' the Alevis as the offspring of Armenians (i.e, 'not true Turks', 'potential traitors' by their 'race', etc.).
25. Cf. Langer (2008).
26. In 2006, a conference was held dealing with historical and recent developments of this so-called *ocak*-system. The papers, investigating topics ranging from the interpretation of historical sources up to modern education programmes for *dede*s are about to be published (Karolewski/Langer/Motika (forthc. 2010).
27. In order to investigate different forms of transmission and reception of Alevi ritual (knowledge) a workshop was held at Heidelberg in October 2007. The papers deal with principal modes of transmission — oral, scriptural, mimetic — or combinations of the three, from pre-modern times to the present (see Karolewski/Langer/Ursinus (forthc. 2010).

References

Ackermann, A. 1997. 'Ethnologische Migrationsforschung: Ein Überblick', *Kea: Zeitschrift für Kulturwissenschaften* 10 (= Ethnologie der Migration): 1–28.

———. 2003. 'Yeziden in Deutschland: Von der Minderheit zur Diaspora', *Paideuma: Mitteilungen zur Kulturkunde* 49, 157–77.

Aydın, A. (ed.). 2000. *CEM Vakfı, Anadolu İnanç Önderleri, Birinci Toplantısı (16–19 Ekim 1998, İstanbul): Dedelerin, Babaların, Ozanların Görüş ve*

Düşünceleri. (CEM Vakfı Yayınları, 4; Alevi — Bektaşi — Mevlevi İnanç Önderleri Toplantıları Dizisi, 1) Yenibosna — Bahçelievler — İstanbul: CEM Vakfı (Cumhuriyetçi Eğitim ve Kültür Merkezleri Vakfı)

Aydın, A. (ed.). 2003. *CEM Vakfı, İslamiyet, Alevilik, Dede(ler) ve Babalar: CEM Vakfı Anadolu İnanç Önderleri Üçüncü Toplantısı Anısına, 8–9 Kasım 2003, İstanbul*. Kültür ve Turizm Bakanlığı'nın Katkılarıyla. (CEM Vakfı Yayınları, 7; El Kitapları Dizisi, 1) Yenibosna — Bahçelievler — İstanbul: Cem Vakfı (Cumhuriyetçi Eğitim ve Kültür Merkezi Vakfı).

———. n.d. *CEM Vakfı Anadolu İnanç Önderleri İkinci Toplantısı (12–14 Mayıs 2000, İstanbul): Alevi İslam İnancının Öncüleri Dedeler, Babalar, Ozanlar Ne Düşünüyor?*. (CEM Vakfı Yayınları, 6; Alevi – Bektaşi – Mevlevi İnanç Önderleri Toplantılar Dizisi, 2) Yenibosna – Bahçelievler – İstanbul: Cem Vakfı (Cumhuriyetçi Eğitim ve Kültür Merkezi Vakfı).

Baumann, M. 2003. *Alte Götter in neuer Heimat: Religionswissenschaftliche Analyse zu Diaspora am Beispiel von Hindus auf Trinidad*. Marburg: diagonal-Verlag (Religionswissenschaftliche Reihe, 18).

Bayraktar, M. 2006. 'Bir Arslan Adam', In: *Yeni Mesaj*, ed. by Bağımsız Türkiye Partisi, Küçükçekmece – İstanbul: İcmal Yayıncılık ve Reklam-cılık San. Tic. Ltd. şti. (03.06.2006); http://www.yenimesaj.com.tr/index.php?haberno=6013187&tarih=2006-06-03 (accessed 14 December 2007).

Dressler, M. 2006. 'The Modern Dede: Changing Parameters for Religious Authority in Contemporary Turkish Alevism', in G. Krämer and S. Schmidtke (eds) *Speaking for Islam: Religious Authorities in Muslim Studies*, pp. 269–94. Leiden, Boston: Brill.

Halm, H. 1982. *Die islamische Gnosis: Die extreme Schia und die ´Alawiten* (Die Bibliothek des Morgenlandes). Zürich, München: Artemis.

Hodgson, M.G.S. 1965. 'Ghulât' in *The Encyclopaedia of Islam. New Edition*. Vol. II: *C–G*. Leiden; London: E. J. Brill.

Karolewski, J., Langer, R. and Motika, R. (eds) (forthc. 2010) Ocak *und* Dedelik*: Institutionen religiösen Spezialistentums bei den Aleviten*, (Heidelberger Studien zur Geschichte und Kultur des modernen Vorderen Orients). Frankfurt am Main et al.: Peter Lang.

Karolewski, J., Langer, R. and Ursinus, M. (eds) (forthc. 2010) *Reception Processes of Alevi Ritual Practice Between Innovation and Reconstruction* (Heidelberger Studien zur Geschichte und Kultur des modernen Vorderen Orients). Frankfurt am Main et al.: Peter Lang.

Kieser, H.-L. 2000. *Der verpasste Frieden: Mission, Ethnie und Staat in den Ostprovinzen der Türkei 1839–1938*. Zürich: Chronos Verlag.

———. 2005. '*Alevilik* als Lied und Liebesgespräch: Der Dorfweise Melûli Baba (1892–1989)' in: R. Langer, R. Motika, M. Ursinus (eds) *Migration und Ritualtransfer: Religiöse Praxis der Aleviten, Jesiden und*

Nusairier zwischen Vorderem Orient und Westeuropa, (Heidelberger Studien zur Geschichte und Kultur des modernen Vorderen Orients, 33), pp. 147–61. Frankfurt am Main et al.: Peter Lang.

Kreyenbroek, P.G. 1995. *Yezidism — Its Background, Observances and Textual Tradition,* (Texts and Studies in Religion, 62), Lewiston, N.Y. et al.: The Edwin Mellen Press.

Langer, R. 2006. 'Das Reframing alevitischer Gemeinderituale im Kontext von Ritualtransfer und Migration' in H. Jungaberle, J. Weinhold (eds) *Rituale in Bewegung: Rahmungs- und Reflexivitätsprozesse in Kulturen der Gegenwart* (Performanzen: Interkulturelle Studien zur Ritual, Spiel und Theater = Performances: Intercultural Studies on Ritual, Play and Theatre, 11), pp. 129–44. Berlin, Münster: Lit Verlag.

———. 2008. 'The Alevi Animal Sacrifice (*Kurbân*) Between Professionalization and Substitution: Recent Developments in the Context of Migration and Urbanization (with 9 photographs of Christian Funke)' in C. Ambos, A. Michaels, E. Stavrianopoulou (eds) *Transformations in Sacrificial Practices: From Antiquity to Modern Times. Proceedings of an International Colloquium, Heidelberg, 12–14, July 2006,* (Performanzen: Interkulturelle Studien zur Ritual, Spiel und Theater = Performances: Intercultural Studies on Ritual, Play and Theatre, 15), pp. 193–214. Berlin, Münster: LIT Verlag.

———. (forthc. 2010). 'Ritual Practice in an Alevi Village: Oral History Sources — A Preliminary Field Report', in J. Karolewski, R. Langer, M. Ursinus (eds) *Reception Processes of Alevi Ritual Practice Between Innovation and Reconstruction,* (Heidelberger Studien zur Geschichte und Kultur des Vorderen Orients), Frankfurt am Main et al.: Peter Lang Verlag, 59–70.

Langer, R., Lüddeckens, D., Radde, K., Snoek, J. 2006. 'Transfer of Ritual', *Journal of Ritual Studies* 20, 1, 1–10.

Langer, R., Motika, R., Ursinus, M. (eds) 2005. *Migration und Ritualtransfer: Religiöse Praxis der Aleviten, Jesiden und Nusairier zwischen Vorderem Orient und Westeuropa* (Heidelberger Studien zur Geschichte und Kultur des modernen Vorderen Orients, 33). Frankfurt am Main et al.: Peter Lang.

Langer, R., Simon, U. 2008. 'The Dynamics of Orthodoxy and Heterodoxy: Dealing with Divergence in Muslim Discourses and Islamic Studies', *Die Welt des Islams* 48, 3–4, 273–88.

Moosa, M. 1988. *Extremist Shiites: The Ghulat Sects,* (Contemporary Issues in the Middle East). Syracuse, N.Y.: Syracuse University Press.

Motika, R. and Langer, R. 2005. 'Alevitische Kongregationsrituale: Transfer und Re-Invention im transnationalen Kontext', in R. Langer, R. Motika, M. Ursinus (eds) *Migration und Ritualtransfer: Religiöse Praxis der Aleviten, Jesiden und Nusairier zwischen Vorderem Orient und*

Westeuropa, (Heidelberger Studien zur Geschichte und Kultur des modernen Vorderen Orients, 33), pp. 73–107. Frankfurt am Main et al.: Peter Lang.

Nestmann, L. 2002. 'Die ethnische Differenzierung der Bevölkerung der Osttürkei in ihren sozialen Bezügen — Auswertung der 'Köy Evanter Etüdleri' des Ministeriums für Dorfangelegenheiten', in P.A. Andrews (ed., with the assistance of Rüdiger Benninghaus) *Ethnic Groups in the Republic of Turkey* (Beihefte zum Tübinger Atlas des Vorderen Orients. Reihe B (Geisteswissenschaften), 60.1) Wiesbaden: Ludwig Reichert: 543–581.

Paul, I. and J. Zimmermann 2005. 'Zur Funktionalität des *Cem*-Rituals als Instrument alevitischer Identitätsstiftung in der *Cem Dergisi*', in R. Langer, R. Motika, M. Ursinus (eds) *Migration und Ritualtransfer: Religiöse Praxis der Aleviten, Jesiden und Nusairier zwischen Vorderem Orient und Westeuropa* (Heidelberger Studien zur Geschichte und Kultur des modernen Vorderen Orients, 33), pp. 175–202. Frankfurt am Main et al.: Peter Lang.

Platvoet, J.G. 1995. 'Ritual in Plural and Pluralist Societies: Instruments for Analysis' in K. van der Toorn and J. G. Platvoet (eds) *Pluralism and Identity: Studies in Ritual Behaviour*. (Studies in the History of Religions [*Numen* Book Series], 67) Leiden et al.: E.J. Brill: 25–51.

Schiffauer, W. 1987. *Die Bauern von Subay: Das Leben in einem türkischen Dorf*. Stuttgart: Klett-Cotta.

———. 1991. *Die Migranten aus Subay: Türken in Deutschland, eine Ethnographie*. Stuttgart: Klett–Cotta.

Shankland, D. 2003. *The Alevis in Turkey: The Emergence of a Secular Islamic Tradition*. London, New York: RoutledgeCurzon.

———. Çetin, A. (forthc. 2010) 'Alevis in Europe: Changing *Dede–Talip* Relations', in J. Karolewski, R. Langer, R. Motika (eds) Ocak *und* Dedelik*: Institutionen religiösen Spezialistentums bei den Aleviten*, (Heidelberger Studien zur Geschichte und Kultur des modernen Vorderen Orients). Frankfurt am Main et al.: Peter Lang.

Sökefeld, M. 2005. '*Cem* in Deutschland: Transformationen eines Rituals im Kontext der alevitischen Bewegung', in R. Langer, R. Motika, M. Ursinus (eds) *Migration und Ritualtransfer: Religiöse Praxis der Aleviten, Jesiden und Nusairier zwischen Vorderem Orient und Westeuropa*, (Heidelberger Studien zur Geschichte und Kultur des modernen Vorderen Orients, 33), pp. 203–26. Frankfurt am Main et al.: Peter Lang.

Stausberg, M. 2001. 'Kohärenz und Kontinuität — Überlegungen zur Repräsentation und Reproduktion von Religion', in M. Stausberg, O. Sundqvist, A. van Nahl (eds) *Kontinuitäten und Brüche in der Religionsgeschichte: Festschrift für Anders Hultgård zu seinem 65. Geburtstag am 23.12.2001* (Reallexikon der germanischen Altertumskunde: Ergänzungsbände, 31), pp. 596–619. Berlin, New York: de Gruyter.

Ursinus, M. 2003. 'Osmanen', in *Religion in Geschichte und Gegenwart: Handwörterbuch für Theologie und Religionswissenschaft*, Vol. VI. Tübingen: Mohr Siebeck: 721–22.

Vertovec, St. and Cohen, R. 1999. 'Introduction', in St. Vertovec and R. Cohen (eds) *Migration, Diasporas and Transnationalism* (The International Library of Studies on Migration, 9; Elgar Reference Collection), pp. xiii–xxviii. Cheltenham et al.: Edward Elgar Publishing.

Waghorne, J.P. 2004. *Diaspora of the Gods: Modern Hindu Temples in an Urban Middle-Class World*. Oxford et al.: Oxford University Press.

Yaman, A. 2006. *Kızılbaş Alevi Ocakları (= Kizilbash Alevi Ocaks)*. 1. Baskı. (Elips Kitap, 267). Ankara: Elips Kitap.

Zimmermann, J. (forthc. 2010) 'Speaking About Rituals: (Re)invention of the *Ayin i Cem* in Alevi Online Discussion Forums', in J. Karolewski, R. Langer, M. Ursinus (eds) *Reception Processes of Alevi Ritual Practice Between Innovation and Reconstruction* (Heidelberger Studien zur Geschichte und Kultur des modernen Vorderen Orients). Frankfurt am Main et al.: Peter Lang.

5

Sunni Concepts of Ritual Purity in a Contemporary Diaspora Context

Udo Simon

Being associated with Islamic ritual practices, purity is a notion Muslims are usually quite familiar with. This holds true even for those Muslims whose interest in religion is rather limited as purity is a part of their cultural heritage. In this essay, I first outline the central aspects of ritual purity in Islam and its related issues. In the second part, focussing on the situation in Germany, I shall be looking at some modern sources that are relevant in the process of transferring those concepts of purity to the West. Finally, I shall discuss the role of thematic corridors based on the recognition of a central idea as a point of reference for Muslims in the diaspora. Classical and modern scripts show a remarkable persistence. They form a 'corridor of rules' that can serve as a resource for personal decision making and allow the believer a degree of agency and flexibility that impacts on ritual dynamics.

The Range of Purity-related Issues in Muslim Heritage

As a rule, Islam is seen as a religion which very strongly emphasises unity and simplicity. Its message is supposed to be easily comprehensible for everyone. Monotheism itself implies the idea of unity. In the case of Islam, unity is represented by means of the notion of *umma*, the community of believers which has to be maintained under all circumstances. This ideal is constantly repeated and forms an integral part of the common Islamic self-conception, even though the facts tell another story. Undermining the unity of the *umma* — for instance by abandoning Islam and converting to another religion — is considered a serious threat and grave sin and requires drastic punishment.[1] Yet, whenever I happened to attend a discussion about religious issues, for instance about certain aspects of worship, how to behave as a Muslim, what it means to be a true Muslim, or what constitutes real Islam, differences in opinion occurred quickly. The same impression can be gained when consulting a textbook on religious law. Along with detailed prescriptions for religious practice and regulations for everyday life, one finds a remarkable repertoire of legal techniques to mitigate these stipulations or principals.[2] That the assumed uniformity of Islam is a persistent fiction becomes evident not only by looking at the local variety of popular Islam, but also by paying attention to the flexibility of regulations and the wide range of compensative and substitute acts. Thus, as opposed to the simplicity and rigidity of theory and practice presumed both from an emic and an etic perspective, there is a rich casuistry in issues of detail. This also holds true for Islamic conditions for maintaining or gaining ritual purity (*ṭahāra*).[3]

Islamic purification practices, as prescribed by religious law, are preparative preliminaries mainly to prayer. At the same time they are classed with various other services dedicated to God. In juridical handbooks, ritual purification is treated as the first of these services (*'ibādāt*), followed by prayer, fasting, almsgiving and the pilgrimage to Mecca. Legally, ritual impurity is of two kinds — minor (*ḥadath aṣghar*) and major (*ḥadath akbar*) — and correspondingly there is a minor ablution (*wuḍū'*), i.e., washing one's hands, arms, face and feet, and a major ablution (*ghusl*), i.e., a complete washing of the whole body, both of which serve to re-establish ritual purity. Moreover, a substitute purification with clean sand (*tayammum*) is part of the system. Under specific conditions, it may be enough for a worshipper to merely strike the earth and symbolically wash to fulfil his or her duty. The minor ablution is made necessary by a number of acts and states which are combined with body emissions (urinating, defecating, emission of prostatic secretions and secretions of the Cowper's, respectively the Bartholin's glands; according to many bleeding and vomiting), body contact between the sexes (for some also touching one's own genitals), or a loss of mental control (insanity, sleep; for some even laughter). The major ablution is obligatory after sexual intercourse accompanied by ejaculation (one condition being sufficient according to most jurists), and is also required after menstruation and childbirth. Furthermore, *ghusl* is part of the burial rite and marks the passage in the case of conversion to Islam. Moreover, Muslims have to avoid a whole set of impure substances (*najasāt*), some of which come along with the above-mentioned acts and states. In case contact could not be avoided, the traces of these substances must be removed by certain prescribed measures. There is general consensus among doctors of religious law about the impurity of the flesh of swine,[4] carrion of warm-blooded animals not living in water, blood of an animal that does not live in water, and urine and excrement of human beings. Most jurists add alcohol and dogs to the list. Vomit, pus and also semen are often included, though their status is debated.

Other contexts that may be associated with purity comprise circumcision, the term for which is usually taken from the root *ṭ - h - r*, e.g., *taṭhīr* 'making pure', fasting which might be seen as a purification of the self, and almsgiving as an act of cleansing wealth and extinguishing sins.

In a broader sense, from the very beginning Islam was conceptualised as a purification movement meant to cleanse Abraham's religion from the degeneration caused by pre-Islamic paganism, Judaism and Christianity. Preserving continuity and, at the same time, marking the difference between Muslims and the preceding monotheistic religions is a characteristic feature of the formative phase of Islam that has left traces in ritual stipulations as well.

Several contemporary Islamic movements emphasise purity as a central concern. *Purification* and *dynamisation* are key-words of the Muhammadiyah movement, Indonesia's second-largest Muslim organisation, which is determined to 'purify faith from superstitions as well as to cleanse ritual observances of innovations' (Anwar 2005: 31). And for the Tablighis, detailed methods of religious practices, perfection in observance of prayers and purity of intention are main aspects of faith.[5]

Purity is a key concept for Islamists as well. Using the purity mindframe as a means of demarcation they feel a vocation to cleanse society from the alleged 'filth' of disbelief, materialism, capitalism or Western culture in general. While it is not very surprising that purity is a major concern of Islamists the impact of purity-related concepts on the 'average' Muslim in different parts of the world is still to be investigated.

From the point of view of most Westerners — and a lot of non-Westerners, too — purity seems to be a pre-modern concept. It comes close to the quality of a feeling. Its mental representations are connected to visual associations such as clear water, freshly fallen snow, or a blue sky, and emotions evoked by images of this kind. Nevertheless, the notion of Mary's purity, for instance, persists in Catholicism until today. Protestant Americans also seem to have a concept of purity, often linked to the ideals of liberty and unity. And the same notion is part of the ideological framework of neo-traditional Hinduism. The idea of purity has a remarkable persistence, both across cultures and through times.[6]

Concepts of ritual purity, as a rule, are paralleled by conceptions of purity as a social category. In this sense, purity is a quality associated with roles and positions within a society that especially impacts on gender relations and sexuality.[7] On a third level, standards of profane cleanliness are linked to both the religious and the social concept of purity. These three levels are interrelated and back each other both in terms of their embedding in everyday life and their justification. For instance, the obligation to wash five times a day in preparation for prayer might have been conducive to establishing certain standards of hygiene in the Muslim world. From the Medina period onward, everyday practices have been increasingly regulated and classified in terms of religion. In fact, a non-Muslim is said to have alleged to a companion of the prophet: 'Your Prophet has taught you everything, even defecation' (Ibn Qayyim 34). Yet, purity-related restrictions applying to body, clothing, places, communication and so forth may also be rooted in an archaic system of social order preceding the canon of religious stipulations. Such a set of regulations is organised in schemes of standardised, and sometimes 'ritualised', behaviour passed on within families in the process of socialisation. Local customs and traditions form the conditions of Muslim life far more than the abstract religious law of Islam.[8] As a consequence, two systems of rules have to be balanced. On the other hand, the option of two frames of reference is a resource of social flexibility. In any case, linking social values and interaction rules to the religious sphere enhances their legitimacy.

Muslims are commonly quite conscious of the existence of a translocal framework of regulations, the details of which they are not expected to fully understand. If we turn now to these translocally accepted scripts and sources, the prescriptions relating to ritual purity could be classified as (*i*) regulations which are mentioned in the *Qur'ān* and *ḥadīth*, i.e., accounts of the prophet's words and practice, (*ii*) regulations deduced from these sources which the jurists agree upon, and (*iii*) issues which remain in dispute. Thus, in the vast literature of the four generally acknowledged legal schools of Sunni Islam, stipulations are combined with reasoning. Especially the so-called *ikhtilāf* literature, a genre dedicated to differences of opinion, mirrors debates on topics such as intentionality or the rationality of ritual actions.

While prayer is undoubtedly a ritual act addressed to God, ritual cleansing, because of its double function as a sacral and profane action, is a more problematic case. Ash-Shāfi'ī (died 820), the founder of one of the four major legal schools, states that washing a dirty part of the body is not a valid act of worship.[9] He refers to the major ablution as an inexplicable way through which God is worshipped by his creatures. To prove this, he points to the stipulation that a man has to perform major ablution after cohabitation with his wife, while not being obliged to do so after contact with the blood of a swine.[10] Some critical authors address the fact that a believer is never regarded as substantively impure and, therefore, cleansing what is already pure seems rather absurd. While Islamic scholars usually associate a multiplicity of advantages with the rites of ablution as such and elaborate on their social and personal benefits in general terms, the majority seems to agree that for the prescribed details of ritual performance, such as time, number of applications, duration and so forth, no stringent explanation can be found. Others put prescribed rites in rather symbolic frames of reference. For the mystics, ritual washings are symbols of the purification of the soul. In this context, *ikhlāṣ* is a key concept that stands for exclusive worship and pure devotion to God, as well as for absolute purity and unity of intention. The short *Sūra* 112 of the *Qur'ān* entitled *al-Ikhlāṣ* is a firm confession of the strictest monotheism.

The notion of *ikhlāṣ* is also a concept underlying the thoughts of al-Ghazālī (died 1111), outstanding theologian and mystic of medieval Islam, and an acknowledged authority till this day. At the beginning of his work *Mysteries of Purity*, he cites the words of the prophet, 'Religion was founded on cleanliness', and 'Purification is one half of belief',[11] a standard opening of texts dealing with ritual purity. Then he presents a concept of purity that comprises four stages. The first stage is the purification of the body from excrements, impurities, and bodily discharges. The second stage is the purification of the bodily senses from crimes and sins. The third stage is the purification of the heart from blameworthy traits and reprehensible vices. The fourth stage is the purification of the inmost self (*sirr*) from everything except God. This last stage is that of the prophets and saints.[12]

In addition to this spiritualised concept, he gives detailed advices for external cleanliness to the extent that the prophet would have ordered manicuring nails every forty days. A purification act should be commenced with the use of the tooth-pick, because the mouth is the pathway of the *Qur'ān*.

Moreover, al-Ghazālī lists ten precepts for visiting the bath-house, including good intention, stepping into it with the left foot first and saying 'I seek refuge in God against Satan the accursed, the filthy, the impure', and not reciting the *Qur'ān*. Other rules have gender-specific implications, such as the following: 'It is unlawful for the man to enter the bath-house without a veil, and it is unlawful for the woman to enter therein except after childbirth or when sick'.[13] Here, the theme of ritual purity is extended into the realm of social order that regulates interaction. In addition to the relationship of God and man which is at the centre of the cleansing rites, profane contacts between human beings, and especially between men and women, are restricted in terms of purity regulations.

On the other hand, he objects to the obsession of those who go to the extreme in the study of purity rules. The caliph 'Umar once performed his ablution with water from a jar which belonged to a Christian woman. As the author states, in his own time, quite a few people would call 'Umar filthy and disdain from eating with him at the very least.

Al-Ghazālī frowns on excessive cleaning and the use of paraphernalia, like special overshoes, veils, et cetera. Those practices would become evil when they are made a fundamental part of religion.[14] Combining detailed advices and the rejection of exaggeration, al-Ghazālī concludes that 'the principle of purity is lenience and all that was innovated therein is a whispering (of the devil) which has no foundation'.[15] In sum, al-Ghazālī represents a position which combines a highly spiritualised notion of purity aligned with a code of conduct that is deduced from the practice of the prophet. Too much emphasis on external cleanliness is rejected.

The whispering of the devil resulting in unreasonable obsessions is also the main topic of a famous work by another well-known theologian, the Ḥanbalī jurist Ibn Qayyim al-Jawziyya (d. 1350), who was a disciple of Ibn Taymiyya. He condemns exaggeration in any act of purification. In his opinion, the Muslim *umma* should set the example of a balanced community that avoids both excessiveness and negligence (Ibn Qayyim 62). Always endangered by religious innovation, it is the unified community of the believers which guarantees protection from extreme positions that would lead to the formation of sects. More generally, the assessment of Islam as a religion which takes the middle way between Judaism and Christianity is a well-known theme in Islamic religious thought, and also includes ritual matters.

In an *ikhtilāf* work on juridical issues of the twelfth century, Ibn Rushd (d. 1198), the commentator of Aristotle, known under the name of Averroes in the West, first enumerates the five modes of acting which form the analytical framework of Islamic religious law: obligatory, recommended, permissible, reprehensible and prohibited. Presuming the general obligation for purifying, Ibn Rushd discusses issues such as (*i*) whether intention (*niyya*) is a requisite condition for ablution; (*ii*) washing hands before touching utensils for purification; (*iii*) the area to be washed; (*iv*) the number of washings; (*v*) the sequence of the acts of ablution; and (*vi*) the continuous performance of the acts. Other issues are the kinds of water used, or factors invalidating ablution, such as sleep, touching women, touching one's private parts, eating food prepared over fire,[16] laughing during prayer and so on.

Let me point out two more issues frequently addressed in handbooks dealing with religious observances. Concerning the question whether purification is a prerequisite for touching a copy of the *Qur'ān*, Ibn Rushd holds that since there is no evidence in the Holy Book or in the *sunna*, the matter is to be left to the original rule of non-liability, which is permissibility.[17] The other question is related to the consequences of sleep for the validity and efficacy of ablution. Three opinions are cited. For one group of jurists, sleep is a factor of annulment of ritual purity, no matter whether it is of short or long duration. Therefore, ablution must be repeated. Another group makes a distinction between a light short sleep and a long deep sleep. A third group simply leaves it up to the individual decision of the believer.[18] Both the topic of touching the *Qur'ān* and the impact of mental states on the validity of ritual action have remained subjects of discussion in the discursive field of Sunni Islam up to the present day. Finally, in this book again the discussion of purity-related issues ends with a detailed toilette etiquette. As a matter of course, Ibn Rushd, the philosopher, adds those issues to sophisticated juridical discussions.

In short, purification acts may range from merely striking the ground before wiping one's hands and face to excessive washings. This variety depends on circumstances such as the believer's physical condition, or the environment he or she is moving in, but not at least on religious conscience, individual choice and personal interpretation of the heritage.[19]

The Reception of Purity Concepts in the Context of Muslim Diaspora in Germany

The following lines briefly touch upon the question of how the cultural-religious heritage is interpreted and exploited under the conditions of social change caused by migration.[20] While investigating the relevance of the complex notion of purity in a contemporary diaspora context, we come across communications about general ethical values and specific issues like the permissibility of make-up, or the use of gelatine in food and pharmaceutical applications.[21]

To be sure, Muslim communities in Western societies are not homogeneous. They are divided into different milieus and life-style groups just like the dominant societies. Attitudes towards religion vary from a kind of cautious atheism to the 'sacralization and transcendentalization of social norms' (Arkoun 1994: 62) that even turns wearing a beard into a service to God. In this context, the notion of purity may be an instrument to mark the boundaries of the community, or it may be applied to shield and preserve the traditional way of life. On the other hand, Sufism seems to be a resource for an undogmatic and even pantheistic interpretation of Islam transcending all boundaries. As such, non-institutionalised Sufism is an open concept capable of integrating all kinds of spirituality. In this context purity may loose its exclusive Islamic character, and be put on the same level with a high degree of spirituality. Though in many cases based on a vague personal interpretation of what Sufism is, this attitude matches very well with a trend towards individual religiosity in the West that refuses to accept a given dogma. Notably, hierarchically organised Sufi orders that are often enough also acting in the political sphere take quite the opposite stance towards individuality.

Just as the cleanliness of the household is a domain of women, 'purity' is a norm related to their conduct. We know from empirical research (Boos-Nünning and Karakaşoğlu 2005: 359) that the majority of young women with a Turkish migration background in Germany uphold the ideal of premarital virginity. Moreover, most of them do not take into consideration marriage to a German or non-Muslim. There is a multiplicity of reasons for this attitude ranging from parental influence, group pressure and marriage restrictions, to a need for laying stress on those aspects of Muslim identity which seem to justify a claim for moral superiority over non-Muslims. While they appreciate living in Germany, and would consider Germany their home, many of these women reject assimilation in terms of clothing and eating.

Practices such as slaughtering animals according to the rules of religious law gain further importance within the complex process of combining the advantages of structural integration with the preservation of identity. Along with the increasing perceptibility of Islamic practice in semi-public and public spaces, a need for explanation and justification comes to be felt both within the immigrant communities and as a response to outside requirements. And a skeptical view of unquestioned convention as guiding principle of their parents' religious life gives rise to some young Muslim's quest for the 'true' and 'pure' Islam and stimulates attempts to bring into accordance stipulations and rationality.[22] The recourse to the formal legal opinions (*fatāwā*) of experts promises a more systematic and methodical deduction of norms and rules than ethnic tradition offers. Those opinions of contemporary, or sometimes old, authorities reflect the vast corpus of classical Islamic religious law.

As for the social consequences of purity-related attitudes, some choices and contacts of Muslims in Germany may be influenced by Islamic criteria, for instance, the choice of a doctor, a sports club, or a hairdresser. Very few Muslims buy meat from a German butcher whereas the demand for *ḥalāl* food, i.e., food that meets the purity standards, is steadily growing.

Predictably, a number of Islamic symbols which may not be of eminently theological interest but particularly illustrate religious identity will be upheld in diaspora, namely the avoidance of pork, slaughtering, fasting, mosque minarets, and — to some extent — the headscarf. For some Muslims, leaving aside other regulations and concentrating on these practices and signs may open up space for participation in the majority.

Let us turn now to contemporary sources and see what writers of some influence on Muslims in the diaspora tell us about purity and related issues like touching the *Qur'ān*, or entering a bathhouse. Just a few years ago, poorly designed brochures intended as guidebooks for everyday life, most of them written in the mother tongue of the immigrants, were the prevailing sources of information. Today, we can find voluminous presentations of religious law in several European languages. Citing a few voices that are heard in Germany I refer to publications of the last five years for the most part.

In a book entitled *The Lawful and Prohibited in Islam* which has been published in several languages, the omnipresent Muslim scholar, preacher, and al-Jazīra TV educator Yūsuf al-Qaraḍāwī lays special stress on cleanliness, but seldom speaks of purity. Quoting the prophet's word 'Cleanse yourself, for Islam is clean', he holds that 'This emphasis on cleanliness is not to be wondered at in a religion which makes cleanliness the key to its principle form of worship' (Qaraḍāwī 1960: 64).

He is implicitly developing a chain of dichotomies that leads from the opposition of good (*ṭayyib*) or bad to pure or impure and finally results in the opposition of forbidden and allowed. The reason for God's prohibitions lies in the impurity and harmfulness of things. God 'has neither permitted anything except what is pure nor has He prohibited anything except what is impure'.[23] The Muslim is not required to know exactly what is unclean or harmful in what God has prohibited. Doubtful things are to be avoided.

Al-Qaraḍāwī sees cleanliness and beautification as characteristics of Islam. Thus, remarks on body care are followed by regulations on clothing and adornment. His concept of cleanliness also includes the view that a woman who enters a public bath without a valid reason or need is committing a forbidden act. Furthermore, his idea of how a Muslim woman should conduct herself does not allow any intermingling with men in such a way that their bodies come in contact or that men could touch women, as it happens in movie theatres, university classrooms, buses and the like.

Yaşar Nuri Öztürk is an eminent Turkish theologian and author of more than thirty books, some of which have also been translated into English and German. He is known among Turkish immigrants in Western Europe for both his religious writings and his political activities. Öztürk calls the verses of the *Qur'ān* dedicated to ritual purity 'a wonderful example for elasticity.'[24] Due to this elasticity stipulations could be observed in spite of continuously changing circumstances and surroundings. Thus, reforming Islam should not be necessary if Muslims would only become aware of its flexibility and leave the definition of obligation to the individual decision of the believer. Here, flexibility is an argument against reform. In his view, change is directed to the personal level only. In other words, religion is restricted to the private sphere. This position fits very well into the concept of Turkish secularism.

For Öztürk, health is a major issue in connection with prescribed washings. As regards touching the *Qur'ān* in a state of ritual impurity he holds that ritual purity is not obligatory. Complicating the reading of the Holy book through artificially constructed obstacles contradicts the intention of Islam, he says.[25]

Another Turkish author and religious activist Adnan Oktar, known under the pen name Harun Yahya, is said to have a record of more than two hundred books. While stressing the consistency between the *Qur'ān* and modern science he vehemently advocates creationism against the theory of evolution. His guide for the modern Muslim youth entitled *24 Hours in the Life of a Muslim* links purity with external order.[26] 'In conformity with the teachings of the *Qur'ān*, believers will be clean and well-groomed, not for the sake of other people, but because this is what Allah likes'. And further: 'God has created in His slaves some imperfections to remind them of their dependence on Him'. In his view, cleansing is a constant reminder of the inferiority of human beings. The believer 'knows that God loves cleanliness and clean people, he sees washing himself as an act of worship and hopes to gain His pleasure'. Finally, Yahya combines personal cleanliness with ideas about environmental protection. Environmentalism linked to Islamic conceptions of the responsibility of mankind for nature seems to be a future development that draws upon purity-related ideas.

Ahmad Reidegeld's *Handbuch Islam* is the first comprehensive handbook on religious duties according to the legal schools published in German. Reidegeld is a German convert, and converts are often highly respected because their religiosity is based on conviction rather than on tradition. Moreover, they represent a perspective on the dissemination of Islam in German society through convincing the majority rather than demographic change. Converts play an important role in adopting and transforming the classical heritage and possibly will form a new generation of speakers for the Muslim community in Germany. This is likely to be a source of religious dynamics in the times to come.

Reidegeld characterises purity as a 'matter of utmost importance, something that is decisive for the realisation and maintenance of religion' (Reidegeld 2005: 231). The term a *ṭahāra* is applied to both ritual purity and physical cleanliness, covering the whole range from epilation and beard care to clothing and cleanliness of places. Interestingly enough, the gender aspect is not addressed prominently. Some ritualised form of avoidance is recommended: reciting the *Qur'ān* and speaking in the toilet and similar unclean places in general is said to be very bad behaviour. Spatial order has to be taken into account, toilets must not be orientated towards Mecca nor should the believer be so when using them. Concerning the touching of the *Qur'ān*, Reidegeld tends towards the view that a copy can only be left to a non-Muslim if he or she is willing to execute purification rites according to the rules of *ṭahāra* (ibid.: 193). In sum, by adjusting religious practice to religious law Reidegeld's work is a contribution to systematising religion based more on a juridical than on an ethnic, or cultural tradition. In a sense, a convert's situation is parallel to the situation of second or third generation immigrants who are about to break away from cultural traditions that guided the lives of the first generation but want to keep and discover their religion. Both may refer to the authority of religious law if customs are not or no longer the basis for the control of social life.

It may sound paradoxical, but the more detailed regulations are, the more they seem to admit exemptions. As a consequence, a Muslim may refer to law in order to escape convention. The ambivalence of the given situation and at the same time a future perspective is expressed in the following words of Halima Krausen, a well-known convert and theologian of Islam in Germany who provoked a public debate on the possibility of female Imams.

> We follow the standardised instructions of Muslim teachers from the formative period of Islam, whose details can vary from one school to another. And at least in the diaspora, we tend to feel the need to simplify even those differences for the sake of Muslim unity, rather than to use the dynamic which they offer as a way of deepening the riches of our spiritual and cultural life.[27]

Conclusion

To sum it up, Muslim communications about purity range from sophisticated debates on the rationality of ritual actions to more or less detailed advices for highly profane cleaning activities. They form, both in synchronical and diachronical perspective, a comprehensive repertoire of positions to refer to, and constitute at the same time the discourse of rules throughout the times. I would like to use the term 'Regelkorridor' in order to denote a corridor of rules and regulations which reflects the integration of various interpretations and controversies over a basic idea and its related issues. This thematic discourse is fuelled by negotiations in which the notion of purity is instrumental for claims to power, superiority, distinction, agency, legitimacy and so forth. At the same time it is an aggregation of arguments to draw upon in the process of negotiating. Given the above-mentioned degree of flexibility and variety, this may happen in the form of reactivating some preformed positions and designing them according to actual social constellations. The diaspora is certainly one of them. Thematic corridors like the purity discourse can provide arguments and tools to master the process of acculturation, or, conversely, to foster segregation from the majority. Everyone moving within this corridor can regard himself or herself as a Muslim or Muslima. Of course, there are always voices claiming to know better what true Islam requires. But in the end, the mere acceptance of the general obligation to purify makes one part of the system. And even those who do not only criticise preoccupation with ritual purity, but the whole of ritual obligations — a position that is not unknown in Islamic heresiography[28] — take part in the discourse while at the same time marking the edges of the corridor. Such a corridor, founded on the recognition of a basic idea or claim, constitutes something like a cultural unit of its own. The more it corresponds to elementary functions of social life the more lasting it should be.

Just like other religions and belief systems, Islam, as reflected in its scripts and collective frames of reference, is characterised by a shared repertoire of figures and fictions, a set of possible views on the world, man, and history, and a number of corridors of regulations. Interests may clash and players may change, as long as they use the same playground the integrity of the community is preserved. In the sense that discourses of the above kind are points of reference for all Muslims, indeed, one can speak of a unity of Islam.

In describing the conditions of modernity, contemporary cultural studies tend to assume that in a globalised world the 'classical' sources are of very little relevance. At best they provide some catchwords, while the real economic, political and social changes proceed independently of their existence. I prefer a perspective on sources as a vital part of the cultural system.[29] People know that there is something in the background, available in case of need, a heritage which may be drawn upon when required, a safe haven, in a way.[30] The return to the cultural heritage is a common strategy in periods of change.[31]

As a rule, few people study this heritage in the form of sophisticated philosophical, theological, or juridical texts. At the most, it appears in a popularised and simplified form of which the *Ilmihal* genre may be an example, a kind of Muslim catechism, or guide or manners and morals, duties and believes. For no small number of Turkish Muslims in the diaspora, especially the women, this genre is a starting point to go further into an issue in question. Thus, it is not unlikely that religious law as a transculturally accepted resource for common Islamic standards will gain importance at the expense of ethnicity as decisive factor in the formation of identity. And it is not unlikely that, in the long run, it will be used by immigrants as a tool for adapting to diaspora surroundings by referring to those positions within the heritage that appear most suitable for that, rather than for marking off boundaries.

◈

Notes

1. This is not clearly deducible from the *Qur'ān*. Qur'ānic passages speak of penalty in the hereafter. Regulations of the *sharī'a* calling for the death penalty are deduced from *hadīth* literature.
2. Take, for example, *takhfīf*, alleviation with regard to ritual duties, or *rukhsa*, exemption or dispensation, e.g., from observing the dietary laws. There is a prevalent opinion among Muslims that man is weak, and God does not want to burden his servants with duties they cannot perform.
3. Unlike the situation in other disciplines of Cultural Studies, in Islamic Studies the purity complex has only recently reappeared as a subject of scholary work after a long period in which the Islamic stipulations were simply explained by tracing them back to the Jewish standards. For older literature see Wensinck (1910, 1914), for newer literature especially Gauvain (2005), Katz (2002, 2005), Maghen (1999, 2004), Reinhart (1989), also see Bousquet (1949, 1950).
4. In 2006, the interpretation of the taboo on pigs was negotiated in the course of the controversy between secularism and Islamic orientation in Turkey. Newspapers had reported that public TV broadcaster TRT had decided to ban Walt Disney's adaptation of Winnie the Pooh from screens because one of its heroes is a piglet. The broadcaster is controlled by the Turkish government which is dominated by the moderate Islamic AKP party. TRT has denied those reports and said they aim to discredit the institution. Pigs as symbols of impurity are also instrumental in conflicts arising, and being fuelled, in the context of immigration. For instance, Roberto Calderoni, a far-right Italian senator and former minister, caused some public attention in September 2007 by threatening that he would be ready to walk with a pig over a site where a mosque was planned to be built in order to 'defile' the ground, and in doing so make the construction impossible which would help to prevent 'the Islamicisation of the Bologna plain'. See http://www.corriere.it/Primo_Piano/Politica/2007/09_Settembre/13/calderoli_maiale_day.html>and<http://www.corriere.it/Primo_Piano/Politica/2007/09_Settembre/14/allam_calderoli_islam.html (accessed 25 November 2007).
5. Ideological rigidity, of course, is not a characteristic of several Islamic movements alone. For fundamentalism in general see Almond et al.

(2003), for puritan movements Beek (1988), for contemporary Hindu nationalist movements Bhatt (1997).

6. Interestingly, recent research states a psychological association between physical and ethical cleanliness at a very basic level. As the Canadian psychologists Zhong and Liljenquist have shown, threats to moral 'purity' activate a need for physical cleansing, which can assuage moral emotions and reduce direct compensatory behaviour.
7. See Schiffauer (1983: 93) for gender norms in rural Turkey and an example of conflict arising from their transfer into a German context; also see Bouhdiba (1985) and Maghen (2004b).
8. Local customary law has been integrated to a certain extent into classical law under the notion of *'urf*.
9. See Katz (2005: 117); for discussions on the status of ritual and the incomprehensibility of divine law 113. For a distinction between rational and non-rational forms of worship with regard to purification see Ibn Rushd (150–51).
10. For relevant citations from ash-Shāfi'ī's *Kitāb al-Umm* see Maghen (1999b: 239).
11. Ghazālī 125; trans. 1. The former tradition is deemed to be 'weak'. Another famous mystic, Ibn al-'Arabī (d. 1240), wrote a similar and even more detailed work also entitled *Asrār aṭ-Ṭahāra*, trans. Eric Winkel (1995) *The Mysteries of Purity*, Notre Dame: Cross Cultural Publications.
12. Ghazālī 126; trans. 2–3; cf. also Jabre (1985: 156). In the last stage the mind has undergone the purification from the categories of time and space.
13. Ghazālī 140; trans. 72.
14. Ghazālī 127; trans. 9. Some religious women's practice of constantly wearing gloves for purity reasons is a parallel in a way.
15. Ghazālī 128; trans. 17.
16. The majority of the jurists agree on dropping this as an invalidating factor.
17. Ibn Rushd 86; trans. 41.
18. Ibn Rushd 73–76; trans. 34–36.
19. Moreover, it is commonly held as not illegitimate to temporarily change one's *madhhab*, i.e., the legal school to which one belongs by birth, for reasons of easing one's obligations. Even though few people can name the differences of the legal schools in detail they know that there are alternatives.
20. The history of post-war immigration of non-German immigrants to Germany is usually divided in four phases: (*i*) recruitment of foreign labour in times of economic prosperity (1955–1973), (*ii*) a phase of consolidation (1973–1980) when, caused by economic decline, the

number of guest-workers were supposed to be reduced while at the same time immigrant milieus established themselves through family reunion and birth rate, (*iii*) a phase of resistance (1981–1998) to the acknowledgement that the country showed features of a multicultural society, and guest-workers had become immigrants, a phase also of a high influx of asylum seekers, (*iv*) the phase of acceptance from 1998 onward, when politics made adjustments to the situation of Germany as a *de facto* immigration country (see Geißler 2006: 235–37). In today's Germany about 19 per cent of the population has a migration background, in some big cities the number amounts up to 40 per cent of the young people. Among an estimated number of 3 to 3.3 million Muslims, approximately 2.7 million people from Turkey form the most important immigrant group of non-German origin. More than half of the Muslims feel themselves excluded from German society in one way or the other. Religious orientation plays a more prominent role in immigrant communities than it does within the majority, Muslims being slightly at the fore. More important, this role seems not to be decreased by the change of generations. See Worbs and Heckmann (2003) and, despite some methodological shortcomings, Brettfeld and Wetzels (2007).

21. Gelatine has become one of the main issues discussed in internet chats and Muslim circles because it is suspected of containing impure substances.
22. As mentioned above, attempts to make religion consistent with rationality, or rather rationality with religion, are not new. In the course of the last two centuries the challenge of modernity has stimulated the old quest for rationality, if not both was set on the same level. For a Muslim physician's view of the beneficial and curative effects of purification and prayer on health see Souidan (1976).
23. Qaraḍāwī (1960: 21); trans. 44. online http://www.witness-pioneer.org/vil/Books/Q_LP/sub 1.4 'The prohibition of Things Is Due to Their Harmfulness' (accessed 31 August 2007); Germ. trans.44. Al-Qaraḍāwī's is not consistently as rigid as commonly supposed. For instance, in the above mentioned controversy over gelatine he held for a long time that it is not a forbidden substance. Notably, in diaspora this position has been neglected even by those who generally follow his views.
24. Öztürk (2001 [1989]): 75; Germ. trans. 73.
25. Öztürk (2001 [1989]): 143; Germ. trans. 141.
26. For all citations see Yahya (2003: 20–22). First published in 2003 as *Müminin 24 saatı*, Istanbul: Global Yayıncılık. It is also available online in several languages: http://www.harunyahya.com/kids/24hours2.html; http://www.harunyahya.org/cocuklar/muminin_24_saati/muminin_24_saati7.html; <http://www.harunyahya.com/de/

kinder/24stunden_muslim/24stunden_muslim01.php (all accessed 31 August 2007)

27. See http://www.qantara.de/webcom/show_article.php/_c-307/_nr-24/i.html (accessed 31 August 2007).
28. For non-conformist views in medieval Islam see Stroumsa (1999: 84 and 135). One of those freethinkers even compared Muslim rituals to those of 'pagan' Indians.
29. After having stated that a lot of scholars in contemporary Islamic studies show little interest in the textual basis of religious law (*fiqh*), Benkheira (1999: 65) takes a similar position: 'contre-courant de ce point de vue, on propose ici de considérer le fiqh non comme un eventuel complément à l'étude des sociétés d'islam mais comme une condition d'existence de ces sociétés'. Cf. also Rao (2006: 159) who sees the meanings given to rituals as 'part of a cultural repertoire in which connections between the various domains of life are established and negotiated.'
30. See Gellner (1981: 53) and passim, who describes the widespread awareness of the existence of higher standards as a decisive psychological factor of folk and popular Islam. People know that the way they practice Islam is just a compromise and the ideal lies elsewhere.
31. In this sense, ritual is a stabilising factor in the process of adapting to changing conditions and circumstances, or, as Michaels (2007: 255) puts it, the advantage of preserving rituals is 'dass der Mensch so die Fähigkeit zur Veränderung und die Notwendigkeit der Bewahrung, von Revolution und Tradition, bewältigen kann.'

References

Almond, G.A., Appleby, R.S. and Sivan, E. 2003. *Strong Religion: The Rise of Fundamentalisms Around the World.* Chicago: University of Chicago Press.

Anwar, S. 2005. 'Fatwa, purification and dynamization: A study of tarjih in Muhammadiyah', *Islamic Law and Society*, 12 (1): 27–44.

Arkoun, M. 1989. *Ouvertures sur l'Isiam.* Paris: Jacques Granger; trans. R.D. Lee 1994. *Rethinking Islam: Common Questions, Uncommon Answers.* Boulder: Westview Press.

Beek, W.E.A. van (ed.) 1988. *The Quest for Purity: Dynamics of Puritan Movements.* Berlin, New York, Amsterdam: Mouton de Gruyter.

Benkheira, H. 1999. 'Le rite à la lettre: Régime carné et normes religieuses', in P. Bonte, A.-M. Brisebarre and A. Gokalp (eds) *Sacrifices en Islam: Espaces et temps d'un rituel*, pp. 63–91. Paris: CNRS Éditions.

Bhatt, C. 1997. *Liberation and Purity: Race, New Religious Movements and the Ethics of Postmodernity.* London: UCL Press.

Boos-Nünning, U. and Karakaşoğlu, Y. (eds) 2005. *Viele Welten leben: Zur Lebenssituation von Mädchen und jungen Frauen mit Migrationshintergrund*. Münster: Waxmann.

Bouhdiba, A. 1985. *Sexuality in Islam*. London: Routledge and Kegan Paul.

Bousquet, G.-H. 1949. *Les grandes pratiques rituelles de l'Islam*: Paris: Presses Univ. de France.

———. 1950. 'La pureté rituelle en Islam', *Revue de l'histoire des religions* 138: 53–71.

Brettfeld, K. and Wetzels, P. 2007. *Muslime in Deutschland. Integration, Integrationsbarrieren, Religion sowie Einstellungen zu Demokratie, Rechtsstaat und politisch-religiös motivierter Gewalt. Ergebnisse von Befragungen im Rahmen einer multizentrischen Studie in städtischen Lebensräumen*. Berlin: Bundesministerium des Innern.

Gauvain, R. 2005. 'Ritual Rewards: A Consideration of Three Recent Approaches to Sunni Purity Law', *Islamic Law and Society*, 12 (3): 333–93.

Geißler, R. 2006. *Die Sozialstruktur Deutschlands*, 4th edn, Wiesbaden: VS Verlag für Sozialwissenschaften.

Gellner, E. 1981. *Muslim Society*. Cambridge: Cambridge University Press.

al-Ghazālī, Abū Ḥamid Muḥammad Ibn Muḥammad (n.d.) *Iḥyā' 'ulūm ad-dīn*, vols. I–V. Bayrūt: Dār al-Ma'rifa, vol. I *Kitāb Asrār aṭ-ṭahāra*; trans. Nabih Amin Faris (1970; 1st edn 1966). *The Mysteries of Purity*: Lahore: Sh. Muhammad Ashraf.

Ibn Qayyim al-Jawziyya, Muḥammad Ibn Abī Bakr. 1994. *Al-Waswasa*, ed. Aḥmad Sālim Bādwaylān. Riyāḍ: Dār Ṭuwayq.

Ibn Rushd, Abu l-Walīd Muḥammad Ibn Aḥmad. 1995. *Bidāyat al-mujtahid wa-nihāyat al-muqtaṣid*, vols I–IV ed. Mājid al-Ḥamawī, vol. I *Kitāb aṭ-Ṭahāra wa-ṣ-ṣalāṭ*; trans. Imran Ahsan Khan Nyazee, reviewed by Mohammed Abdul Rauf 2006. *The Distinguished Jurist's Primer*. Reading: Garnet.

Jabre, F. 1985. *Essai sur le lexique de Ghazali*: Beyrouth: Publications de l'Université Libanaise.

Katz, M.H. 2002. *Body of Text. The Emergence of the Sunni Law of Ritual Purity*. Albany: State University of New York Press.

———. 2005. 'The Study of Islamic Ritual and the Meaning of Wuḍū'', *Der Islam* 82: 106–45.

Maghen, Z. 1999a. 'Close encounters: Some preliminary observations on the transmission of impurity in early Sunni jurisprudence', *Islamic Law and Society* 6 (3): 348–92.

———. 1999b. 'Much Ado about *Wuḍū'*', *Der Islam* 76 (2): 205–52.

———. 2004a. 'First Blood Purity, Edibility, and the Independence of Islamic Jurisprudence', *Der Islam* 81(1): 49–95.

———. 2004b. *Virtues of the Flesh: Passion and Purity in Early Islamic Jurisprudence*. Leiden: Brill.

Michaels, A. 2007. 'How do you do?' Vorüberlegungen zu einer Grammatik der Rituale', in H. Schmiedinger and C. Sedmak, *Der Mensch — ein 'animal symbolicum'? Sprache-Dialog-Ritual*, pp. 239–58. Darmstadt: Wissenschaftliche Buchgesellschaft.

Öztürk, Y.N. 2001; 1st edn 1989. *400 soruda islam*. Istanbul: Yeni Boyut. Germ. trans. 2000. *400 Fragen zum Islam, 400 Antworten. Ein Handbuch*. Düsseldorf: Grupello.

al-Qaraḍāwī , Y. 1960. *Al-Ḥalāl wa-l-ḥarām fī l-islām*. al-Qāhira: Dār Iḥyā al-Kutub al-'Arabiyya. 1st edn 1989; Germ. trans. 2003. *Erlaubtes und Verbotenes im Islam*. München: SKD Bavaria.

Rao, U. 2006. 'Ritual in Society', in J. Kreinath, J. Snoek and M. Stausberg (eds) *Theorizing Rituals: Issues, Topics, Approaches, Concepts*, pp. 143–60. Leiden, Boston: Brill.

Reidegeld, A. 2005. *Handbuch Islam. Die Glaubens- und Rechtslehre der Muslime*. Kandern: Spohr.

Reinhart, A.K. 1989. 'Impurity no danger', *History of Religions*, 30 (1): 1–24.

Schiffauer, W. 1983. *Die Gewalt der Ehre: Erklärungen zu einem deutsch-türkischen Sexualkonflikt*. Frankfurt am Main: Suhrkamp.

Souidan, M.Z.A. 1976. *Prayer in Islam: Hygienic, Preventive and Curative*. Cairo: Souidan.

Stroumsa, S. 1999. *Freethinkers of Medieval Islam*. Leiden, Boston, Köln: Brill.

Wensinck, A.J. 1910. 'Die Herkunft der gesetzlichen Bestimmungen die Reinigung (*istindjā'*) oder (*istiṭāba*) betreffend', *Der Islam* 1: 101–02.

———. 1914. 'Die Entstehung der muslimischen Reinheitsgesetzgebung', *Der Islam* 5: 62–80.

Worbs, S. and Heckmann, F. 2003. 'Islam in Deutschland. Aufarbeitung des gegenwärtigen Forschungsstandes und Auswertung eines Datensatzes zur zweiten Migrantengeneration' in Bundesministerium des Innern (ed.) *Islamismus*, pp. 133–220. Berlin: Eigenverlag.

Yahya, H. 2003. *24 Hours in the Life of a Muslim*. London: Ta-Ha Publishers.

Zhong, Chen-Bo and Liljenquist, K. 2006. 'Washing away your sins: Threatened morality and physical cleansing', *Science* 313: 1451–52.

&6

Old Rituals for New Threats
Possession and Healing in the Cult of Śītalā*

Fabrizio M. *Ferrari*

Smallpox was eradicated in India on 23 April 1977. But despite the action of colonial authorities first, and the World Health Organisation (WHO) Global Commission for the Certification of Smallpox Eradication later, the cult of Śītalā, the 'smallpox goddess', has persisted. Śītalā is still celebrated to prevent diseases such as fevers, measles, malaria and tuberulosis. Further, with the spread of acquired imnuno deficiency syndrome (AIDS) in the 1980s, she started to be worshipped as an AIDS-goddess. A similar phenomenon is found in Karnataka where a new deity, AIDS-ammā (lit. 'Mother AIDS'), was created in 1997 by a local schoolteacher to instruct the rural population on the risks of human imnunodeficiency virus (HIV). AIDS-ammā and Śītalā represent the artificial and natural adaptation of South Asian 'plague goddesses' and the response to a new threat. But if in the former case, contraception and hygienic norms are promoted as *pūjā,* in the cult of Śītalā devotees tend to believe their faith will protect them and look at contagion as a (desirable) form of possession. As it was for smallpox, when variolation was preferred to vaccination, the contact with the goddess is looked upon as a form of love and can be therefore sought for.

Focussing on a specific cultural environment, rural West Bengal, where the goddess is endemic, I re-read the cult of Śītalā from the insider's perspective. My research will avoid a pan-Hindu reading of the goddess and her worship, an approach which has invariably led to disturbing generalisations. What I discuss here is the way Śītalā is worshipped and understood in the districts of southern West Bengal in a period of time which spans from the end of 2001 to the beginning of 2007.[1] I am aware that the goddess is worshipped in Pakistan, Nepal, Bangladesh and other Indian sites (e.g., Varanasi, Delhi, Gurgaon, Jaipur, etc.) following different patterns and for different reasons. A rich scholarly literature informs us about this ritual dimorphism. But it will be unfair to my many informants as well as intellectually dishonest to change such perspective only because elsewhere Śītalā is worshipped mainly (and not only) as a pox goddess, a protector of children, a dispenser of wealth, et cetera. Goddesses like Śītalā should be studied as integral to the vernacular tradition they belong to and discussed as local products of that variegated knowledge which constitutes folklore.

To compensate the limitations resulting from a strict phenomenological approach, I analyse the 'language' of the cult and the meta-narratives generated through it. In the first part of the essay, I go through the academic literature on Śītalā in order to point out: (*i*) how the goddess has been understood and 'translated' by Western and South Asian scholars; and (*ii*) how she ended up being totally identified with smallpox. Such an approach will be conducive to discuss, in the second part, the ritualism behind the cult of Śītalā, with particular reference to the role of ritual specialists: variolators (until the eradication of smallpox) and folk healers. I specifically address the concepts of illness and ritual healing as cultural constructs opposed to the sociological explanations of the *Śītalā-pūjā* as a way to justify the presence/absence of disease or to mirror an insider/outsider conflict (vaccination/variolation, coloniser/colonised, *dharma*/*adharma*). In particular, I examine the Bengali concept of illness as possession, a desirable state of grace which requires ritual action to celebrate — rather than to let go — the presence of the goddess. In the last part of this study, I consider the adaptations that occurred to the cult of Śītalā in Bengal after the eradication of smallpox and the insurgence of AIDS. By comparing ancestral religious rituals (*Śītalā-pūjā*) with ritualised knowledge (as in the case of AIDS-ammā), I show how the latter fails to respond to the needs of villagers, who eventually turn onto Māriyammaṉ, the local 'plague goddess', as their only resource.

The Making of the Smallpox Goddess

Śītalā is widely known as the 'smallpox goddess' or the 'goddess of smallpox'.[2] For at least three centuries missionaries, travellers, soldiers, traders and scholars have largely used these labels to the point that they have now become customary. European languages bear witness to this as they all use the same semantic construct: 'dea del vaiolo' in Italian, 'diosa de la viruela' in Spanish, 'deusa da varíola' in Portuguese, 'déesse de la variole' in French, 'Göttin der Windpocken' in German. It is thus reasonable to say that, at least in non-Indic languages, Śītalā is definitely the 'smallpox goddess'. But what happens when Śītalā is mentioned by *deśis* in a *deśi* context? Does 'smallpox goddess' remain an acceptable rendering? What do Bengali villagers mean when they say 'Śītalā'?

Indic dictionaries invariably translate Śītalā as 'smallpox' first, and in second instance 'the Cold One', an epithet of the 'goddess of smallpox'. Lexicographers therefore tend to identify the disease with the goddess, and/or vice versa. But this is not so for devotees who explain Śītalā as *vasanta roger adhiṣṭhātrī*: '[she] who controls the Vasanta fever.'[3] In Bengali *adhiṣṭhātrī* is '[...] a controller, one who holds; a possessor, an occupier' (Biswas 1999: 18). According to my informants, Śītalā is not to be identified with disease, as the label 'smallpox goddess' seems to imply. Smallpox, measles and fevers exist independently, and they are already inside our body — though inactive. Śītalā simply controls them, as many of her names suggest. Further, she is rarely said to be an infecting presence. The conditions of illness are explained by locals in terms of weight (*bhar*) and/or heat (*tapas*). Those features which Western medicine calls 'symptoms' are a sign of Śītalā activating presence. Alternatively, they are believed to be visiting spirits, belonging to and controlled by the goddess. Śītalā is more likely a 'removing goddess' (*apanodanakāriṇī devī*), with reference to misfortune.

During my periods of fieldwork in West Bengal (2000–2003), I have been able to collect a number of names of the goddess which I eventually arranged into five categories:

(*i*) names implying a maternal condition: Mā, Ammā, Āi, Padmāvatī Mā[4] (Mother [born from] a lotus), Choṭi Mā (Small Mother), Baṛī Mā (Great Mother) and Moṭi Mā (Pearl Mother);

(*ii*) names implying a relation with a particular season: Vasanta Rāy[5] (Queen of Vasanta), Vasanta Buṛī (the Beldam of Vasanta) and — among Munda speaking tribes — Māgh-boṅga[6] (Spirit of Māgh);

(*iii*) names implying a relation with a particular disease: Rog Rāy (Queen of fevers), Vyādhipati (Queen of epidemics), Phapholevālī (She of the vescicles), Guṭikā (Pustule), Roger Jananī (Mother of fevers), Kalejavālī (She [who attacks] the liver).

(*iv*) honorific titles: Ṭhākurāṇī (Notrê Dame),[7] Jāgatrānī (Queen of the World), Karuṇamāyī ([She who is] Full of Mercy), Maṅgalā (the Auspicious One), Bhagavatī (the Blessed One), Dayāmāyī ([She who is] Full of Grace).

(*v*) names primarily belonging to other goddesses: Baṇ Bibi (Lady of the forest), Manasā (the 'serpent goddess'), Olā Bibi (Lady of Flux, i.e., 'goddess of cholera'), Maṅgal Caṇḍī (an auspicious form of Caṇḍī), Vasanta Caṇḍī, Raktāvatī ([She who] holds the blood, i.e., 'goddess of blood infections'), Ṣaṣṭhī, Hāritī and Parṇaśavarī. Other goddesses associated with the function of controlling diseases or death and sometime identified with Śītalā are Mātaṅgī, Mahākālī, Jyeṣṭhā, Cāmuṇḍī and Kālarātrī.

The label 'smallpox goddess' is not entirely satisfactory for three main reasons. First, Śītalā is never explicitly called so by local people. In Sanskrit medical literature smallpox is *masūrikā* (*virus Variola major*) and *kṣudra roga* (*virus Variola minor*).[8] But Śītalā is not known as, for instance, *masūrikā devī*. Second, the goddess controls a great deal of diseases among which smallpox was just the deadliest one. In Bengal, Śītalā is the 'controller' of ailments such as syphilis (*upadaṅgaś rog*), malaria and fevers (*jor, rog*), measles (*milāmilā* or *hām vasantā*), chickenpox (*pāni vasantā*), diarrhoea (*dāsta*), skin eruptions (*cāmudal*), leprosy (*visphoṭa*), cholera (*olāuṭhā*), vomit (*vaman*), tuberculosis (*yakṣārog*), blindness (*andhatvā*) and vitiligo (*śvetīrog*).[9] Third, and most important, the label 'smallpox goddess' implies an identity with the disease, a concept which is actually missing in the minds of local people. This central concept was recognised by Monier-Williams as early as 1879 when he described Śītalā as 'the Mother who *presides over* small-pox, and *may* prevent small-pox, cause small-pox or be herself small-pox.' (Monier-Williams & Coote 1880: 120; emphasis mine).

The iconography of the goddess offers a further chance to examine the controlling power of the goddess. Śītalā, when

Figure 1: Śītalā, Traditional Print, Śītalā-mandir, Dasashwamedh-ghat, Varanasi.
Source: All photographs by the author.

Figure 2: Śītalā-mā, Dharmatala Śītalā-mandir, Kolkata.

Figure 3: Śītalā-pūjā in the Dharmatala Śītalā-mandir, Kolkata.

Figure 4: Śītalā Protecting Bottled Water from Pollution, Tea Stall, Lal Bazar, Kolkata.

anthropomorphically portrayed, is always represented as a fair-complexioned virgin riding an ass (*gādhā*), crowned with a winnowing fan (*śūrpa*), holding a short broom (*jhāṛu*) in her right hand and an earthen pitcher (*khālśī*) in her left (See Figures 1 and 2).[10] Although these items have been carefully discussed, nobody has ever questioned so far the meaning of her mount (*vāhana*).[11] Donkey in Bengali is *gādhā*, a *tadbhāva* (altered) word from the Sanskrit *gardabha*. From this word comes *gardabhaka*, 'anybody or anything resembling an ass' but also 'a cutaneous disease (eruption of round, red, and painful spots).' (Monier-Williams 1997: 349). Such a definition closely resembles a sarcoid, a benignant tumour involving connective tissue (muscle, sub-cutaneous tissue, etc.) which frequently appears on donkeys. Sarcoids, dry, scaly masses, tend to ulcerate and bleed, like big smallpox pustules. Verrucous sarcoids, the most common on donkeys, often occur on the head, chest, shoulder and under-leg and, lacking hair, they are not difficult to spot. Their growth mostly appears in spring and early summer, when smallpox used to erupt in Bengal. Although changing factors must be considered (dietary change, increased ultraviolet light, fly strike, changing routine and stress levels), sarcoids — and cutaneous diseases in general — are firmly believed to be caused by solar rays, as smallpox. By riding — i.e., controlling — a donkey, Śītalā shows her power over a dreadful disease and the seasonal variations which affect the life of the village.

The Smallpox Myth

The most common titles of the goddess are maternal (Mā, Choṭi Mā, Baṛī Mā, Moṭi Mā and Buṛī Mā) and together with the name Śītalā they are explained by Indologists and anthropologists to be deflectors of smallpox (Junghare 1975: 298 and Kolenda 1982: 229, among the others). In turn, Bengali people when asked about the meaning of the word 'Śītalā', simply explain it as 'cold' or 'coldness'. Choṭi Mā is not compulsorily a milder form of the disease nor is Baṛī Mā a deadly haemorrhagic smallpox attack.[12] Rather, the two titles are used to indicate the goddess as *kanyā* ('virgin', 'maiden') and Mother, or simply recent or older *mūrtis* (icons, images of the deity).

A long list of scholars[13] claimed that Śītalā is an euphemistic name, 'an attempt to ward off the goddess's fire as she rages through the Bengali countryside [...].' (Nicholas 2003: 230). But Śītalā is actually and intrinsically cool. The goddess is both 'She who is cold' and 'She who cools', as translated by Wadley (1980: 35), who emphasised Śītalā's role as a village mother rather than that of a plague deity (1980: 33). Filippi too (2002: 196) retained Wadley's translation ('Colei che rinfresca'), but he made reference to a Yogic form of *prāṇayāma* (*śītalī*, a cooling technique), to high fever shivering and to the therapeutic action of the goddess directly on the patient through stale edibles and cold baths. These explanations are unsatisfactory. The former refers to a tradition which is basically alien to the Bengali (and I would say South Asian) farming societies. In the latter two cases, the perspective should be inverted. The majority of my informants agree in saying that cold waters and cooling edibles are offered to Śītalā, not to the ill person. This is because the diseased person is the goddess, quite literally.

Ultimately, the translations of popular names for smallpox represent, in my view, a case of disturbing inductive exegesis. I suspect this interpretation is a sort of Western Orientalist fascination which drove us to see the germs of disease every now and then. In Bengali, smallpox is known as *vasantā rog* (spring fever), *guṭi vasantā* (spring vesicle), *icchā vasantā* (Spring's will), *māyer dayā* (the mother's grace), *māyer khelā* (the mother's play) and *devir cumu* (the kiss of the goddess). Although for a Western observer such periphrases indicate a state of disease (organic dysfunction), to a local they are a 'performance of the sacred' (*dharma karma*), i.e., illness (functional dysfunction) (cf. Hahn 1984: 2; also Wilce 1997: 353). The difference is highly relevant, especially in a ritual context.

The 'breaking up of strength' (*rog*) and the psychological confusion (*khelā*) experienced by 'patients' are believed to be signs of the goddess's presence. The touch of the goddess, her grace and kisses are not always at the origin of sickness and bodily sufferance, but convey a series of manifestations which are related to possession phenomena. For this purpose it is relevant to observe that one can be possessed by Śītalā (i.e., one can be Śītalā) without suffering any organic disease. This is particularly evident in the case of on-stage performances, when actors who play the goddess are possessed by Śītalā, who descends on them (Katyal & Kishore 2001: 100). Śītalā's priests are always present before and after dramatic representations of the goddess's myth, as they have to consecrate the stage and the bodies of the actors.

Identifying previous interpretive and methodological errors is not a mere critical exercise. Rather it enables us to inquire into reasons and causes of a complex ritual system which — due to its setting (borderline Sanskrit culture) and the lack of updated ethnographies — is still in need of careful examination. My criticism towards theories built on the 'smallpox goddess' and the 'smallpox myth' aims at resolving unfinished problematics, namely the general understanding of illness as possession (a privileged condition) and healing as *pūjā*.

Śītalā's Ritual Specialists: Illness, Possession and Healing

The Bengali concept of possession is still little explored.[14] As in other similar contexts, possession can be broadly defined as a non-ordinary psychophysical condition in which an individual exhibits 'new and different sets of memories, dispositions, and skills' (Becker 1993: 11). In Bengal, these occurrences are imputed to the visit of a loading entity. When 'patients' (*rogī*) are asked about their condition, they use expressions like: *ālgār kichu/kono eseche*, 'something/someone loose has come'. The descent of the goddess is explained as an activating force, a *śakti*, and more precisely as 'weight' or 'pressure' (*bhar*). Such a concept has been translated so far as 'possession'. In fact Śītalā does not 'take possession' of human beings. To my informants, the action of the goddess is better explained in terms of 'filling' (*bharā*) the body. What we interpret as an organic imbalance is a load which causes pressure and then heats (*tāpāno*) one or more persons. Only a small number of informants referred to the same concept as *āveśa*, lit. 'confounded state of mind', 'frenzy'.[15] The term, which in the psychiatric jargon indicates an obsessive behaviour, comes from the Sanskrit lexeme *a√viś* which means 'to enter, to come into; to take possession'. Another word to indicate a state of possession imputed to Śītalā is *apadṛṣṭi*, lit. 'a glance coming from above'. The very same experience is also described as *avatāra* (descent), *darśana* ('vision') or, by my Muslim informants, as *najar* ('sight', from Persian *naẓar*). I am therefore inclined to believe that in the case of Śītalā, people are 'oppressed' or 'burdened' rather than 'possessed', and by no way are they considered — or consider themselves — victims.[16] But to 'oppressed' people neither is Śītalā believed to be at the origin of contagion, nor is illness interpreted as an organic dysfunction (disease). Rather they agree in saying that illness is a sleeping entity which is already inside the body (Cf. Sujatha 2007: 176).

In rural Bengal, the presence of Śītalā is acknowledged both psychologically (possession, either voluntary or not) and physically (contagion). Although such occurrence may result in long-lasting health sequelae (blindness, scars, respiratory problems, encephalitis, osteomyelitis variolosa, arthritis and malformed bones), or even death, the goddess must be greeted and welcomed. In the cult of Śītalā two kinds of ritual specialists can be identified: variolators and village-level practitioners (folk healers).

Variolators served as the only available remedy against poxes in South Asia until the advent of the first vaccination campaigns by the British (1868–69, 1872–74, 1877–79, 1884–85). But variolation and vaccination were not so different. Both were grounded on the principle that once a patient contracts pox he/she develops immunity. Variolators' technique consisted in the cutaneous inoculation of infected dried pus extracted one year before from human smallpox victims' scabs or pustules and aiming to result in a milder form of smallpox.[17] The vaccine, instead, was fresh and collected from infected bovines. Despite the success of vaccination,[18] variolation remained the preferred practice in South Asia to the point that British Government had to outlaw it in 1865.

Several theories have been pronounced so far in order to explain the hostility of village India towards vaccination. Brimnes (2004) sees in it a form of resistance towards the coloniser. Arnold (1993: 133), in turn, sees in vaccination a violation of the body while variolation was meant as an invocation to the goddess.[19] Vaccination had socio-economic implications as well. Variolators charged an affordable fee (females were usually charged half that of males), but vaccination — even though dispensed free of any charge by British authorities — was looked upon with suspicion, especially by upper castes. Vaccination initially transferred bodily lymph from one body to another, an extremely polluting event since low/out-castes were often the only vaccinifers available. But even when the substitution of the arm-to-arm with calf lymph vaccination was made, suspicion was not erased, as many Hindus looked at this practice as a form of cruelty towards holy cows (Chacko 1980: 15, Arnold 1993: 142). Also, according to a widespread belief, people thought that 'the practice of taking down personal details of every vaccinated person was a prelude to either a captivation tax or transportation' (Brimnes 2004: 210). Smallpox vaccine ended up becoming a psychosis to the point that: '[m]any were convinced that the actual aim of these vaccines was the destruction of the race as well as of religion.' (Bose 2006: 40). In Bengal, both Hindus and Muslims looked at vaccination as a threat to their religion (Bhattacharya et al. 2005: 66–69) while Brahmins who relied on variolation fees tried to dissuade people to take the free-dispensed vaccine (Wujastyk 1987: 153). Further, ill-effects of vaccination were given great and protracted attention as peasants could not afford missing work due to vaccination side-effects (fever or sepsis) (Bhattacharya 2001: 256). Within two years of the official introduction of the smallpox vaccine in India (1802), British surgeons and civil servants were already complaining about major problems in distributing it.

Brahmins are reported to have acted as variolators (*Śītalā-pūjak*s), but the large majority of variolators belonged to low castes such as *mālin*s (gardeners) or *nāpit*s (barbers). They were known as *ṭikā cikitsāk*s, 'marking doctors', or *dehuri*s. Both *Śītalā-pūjak*s and *dehuri*s were considered *pūjarī*s, without any regard for their actual caste. Most importantly, they were not considered enemies of the goddess. Variolation was a way to celebrate the living goddess, not to reject her, as vaccination was instead looked at. The presence of variolators coincided with that of Śītalā and their performance followed a strict ritual agenda.

Variolation was indeed a *Śītalā-pūjā* in which the goddess was awakened, invited and worshipped as an immanent presence in the village. The 'patient' was literally equated to Śītalā and the room where s/he was lying was her abode. Invocations in form of *vandhanā*s (bonding prayers), *nāmḍāk*s (loud calls) and *mantra*s in corrupted Sanskrit (extrapolated from *Śītalā-maṅgal-kāvya*s) were conducive to the process of *ākarṣaṇa* (lit. attraction, also awakening, of the goddess). Once the presence was ensured, the variolator proceeded with the next phase, inoculation, a ritual explained as *sthāpana*, the stabilisation and installation of the goddess into the hosting body. It was so that the 'patient' became the *mūrti* of the goddess and the room in which s/he was confined Śītalā's temple. Fever and shivering were regarded as a tangible sign of the presence of the goddess. For those killed by smallpox (or other diseases) there was no cremation, as it was believed to enrage the goddess.

After inoculation, stale edibles, meat (during epidemics) and specific offerings were presented:

(*i*) Cold water (either swallowed or used for baths) or cold infusion of fenugreek (*methinī*), anise (*mauri*), liquorice (*madhuka*), white sandal (*sitacandan*), different kind of jasmines or juice of *bāsā* (*Justicia gandrussa*).
(*ii*) Vegetarian offerings: leaves, flowers and branches of selected trees — *nīm* (*Azadirachta indica*), *akhaṇḍa* (*Calotropis gigantes*), *bel* (*Aegle marmelos*), *aṣvahu* (*Ficus bengalensis*), *sāl* (*Shorea robusta*) and *gāmār* (*Gmelina arborea*), limes, coconuts, bananas, cucumbers, flour and *naibedya* (raw fruits and vegetables mixed with uncooked rice, milk and curd and presented stale to the goddess).
(*iii*) Cold dairy products: donkey's milk,[20] curd.
(*iv*) Blood and raw meat of goats, piglets, chickens, ducks, fowls, fishes (*rui*, *māgur* and *boyāli*) and (occasionally) buffaloes.
(*v*) Miscellanea: shell-powder, incense powder (i.e., cold fire), *cāmars* (a fly whisk obtained from bovines' tail and used to winnow the goddess),[21] *nāmaboli* (devotional scarves with the names of a particular deity printed on), coins.

Outside the newly consecrated *mandir*, women were engaged in drawing traditional sketches (*alpanās*) as a parallel form of worship. Musical performances (especially loud drum rolls), singing and telling stories (*kathā*) of Śītalā were also related activities, responding to the patterns of the *Śītalā-vrata* tradition performed by women in Bengali villages (Bidhyābinod 1408 BS: 146–147; Majumdār 1991: 112).

Bengali folk healers show relevant differences. Untrained and without a specific initiation, mostly women in gender, they invariably belong to the lowest social strata (*ḍoms*, *hāḍis*, *bāgdīs*, *śũṛīs*, *bāitis*, *cāmārs*, *nāpits*) including local tribes (Santals, Bhumijs, Mundas, Oraons). These ritual specialists, known as *khālśīs* (vessels), *dhāis* (midwives), *ojhās*, *rojās*, *jhupars*, *gunins* or just *bhardhārīs* (women who can be 'possessed'), communicate with the goddess in a state of (self-inducted) trance and act like shamans or oracles. They suffer, or have suffered, from the disease they claim to be able to cure and instruct their customers on healing methods, prophylactic techniques and the kinds of offerings to be presented. Although they have a crucial role in the healing process, they seldom act as 'priests', a role which belongs to Brahmins. Ritual purity is not a matter of concern during *Śītalā-pūjās*, yet folk healers are generally considered less pure than *pūjārīs*. Reasons vary, but informants suggest gender, social status/profession, tribal origin and individual behaviour (both in a lay and ritual context) may affect the perception of these ritual specialists in terms of purity. The belief in the efficacy of their methods, or the need to have them operating along with *pūjārīs*, is however solid.

The ritual patterns followed by folk healers is extremely variable as states of possession — the *sine qua non* of their technique — can be achieved through different practices: image worship, meditation, repetition of *mantras*, smoking hemp, fasting and forms of 'self-torture' (beating, piercing, hook-swinging, rolling on the soil, etc.). Possession — once achieved — is conducive to an oracular performance, where remedies are individuated and presented to the 'patient(s)': *mantras*, herbal preparations, water from selected ponds/rivers, ashes from fire, or standard *prasād*. One aspect of the healing technique of folk healers is however unconditional: the actual necessity to *feel* the disease, or in local terms, to host (i.e., 'to be filled with') the goddess. This is occasionally explained as *sādhana*.

The main difference between variolators and folk healers lies in the object of 'possession'. On the one hand, variolators were never possessed by the goddess. They acted as ritual facilitators in order to let the goddess descend on somebody else. They coordinated the paraphernalia for the worship *on behalf of* the village and finally — after confirmation — allowed a safe detachment. On the other hand, folk healers' ritual technique does not directly address the 'patient'. Individual ritual actions are conducive to a descent (*avatāra*) of the goddess on the healer him/herself. The performance following this is subject to a number of variations and do not adhere to any specific ritual agenda. Healers describe it as an inner struggle *for* the 'patient'.

Both in the case of variolators and in that of folk healers, the goddess is required to be alive in the village. Illness, the local cultural understanding of a state of grace (*māyer dayā/khelā*), is already present in each and every body (i.e., in the village) but needs to be activated. Śītalā's ritual specialists — though in different ways — ensure such presence and also allow a dialogue. To Bengali villagers, organic dysfunctions — i.e., diseases — are signs which ask to be interpreted. Hence the oracular features of ritual specialists who not only have to prepare an arena for an auspicious manifestation, but also have to reiterate the dependency of the village on the goddess as mother. The possessions of the 'patient' as well as that of the healer are thus welcome phenomena and are often sought for. Although the idea of 'ritual contagion' is at odds with allopathic medicine, the reasons behind these practices appear clear if we consider the motivations of the insider. Despite radical mutations as the eradication of smallpox and the insurgence of new deadly contagious diseases, *Śītalā-pūjā* will prove to be a solid and durable ritual system.

AIDS-Goddesses: Artificial and Spontaneous Theophanies

The eradication of smallpox happened more than thirty years ago, yet Indologists and anthropologists have almost exclusively focussed their researches on the 'smallpox myth' and the 'smallpox goddess'. New trends in the worship of Śītalā must however be considered. The comparison between the recently created AIDS-ammā in Karnataka and the spontaneous transformation of Śītalā into an AIDS goddess offer the opportunity to examine the South Asian cultural understanding of healing as ritual versus the social/state-notion of ritual as a mean to transmit information.

The case of AIDS-ammā (lit. 'AIDS-mother') perfectly embodies the latter condition. The goddess was created by a science high school-teacher, Mr H.N. Girish, who built a temple in Menasikyathana Halli village (Mandya District, Karnataka), on 1 December 1997, World AIDS day.[22] AIDS-ammā is meant for worship but the intention of her creator is to spread prophylactic knowledge among the rural population. At the base of the shrine a Kannada inscription defines the site as a 'Scientific Temple'.

A humble hut made of *nīm* branches stands over a six feet square stone-pavement at whose centre is placed a four feet white stone slab with the stylised silhouettes of a man and a woman. According to an online report written by a witness:

> Girish intended the figures of the man and woman to represent religion, and the red circle to represent the HIV, or, more generally, science. On the stone pillars to the right of the shrine, he painted slogans, kernels of information he got from the World Health Organization. (Portnoy 2000)

Mr Girish admitted he created AIDS-ammā following the model of Māriyammaṉ, the 'smallpox goddess' of Dravidian-speaking India. However, remarkable differences are noticeable. AIDS-ammā neither causes nor heals AIDS, neither possesses nor does she claim miracles. Unlike 'natural' plague goddesses, she is just expected to give villagers a 'clear mind.' Villagers have been instructed to repeat in a mantric fashion such formulae like: 'Please AIDS-ammā, bless me with information' (Portnoy 2000). The urgent need for spreading knowledge led Girish to create such a goddess.

The urge can be well understood if we take a glance at India's HIV and AIDS statistics. The first case of AIDS in India was certified in 1986 in Chennai (Tamil Nadu) among sex workers. By the end of 2002 nearly 4.58 millions had contracted HIV, but according to many non-governmental organisations (NGOs) working in the field such numbers do not reflect the actual situation.[23] The WHO Regional Office for South and South-east Asia, at the end of 2005 estimated the number of PLWAH (people living with AIDS/HIV) in India to be 5.1 million, a number second only to South Africa. Six states in the country, namely Andhra Pradesh, Karnataka, Maharashtra, Manipur, Nagaland and Tamil Nadu, bear the highest burden. In this tragic landscape, AIDS-ammā was desired to be an educational project. By worshipping her, people are expected to acknowledge common misconceptions such as the belief that women are the main carriers of HIV (depending on the fact that AIDS, in India, is mostly a hetero-sexually transmitted disease and prostitutes are the major vehicle) and abandon the practice of ostracism.

But knowledge (i.e., acquiring new information) is not an issue for the villagers of Menasikyathana Halli, at least in a ritual context. It has been observed that the worship of 'plague goddesses' in general is not strictly performative religion (i.e., ritual). Rather it is performative knowledge (Appfel-Marglin 1990: 126–130; Naraindas 2003: 307). Dimock (1982: 195) goes even further when he defines the worship of Śītalā after epidemics a 'divine pedagogy.' These theories however are not entirely convincing. During my periods of fieldwork, I was able to observe that — at least in a Bengali context — the opposition between *jñāna* and *ajñāna*, rather than identifying knowledge and ignorance, defines states of 'consciousness' and 'uncosciousness', with reference to illness and or/possession. The same has been noticed by Wilce (1997: 356) who worked in Bangladesh and talks about loss of control as a way to reinforce the internal dynamics of the village.

Coming back to AIDS-ammā, prophylactic knowledge is explained in culturally understandable terms for social purposes. The outcomes of this operation have produced some results so far. Following the interest of local and national newspapers and Indian broadcasting networks, in December 1999, hundreds of people in the Southern Indian state of Karnataka have taken part in a religious procession to mark the annual World AIDS Day. Students from a number of schools and their teachers joined together with villagers (mostly women and their children). According to the consolidated *vrata* tradition, students took a vow to educate villagers on HIV transmission and AIDS, and to prevent the further isolation of those already infected.[24] Information, in this case, is transmitted following consolidated ritual patterns (the *vrata*) although one may doubt the effective understanding — thus validity — of the information transmitted.

The situation in West Bengal is quite different. A specific AIDS-goddess does not exist. Local Śītalās started to be sporadically worshipped from the mid-1990s to keep away AIDS. But unlike the Karnataka AIDS-ammā, Śītalā has fully maintained her features. She is believed to cause ('awake', 'play with') AIDS and at the same time she is invoked as a remover.

According to my fieldwork in rural West Bengal, AIDS tends to be seen as the result of an erratic social and ritual behaviour.[25] Among less-educated people, AIDS is a punishment for not regularly worshipping the goddess and the acceptance of a modern/Western lifestyle, especially for what concerns inter-gender relations. The awareness that AIDS is a sexually transmitted disease is not sufficiently rooted (Pallikadavath et al. 2006: 44). Informative leaflets in Bengali and other local languages are distributed by governmental institutions, hospitals, NGOs and schools, but ancestral beliefs remain obstinate. In rural communities illness is invariably related to the descent of deities and spirits. Further, the existence of sexual taboos makes it difficult to explain that a disease — considered a state of possession — can be caused by sexual activity.

Śītalā is believed to descend on her sons and daughters and activate AIDS, as she used to do with smallpox. The persistence of this pattern has lead Śītalā's devotees to believe in the possibility of recovery from HIV positiveness thorough worship (*pūjā*) and sacrificial offering (*balidān*). Contagion is not always seen as a life-threat, but a sign of the presence of the goddess. In fact, it can be a privileged condition. Devotees continue to look at contact with the goddess as an inevitable experience, generally meant as a form of love, in both maternal and sexual terms.

PLWAH tend to be ostracised, yet the belief that these people live in a state of possession — or at least in a condition of closeness to the goddess — persists. As smallpox victims were totally identified with Śītalā, so it is for HIV/AIDS. They are experiencing the 'kiss of the goddess', an extreme form of love which can eventually devour them. To summarise, the Bengali case proves that where Śītalā is related to AIDS, PLWAH:

(i) believe in recovery;
(ii) believe and are believed to live in a state of possession;
(iii) can be identified with healers;
(iv) can be asked for responses on how to heal other people from HIV/AIDS;
(v) occasionally admit they are happy with their condition as it gives them social recognition.

It is particularly interesting here to observe how the 'patient' — once again — becomes the healer, a role which is validated by the presence of the goddess. Although more data are to be collected, the desire to be a medium of the goddess (i.e., to be HIV positive) can be variously interpreted. On the one hand, due to the social environment and the condition of extreme deprivation of some of my informants, I suspect such a claim can be looked at as a way to avoid ostracism and to get a minimal source of living. On the other, when publicly recognised as healers, they are no longer infected bodies but blessed people. They are entitled to a compensation for their profession, a trade which locals, without malice, call *byabasā*, business (cf. Wilce 1997: 356). Although the occurrence of this phenomenon is still limited, it poses interesting questions. Is, after all, the belief that PLWAH are mediums of the goddess a sort of individual self-defence mechanism? Or should we look at the claims of 'seeking for AIDS' with legitimate concern? If it is true that some people simply adapt themselves to a particular cultural background, it is also true that others, especially in the more extreme cases of deprivation, would be willing to seek for contagion in order to become village healers, a dramatic way to earn social recognition and an income.

Conclusion

Over the preceding pages two principal aims have been accomplished. The first was to question previous 'translations' of the goddess Śītalā and to offer a more reliable interpretation of her presence in Bengali villages. The second was to demonstrate the existence of an Orientalist 'smallpox myth', that is the tendency to identify Śītalā with smallpox (or disease), an approach which much affected the scholarly literature on the subject. This led to an analysis of *Śītalā-pūjā* as a celebrative — rather than strictly 'healing' — ritual process aiming to invite, establish and host the living goddess. Possession, which to devotees is Śītalā's loading descent, is the *sine qua non* to establish a dialogue. Hence the oracular feature of *Śītalā-pūjā*. The goddess is hosted in a living body, whether a (inoculated) 'patient', a (self-possessed) healer or an on-stage performer (actor). The possessed becomes the living goddess and the space around him/her is consecrated as a *mandir*.

A further element of significance that has emerged is the divide existing between the cultural understanding of ritual and its social usage in contemporary South Asia. The creation and worship of an artificial goddess like AIDS-ammā is highly significant. Although practitioners engage themselves in ritual offerings to AIDS-ammā, what is actually missing is a dialectics of power. Unlike natural plague goddesses, AIDS-ammā in not a *śakti*. According to both Sanskrit and vernacular sources, Śītalā — and women in general — have to fight for recognition; their power derives from suffering.

This is why their power often generates weakness or, in other terms, illness (*durbalatā*). AIDS-ammā was born in anomalous context. On the one hand there is no supporting myth. On the other, she just borrowed elements from the local plague-goddess (Māriyammaṉ). She has no *śakti* to give, as her power is turned by non-ritual specialists into lay knowledge, i.e., information. Conversely, the ritual process performed by Śītalā's mediums aims at conferring *śakti* upon the village, even though this is a an affected power. The presence of the goddess, illness (or disease to Western eyes) in a ritual arena is interpreted as the goddess's mercy (*karuṇa*) and grace (*dayā*) and a form of *prasād*, the leftover of ritual food-offering (*bhoga*) presented by the village to the goddess.

It thus appears that diseases are not the mere caprice of a powerful goddess, as previously theorised. Functionalist (Arnold 1993: 157 and Nicholas 2003: 166–167) and structuralist (Wadley 1980: 33 and Dimock 1982: 95) interpretations of the presence of Śītalā as a popular explanation of a catastrophic phenomenon or an agent of established dichotomies simply do not fit the context. Not only do these interpretations elude the discourse on Śītalā's mediums as ritual specialists, but they also maintain the Orientalist perspective of the cult of Śītalā as 'humoral (naturalistic)' and 'theurgic (religious)', as observed by Appfel-Marglin (1990: 115–116).

Finally, the ritualism underlying the cult of Śītalā bears witness to the continuity and deep embeddedness of endemic ritual patterns within South Asian communities. By analysing the indigenous understanding of Śītalā, the differences between illness (a cultural construct) and disease (a biomedical condition) and the way healing is meant to be a ritual offering (*karman*) to restore an order (*dharma*), I tried to present a more accurate portrait of one of the most popular forms of devotion in South Asia. While previous scholarship showed itself particularly keen to explain Śītalā as a theophany of disease generated by fear (i.e., a response to the irrational) or as a manifestation of the untamed and terrifying sacred feminine, I examined Śītalā as a village deity (*grāmya devatā*) of agricultural communities. The mechanics at the origin of her relation with illness are the result of the last phase of the agricultural cycle, i.e., decaying and absence of resources. As I have explained elsewhere (Ferrari & Refolo 2005: 16 and Ferrari 2007b: 211), Śītalā is not a demiurge, but an agent of renovation.

She is not responsible for the creation. The process of identification of the threefold agricultural cycle with the cosmogonic myth — creation (*sṛjan*), maintenance (*pālan*) and destruction (*saṃhār*) — is extraneous to Śītalā's narratives. Village deities are pragmatic, they are only concerned with worldly affairs and their ritual arena does not recreate any primordial act of sacrifice. Śītalā embodies the fertility cycle which is actualised at all levels of the Bengali farming society: religion, economy, welfare, development and population. She reflects the ancestral bond between the earth and the village. And agriculture, as theorised by Gramsci (2005: 74), has maintained a powerful psychological bondage within the society.[26]

The *Śītalā-pūjā* is a set of rituals aiming at confirming a presence, a performance of the sacred which is ensured by specific ritual specialists. Powerful psychological motivations combined with environmental and seasonal changes produce macrocosmic imbalances. These result in forms of physical and mental alterations which to Bengali villagers are due to a loading descent, a natural phenomenon which mirrors the presence of the goddess and her requests. Healing is therefore a necessity not because it aims to recover a patient, rather because it systematically addresses the needs of the village.

◈

Notes

* I am thankful to Dr Anna King who invited me to present an early version of this paper at the 31st Spalding Symposium on Indian Religions, Jesus College, University of Oxford. An abridged form of this eassy is published in *Religions of South Asia*, 1(1), 81–106, 2007. My thanks go to Prof. Jeffrey Kripal, Dr Lynn Foulston, Dr Caroline Osella and Prof. Ron Geaves for their insightful remarks. Special thanks go to Dr Alex McKay, whose expertise and passion for Śītalā-mā were highlyinspiring. My conversation with Dr Ram Varmha on plagues and donkeys in South Asia were also extremely useful. Finally I wish to express my sincere gratitude to the British Academy which awarded me with an Overseas Conference Grant to present my research at the 5th International Conference of Asia Scholars in Kuala Lumpur, Malaysia (August 2007). As convenor of the panel

'Causes and Cures in Health Care in Asia', I had the chance to meet specialists in the field of medicine and medical anthropology and discuss the cult of Śītalā from a strictly biomedical perspective.

1. Fieldwork has been conducted in the following site (in order not to reveal sources, only police stations, *thānas*, are given): Bishnupur, Jaypur, Kotalpur and Indas *thānas* (Bishnupur subdivision, Bankura district), Ketugram, Katoya, Mangalkot *thānas* (Katoya subdivision, Bardhaman district), Ausgram *thāna* (Uttar Sadhar subdivision, Bardhaman district), Faridpur, Kanksa *thānas* (Durgapur subdivision, Bardhaman district), Asansol, Raniganj *thānas* (Asansol subdivision, Bardhaman), Ilam Bajar, Bolpur, Nanur *thānas* (Bolpur subdivision, Birbhum district), Sainthya, Siuri, Khyarasole, Rajnagar *thānas* (Sadar subdivision, Birbhum district), Mayureshwar *thāna* (Rampurhat subdivision, Birbhum district), Bangaon *thāna* (Bangaon subdivision, North 24-Parganas district), Swarupnagar *thāna* (Basirhat subdivision, North 24-Parganas). Additional fieldwork has been conducted in Kolkata (West Bengal), Varanasi (Uttar Pradesh) and Kathmandu (Nepal).
2. The name Śītalā is mainly used in northern, central and eastern India. Goddesses with similar features are Hāritī and Parṇaśavarī in the sub-Himalayan areas, Mriyammaṉ in Dravidian-speaking India, Āi in Assam and Ṭhākurāṇī in Orissa. Local 'plague goddesses' can be found in almost every village across South Asia with uncountable names.
3. Vasanta is the Spring season (mid February–mid April) when smallpox prepared to burst off.
4. Such a title is generally refers to Manasā, the 'serpent goddess'. Maity (2001: 271) notes that in some (unspecified) villages of West Bengal, when the first symptoms of epidemics appeared, Manasā is invoked as Śītalā.
5. In Basu (1405 BS: 99–102), Basanta Rāy is an independent male deity.
6. Māgh (March/April) is one of the Spring months when smallpox used to strike Bengal.
7. I am indebted to Dr Francesco Brighenti (Utkal University, Bhubaneshwar, Orissa) for this beautiful rendering.
8. See *Suśruta-saṃhitā* (XIII: 1–2; 9 XIII: 30, 36; XX: 19) and *Caraka-saṃhitā* (XI: 94; XII: 93), *Aṣṭāṅgahṛdaya-saṃhitā* (II, 5: 111) of Vāgbhaṭa and *Nidāna* (LIV) of Mādhavakara.
9. All these diseases are administered by minor deities: Olāi Caṇḍī/Bibi: goddess of cholera (in her Hindu and Muslim variant), the *causaṭṭī rogas* (the sixty-four epidemics), the *sāt bhagnīs* (the seven sisters), Gheṇṭu (the spirit/god of itch, pimples and skin diseases), Raktāvatī

(goddess of blood infections), Dharma Ṭhākur (a fertility god/spirit who causes and heals from viral blindness, vitiligo, leprosy and barrenness).

10. Śītalā is generally represented with two arms. Occasionally she may be a four-armed maiden holding a jar, a broom, a lotus and a conch. Alternatively the palm of the fourth hand is placed on the head of the donkey.
11. Few notes on the donkey can be found in: Bhaṭṭācāryya (1997: 155), Bang (1973: 85–87), Svāmī Nirmalānanda (1390 BS: 170), Auboyer & De Mallmann (1950: 213–14).
12. The prevalent form of smallpox in South Asia was virus Variola major which manifested in a variety of forms, the deadliest being haemorrhagic smallpox. Virus Variola minor — or alastrim — was a less severe form of the same disease, endemic in Europe and North Africa.
13. See: Arnold (1993: 123), Babb (1975: 130), Dimock (1982: 184), Neog (1994: 52) and Stewart (1995: 389), Nicholas (2003: 230, fn. 16), among the others.
14. Bhattacharyya (1986), Carrin (1999), McDaniel (1989), Smith (2006: 119–20).
15. One of my informants translated this term for me in English as 'trance'.
16. The same can be observed in the worship of 'disease goddesses/spirits' in Dravidian-speaking India. As Foulston observes (2003: 141): 'The possession by a deity is referred to in Tamil as *iraṇku*, to 'descend' on a person, who is then referred to as a *cāmyāti* or 'god dancer'.' In Burrow, T. & Emeneau, M.B. (1984: 51), the same verb is explained as follows: '*iraṇku* (*iraṇki-*) to descend, alight, fall (as rain), disembark, settle into place, halt, abate (as poison, small-pox, etc., which are supposed to pass away from the head downward), bow respectfully, fall from a high state.'
17. Variolation is neither related to Ayurvedic medicine nor to any other Indian medical system. Cf. Greenhough (1980), Holwell (1971: 151), Shepherd McClain (2005: 102–03). Smallpox Commission of Bengal (1850), Stewart (1844).
18. Variolation was still a risky practice (2–3% of those variolated died) while vaccination, despite the existence of adverse effects, revealed to be a safer technique. See Belongia (2003: 89–90) and Bhattacharya (2006: 101–02) for more details on vaccination counter effects.
19. Glynn & Glynn report that '[i]n one area of Nepal where smallpox spread unusually rapidly, it turned out that the inhabitants were members of a sect that refused vaccination and believed that children with smallpox were possessed by the goddess and should be granted every wish — including the wish to visit relatives.' (2004: 212–13).

20. See Mukhopadhyay (1994: 25) who quotes a letter by Dr Samir Kumar Cakravorti to the Government of West Bengal (03/09/1987). Donkey's milk is explained to be widely believed to be a valid cure against smallpox, especially for children. According to Bang (1973: 86), this was also injected into the patients' arms by marking doctors.
21. The *cāmar* itself is worshipped as a proper *mūrti* and women often dance in front of it (Hāphij 1978: 94). A similar dance is performed by women around the pot (*khālśī, ghat*). On winnowing practices see also Katyal & Kishore (2001: 97) and Naraindas (2003: 313).
22. On AIDS-ammā, see http://www.twfindia.com/offTrackDetail1_17.07.04.asp; http://www.news.harvard.edu/gazette/2000/02.24/AIDS.html (accessed 18 November 2007).
23. More information can be obtained by the Web Site of the National Aids Control Organisation (http://www.nacoonline.org) who work with the Ministry of Health and Family Welfare, Government of India. See also the WHO (World Health Organisation) Regional Office for South and South-east Asia at the following link: http://www.who.int/hiv/countries/en/ (all websites accessed 18 November 2007).
24. http://news.bbc.co.uk/1/hi/world/south_asia/545405.stm (accessed 18 November 2007).
25. This tendency is common to village India. An example of spirits' anger as a result of transgression is presented in Nichter (1987: 411).
26. In doing so, not only do I maintain the insider's perspective which looks upon the goddess as a mother, but I also justify the recurrence of pompous Śītalā-*pūjās* in a critical moment of the year, between the fertilisation of the earth (*gājan*) and the menses of the earth (*ambuvācī*), when the soil is supposed to rest and expectations for the new agricultural year are higher.

References

Appfel-Marglin, F. 1990. 'Smallpox in Two Systems of Knowledge', in F. Appfel-Marglin and S.A. Marglin (eds), *Dominating Knowledge: Development, Culture, and Resistance*. Oxford, Clarendon Press, 102–44.

Arnold, D. 1993. *Colonizing the Body: State Medicine and Epidemic Disease in Nineteenth-Century India*. Berkeley, University of California Press.

Auboyer, J. and de Mallmann M.T. 1950. 'Śītalā-la-froide: déesse indienne de la petite vérole'. *Artibus Asiae*, 13 (3): 207–27.

Babb, L. 1975. *The Divine Hierarchy: Popular Hinduism in Central India*. New York, Columbia University Press.

Bang, B.G. 1973. 'Current concepts of the smallpox goddess Śītalā in West Bengal'. *Man in India*, 53 (1): 79–104.

Basu, G. 1405 BS. *Bāṅglār laukik debatā,* Kolkata. Dey's Publishing.

Becker, C.B. 1993. *Paranormal Experiences and Survival of Death.* Albany, SUNY Press.

Belongia, E.A. 2003. 'Smallpox Vaccine: The Good, the Bad, and the Ugly'. *Clinical Medicine and Research,* 1 (2): 87–92.

Bhaṭṭāchāryya, H. 1997. 'Śītalā', in *Hinduder debadebī,* vol 3, Kolkata. Firma KLM, 150–55.

Bhattacharya, S. 2001. 'Re-devising Jennerian Vaccines? European Technologies, Indian Innovation and the Control of Smallpox in South Asia, 1850–1950', in B. Pati and M. Harrison (eds), *Health, Medicine and Empire: Perspectives on Colonial India,* pp. 217–69. New Delhi, Orient Longman.

———. 2006. *Expunging Variola: The Control and Eradication of Smallpox in India, 1947–1977.* New Delhi, Orient Longman.

Bhattacharya, S., Harrison M., Wordboys M. 2005. *Fractured States: Smallpox, Public Health And Vaccination Policy In British India 1800–1947.* New Delhi, Orient Longman.

Bhattacharyya, D. 1986. *Pāgalāmi: Ethnopsychiatric Knowledge in Bengal.* Maxwell School of Citizenship and Public Affairs, Syracuse, New York.

Bidhyābinod, K. (ed.) 1408 BS. *Bṛhat bāromese meyeder bratakathā,* Kolkata, Akshay Library.

Biswas, S. 1999. *Samsad Bengali English Dictionary*. Calcutta: Sahitya Samsad.

Bose, P.K. (ed.) 2006. *Health and Society in Bengal: A Selection from Late 19th-Century Bengali Periodicals.* New Delhi and London: Sage Publications.

Brimnes, N. 2004. 'Variolation, Vaccination and Popular Resistance in Early Colonial South India', *Medical History,* 48: 199–228.

Burrow, T. and Emeneau, M.B. 1984. *A Dravidian Etymological Dictionary.* Oxford, Clarendon Press.

Carrin, M. 1999. 'Reasserting identity through suffering: healing rituals in Bengal and Karnataka', in M. Carrin (ed), *Managing Distress. Possession and Therapeutic Cults in South Asia,* pp. 90–113. Delhi: Manohar.

Chacko, A.M. 1980. 'A Goddess Defied', *World Health* (May), 14–17.

Dimock, E.C. Jr. 1982. 'A Theology of the Repulsive: The Myth of the Goddess Śītalā', in J.S. Hawley and D.M. Wulff (eds), *The Divine Consort: Rādhā and the Goddesses of India,* pp. 184–203. Berkeley, University of California Press.

Ferrari, F.M. 2007a. 'Love me two times. From smallpox to AIDS. Contagion and possession in the cult of Śītalā.' *Religion of South Asia,* 1 (1), 81–106.

———. 2007b. 'Baciami e uccidimi. Śītalā le madri ambigue del Bengala: amore materno, ira divina ed epidemie', in M. Marchetto (ed.),

Le maschere di dio e l'ira del cielo: divinita' terrifiche e angeli vendicatori, pp. 183–224. Venezia, CaFoscarina.

Ferrari, F.M. and Refolo M. 2005. 'Mito e contagio: per un'analisi comparativa dei *Śītalāmaṅgalkābya* e de *Il Cromosoma Calcutta*', *Annali di Ca' Foscari*, 44 (3): 139–63.

Filippi, G.G. 2002. 'Il movimento della Devī: un'epidemia di possessione collettiva', *Annali di Ca' Foscari*, 41 (3): 191–210.

Foulston, L. 2003. *At the Feet of the Goddess: The Divine Feminine in Local Hindu Religion*. Delhi, Adarsh Books.

Glynn, I. and Glynn J. 2004. *The Life and Death of Smallpox*. London: Profile Books.

Gramsci, A. 2005. *La Questione Meridionale*. Roma: Editori Riuniti.

Greenhough, P. 1980. 'Variolation and Vaccination in South Asia c. 1700–1865: A Preliminary Note', *Social Science and Medicine*, 14: 345–47.

Hahn, R.A. 1984. 'Rethinking "Illness" and "Diseases"', *Contribution to Asian Studies*, 18: 1–23.

Hāphij, A. 1978. *Laukik saṁskār o bengali samāj*. Dhākā: Muktadhār.

Holwell, J.Z. 1971. 'An Account of the Manner of Inoculating for the Smallpox in the East Indies (Reprint of 1767 edition)', in Dharmapal, *Indian Science and Technology in the Eighteen Century: Some Contemporary European Accounts*, pp. 143–63. Delhi: Impex India.

Junghare, I.Y. 1975. 'Songs of the Goddess Shitala: Religio-cultural and Linguistic Features', *Man in India*, 55 (4): 298–316.

Katyal, A. and Kishore N. 2001. 'Performing the goddess: sacred ritual into professional performance', *The Drama Review*, 45 (1), 96–117.

Kolenda, P. 1982. 'Pox and the Terror of Childlessness: Images and Ideas of the Smallpox Goddess in a North Indian Village', in J.J. Preston (ed.), *Mother Worship*, pp. 227–50. Chapel Hill: University of North Carolina Press.

Maity, P.K. 2001. *Historical Studies in the Cult of the Goddess Manasā: A Socio-Cultural Study*. Kolkata, Punthi Pustak.

Majumdār, Ā. 1991. *Meyeder bratakathā*. Kolkata: Deb Sāhitya Kuthir.

McDaniel, J. 1989. *The Madness of the Saints: Ecstatic Religion in Bengal*. Chicago, The University of Chicago Press.

Monier-Williams, M. 1997. *Sanskrit-English Dictionary*, Delhi: Motilal Banarsidass.

Monier-Williams, Sir M. and Coote, H.C. 1880. 'Indian Mother worship', *The Folk-Lore Record*, 3 (1): 117–23.

Mukhopadhyay, S.K. 1994. *Cult of Goddess Śītalā in Bengal: An Enquiry into Folk Culture*. Calcutta: Firma KLM.

Naraindas, H. 2003. 'Preparing for the Pox: A Theory of Smallpox in Bengal and Britain', *Asian Journal of Social Sciences*, 31 (2): 304–39.

Neog, M. 1994. 'The Worship of Ai, the Smallpox Goddess', in *Religions of the North-East*, pp. 50–61. Delhi: Munshiram Manoharlal.

Nicholas, R. 2003. *Fruits of Worship: Practical Religion in Bengal.* New Delhi: Chronicle Books.
Nichter, M. 1987. 'Kyasanur Forest Disease: An Ethnography of a Disease of Development,' *Medical Anthropological Quarterly New Series*, 1 (4): 406–23.
Pallikadavath, S., Sreedharan C., and Stones R.W. 2006. 'Source of AIDS Awareness among Women in India', *AIDS Care*, 18 (1): 44–48.
Portnoy, A. 2000. 'A Goddess in the Making. A Very Hard-to-find Town in India Builds a Shrine to a Goddess for AIDS', http://www.findarticles.com/p/articles/mi_m0GER/is_2000_Fall/ai_66240450 (accessed 14 May 2007).
Shepherd McClain, C. 2005. 'A New Look at an Old Disease: Smallpox and Biotechnology', in M.C. Inhorn and P. J. Brown (eds), *The Anthropology of Infectious Disease: International Health Perspectives*, pp. 97–117. Amsterdam: Routledge.
Smallpox Commission of Bengal, India 1850. *Report of the Smallpox Commissioners, Appointed by Government, with an Appendix, Calcutta, 1st July 1850*. Calcutta: J.C. Sheriff, Military Orphan Press.
Smith, F.M. 2006. *The Self Possessed: Deity and Spirit Possession in South Asian Literature and Civilization*. New York: Columbia University Press.
Stewart, D. 1844. *Report on Small-pox in Calcutta, 1833–34, 1837–38, 1843–44; and Vaccination in Bengal, from 1827 to 1844*. Calcutta: Huttmann.
Stewart, T.K. 1995. 'Encountering the Smallpox Goddess: The Auspicious Song of Śītalā', in D.S. Lopez, Jr. (ed.), *Religions of India in Practice*, pp. 389–97. Princeton: Princeton University Press.
Sujatha, V. 2007. 'Pluralism in Indian medicine: medical lore as a genre of medical knowledge', *Contribution to Indian Sociology*, 41 (2): 169–202.
Svāmī Nirmalānanda, 1390 BS. *Debadebī o tāder bāhan*. Kalikātā: Bhārat Sebāśram Saṅga.
Wadley, S.S. 1980. 'Śītalā: The Cool One', *Asian Folklore Studies*, 39: 33–62.
Wilce, J.M. 1997. 'Discourse, Power, and the Diagnosis of Weakness: Encountering Practitioners in Bangladesh', *Medical Anthropology Quarterly*, 11 (3): 352–74.
Wujastyk, D. 1987. '"A pious fraud": the Indian claims for pre-Jennerian smallpox vaccination', in G.J. Meulenbeld and D. Wujastyk, *Studies on India Medical History*, pp. 131–67. Groningen, Egbert Forsten.

7

Transfer of Ritual in a Local Tradition

Some Observations[1]

Barbara Schuler

This essay is concerned with the question of what happens when a ritual performed within a local tradition is transferred to another setting within the same tradition. It focuses on one type of ritual held in honour of a local goddess and compares the variants within it. I have relied mainly on ethnographical and textual materials as my sources, and sought to turn to account the anthropological insights formulated by Don Handelman in his study of ritual dynamics. I do not, then, aim at suggesting a new line of approach but rather at examining and proving the applicability of parameters set by Handelman to the material collected by me in the southernmost parts of Tamil Nadu, South India. I shall demonstrate by means of the tools at hand how the ritual performed individually by different social groups differs in its inner logic and complexity, in conspicuous agreement with each group's socio-cultural outlook and needs outside the ritual; and in the end draw a tentative conclusion, namely that we witness two main categories of ritual design which can be correlated with the two traditional (emic) divisions of the Tamil social order to which the social groups belong.

Introduction

Once a year a *koṭai* ritual is performed at different times and places in honour of the local Tamil goddess Icakkiyammaṉ[2] who, as her legend relates, is capable of killing, and indeed does so. This *koṭai* festival requires not only that the goddess be brought various gifts (hence the name *koṭai*),[3] but also that her legend be sung.

It is only by doing so that she is made to come into being. Of particular relevance for the discussion in this essay is the fact that the cult of Icakki has become the focus of social and political interests over which three different communities compete with one another. These groups are: first, the influential Vēḷāḷas,[4] who have traditionally been the dominant upholders of the ritual tradition; second, the Nāṭārs, nowadays an economically successful social group, which has traditionally been associated with the bow-song[5] performance of the goddess's legend; and third, an economically weak group, the Barbers (Ampaṭṭars), who traditionally have had no say in ritual matters. Due to social changes, the patronage of the yearly ritual festival is a concern that has come to be shared by the second and third groups. By looking at the ritual practice of these three groups individually, we learn to differentiate the ways in which they impart a dynamic force to their *koṭai* ritual, and to recognise the meaning that is generated from it. Such a comparative view is worthwhile both for those interested in the dynamics of ritual *per se* and those who want to obtain a better understanding of the various cultural attitudes, social realities, needs and perceptions of social groups on the basis of rituals.

By proceeding on the assumption that the forms of the *koṭai* ritual of the three social groups are similar not because each group has drawn on a common source, but because the ritual has to a large extent been adopted from one group and incorporated into the religious practice of another group, we obtain a means of viewing the development of variants and the varying motivation for adopting a ritual. It can be assumed that borrowers will tend to revise the modules they are incorporating into their own *koṭai* ritual, especially when they are taking them from another social group. Similarly, the 'source' ritual may have ritual segments which the members of another group will not wish to adopt, or if they do so, they will perhaps not understand their inner logic. The source ritual is a means of evaluating ritual variants and may alert us to coherent or less straightforward transfers of ritual. It is a crucial guide to a clearer perception of what is and is not adopted.

In this essay, which is largely empirically-oriented and uses the approach of Don Handelman,[6] I shall communicate a number of conclusions concerning the transfer of ritual in a local tradition[7] reached through the comparison of basically one single key element of the ritual under discussion. I shall address the following questions: what happens to the ritual and the bow-song text when they are adopted by another social group? And what happens when the responsibility for them is transferred from a particular social group to a government-affiliated authority? I shall first of all briefly introduce the translocal legend[8] of the goddess. Basing myself on case studies, I shall then present a description and analysis of the ritual of Group One (the Vēḷāḷas). I shall at the same time illustrate the complexity of their ritual by elaborating on its inner design[9] and sequential order. This will be followed by an inquiry into the rituals of Groups Two (the Nāṭārs) and Three (the Barbers) together with a consideration of the corresponding ritual at a temple run by a government-affiliated authority and no longer community-based. I shall then set forth how the selected key element reflects the dynamics and programme of each social group's ritual and that of the government-affiliated authority. Further, I shall also demonstrate how the ritual design is related to the social order. In the final section, I shall attempt, on the basis of the presented material, to draw a number of conclusions, which perhaps can contribute to a theory of the transfer of ritual.

The Text

I shall begin with a synopsis of the epic-length text[10] (*katai*) that forms our primary source material, embedded as it is in the annual *koṭai* ritual. The story (sung by a bow-song group) starts off with a sequence of events that reaffirms a gender stereotype: males kill, females bear babies. But with the tragic murder of a childless woman, the story pattern is inverted. The female who is killed becomes an avenging goddess. She not only kills her own murderer, who formerly was her lover, but also avenges her brother's death, causing thus the extinction of an entire community. What follows is a more detailed account.

> The story begins with the birth stories of the main characters and moves on to the Brahmin priest, who has squandered the entire temple treasury on his lover, a *devadāsi* (temple dancer). When he runs out of money, he is thrown out by the woman's mother. He then leaves the village, but his lover runs after and catches up with him. Further along the way, when she grows tired and falls asleep, he kills her and steals her ornaments. Only a *kaḷḷi* plant[11] is witness to this. The brother of the murdered woman finds her and commits suicide. The

> murderer dies too, bitten by a snake. This first part of the narrative, in which the violation occurs, is only a small fraction of the whole. The major part of the story takes place in the second portion, in which the murdered *devadāsī* becomes an avenging goddess. In this portion, the three persons are reborn: the Brahmin as a merchant's son, with a margosa leaf to protect him from evil, and the murdered lover and her brother as twins of the Cōḻaṉ king. However, the twins turn out to be *pēy*s (hungry spirits)[12] and are abandoned in the forest under a margosa tree (Tamil *vēmpu,* Hindi *nīm*). There the twin brother is murdered by landowning Vēḷāḷas, who cut down the tree in which he has been living as a hungry spirit. The woman swears an oath to take revenge on both the merchant and the Vēḷāḷa landowners.[13] After a long search, she finds the merchant and chases him through the forest to a nearby village, where the seventy Vēḷāḷas live. There the merchant pleads with the Vēḷāḷas to protect him. Then the avenging woman appears before the assembly of the Vēḷāḷas, disguised and with a branch of the *kaḷḷi* plant in the guise of a baby in her arms. She pretends to be the legitimate wife of the merchant and lays claim to him as her husband. Since no decision has been made by the time the sun is setting, the two are locked in a room overnight, in the belief that they are a couple. The merchant, knowing the woman to be a demoness, is afraid, but the seventy Vēḷāḷas promise their own lives as security for his. In the intimate setting of the room, the woman sings the merchant to sleep with a lullaby, thereby convincing the people that all is well. However, when the protective margosa leaf falls from his hand she kills the merchant and escapes by way of the roof. The avenging goddess, in a second move, takes revenge on the Vēḷāḷas by assuming the shape of an old woman who claims to be the merchant's mother. When the Vēḷāḷas come in the morning, they find the man covered in blood and the *kaḷḷi* plant on his chest.[14] The Vēḷāḷas are forced to be true to their word and commit suicide. Then the goddess kills their wives and children with poisoned milk, thus extinguishing all trace of the community. Afterwards she is reunited with her brother.

I hasten to add that this bow-song text — its title is *Icakkiyammaṉ Katai* — cannot fully be understood separately from its performance in the *koṭai* ritual. Ultimately, it is the interpretative potential of the ritual that illuminates and communicates the essential message of the text. I shall be speaking of this ritual here, then, not only as a transformative practice, but also as an indigenous commentary on the bow-song text, while my own anthropological inquiry is an interpretation of that commentary.

Turning now to the initial questions, we shall consider what happens to the bow-song text when it is adopted by another social group. The field research has shown that except for minor modifications the bow-song text as such remains unchanged whenever it has been adopted. When it is performed within the ritual context, however, it becomes quite clear that each social group stages the narrative climax differently. How does this manifest itself? The narrative climax is marked by the fusion of the performance and an act of possession, namely the emergence of the goddess. This emergence, evoked by singing the story of the goddess, does not occur at one and the same point in the rituals of the different social groups, but varies from one to the other. One renowned bow-song bard confirms the difference in emphasis which Group Two (the Nāṭārs) and Group One (the Vēḷāḷas) place with regard to the narrative climax:

> In Nāṭār temples, the *cāmiyāṭṭam,* or the dance of the deity, takes place when the Ceṭṭi merchant is murdered. In Piḷḷaimār [= Vēḷāḷa] temples they don't like this. They want it after their [= the Vēḷāḷas'] death, that is to say, after they went to Kailāsa and received the boon from Śiva. Only then is the power of the deity expected to come.

From my knowledge of the ritual and legend surrounding the goddess, and from the numerous interviews with members of the two groups, I infer that for Group Two, the Nāṭārs, injustice and revenge are the main themes in the legend of the goddess, and obviously ones that also figure prominently in the lives of individual members of the group. In contrast to the Nāṭārs' focus on the ill-treatment and violence done to a person, the privileged landowning Vēḷāḷas are clearly more concerned with the goddess's blockage of fertility and human continuity. In my opinion, the choice of emphasis allows one to draw conclusions about these groups' social identity and economic needs. Unfortunately, given the limitations of this essay, I cannot dwell on this point. Instead I shall proceed to the question raised above relating to the ritual and look into what happens to the ritual when it is adopted by another social group.

The Ritual

Generally we approach a ritual by first establishing its socio-cultural context. However, in this essay I shall follow an approach proposed by the ritual theoretician Don Handelman (2005: 16), who writes 'that a radical way through which to learn of the relationship of ritual to social order is to examine first and foremost what [can be found out about a] ritual in relation to itself.'[15] I shall devote myself, then, to answering the question: How is the ritual organised? This question I shall pose first with regard to the ritual of the Vēḷāḷas,[16] and then, in a next step, draw comparisons with the ritual as practised by the other social groups.

For my comparative study of the *koṭai* ritual of the goddess I am discussing here, I shall take as parameters those of self-organisation, autonomy and complexity, which were introduced by Handelman (2005: 1–32), and inquire into the degree with which they are realised in the ritual of each social group.

The Vēḷāḷas' Ritual

In my field research, which I conducted in 2002 and again in 2003, I intensively analysed the inner logic of the ritual system of the Vēḷāḷas, and discovered it to be a system of astonishing complexity and power that has remained largely unnoticed by the scholarly community.[17] This ritual system of the Vēḷāḷas serves a goddess who is considered to be a split goddess — split, namely, into a younger and an elder sister. Viewed emically, this fragmentation represents two psychological configurations: a wrathful, anti-maternal one reflected in the younger sister, and a harmonised, fertile one reflected in the elder sister. The ritual attempts to heal this split. In this attempt it is a flowerbed (*pūppaṭukkai/pūppaṭaippu*)[18] that commands centre stage.[19] In highlighting the flowerbed segment, however, I do not mean to suggest that other elements are less important, but rather that the flowerbed possesses a remarkable degree of internal dynamic and clearly encapsulates the central idea of the *koṭai* ritual. Its botanical markers, in particular, delineate the transitions which the ritual seeks to produce: away from the highly destructive and menacing aspect of the goddess, very pronounced in the bow-song text, and towards a harmonised — and more importantly, generative and fertilising — presence that serves society. From a psychological point of view, the flowerbed in the ritual system of the Vēḷāḷas reflects a therapeutical concept.

I shall go into this important segment of the Vēḷāḷa *koṭai* ritual, which I have participated in, in somewhat greater detail by first providing a brief description and then an interpretation of it.

> As a direct sequel to the *alaṅkāra tīpārātaṉai* (in our terms, the moment of the goddess's self-recognition and her recognition by others, which eventually brings her to life),[20] the goddess (in the body of a male) comes out of her shrine and descends to the circular, womb-like flowerbed, which is situated in an arena in front of the shrine. S/he is smeared with blazing red *mañcaṇai* paint, indicative of having attained a sexually matured, overheated body. The air is filled with expectation and excitement. People believe that the power of the goddess is felt only on the flowerbed. 'Ammaṉ will come and play (*viḷaiyāṭutal*) on the bed,' they say. Purifying smoke covers the sacred site. An oboe-like *nātasvaram* plays mildly. The drummers and the *nātasvaram* surround the altar-like flowerbed. The flowerbed is gorgeous, with its three layers of plants and flowers: below there is basil (*tuḷaci*) covered with margosa leaves, and above a *Pandanus odoratissimus,*[21] an areca and various other flowers. The body of the *cāmiyāṭi* (the person possessed by the goddess) begins to rock to and fro to the rhythm of the drums (*mēḷam*). The drums start to beat faster, and become dominant. Then s/he gets up from the ground, jumps onto the flowerbed, and in the blink of an eye grabs hold of a handful of the cooling margosa leaves, bites into and chews them. S/he is joyful. The surrounding men perform the *kuravai* (a sound made by flapping the tongue against the palate).[22] The goddess begins to roll around clockwise on the flowerbed. She is extremely joyful. At times the sensual overtones of her behaviour are suggestive of an ecstasy that is, in union with the flowerbed's response, not unlike an orgasmic experience.[23] The goddess cannot look more erotic. Her mouth is crammed full of cooling margosa leaves. She rolls again and again in a circular movement on

> the flowerbed. The heat increases. The *nātasvaram* and drums play with a faster rhythm. The main *pūjāri* shouts: *aṭi, aṭi, aṭi* ('beat, beat, beat [the drum]!'). Men again perform the *kuravai*. Then, all of a sudden, s/he finds and picks the flowers placed in the centre. The goddess smiles happily. She has found and picked the *Pandanus odoratissimus* and areca flowers.

In order to arrive at an appropriate understanding of this ritual segment, a closer look at the acts of rolling on the flowerbed and finding the *Pandanus odoratissimus* and areca flowers is indispensable.

Understanding the rolling on the flowerbed as a key moment of transformation presupposes not only a description of the process, but also an analysis of it. I argue, as already mentioned, that the highly destructive split goddess is invited to reconfigure her broken self on the flowerbed. There is good reason to assume that the flowerbed is the goddess herself; more precisely, another version of her self, one which is fertile. Rolling on the flowerbed is the transformative process itself. I propose that the act of rolling is a three-dimensional movement towards the heart of the goddess's cosmos, the centre of erotic harmony and fertility. In concrete terms, it is a movement into the three layers of the flowerbed towards the centre, the location of the *Pandanus odoratissimus* and the areca flower, flowers which signify sexuality.[24] Finding these flowers is, in our terms, finding and merging with the fertile version of one's self. Thus the rolling on the flowerbed is an outward manifestation of an inward transformative process that leads not only to the goddess's reconfiguration, but simultaneously, and of greater importance for the ritual participants, to a change in her cosmos, which is now seen as profoundly social.

The flowerbed segment is embedded in the sequencing of the ritual at three points: in the first ritual cycle at noon, in the second ritual cycle at 1 o'clock the next morning, and in the third ritual cycle around midday the same day. Each cycle has its own peak moments: in the first cycle it is the flowerbed segment; in the second cycle it is the drinking of a kid goat's blood and the divinatory spinning of a coconut; and in the third cycle it is the goddess's bathing in water mixed with turmeric *(mañcaḷ nīrāṭṭu)*. The three cycles together have a climax of their own, which occurs in the second cycle. The second cycle is at the same time an intensification of the first, since it multiplies the signs and draws the goddess deeper into the ritual. In terms of activity and mood, there is an increase of heat and ritual arousal of eroticism.[25] As regards the individual segments, each one must take place in the specified sequential order. Each of the components is dependent on the one before to do its part towards producing a result. The goddess cannot emerge before she is made aware of herself in the *alaṅkāra tīpārātaṉai*. She must not come out of her shrine before the flowerbed is prepared. Her becoming overheated and eroticised should occur in the middle of the night rather than at noon. The goddess's drinking of the *tuvaḷai* kid goat's blood, and equally important, the divinatory spinning of the coconut for the benefit of childless couples, cannot occur until the goddess has been recomposed and made keenly aware of her fertile self. We can see that single modules cannot be rearranged without doing harm to the integrity and efficacy of the whole.

The ritual system of the Vēḷāḷas is indeed marked by the high degree of its self-containment, its compact wholeness. This is immediately evident not only from the complex circular and three-dimensional movement on the flowerbed, but also from the fact that the ritual courses around and re-establishes a link to the beginning of the legend of the goddess (the birth stories), thus carrying us full circle back from death to human fertility. In doing so, the ritual sets procreation against the fatal denouement of the narrative. Here we see a great ritual dynamic, with the movement being from death to new life. The ritual turns the goddess back upon herself. It is an inner dynamic that works towards change. What comes out at the end is different from what was before. Two points will make this clear: First, the violent goddess, after rolling on the flowerbed, returns to her shrine not bent on destruction, but rather eroticised and otherwise transformed. Second, the kid goat is slaughtered; however, its blood is turned into new life. At the end there are clear signs of a transformed goddess who gives up opposing reproduction, and of transformed goat's blood that becomes foetuses in the wombs of the childless women. The childless women, too, then, are different than before. That this ritual system has repercussions in domestic life is reflected in the divinatory spinning of the coconut, meant to unblock the forces of fertility that have been dysfunctional in the childless couples who have come to ask the goddess for help. With the spinning of the coconut, the ritual opens up to the outside world — to the childless couples, who receive a most direct form of help from the reconfigured and now highly self-aware goddess.

I would propose that this ritual practice manages to do what the split goddess and the childless women — I believe we can view them as analogous — could not have done by themselves. This, in my opinion, is what makes the ritual practice of the Vēḷāḷas most powerful. By building on intimacy and positive emotionality, it allows for an experience that is radically different from the social patterns outside the ritual. Thus the ritual can claim an independent status. In Handelman's (2005: 12) theory of ritual, the otherness of experience within a ritual compared to the experience outside the ritual world is the mark of a ritual which not only manifests a high degree of self-organisation, but is also distinguished by its autonomy and power to bring about change.

The Nāṭārs' Ritual

After this all too brief sketch, I again stress that the argumentation of my comparative study of the Icakki *koṭai* ritual of three social groups is based mainly on one single segment within that ritual, namely that of the flowerbed. This ritual segment offers us some interesting ethnographical material. We find it in the *koṭai* ritual of the Vēḷāḷas and Barbers, but not in the ritual of the Nāṭārs. What does the absence of this ritual segment tell us about the programme of the Nāṭārs' ritual? It seems to me that the absence of the flowerbed segment in the ritual of the Nāṭār community restricts the dynamics of transformation to the bow-song text; that is to say, transformation occurs in the social order rather than in the ritual moment. Thus the motivation is completely different from that of the Vēḷāḷas' ritual, which aims at biological continuity and the removal of infertility and bears the marks of a therapeutically attuned culture. The programme of the Nāṭārs' ritual does not appear to offer a radically different experience, of the type produced by the Vēḷāḷas', but rather concentrates on the world portrayed in the text, a world that mirrors social realities. In this ritual, then, the forces of injustice and revenge command centre stage, and what the ritual attempts to do is to pacify the wild goddess rather than to transform her. In this the Nāṭārs are clearly driven by their need of her protection in cases of conflict. Here informants' statements that the establishment of Nāṭār shrines for this goddess increases whenever there are escalating confrontations between groups over competing interests are worth noting.[26]

The Barbers' Ritual

Having considered the Nāṭār ritual, let us now turn to the ritual of the Barbers.[27] In this ritual practice, unlike in the Nāṭārs', we do find the flowerbed element. Now here the crucial question seems to me to be whether the ritual design of the Barbers' *koṭai* has the same therapeutic, autonomous and transformative qualities as the Vēḷāḷas'. I would answer this in the negative. The two rituals of the two social groups convey two different meanings in the flowerbed segment. In the case of the Barber ritual, this segment suffers a loss of complexity and inner dynamic. This is first of all indicated by the fact that the crucial moment of rolling on the flowerbed is missing. This circular movement immediately lends a heightened degree of integrity to the Vēḷāḷas' ritual, and is, in fact, as inscribed in it, the very transformative process itself. Here, however, it is missing. Therefore I would suggest that radical change is not integral to the Barbers' ritual programme. This, in a sense, is not very surprising, because the Barbers underwent a fundamental shift in their perception of the goddess at the time they adopted the cult. For them she is not the 'hot goddess' of demonic character, a fact which comes out clearly, first in the shift of the timing of the *koṭai* ritual from the hottest and driest season to the windy, rainy month of Āṭi (middle of July till middle of August), and second in the goddess's iconography: she has neither fangs and a trolling tongue nor a baby in her mouth.[28] Hence any radical change in the goddess would be superfluous. But then what is the meaning of the flowerbed ritual here? In my view, the purpose of the flowerbed has been reduced to proving the possessed person's identity with the deity. Here, finding and picking the *Pandanus odoratissimus* flower is concrete evidence that the finder *is* the deity. The fact that the flowerbed and the picking of the *Pandanus odoratissimus* are not exclusively confined to the goddess but also fall within the province of other deities supports the argument.

Various other changes in the Barbers' *koṭai* ritual make for a specific difference that in one way or another is relevant to the very identity of the ritual. For instance, there is a shift from solemnity towards entertainment and spectacular feats, which attract the attention of the gathering: comical acts, the performance of folk arts (for instance, *karakam*) and fire walking (*tīmiti*). Here we must ask ourselves whether these changes do not compromise the ritual's identity? Or in other words: can we still call it a ritual, or should we label it rather an event? Clearly it is a different way of experiencing the ritual action. Bearing in mind what I have briefly outlined here, we may conclude that in comparison with the Vēḷāḷa ritual, the programme of the Barbers' *koṭai* ritual shifts from transformative processes induced by intimacy and positive emotionality towards painful and exhaustive bodily disciplines, as seen not only in the fire walking in the *pūkuḻi* (fire pit) at the peak moment at 2:30 AM, but also in hooks being inserted in the necks and backs of devotees at the start of the festival. The experience undergone within the ritual is thus not radically different from what occurs in the world outside the ritual. On the whole, the ritual shows few signs of either self-containment or self-organisational skill. It is, compared with the Vēḷāḷas' ritual, no longer an undertaking to respond to the text's message. In sum, it seems to me that the ritual programme is less one of transformation, as indicated by the absence of the movement of rolling on the flowerbed. Rather the ritual has an incorporative function. We may see in it the emergence of an integrated Barber (Ampaṭṭar) culture. The establishment of an Icakki *koṭai* of their own some twenty years ago has evidently facilitated the process of coexistence and integration of this low-ranking, politically powerless social group.

The Ritual Organised by a Government-Affiliated Temple Authority

One more question remains to be asked: what happens when the responsibility for the ritual and text is transferred from a social group (in this case, the Vēḷāḷas) to a government-affiliated authority?[29] In terms of the above parameters (self-organisation, autonomy and complexity) the ritual changes greatly. Again the flowerbed[30] segment provides major supporting evidence. The goddess's scattering of the flowers in all directions rather than rolling around on (and into) the layers of flowers and plants marks a clear divergence. Instead of being an internally bound movement through one's own self that ends up back at the point of origin, it is now rather a horizontal movement of dispersion. We may see here a shift from self-enclosure towards opening up to a broader world. The flowerbed segment thus brings out most unambiguously the programmatic change within this design of the *koṭai* ritual, one that is less concerned with radical change and autonomy than in developing the horizontal extension of social and cultural ties, as indexed by visitors from a wide geographical area extending into neighbouring Kerala. This opening up to representatives of cultures and social patterns that have developed along different lines creates a new kind of ritual dynamic that binds people together who depend on revitalisation and resourcefulness. All this necessarily alters the organisational features of the flowerbed segment and, moreover, the relationship between ritual and bow-song text. As to the relationship between ritual and text, it seems to have changed to such an extent that their interaction — and in particular, the ability of the text to flush the goddess out into the open, so to speak — must be called into question. Interestingly enough, in the *koṭai* ritual performed at the government-affiliated (non-community-based) temple, the local story of the goddess, generally presented as a direct sequel to the translocal story, is entirely absent. This is not surprising, since this *koṭai* ritual is probably not meant to serve so much local or caste identity as the cultural identity of the region, a region that, prior to the linguistic division into Kerala and Tamil Nadu in 1956, coincided with Nāñcilnāṭu.[31] Remarkably, the transfer of the ritual to a government-affiliated authority has brought about a change of attitude not only towards the bow-song performance (which no longer generates ritual depth[32]), but also towards individual ritual segments — for instance, the animal sacrifice, the prohibition of which is a demand that was put forward by the authority in charge of the temple. Needless to say, a different mode of perception towards the goddess has emerged here.[33] While iconographically still a demonic *(pēy)* goddess, she is treated as a benevolent one.[34]

The Relation of Ritual Design to Social Order

I have attempted to show in the evaluation above with regard to the Vēḷāḷas' ritual as compared to the Nāṭārs' and Barbers', and of the rituals of social groups as compared to a non-community-based ritual, that while there is a general similarity in ritual procedure, the ritual tradition is not uniform, displaying at least two clearly divergent designs — a fairly self-contained, intimate and solemn one and a more linear, public and entertaining one — that exist side by side. In this section I look at conceptual features of social organisation found in Tamil Nadu, and try to relate the two distinctive ritual designs to the social order existing outside the ritual. Two indigenous social categories which have long been integral to Tamil society can be shown to be useful in this regard: the right-hand and left-hand communities.[35] According to anthropological literature, the right-hand division comprises agricultural and landowning groups, among them the Nāṭārs[36] and Vēḷāḷas[37].[38] In contrast, the left-hand division comprises trading and artisan communities. The Barbers are among these latter groups, which follow professions that afford a certain degree of social interaction.[39] For our discussion, these two divisions have the advantage of serving as a basis for interpreting social behaviour and attitudes. If we proceed on the basis of these right- and left-hand categories, differences in ritual practice among the three social groups, in my opinion, can be convincingly explained. The example of the *cāmiyāṭi,* the person designated to embody the goddess Icakki, can serve to illustrate this. In the *koṭai* ritual of the left-hand Barbers, the *cāmiyāṭi* is a woman. The right-hand Vēḷāḷas, contrarily, designate exclusively males; in the right-hand Nāṭārs' ritual, to be sure, women are possessed, but this is an unforeseen occurrence.[40] These divergences reflect differences in the prestige markers and modesty rules operative among members of the two categories. Among the left-hand service groups such as the Barbers, women enjoy a certain freedom of movement, whereas the right-hand groups, such as the Vēḷāḷas and Nāṭārs, who are particular about all forms of interaction, keep their wives under strict control. Noteworthily, these latter two are the social groups that iconographically depict the goddess we are concerned with in her unrestrained and violent form.

The Vēḷāḷas and Nāṭārs are guided, then, by similar models, but these two right-hand groups nevertheless differ considerably in social prestige and local power.[41] This point is relevant when we examine ritual design in relation to social order. In the Tamil view, material wealth is one kind of power, but only when financial and political power is combined with ritual competence is it considered superior.[42] And it is here that the social groups enter into competition with one another. As I mentioned earlier, the autonomous, high-ranking Vēḷāḷas have traditionally been the main upholders of the ritual tradition of the goddess Icakki, while the Nāṭārs have for their part been mainly confined to the role of performing the bow-song text of the goddess's legend.[43] It is not surprising that the wealth of this latter populous community, as it progressed both socially and economically,[44] should have enabled them to gain a measure of control over the ritual tradition surrounding the *Icakkiyammaṉ Katai* text that they perform, and so to tap this force and direct it according to their own needs and creative potential.

Given that ritual design is intimately bound up with the complexities of group culture, it is important to exercise caution when formulating general theories about it. Although it is not my intention to present a general theory, it is nevertheless necessary to present different possible ways of viewing the interrelation of ritual and social realities. To begin with, we may state that social advancement occurs in the context of competition and tension, and hence there is a corresponding need (as can be seen in the case of the Nāṭārs) for protection from acts of social violence. Landowning peasant-farmers exercise control over the soil and women, depending as they do on the fertility of both.[45] The service group, on the other hand, controls nothing and usually must merely tend to the wishes of others. Each of these social realities, as we can readily see, interacts with the reality given within the ritual[46] and generates its own ritual dynamic, and each force within the ritual dynamic tends towards a distinct outcome. What the Barbers put in and take out is not the same as what the Vēḷāḷas and Nāṭārs do. As we have seen, the former, by means of the ritual,[47] have gained the status of a ritually recognised group within the local area, with a visibly left-hand identity, while the Vēḷāḷas, whose perception is directed towards cyclical processes of dying and becoming, have ensured their biological continuity[48] in an act of procreating themselves anew.[49] The Nāṭārs for their part, as mentioned above, use the transformative force of the bow-song text for negotiating power balances. That transformation for them is meant to occur in the social order rather than in the ritual moment seems logical if we acknowledge the Nāṭārs' identity as a 'community in change.'[50]

From what has been said up till now, it is of little surprise that the low-ranking social groups do not faithfully adhere to the ritual design of the high-ranking Vēḷāḷas. Although the left-hand Barbers, for instance, have adopted all elements from the Vēḷāḷas' ritual tradition, their *koṭai* ritual clearly differs in inner design and in the directedness of its dynamic force.[51] Here the treatment of the flowerbed, which also has come to be a fixed part of the Barbers' ritual, is particularly instructive.

The above sketch of the three social groups, and their classing as either right- or left-hand communities, has shown that the emic right- and left-hand dichotomy is particularly well suited for understanding the relation of ritual design to social order. I argue for a correlation of two main organisational ritual features with the two social categories. There is reason to regard self-containedness,[52] solemnity and depth (which signifies a full immersion into ritual liminality) as the organisational rationale behind the ritual design of the right-hand groups,[53] whereas the rationale behind that of the left-hand group (the design here being quite similar to the non-community-based, government-affiliated ritual) is a more linear, less internally bound one, moving along the surface. Judging in terms of the degree of self-contained wholeness, a marker (as Handelman has suggested) linked with the parameters of inner self-organisation and complexity, the Vēḷāḷas' ritual, which negotiates the issue of human existence itself (rather than social position), exhibits the highest degree among the forms of the ritual dealt with.[54]

Concluding Remarks

As far as I can tell at present, on the basis of the rituals that I have analysed, and on the basis of the interviews I have conducted, there are important differences between the ritual practice of the groups we have been discussing here. My comparative study of their organisation and programmatic features has mainly been based on the flowerbed segment, using the parameters of complexity, independence and wholeness. These parameters, we see, decline in intensity as we move away from the Vēḷāḷas' ritual. The Vēḷāḷa ritual has a reality of its own, a dynamic space quite independent of the social world outside it — with an individual inner logic and a force for radical change that is based on intimacy and emotional empathy, and directed to solving an existential crisis. Such a ritual design is absent in the rituals we have compared it with. The ritual of the other social groups either restricts the scope of the resourcefulness and transformational dynamic it embodies to the bow-song text, a narrated world that is recognisably continuous with social realities outside the ritual (as in the case of the Nāṭārs' ritual), or else (as seen in the Barbers') it suffers a loss of ritual depth and transformation in the priority it assigns to entertainment and spectacular feats. Turning to the ritual for which a government-affiliated authority is responsible, its programmatic ambitions (in comparison to the Vēḷāḷas') shift from a centred, internally-bound movement to a horizontal, extensive one, and so are associated with linear processes[55] and intermixing rather than with cyclical processes and self-reference. The ritual acts here as a cohesive force that unites the heterogeneous rather than the homogeneous, and displays a multiplicity of cross ties.

However, the community–non-community dichotomy does not represent a real parallel to a tradition–modernity continuum. As we move from the more isolated village *koṭai* ritual to the *koṭai* at a government-affiliated shrine along a national highway, we do not necessarily find a ritual practice in the process of modernising (in the latter, possession is still a prominent element); rather one that merely appears as such, in that it is in the process of widening out to a broader, somewhat anonymous world.[56]

Still, everything that I have said can be no more than provisional in nature, since further fieldwork will be necessary to finally confirm this view.

◈

Figure 1: A newly made terra-cotta figure of the goddess Icakkiyammaṉ, to whom a *pūjā* and blood sacrifice is performed. The goddess is wrapped in a red silk sari. She is adorned with several ornaments such as bangles, *meṭṭis* (toe-rings), *cilampus* (anklets), a *mēkalai* (waistbelt, a sign of long life), a *tāli* (the *tāli*, a string, is not necessarily a sign of marriage; in Malabar matrilinear society it was the custom to tie a *tāli* around the neck as a sign of sexual maturation), and earrings. A dot of fresh blood marks the centre of her forehead. Her neck, arms, and face look as if they were smeared with turmeric. She carries a baby on her left arm. Her widely opened collyrium-smeared eyes flash menace. On her head is a colourfully striped crown. Taken by her beauty, one would almost have overlooked her lolling blood-red tongue, her fangs, and the two babies, one crunched between her pearly-white teeth and one pinioned under her feet, and her right arm held head-high with a knife in hand (all signs of her wrathful nature).

Source: All photographs by the author, taken during a Vēḷāḷa *koṭai* ritual in honour of the goddess Icakkiyammaṉ, 7–8 May 2002.

Figure 2: A bow-song (*villuppāṭṭu*) group

Figure 3: The flowerbed (*pūppaṭukkai/pūppaṭaippu*), a key element in the ritual system of the Vēḷāḷas

Figure 4: A possession dance with a flaming torch (*tīpantam*). The burning torch comes from the inner sanctum of the goddess's shrine. There is an increase of heat and ritual arousal of eroticism. The *cāmiyāṭi* (the one who dances the goddess) touches his body lightly with the fire of the torch, brushing the torch past his chest and rotating it over his head and shoulders while dancing. In this segment of the Vēḷāḷas' ritual system, the goddess's inner heat needs to be augmented by an outer heat that is, it may be argued, of a generative and fertile quality.

Notes

1. A version of this paper was first presented at the Nineteenth European Conference of Modern South Asian Studies, Leiden, 29 June 2006.
2. For a thorough study of the goddess Icakkiyammaṉ, who in her texts goes also by the name Nīli, see Schuler (2004). Kaṉṉiyākumari and Tirunelvēli districts (in Tamil Nadu) are the main centres of the cult of this goddess, with Tūṭṭukuṭi (Tuticorin) district a third one of less significance. For an iconographical depiction, see Figure 1.
3. *Koṭai,* the Tamil word for 'gift,' is generally used when referring to the annual festival held in honour of a local deity.
4. The two forms Vēḷāḷa and Veḷḷāḷa are in usage. However, the former is considered to be the older of the two. Vēḷāḷas are also known as Piḷḷaimārs.
5. Tamil *villuppāṭṭu* (*vil,* 'bow' and *pāṭṭu,* 'song') is a genre that only exists in the three southernmost districts of Tamil Nadu. For a thorough

discussion of this tradition, see Blackburn (1980). The bow *(vil)* is the main instrument used in the performance (see Figure 2). It is usually made of a piece of wood taken from the base of a palmyra tree and is about ten feet long. Eleven (and sometimes thirteen or nine) small bronze bells are attached to it by rings. The bow-string is made of twisted hide. The sound of the played bow combines the tinkle of the bells and the resonance of the string, and is achieved by striking the string with a pair of thin sticks, one in each hand. See also Blackburn (1986: 175).

6. I have settled upon the route marked out by Handelman (2004 and 2005) because his (and Kapferer's) is one that offers new approaches to ritual dynamics within anthropology. It is based on a view of ritual as having a 'reality of its own' (Kapferer 2005: 37), and as exhibiting a dynamic that is constantly connecting external (social order) with internal (ritual content) realities, and vice versa (Handelman 2004: 15), or to speak in Kapferer's (ibid.) terms, the 'surface' to the 'depth' (37).
7. I am not aware of studies that shed light on this issue in South Indian local traditions.
8. We have to distinguish between the goddess's translocal story, which is part of every *koṭai* festival held in honour of this goddess, and the local stories about her.
9. The term is used in Handelman's (2005: 12) sense.
10. The core of this narrative goes back at least to the seventh century C.E. since it was recognisably alluded to in the *bhakti* Śaiva work *Tēvāram* (1.45.1), of probably that date (a date that I have taken over from Zvelebil 1995: 682). The story is recounted throughout Tamil literature; see Caṇmukacuntaram (1978); Zvelebil (1989: 297–301); Schuler (2004, Chapter 3). A translation of one of the longest versions of the bow-song text under discussion is offered in ibid. (Section 5.4).
11. On the *kaḷḷi*-milkweed as a metonymic embodiment of infertility, abandonment, and injustice, see Schuler (2004, Section 6.4, Humans and Plants). The intimate relation between *kaḷḷi* plant and (unborn) baby comes out in a lullaby, full of double meaning, that imagines the plant being a baby boy; see my translation of the bow-song text (ibid., Section 5.4, lines N1.2047–2078).
12. The two terms *pēy* and *pūtam* are used interchangeably by the local people, although they convey different meanings. *Pēy* may derive from Prakrit *peya* (Sanskrit *preta*), 'spirit of a dead person,' while *pūtam,* a loanword, corresponds to Sanskrit *bhūta*, 'demon.' In the year 1713, the Christian missionary Bartholomaeus Ziegenbalg referred to *pēys* as 'evil spirits' (see Nabokov 1997: 299), in accordance with the contemporary usage of the word, which, according to the same author (ibid.), '[...] throughout Tamil Nadu [...] characterizes the spirits of

people who [...] met an 'untimely' [...] death [...] which prevented their transit into the hereafter [...].'

13. On the cases of retaliation and the strong sister–brother bond (the latter echoing a matrilinear kinship system, formerly prevalent in the region), see Schuler (2004, Sections 6.2, A World of Oaths and Honour, and the Anguish of Barren Women, and 6.3, The Sister–Brother Bond and the Case of Retaliation).
14. The *kaḷḷi* plant, having turned into a punitive agent, is the embodiment of a curse, the witness of a murder, and, in brief, the exteriorised expression of a violent male–female relationship. By planting it in her former lover's chest, the avenging woman enacts, I propose, an inverse sexual union, an act opposite to a normal, life-producing union.
15. Handelman (2005) proposes to study in the first place '[r]itual in its own right' (1), and to consider only in a second step the ritual's surrounding world. It seems to me that there are good reasons for following this approach for our investigation: I agree with Handelman that a ritual creates its own virtual reality, with its own inner logic; acceptance of this premise naturally puts a view primarily focused on what is practised within the ritual into the forefront of the study.
16. I am greatly indebted to Prof. Don Handelman and Prof. David Shulman, the Hebrew University of Jerusalem, with whom I discussed parts of my visual ethnographical material relating to the Vēḷāḷas' ritual in 2002 and 2003.
17. For a detailed description and analysis of this ritual system of the Vēḷāḷas, see Schuler (2004, Chapter 9).
18. In the Vēḷāḷa ritual, the terms *pūppaṭukkai* (flowerbed) and *pūppaṭaippu* (flower offering) are used interchangeably.
19. For the design of the flowerbed, see Figure 3.
20. Literally, *alaṅkāra tīpārātaṉai* means the 'rotating of a light source in front of an embellished deity.' On the *alaṅkāram* moment that generates self-recognition and recognition by others, see Schuler (2004, Sections 9.3.2 and 9.3.3).
21. Tamil *tāḻampū,* in classical Tamil literature known as *tāḻai* and *kaitai;* Sanskrit *ketakī/ketaka;* Telugu *mugali;* English *screw pine.* For a detailed discussion of this key ritual floral element, see Schuler (2004, Section 9.3.3).
22. Blackburn (1980: 255) states: 'the kuravai ululation [...] contribute[s] to the extreme ritual depth of the possession [...].'
23. On the flowerbed's cultural meaning as a locus of love-making, see references to Sanskrit and Tamil sources in Schuler (2004, Section 9.2.1, Reflections on the First Flowerbed).
24. On the erotic associations of *Pandanus odoratissimus* flowers, see Gupta (2001: 62f).
25. See Figure 4, which captures one moment in this process.

26. The Maṇṭaikāṭu riot in 1987 in Kalkulam tāluk was such a case. This trauma led people to construct a large number of new Icakki temples (personal communication with different informants). This clearly shows that new temples spread fastest precisely where 'competition and resistance [are] most intense,' an observation made by Ludden (1989: 98) with respect to another, earlier political conflict in the seond half of the eighteenth century. It reflects, moreover, the belief in Icakkiyammaṉ as a protectress.
27. A video documentation of a Icakki *koṭai* festival of Group Three (at Śrī Ālamūṭu Ammaṉ temple) by archivist Peter A. Raj is available at the Folklore Resource and Research Centre, St. Xavier's College, Pālaiyamkōṭṭai, Tirunelvēli, Tamil Nadu. On the origin of this particular temple, see Schuler (2004, Section 7.7.1).
28. In keeping with this no animal sacrifice occurs.
29. In this particular case, a government-affiliated authority took over the temple from the Vēḷāḷas as a result of a conflict that arose between the latter and the Nāṭārs.
30. Along with Tamil *pūppaṭaippu,* the Sanskrit term *puṣpāñjali* (flower offering) is in usage in the context of this non-community-based temple run by a government-affiliated authority.
31. Nāñcilnāṭu, lit. 'Land of the Ploughshare,' also known as the land of wet agriculture. For further details, see Blackburn (1980, Chapter 2).
32. The term 'ritual depth' is Blackburn's (1980: 255). I define ritual depth in the present context as what occurs at the moment when the sacred arena is exposed to a synchronised outpouring of exciting drumbeats, the high-pitched singing style of the *villuppāṭṭu* text, and the ongoing possession. This is usually the moment when the goddess has fully emerged and her devotees are engulfed in the depths of her presence. Ritual depth is also accompanied by moments of ambivalence, when opposing cosmic forces are confronted (see Schuler 2004, Section 9.3.4.1). For features of ritual depth in *koṭai* rituals, see Blackburn (1980: 250ff). One of the markers of ritual depth is its triggering the intervention of assistants in cases of observable injury. For general remarks on ritual depth in *villuppāṭṭu* performances, see ibid. (237ff). On the connection between the *pāṭṭu* style and ritual depth, see ibid. (347ff).
33. Admittedly, this attitude is obviously more the official one than that of individual devotees. Even if ideally no animal at all should be killed, on ordinary days the devotees still come to sacrifice a cock to the goddess behind the temple, as I myself witnessed.
34. We may see here a process in which the goddess's *pēy* persona vanishes and the cult of Icakki transforms itself into the *bhakti* worship of a benevolent image of the goddess.

35. The idea of examining South Indian ritual in terms of the system of left- and right-hand communities was first proposed by Handelman (1995: 331ff.) in his article on gender as a 'continuum' in left-hand castes in Andhra Pradesh. — On the emic division of *valaṅkai* (right hand) and *iṭaṅkai* (left hand), see Beck (1970 and 1972); Hardgrave (1969: 23). See also Stein (1985: 469f.), who, elsewhere dating this dual division to the eleventh century — by comparing its character in the Cōḷa and the later Vijayanagara periods (the major ingress of the latter authority into the Tamil land occurring around the fifteenth century; ibid.: 485) — underscores its continuity.
36. The Nāṭārs are generally better known under their earlier community name Shanar. On the community's petition in the nineteenth century to change their official name in all public records to Nāṭār, see Ludden (1989: 194). For the history of this community, see Hardgrave (1969: Preface, x); also Ludden (1989: 46ff). They are a low-caste people who have traditionally engaged in agricultural labour and the tapping of toddy. On the Nāṭārs' exploitation in the eighteenth century, see *Kanniyakumari District Gazetteer* (2002: 183). Nāṭār settlements have tended to be concentrated in dry zones (Ludden 1989: 67). As Ludden remarks: '[...] people in the dry zone [...] lived in a hard world of stiff competition and locally tight sub-jati solidarity' (84). It is of some interest for our discussion that the cultivators of dry land could produce dry crops and cotton independently of water assets, a form of wealth historically in the hands of the Vēḷāḷa and Brahmin elite (Ludden 1989: 95). According to Ludden, the agrarian economy of the dry zone experienced a great boom in the cotton trade during the nineteenth century (159), favoured by the construction of the cotton road in the 1840s (ibid.: 160). The reason for the boom was the high demand in industrial Britain (137). The Nāṭār community profited greatly from this. In the district I conducted research in, the Nāṭārs are the predominant community in three administrative units (tāluks). Only in one tāluk are the Vēḷāḷas in the majority; still, if not in terms of population, then of social-economic dominance, they do form a major community within the district (Blackburn 1980: 59).
37. For the history of the landowning peasant elite community of the Vēḷāḷas, see Ludden (1989: particularly pp. 67, 85ff).
38. On the two groups' right-hand affiliation, see Beck (1972: 8ff., 12); and Hardgrave (1969: 23).
39. Hardgrave (1969: 23) places the Barbers among the right-hand subcastes (which seems doubtful), but Beck's (1972: 5; 9) study of right- and left-hand subcastes classes them mainly (if not exclusively) among the left-hand bloc.

40. Based on his studies of the epics of the right- and left-hand communities, Rao (1986: 147; 1989: 113f.) terms the two divisions of communities respectively male-centred and female-centred.
41. Although the Nāṭārs are more numerous in the region I did research in, the landed Vēḷāḷas are dominant in terms of local political power.
42. Beck (1972: 8).
43. Most of the palm-leaf manuscripts of the *Icakkiyammaṉ Katai* are in their hands. The group has always been professionally linked with palm trees, and therefore has had easy access to this writing material (see Ludden 1989: 46f.).
44. On the changing economic and social realities of the Nāṭārs, see the thorough analysis in Hardgrave (1969).
45. Note that Tamil landowning communities associate women 'with the fertility of the soil' (Rao 1986: 143).
46. Cf. Handelman (2004: 15), where the notion of a dynamic 'Möbius framing' is introduced into the theory of ritual.
47. Pecuniary considerations may underlie its programme, for the success of a *koṭai* festival means success in fund-raising.
48. Viewed in terms of contemporary demographics, the decline in the birth-rate among Vēḷāḷas as women enter the job market may indeed be cause for worry among members of the community, who stand to lose political power to other social groups.
49. It can be assumed that this act, the aim of the Vēḷāḷas' effort to transform the anti-maternal, vengeful goddess, is in direct response to their total extinction that is culturally remembered in the bow-song text *(Icakkiyammaṉ Katai)*.
50. This description of them by Robert Hardgrave, Jr. serves as the subtitle of his 1969 study.
51. In my opinion, the left-hand Barbers tend to imitate Brahmin mannerisms rather than Vēḷāḷa behaviour. One reason for this may be that the Brahmins belong to a neutral division, without affiliation to either the right or left bloc. Another reason may be that they perhaps consider the Vēḷāḷas ritually inferior, given their sacrifice of animals.
52. Handelman (2005: 17) uses the term 'self-closure.'
53. The degree of this can vary, however. That self-containedness is determinative of the design of the Nāṭārs' ritual seems logical if we acknowledge the Nāṭārs' group identity as 'developing a subculture that is both insular and traditional' (Blackburn 1980: 65).
54. This self-containedness of the Vēḷāḷas' ritual, in a sense, has a counterpart in an arrangement of verse called *toṭarnilai,* which follows a principle of continuity and connectedness. One characteristic *toṭarnilai* type is the well-known poetic arrangement called *antāti,* a

word deriving from Sanskrit and literally meaning 'end and beginning.' (In a poem following this scheme the final syllable or word of one verse is repeated to begin the next one.) On this type, featured in the *Taṇṭiyalaṅkāram* (an anonymous work published by the South India Saiva Siddhanta Works Publishing Society, 1967), see Manuel (1997: 168f., 594).

55. The organisers who provide the input are different from those who experience the outcome.
56. The temple located along a national highway has developed an aggressive fund-raising campaign, stopping cars, buses and trucks and demanding donations from all travellers.

References

Beck, B.E.F. 1970. 'The Right-Left Division of South Indian Society', *The Journal of Asian Studies* 29.4: 779–98.

———. 1972. *Peasant Society in Koṅku: A Study of Right and Left Subcastes in South India*. Vancouver: University of British Columbia Press.

Blackburn, St. H. 1980. 'Performance as Paradigm: The Tamil Bow Song Tradition', Ph.D. thesis, University of California, Berkeley.

———. 1986. 'Performance Markers in an Indian Story-Type', in St. H. Blackburn and A.K. Ramanujan (eds) *Another Harmony: New Essays on the Folklore of India*, pp. 167–94. Berkeley: University of California Press.

Caṉmukacuntaram, Cu. (ed.) 1978. *Paḻaiyaṉūr Nīli Katai*. Madras: Manimekalai Piracuram.

Gupta, Shakti M. 2001. *Plant Myths and Traditions in India* (revised and enlarged). New Delhi: Munshiram Manoharlal.

Handelman, D. 1995. 'The Guises of the Goddess and the Transformation of the Male: Gangamma's Visit to Tirupati and the Continuum of Gender', in D. Shulman (ed.) *Syllables of Sky: Studies in South Indian Civilization in Honor of Velcheru Narayana Rao*, pp. 283–337. Delhi: Oxford University Press.

———. 2004. 'Re-Framing Ritual', in J. Kreinath et al. (eds) *The Dynamics of Changing Rituals: The Transformation of Religious Rituals within Their Social and Cultural Context*, pp. 9–20. New York: Peter Lang.

———. 2005. 'Introduction: Why Ritual in Its Own Right? How So?', in D. Handelman and G. Lindquist (eds) *Ritual in Its Own Right: Exploring the Dynamics of Transformation*, pp. 1–32. New York: Berghahn Books. (Also in *Social Analysis* 48.2, 2004.)

Hardgrave, R.L., Jr. 1969. *The Nadars of Tamilnad: The Political Culture of a Community in Change*. Berkeley: University of California Press.

Kanniyakumari District Gazetteer 2002. Chennai: The Director of Stationery and Printing on behalf of the Government of Tamil Nadu.
Kapferer, B. 2005. 'Ritual Dynamics and Virtual Practice: Beyond Representation and Meaning', in D. Handelman and G. Lindquist (eds) *Ritual in Its Own Right: Exploring the Dynamics of Transformation*, pp. 35–54. New York: Berghahn Books. (Also in *Social Analysis* 48.2, 2004.)
Ludden, D. 1989. *Peasant History in South India*. Delhi: Oxford University Press.
Manuel, I. 1997. *Literary Theories in Tamil*. Pondicherry: Pondicherry Institute of Linguistics and Culture.
Nabokov, I. 1997. 'Expel the Lover, Recover the Wife: Symbolic Analysis of a South Indian Exorcism', *The Journal of the Royal Anthropological Institute* (N.S.) 3: 297–316.
Rao, V.N. 1986. 'Epics and Ideologies: Six Telugu Folk Epics', in St. H. Blackburn and A.K. Ramanujan (eds) *Another Harmony: New Essays on the Folklore of India*, pp. 131–64. Berkeley: University of California Press.
———. 1989. 'Tricking the Goddess: Cowherd Kāṭamarāju and the Goddess Gaṅga in the Telugu Folk Epic', in A. Hiltebeitel (ed.) *Criminal Gods and Demon Devotees*, pp. 105–21. Albany: State University of New York Press.
Schuler, B. 2004. 'Of Death and Birth: Icakkiyammaṉ, a Tamil Goddess, in Ritual and Story' Ph.D. thesis, University of Hamburg. (2009. Wiesbaden: Harrassowitz; Ethno-Indology. Heidelberg Studies in South Asian Ritual, with a film on DVD.)
Stein, B. 1985. *Peasant State and Society in Medieval South India*. Delhi: Oxford University Press.
[Tēvāram of Ñāṉacampantar]. *Hymnes Sivaites du Pays Tamoul*. 1984. Vol. 1, edited by T.V. Gopal Iyer and F. Gros. Pondichéry: Institute français d'indologie.
Zvelebil, K.V. 1989. 'Some Tamil Folklore Texts: Muttuppaṭṭaṉ Katai, Kāttavārayaṉ Kataippāṭal, Paḷaiyaṉūr Nīli', *Journal of the Royal Asiatic Society* 2: 290–303.
———. 1995. *Lexicon of Tamil Literature*. Leiden: E.J. Brill.

Part II
Psychological Aspects of Ritual

8

The Uses of Ritual

Sudhir Kakar

The preferred data for a psychoanalyst from which he seeks to derive insights that may contain the potential for further generalisation are his case histories. And the case history I am going to use in trying to understand the uses of a ritual is my own. My understanding of ritual, then, is inextricable from my own experiential background which I will try to articulate although I am acutely aware that all such articulations are fated to remain incomplete.

My childhood memories of rituals derive from the house of my grandparents, a dark three-storied house in a narrow lane off a main bazaar of Lahore, a house with little space but much warmth, which was the site of many ritual festivities. The rituals were celebrated within a typical Indian extended family, a sprawling collection of my father's dozen brothers, sisters, cousins and assorted uncles and aunts on visits that in some cases could extend over a year. My childhood memory of rituals is of gaiety and excitement interspersed with solemn interludes. I have a vague recollection of ritual specialists, the *pandits* and *pujaris*, who presided over some of the religious rituals and a much more vivid memory of the kitchen, full of women, that was in action from early morning till night, a source of steaming hot delicacies coming out of deep-bottomed frying pans.

My memory of rituals is also inseparable from the stories around them, stories told by one or another aunt as I drifted off to sleep at night, fighting my tiredness all the way. The stories, narrating the origins of a ritual and warning against misfortunes in store for those who neglected its proper performance were legends from the epics but also folktales about princes and princesses, and magicians who turned them into birds and animals and back again into people.

My earliest association with a ritual, then, is of a time outside the reality of everyday life, a time of excitement and enchantment, an experience suffused with a warm glow, filled with light even if not with Enlightenment.

It was my father who introduced (Western) Enlightenment into my experience of rituals. My father was an uncompromising rationalist who looked down upon religious rituals as superstitious relics of bygone eras of which modern man was well rid. A civil servant by profession, my father was the first of his family to immigrate from a bazaar into the Indo-Anglian world of the Raj, the world of Civil Lines and army cantonments, of clubs and picnics. Temperamentally incapable of being moved by religion or the beauty of Indian ritual, art or music, and with a strong belief in rationality as the desirable principle of ordering human affairs, he readily identified with his British superiors whom he saw as valiant fighters against the decay of an Indian society riddled with magic and superstition. My father was also a gentle, considerate man who never objected to my mother's temple visits or interfered with her rituals although we were all aware of the distaste with which he regarded these activities. The only rituals he acknowledged as being of some value were those marking the major transitions of life: birth, marriage and death. These, he said, were valuable not because of their worthless religious content but because they made us pause before the enduring mysteries of human existence.

My own stance towards ritual, as one can easily comprehend, was ambivalent. I loved participating in the ritual life of my grandparents' house. Even in our small nuclear family, I loved helping my mother in her preparations for Diwali or Rakhi. I enjoyed the measured unfolding of a familiar sequence of actions, the coming together of people one loved and was loved by, the solemnity of the occasion which soon gave way to gaiety and abandon, the feeling of being pulled out of ordinary life into a magical space where time had stopped — all of which were greatly seductive to the young child. Yet, on the other hand, like any other boy I could not wait to become a grown-up man and felt impelled to adopt the attitude towards ritual of the adult I admired most — my father.

My father's attitude towards ritual was reinforced by my beginnings as a psychoanalyst. Psychoanalysis is rightly called the hermeneutics of suspicion and Freud was indeed, in the words of the French philosopher Paul Ricoeur, a 'master of suspicion'. In relation to ritual, psychoanalysis naturally refuses to accept the religious explanation of ritual which, for me, is enshrined in the stories I heard as a child. A classical, Freudian analyst, then, is not interested in what a particular ritual reveals but in what it conceals; in other words his intellectual excitement will lie in ferreting out the unconscious content the ritual is defending against. The fact that in this enterprise psychoanalysts can and sometimes do 'go over the top', coming up with fanciful explanations that strain every nerve of credulity, is seen as an acceptable risk of the analytic enterprise.

As a budding analyst, I learnt that when psychoanalysts talk about ritual they do not mean it in the way scholars of religion and anthropologists sometimes do: a ceremonial form that deepens the individual's connection — with nature, community and the sacred — and from which the individual emerges purified and with a sense of awe and significance. For them, ritual means the actions of a person suffering from an obsessive-compulsive disorder, someone who is subject to a panic attack if he deviates even the slightest bit from a rigid routine. He or she may be someone who, for instance, is enslaved to the hand-washing ritual, scrubbing his or her hands raw in a tortured solitude, yet never feels that they are ever clean. I would not, however, summarily dismiss the psychoanalytic view of religious ritual as originally obsessional in intent simply out of hand. The preoccupation with creating an order out of a threatening chaos, which is the hallmark of the obsessional, is also reflected in theories of the anthropologist Mary Douglas and the scholar of religions Roy Rapaport which, too, stress the ordering function of ritual (Douglas 1966; Rapaport 1979). Analysis may be revealing to ritual merely its caricature. Yet it is a revelation that is important in making us aware of the ever-present possibility and danger of a ritual resembling its distorted double.

As a child, then, ritual was an amalgam of superstition, mystery and exhilaration and as a young adult in psychoanalytic training it carried connotations of mental illness. Even at that time I sensed, though, that psychoanalysis was leading me away from my native Indian imagination — full of myths and marvels, many of them around ritual activity and performance — into an iconoclastic way of seeing the world where, if one looked hard and deep enough, all gods have feet of clay. It is only now, as I get older, that even as

I continue to keep faith with Freud's suspicious vision, I become less and less enamoured of the bargain I made when I was young. Perhaps it is true that innocent eye sees nothing. On the other hand, the view of the suspicious eye remains partial.

My father's attitude towards ritual is not difficult to understand. I have said he was an old-fashioned rationalist although the adjective 'old-fashioned' for someone who considered rationality synonymous with modernity would have certainly annoyed him. He was very much a Macaulayian product who idealised modern West — i.e., the confident, imperial West of the first half of the twentieth century — and had swallowed one of its myths that the core of a ritual is rigid precision. As a young man, he had been influenced by the reformist Arya Samaj Movement which, in turn, had incorporated the Puritan belief that ritual is mere empty form without true religious content, that rituals are only husks or empty shells. Times have changed. His modernism has given way to a post-modernism (with its own myths) and to pervasive doubts in what had been his certainties. Over the years, as a layman rather than a scholar of rituals, I have come to appreciate the uses of ritual and have moved to an intellectual position that is far removed from that of my father. Yet remnants of his stance towards ritual are stuck in my own psyche, like a food particle lodged between teeth, constantly explored by an uncomfortable tongue. Today, I can appreciate the significance of rituals in human life yet, at the same time, I cannot help but suspect ritual specialists — less the scholars than the professionals — of a nostalgic conservatism, of championing faded or dead rituals that have little relevance for the world we live in. I can be an enthusiastic participant in the celebration of rituals but have also developed a fine antenna for rituals that are truly empty, where the letter has triumphed over spirit. In fact, even as a participant in a ritual activity, I am sometimes so busy operating my own private radar, scanning for signs of a fake, routinised performance, that I may easily miss the central import of a particular ritual. It is as if I want to confirm my father's views on ritual at the same time as I want to refute them.

Now, of course, there is a vast variety of rituals. There are the rituals of daily life; for instance, the family ritual of coming together for a meal. And then there are the once in lifetime ceremonies around major life events that sponsor our transition from one cultural status to the other. There are healing rituals and academic rituals, political and judicial rituals, rituals of war and rituals of peace, rituals of sport and rituals of science, and so on. I am not a taxonomist by temperament and will not seek or dwell upon criteria for their classification but come to the main theme of this essay: the psychological uses of ritual.

Now there is a widespread agreement among scholars in ritual studies that rituals are important for the formation of identity on cultural, social and personal levels. Psychologically speaking, the value of a ritual lies in the degree to which it contributes to strengthening a person's sense of identity. This contribution can be to the individual aspect of personal identity, for instance, in rituals that encourage us to look at and lend significance to our life cycle by emphasising its beginning, transitions, end, as also its connection to nature and the cosmos. Or the strengthening may be of the group aspect of personal identity through rituals that accent our connection to others who belong to our family, caste, creed, tribe, nation and so on. These teach us our group's sanctioned ways of doing things, heightening the sense of 'us' while at the same time excluding outsiders, 'them', who do not know the right way. Another psychological classification can be between those rituals that defend or protect our sense of identity against a perceived danger by closing the psyche, and others that augment personal identity by opening the psyche to novel experiences. In my personal mythology, I like to think of the former as 'father rituals' while the latter are 'mother rituals'. The protective, conservative rituals can of course degenerate into rigid compulsions such as the persistent hand washing while the enhancing, transformative rituals are in danger of slipping into a delusional grandiosity. In a somewhat more theoretical aside, what I am highlighting here is a vexing problem of ritual studies, namely the uniting of the conservative and transformative functions of ritual activity.

When I look back at my own erratic engagement with rituals, I see that the rituals that were most vital, that made me feel most alive, combined both these qualities in a psychologically energising moment. In other words, these were rituals that closed certain threatening experiences of psychic danger while they simultaneously opened the psyche to experiences that produced a distinct sense of self which is difficult to put into words but is approximately captured by such terms as 'wonderment' 'enchantment', 'awe' or 'a sense of the sublime'.

Here, I will give only two illustrations of rituals where the two aspects that appear contradictory, in fact, turn out to be complementary, where the closing and opening of experience are not mutually exclusive but combined. Let me begin with a quiet ritual that is familiar to most of us, either from our memories of being a child or from our adult life as a parent, or both.

It is night. The 4-year-old boy is in his bed but not yet asleep. He is waiting for his mother to put him to sleep. The household is becoming quieter, preparing to see off yet another day. The mother comes in and sits down on the bed, in her usual place where they can look at each other while she tells him a bedtime story. From her sigh of contentment as she squats down cross-legged on the bed, folding her feet under her, the boy senses that she is more relaxed today, that as she begins the story which he has heard many times before, her engagement with him is less coerced by duty and is more an expression of a free choice. She *wants* to be with him, just the two of them. For her, the bedtime ritual is also a safe haven from the demands and tensions of the large family. She takes obvious pleasure in repeating those familiar step-by-step actions that will lead to his falling asleep. In the beginning, he sometimes interrupts her narration, correcting her when she makes a mistake, reminding her of an omission, but slowly the ambience of the bedroom changes. An invisible net of safety descends around the bed, cocooning mother and child in its folds even as night obliterates the familiar landmarks of the day. The sounds outside the house, the barking of stray dogs, the whistle of the engine as the night train to Delhi pulls out of the train station, seem to come from far away. Occasionally, the mother's hand caresses his hair as her story-telling voice washes over him, arming him against the approaching blanking of consciousness. He is no longer afraid of the free rein sleep will give to the approaching unknown and its possible terrors. As they look at each other in a mutual affirmation, his mother's face glowing with an inner light as it bends over his, the child not only senses an absence of fear in the room but a presence of something extraordinary yet utterly familiar, an enchantment that suffuses the last moments of his waking consciousness. Later, as an adult, he will find a name for these remarkable moments of the bedtime ritual. They were, he would now say, marked by the presence of what the psychologist William James called the *numinous*, a magical quality which, at bedtime every night, transformed his mortal mother into a hallowed and beneficent divinity.

My second example is a much louder one. It is of a ritual performance involving possession and healing. These rituals can take place in healing spaces such as temples and *dargah*s especially known for this purpose or they can be characteristic forms of worship, such as the possession dance and drama in south-western India where male ritual specialists dress as and become possessed by the spirit of fierce goddesses during temple festivals. These rituals, like all others, certainly lend themselves to psychological interpretation. Indeed, I too have interpreted some of the healing rituals in a north-Indian temple and in the Oraon tribals of Jharkhand in an earlier work (Kakar 1982, chs. 3 and 4).

Here, though, my focus is not on psychological interpretation of either the content or context of a ritual but on what makes a ritual come alive. I want to emphasise the experience of rituals rather than their explanation. Or, to be more exact, I would like to give precedence to the interpretation of experience than of content. The rituals I have talked of above are infinitely more dramatic than the story-telling ritual of bedtime. They are often in the form of a polyphonic play, with voices of the shaman or the exorcist, of possessing spirits or deities, of the patient, speaking singly or in a cacophonic bedlam. These are voices that are raised in anger, can threaten, shout, plead. The purely healing ritual may be accompanied by a great deal of movement; rhythmic swaying of the upper half of the patient's body or a violent sideways shaking of the head, unexpected dancing movements of the patient or the shaman, beatings that are self-administered or are the province of the healer, and so on. In the temple festival rituals of Kerala, as described by Sarah Caldwell, ritual specialists enact the mythic deeds of the goddess in a possession trance, providing devotees with a direct experience of the goddess in living form (Caldwell 2001). Speaking from my own experience, I can testify that such a ritual, with its embodied deities or spirits from another world, can produce a mild state of altered consciousness in even the most skeptic of onlookers. The dramatic aspect of these healing and worship rituals is certainly one reason why they can shake an onlooker's habitual way of experiencing the world, give ordinary reality a significance it did not have earlier, even when he *knows* that what he is witnessing is just a 'drama', a performance.

Being part of an audience in such rituals is another reason for the mildly altered feeling of consciousness, essentially the feeling that one's normal psychological defences and controls have been weakened and one's sense of identity has become shaky. In other words, one is more open to influences, both threatening and beneficial. Or, if you will, to use another vocabulary, there is a feeling of vulnerability to both malignant and helpful spirits, to protective and fierce deities. The touch and press of other bodies is only one of the stimuli that hammer at the sense of individual identity with an intent to weakening it. Other excitations, channelled through vision, hearing and smell are as much involved in this assault as are the more subliminal exchanges of body heat, muscle tension and body rhythms that take place when one is part of a large group or crowd. The weakening of identity goes hand-in-hand with a relaxation of controls over impulses and emotions and a gradual abandonment of critical faculties and rational thought processes; in short, there is a regression to mental states of early life. In this highly receptive and, yes, also expectant state, I have often felt the menace of the patients' possessing spirits even while being aware that the menace is a projection of my own internal state, the surfacing of my own 'evil' from unconscious depths as my defenses are relaxed. And then, as the ritual proceeds further, the threats recede. What comes to the fore is the vision of a deeply beneficent universe to whose care all disturbances of body or mind have been entrusted. Once again, as in the bedtime ritual of the child, we encounter those magical moments which bring these rituals to pulsating life. These are moments that can take birth only if the mind senses and closes to a situation of psychic danger while simultaneously opening up to unknown but beneficent forces.

Rituals for me, then, at least the ones I consider 'alive' and psychologically the most valuable, are not symbolic of something else. They are not gateways to other worlds or doors to other realities. They are not stimulants to 'deeper spiritual appetites' but, along with poetry, music and art, they are all we have to satisfy these appetites. We have called the arresting, transformative moments of rituals magical, and that is what a truly alive ritual does: it conveys the experience of magic, of enchantment — nothing more, nothing less. One can say about a ritual what the great jazz trumpeter Duke Ellington said about jazz, 'It don't mean a thing, if it ain't got that swing'. The peril a ritual transforms is as illusory as the safety it conjures. A ritual is an illusion, yes, but a necessary and even desirable illusion that lights up the narrow, mundane world of daily existence, a world which has always been inadequate to our experience and unequal to bear the burden of our hopes. For a brief period of time, it lets us transcend what the Irish poet William Yeats called 'the desolation of reality'. Yet, however much I, and modern man, may long for that early stage of life where the magic of ritual was taken for granted, I also know that a return to ritual experience characterised by the childish naiveté of idealised, simple and literal forms is impossible. Perhaps all one can aspire to in relation to ritual is what Paul Ricoeur suggested a believer could achieve in relation to his religious faith: a 'second naiveté', a sophisticated, adult, reflective affirmation of ritual that never lets go of a necessary, corrective suspicion.

◈

References

Caldwell, S. 2001. *Oh Terrifying Mother: Sexuality, Violence and Worship of Goddess Kali*. New York: Oxford University Press.

Douglas, M. 1966. *Purity and Danger: An Analysis of Concepts of Pollution and Taboo*. London: Routledge and Kegan Paul.

Kakar, S. 1982. *Shamans, Mystics and Doctors*: A psychological Inquiry into India and its Healing Traditions. New York: Knopf.

Rapaport, R.A. 1979. 'The Obvious Aspects of Ritual', in *Ecology, Meaning and Religion*, pp. 175–221. Berkeley, CA: North Atlantic Books.

9

Dynamic of Emotions and Dynamic of Rituals

Do Emotions Change Ritual Norms?

Angelos Chaniotis

Emotional Explosions During the Performance of Rituals

The very first word of Greek literature is a word of strong emotions: *menis*, wrath (*Ilias* 1.1; Muellner 1996). And the very first personal voice in Greek poetry, that of the lyric poet Archilochos around 650 BC, is the voice of a man who addresses his *thymos*, his spirit, urging it to control the emotions, to feel neither too much joy nor too much sorrow, but rather to understand the rhythm of life (West 1993: 11 frg. 128). Emotions are of crucial importance for the understanding of the social, political and cultural life of the Greeks, but they were not the only factor that dominated their life.[1] Their private and public conduct was subject to strict norms and was to a great extent determined by rituals.

The spontaneity of emotions unavoidably collides with the normative power of rituals in a variety of situations: when a man is mourning for his only son, a fallen soldier, while his city joyfully offers a thanksgiving sacrifice for a victory; when the harvest festival approaches and a farmer has just lost a mortgaged piece of land; when during a procession a poor woman is reminded that only the daughter of a wealthy family will carry the sacrificial basket;[2] when a defeated athlete attends a festival among the common citizens and watches his victorious competitor marching on the head of the procession;[3] when a woman observes the neighbour whom she hates officiate in a ritual as a priestess; when a community is obliged to celebrate a festival after a devastating defeat in war or a natural catastrophe. When a norm prescribes that only a boy whose parents are both still alive (*pais amphithalles*) shall have the honour to carry a sacred object and sing hymns (e.g., Sokolowski 1955: no. 32), every orphan in the city is bitterly reminded of her/his unfortunate situation. I could go on describing situations in which the impersonal, timeless norms, which prescribe the performance of rituals, collide with the feelings of the individuals who perform them.

The Greeks often found themselves confronted with this problem. In 514 BC, the Athenians were preparing for the celebration of their greatest festival, the Panathenaia. Their city was ruled by the sons of the popular tyrant Peisistratos. Hipparchos, one of them, was in love with the young aristocrat Harmodios, but had no success in his attempts to seduce him. So, he took revenge on him by insulting his sister. He first invited her to serve as bearer of the sacrificial basket in the procession, but when the girl came he sent her away telling her that she was unsuitable for this honorary service. Harmodios could not bear this loss of face. Together with his lover, Aristogeiton, he murdered Hipparchos on the day of the festival, just before the procession began. Harmodios was immediately killed by the bodyguards, Aristogeiton was executed later (Thucydides 6.54–59). An explosion of emotions — disappointed love, sense of honour, affection, solidarity and revenge — made a festival unforgettable. In a sense, this incident also changed the ritual. The murderers of Hipparchos were later celebrated as tyrannicides and founders of the democracy (Taylor 1992); their deed transformed Ahena's festival into the anniversary of the tyrant's murder. The privileges awarded to the descendants of the tyrannicides remained valid for another eight centuries.

Rituals, as emotionally loaded activities, often intensify pre-existing tensions among persons and groups. It occasionally occurred that festivals and other celebrations were disturbed by violent events, such as the one described above (Chaniotis 2006: 211–2). But this indirect impact of emotions upon rituals, intriguing as it may be, is not the subject that I should like to treat in this essay. I shall argue that both emotional experiences and the close observation of emotional responses to rituals were factors that could lead to the modification of pre-existing rituals or even to the creation of new ones. This is not an easy task. That ritual norms intended to provoke certain emotions among the participants in a ritual, is not hard to demonstrate. But can we also detect whether the emotions prescribed by the norm were at odds with the prevailing mood during the individual performance of a ritual? And is it possible to prove that a ritual changed under the influence of a particular emotional event? Our source material usually provides information about how rituals should ideally be preformed, not about how they were actually performed in particular situations. But despite the scarcity of the evidence, this enterprise is worth undertaking.

Emotional Frame and Manipulation of Emotions in Rituals

Kallimachos, a poet living in Alexandria in the early third century BC, is known as the composer of hymns — performative ritual texts intended to be sung during festivals. His *Hymn on Apollo* describes the emotions of the worshippers anticipating the god's imminent arrival to Delos, the sacred island where he was born. In the first verses, the poet observes the movement of the sacred palm tree and the flight of the birds — signs that the god is approaching. With the sacred cry *euphemeite* — literally: 'use good language', 'speak pious words' (Stehle 2004: 103; Chaniotis 2009a, 201) — the poet urges the worshippers to use the words appropriate to this ceremony, words that would not disturb the communication with the god and would not present an obstacle to his coming. Nothing should disturb the joy of this moment; even Achilles's mother, Thetis, eternally mourning for her son's death, even she has to postpone her lament as soon as she listens to this ritual cry; even a goddess's sad voice was banned from the celebration.

Kallimachos's hymn reflects ritual norms. It reflects the preoccupation of the expounders of Greek sacred law not only with ritual gestures and ritual acts, but also with the general mood of those who attend the ritual. That emotions are important for the performance of rituals did not escape the attention of the Greeks — the ritual experts who composed the sacred regulations, the poets who wrote the ritual texts, and the men of letters who observed and commented on the performance of rituals. Greek sacred regulations never directly prescribed emotions to the worshippers, but many of the measures they took were intended to intensify emotions. For instance, the abstinence from food increased the anticipation of the climax of a festival, the conviviality of the sacrificial banquet. Married women who celebrated the festival of the Thesmophoria temporarily returned to the status of the bride; they were obliged to abstain from sex during a celebration full of sexual symbolisms, thus being prepared for the return to the normality of marital life (Versnel 1994: 240–48, 276–88). The emotional differentiation of rituals was reflected in the selection of musical instruments and musical accompaniment, and the instruments varied depending on the occasion — procession, funeral, wedding, sacrifice, banquet, et cetera — thus marking and stimulating the participants (Nordquist 1994; Brand 2000). If those in mourning were excused from religious service such as the singing of hymns in Stratonikeia (second century AD), it was because their emotions were taken into consideration (Sokolowski 1955: no. 69). Even the 'emotions' of animals were manipulated before their ritual killing. The sacrificial animals were lead in the procession well fed and decorated, creating the illusion of willingly going to their death (Hotz 2005a); the sound of the flute covered their screaming while they died, the incense covered the smell of blood and excrement.

Rituals were also intended to manipulate the emotions of the deities, to whom they were primarily addressed. Let us take, for instance, one of the most elementary rituals: prayer. Greek prayers aiming at harming an opponent occasionally applied the persuasion strategy of 'slander', which magical handbooks designate as *diabole* (Graf 1996: 163–6). This kind of prayer attempted to make the god angry and direct his anger against the opponent. A magical papyrus, e.g., advises the *defigens* (the person who curses) to accuse his opponent of having burnt the papyrus bed of the god Osiris and eaten sacred fish (*Papyri Magicae Graecae* LVIII). Indeed, this very recipe was applied in a curse tablet, allegedly from Rome: in the name of the god Osiris, the *defigens* ordered a man who had died prematurely (*aoros*) to haunt a certain Nikomedes whom he accuses exactly with these charges (Jordan 2004). Another magical recipe recommended to a man in love, directs the anger of a goddess against the woman who had broken his heart by accusing her of insulting the goddess (*Papyri Magicae Graecae* IV 2471–9):

> She is the one who slanderously spoke of your sacred secrets, revealing them to mortals. The NN, not I, is the one who said: 'I saw how the goddess left the heavenly dome and called out an inappropriate name, walking on the earth without sandals, carrying a sword.' The NN is the one who said: 'I saw the goddess drinking blood'.

The goddess, furious at the revelation of her mysteries, was expected to conform to the *defigens's* wishes and pursue the object of his obsession until she would fall in love with him. A grave stele of a 15-year-old boy in Asia Minor, inscribed with an appeal to divine justice and revenge, is another example of the manipulation of divine emotions in prayer (Marek 2000: 137–46): 'Lord the Almighty, you have made me, but an evil man has destroyed me. Revenge my death fast!' In order to attract the god's personal interest in this affair, the author of this text made the god a victim of the offender. The crime, as he presents it, was not just the killing of the boy by an evil person but the destruction of the god's personal creation. Thus the punishment became the god's personal affair. Also flattery, by stressing the god's unlimited power, is part of the persuasion strategy. In a subtle way, the god was invited to prove his endless power not only by punishing the murderer, but by afflicting the punishment fast (Chaniotis 2009b, 127). We observe the same strategy also in a 'prayer for justice' from Asia Minor (Versnel 2002: 55–6). A victim of theft, probably a woman, attempted to motivate a goddess to act, by making her the owner of the lost property. The goddess had every reason to act — or lose face:

> I dedicate to you, Mother of the Gods, all the golden objects which I have lost; in order that she [the goddess] will investigate [the matter] and reveal everything, and in order that those who possess them will be punished in a manner worthy of her power, so that she [the goddess] will not look ridiculous.

That the emotions of the participants in a ritual were to be taken into consideration by those who composed the norms for its performance is evident, e.g., in sacred regulations concerning processions (Chaniotis 1995). How such regulations constructed the emotional frame for a successful ritual can be observed in a representative normative ritual text, a decree of the city Antioch on the Pyramos (c. 160 BC). The text gives the following instructions for the performance of a procession (Sokolowski 1955: no. 81).

> On the day, on which the altar was founded, a procession as beautiful and glamorous as possible shall take place every year, leading from the altar of the council to the sanctuary of Athena. The procession will be headed by the *demiourgos* [the highest official of the city] and the *prytaneis* [the members of the council]. They will offer a sacrifice of a cow with gilded horns to Athena and to Homonoia [the Concord]. The priests, all the other magistrates, the winners of the athletic contests, the supervisor of the gymnasium with all the ephebes and the young men, and the supervisor of the boys with all the boys, shall attend the procession. This day will be a holiday; all the citizens shall wear garlands. All shall be released from work, the slaves shall be released from chains. The magistrates and the winners of the contests shall gather in the sanctuary of Athena, all the other citizens will gather in groups according to the civic subdivisions [the tribes]. The *hieromnemon* [a sacred official] and the presidents of the tribes will be responsible for order on this day [...]

These prescriptions aimed at creating a joyful frame for the celebration (Chaniotis 2006, 212–3). The citizens wore white clothes and garlands, the magistrates their most glamorous garments. Neither envy caused by social inequality nor conflicts should undermine the celebration of concord. The slaves were, therefore, released from their chains; legal disputes were not allowed. The procession was lead by persons who represented success: the elected magistrates, the victorious athletes. The citizens were to gather in small groups of people who know one another and would not be puzzled, embarrassed or annoyed by the presence of foreigners (see below). Similarly, a sacred law concerning the festival of Asklepios in Lampsakos (second century BC), released the slaves from work and forbade loans and trials on that day (Sokolowski 1955: no. 8).[4] In Magnesia on the Maenader no lawsuits were allowed on the day of a festival (Sokolowski 1955: no. 33).

Dangerous Emotional Tensions

The Greek ritual experts also knew that men and women went to rituals to show off, to watch and to be seen. An individual in a Hellenistic comedy (known from a Roman adaptation) explains (Plautus, *Poenolus* 191–3): 'I am going to the temple of Aphrodite [...] ; the festival of the Aphrodisia is celebrated today [...] I want to please my eyes at the beauty of the girls.' And a Hellenistic poet, Theocritus, describes in a poem (*Idyll* 2) how a woman recalls a procession in honour of Artemis, during which she for the first time encountered her lover (Chaniotis 2006: 226–7; Petrovic 2007: 57–113):

> Theumaridas's Thracian nurse, now dead and gone, that dwelt at my door, had begged and besought me to come and see the procession. And I, unhappy wretch, went with her, wearing a fair long linen dress, and Klearista's fine wrap over it. [...] And when I was come already midway on the road, where Lykon's is, I saw Delphis and Eudamippos walking together. More golden than helichryse were their beards, and their chests brighter far than thou, O Moon, for they had lately left the manly labour of the gymnasium. [...] I saw, and madness seized me, and my hapless heart was aflame. My looks faded away. No eyes had I thereafter for the procession [...].

If this woman's gaze was attracted by beauty, valuables attracted the interest of thieves and luxury provoked envy and distracted attention from the ritual. As a sacred law from Kios puts it (Sokolowski 1955: no. 6): 'Leave the gold jewels at home; for they are expression of silly vanity; they make some people to enemies, they cause the gossip of others.'

The prohibitions included in sacred regulations give us an idea of the real world of ritual practice: women pushing one another in nocturnal celebrations (Sokolowski 1955: no. 61: 'when the torches are carried the women should not push one another') or discussing the purple and colourful garments or the excessive make-up of others;[5] individuals attempting to intrude in an exclusive circle of worshippers and get a share of the sacrificial meet (cf. Sokolowski 1969: no. 173 lines 14–18: 'those who welcome the worshippers can easily control the people who are allowed to attend the sanctuary'); drunk priests and magistrates (Lupu 2005: no. 22: 'a priest shall not drink'; cf. Sokolowski 1969: no. 83 and 94; Lupu 2005: no. 14); prostitutes exhibiting themselves to customers along the processional road (Graham 1998; Henry 2002); men turning their eyes to the see-through clothes of women[6] and thieves turning theirs to the purse and the gold jewels of inattentive worshippers;[7] quarrels, insults, bleeding noses. Bad experience with such problems — envy, greed, hatred, insults, political opposition, sexual tensions, theft — was the origin of normative interventions dealing with potential tensions among the participants in rituals. In addition to general measures concerning order,[8] norms concern among other things the limitation of the participants (see below), wine consumption before or during a ritual, the appropriate clothes, the carrying of valuables, et cetera. If the sacred laws of the Hellenistic period determine in detail the exact place of the participants in the procession, it was not only in order to express hierarchical positions, but also because this must have been one of the most common causes for quarrels among men with a particular sensibility towards issues of honour. There were rules even for the exact sequence of the sacrificial animals. At Bargylia (Asia Minor), a 'beauty contest' among the cows, that had been raised under the responsibility of the various subdivisions of the community, determined their position in the procession (Zimmermann 2000; Hotz 2005b).

The indignation caused by intruders in a sacrificial feast can be clearly recognised in the strong emotional language used in a decree of the small community of Olymos (Asia Minor, late second century BC Sokolowski 1955: no. 58). Although participation in the sacrifices and other acts of worship was reserved to the members of the three subdivisions of the citizen-body, some honorary members of the subdivisions claimed for themselves the right to participate in the gatherings of the citizens:

> some of them only dared [*tetolmekasin*] to attend the sacrifices; however, others even dared occupy the offices of the sacred official, the priest, and the prophet. The rights of the people and the care of the gods were violated in an impious way [*asebemata synebe*] through this shameless appropriation of rights which they did not deserve [*ek tes ton methen prosekonton anaidous amphisbeteseos*].

The decree hoped to put an end to this 'evil pretence' (*mochthera pareuresis*). The primary and original function of most norms limiting the circle of the participants in rituals by banning outsiders (stained persons, foreigners, suppliants, etc.), and in some case women, was to exclude sources of impurity;[9] they eventually reduced the danger of conflicts and distraction (Chaniotis 2006: 237).

Similarly, the ban of certain objects from celebrations originates in taboos concerning ritual purity and not in the fear of disorder and tensions. For example, iron objects and weapons were banned probably because of their association with war, violence and blood (Sokolowski 1962: nos. 59 and 60). The association of 'binding' with magic and curses is the most plausible explanation for prohibitions concerning belts, bound hair, bound shoes and rings.[10] If such taboos co-exist with prohibitions concerning valuable objects and colourful clothes, this does not mean that the latter had the same origin and significance. We should rather suspect that traditional taboos were re-interpreted and associated with order. For instance, by prohibiting the presence of weapons in a sanctuary, the authors of sacred laws paid respect to an old tradition. Simultaneously, they also prevented the use of weapons during violent conflicts, which are known to have occurred during celebrations. Although private clubs were, in theory, based on friendship and concord, their rituals (sacrifices, drinking parties, banquets and other celebrations) were often disturbed by quarrels, especially after the consumption of wine (Arnaoutoglou 2003: 101–2 and 156). The statutes of a club of worshippers of Hercules (Athens, c. AD 100) state: 'if anyone engages in a fight in the association, on the following day the one who started the fight shall pay a fine of ten drachmas; the one who joined it shall pay five drachmas.' Those who did not pay the fine were excluded from the club. One of the most important pieces of evidence for such measures concerns the rituals of a private cult association, the Athenian Iobakchoi, the worshipers of Dionysos. An inscription preserves the statutes of the association and a protocol of the meeting, during which they were approved (AD 178). One of the primary concerns was the celebration of convivial gatherings on the ninth day of every month and on the festive days dedicated to Dionysos in a peaceful and orderly manner (Sokolowski 1969: no. 51; Baslez 2004: 118–20; Chaniotis 2006: 232–4):

> No one is allowed to sing, to be loud or applaud in the dining room; the distribution [of wine] should take place in an orderly and quiet manner under the instructions of the priest or the chief Bakchos [...] If someone starts a quarrel or does not behave properly or goes to another bed or insults someone or uses defamatory words, the victim of the insult or of the defamation should present as witnesses two members, who can declare under oath that they have heard

> how this person has been insulted and defamed; and the one who has insulted or defamed shall pay to the club 25 drachmas as a fine. And the one who has started a quarrel should pay the same amount of 25 drachmas; these persons are not allowed to attend the gathering of the Iobakchoi until they have paid the fine. And if someone reaches the point of striking others, the member who has been struck will submit a written accusation to the priest or the vice priest, who is then obliged to call an assembly; and the Iobakchoi should pass a judgement upon vote under the guidance of the priest, and in addition to any other punishment they should determine the period during which the convict will not be allowed to attend the gatherings, and a fine of up to 25 denarii. And the person who has been beaten will be subject to the same punishment, if he publicly accuses him, instead of declaring the incident to the priest or the chief Bakchos. The person responsible for order who neglects to expel those who quarrel will be subject to the same punishment. [...]

The club's primary aim was not the cult of Dionysus, but drinking together. Pre-existing tensions among the members received additional input from wine consumption and lead to quarrels, insults and even open violence during the regular meetings. We notice the efforts of the club to keep these tensions unnoticed by others. The statutes introduced the following rule (lines 136–46):

> A *eukosmos* ['the man responsible for good order'] shall be elected by lot or appointed by the priest. He shall bring to those who behave in a disorderly manner or makes trouble the *thyrsos* [the distaff] of the god; the one to whom the distaff is brought should leave the dinning place, if the priest or the president of the club consents. If he disobeys, the 'horses' [a kind of club police] who will be appointed by the priests, shall carry him outside of the gate and he should be liable to the fines determined for those who are engaged in fights.

There can be no doubt that the reform of the statutes followed upon a crisis in the club. The acclamations, which the members cried out when the statutes were approved, allude to this crisis. The acclamation 'Strength and order in the club!' presupposes the danger of falling apart and the lack of order. The acclamation 'Now we are happy!' presupposes a distressful situation, which had now come to an end. Such problems did not occur in this Bakchic association only. Another association made a dedication on behalf of concord — obviously this was what the club was lacking (*IG* II^2 4985). Quarrels and disorder also threatened another association dedicated to friendship and to the commemoration of the dead (*IG* II^2 1369 lines 40–1: 'if we observe someone instigating quarrels and trouble [...]'). Measures against quarrels, which threatened the rituals of commensality, are also attested in another decree of an Athenian association (*SEG* XXXI 122; Lupu 2005: 177–90 no. 5; c. AD 121): 'if anyone engages in a fight in the association, on the following day the one who started the fight shall pay a fine of five drachmas; the one who joined it (shall pay) five drachmas.'

Emotional Experience and Modification of Funerary Rituals

A fascinating group of inscriptions found in Asia Minor contain the confessions of true or imaginary sinners.[11] These confessions were made publicly during complex ceremonies, which included the confession of the sin and the praise of the god, often with the use of a very emotional language (Chaniotis 2009b). Some of the texts end with a sort of catechesis, in which the repented sinner loudly instructs the audience present at the ceremony not to underestimate the power of the gods. In one of the texts the sinner explains (Petzl 1994: no. 123):

> With purifications and sacrifices I have propitiated the lord, in order that he may save my body (my life); and finally, he restored my health. For this reason I instruct: No one should eat the meat of a sacred goat that has not been sacrificed, because otherwise you will suffer the same punishment.

The priests, who inscribed this text, exploited an individual experience in order to endorse a ritual norm (abstinence from a particular type of food). Similarly, the authors of the sacred regulations hitherto presented took into consideration problems which could and did arise during the performance of a ritual due to emotional tensions, and modified the ritual norms accordingly. If we look for evidence that a very particular emotional experience, collective or individual, changed a ritual — not its performance in a single instance, but the way it was performed in the future — we have to turn to funerary rituals, which are dominated by emotions.

Indeed, we can plausibly argue that experiences had during a particular funeral influenced the further development of funerary rites. The introduction of strict rules concerning funerals and lament from the seventh century BC onwards (Engels 1998; Frisone 2000 and 2004; Kavoulaki 2005; Stavrianopoulou 2005) must be connected with the extremely pompous funerals of aristocrats, the provocative display of power and wealth, the equally provocative demonstration of emotions, the performance of professional mourners, and the shocking destruction of life (through sacrifices) and of valuables (through burning on the funeral pyre or deposition in the grave). Some of the relevant sacred regulations are concerned with pollution and try to keep the circle of the persons polluted by death limited (Parker 1983: 35–48). Others limit the renunciation rituals, the expenses of the funeral, and the public display of wealth (e.g., Sokolowski 1969: no. 97). In some cases, these laws were status oriented; for instance, the sumptuary law of Demetrios of Phaleron (Athens, late fourth century BC) seems not to have applied to foreigners (Hallof and Stroszeck 2002). Some prohibitions allow us to infer the emotional scenes, which the ritual experts wanted to prevent: the loud and inarticulate screaming of the women in the streets; stopping of the funeral procession on every corner with loud lament; mourning on the graves of persons deceased a long time ago; and continuation of excessive grief for months. One of the earliest of such laws survived in two copies, at Panopeus (sixth/fifth century BC; still unpublished; Camp 2003: 184–5) and in Delphi (mid-fourth century BC; Sokolowski 1969: no. 77; Rougemont 1977: 26–85 no. 9):

> They shall carry the dead covered, in silence [cf. Sokolowski 1969: no. 97]; they shall neither stop at any corner nor put the corpse down; they shall not scream outside of the house or before they have reached the grave. They shall neither lament nor scream at the graves of those who had died in the past, but they shall go home, except for the closest family members and the cousins and the stepparents and the grandchildren and the children-in-law. They shall neither woe nor scream, neither on the next day, nor on the ninth day, nor on the anniversary.

Another law from Gambreion prescribes (third century BC.; Sokolowski 1955: no. 16; Stavrianopoulou 2005):

> The women in mourning shall wear a dark garment, not made dirty [probably an allusion to the custom of throwing ashes and earth as sign of grief]; the men and the boys who mourn shall also use a dark garment, if they do not wish to wear a white garment. They should perform the customary rites for the dead for three months at the most, but on the fourth month the men shall stop the period of grief, the women in the fifth month.

Such normative innovations responded to the emotional impact funerary rituals had in relatively small communities. Scenes of excessive and loud mourning disturbed normality; the provocative demonstration of power and wealth caused envy; the lament of one family renewed the pain of another.

A law from Thasos (around 400 BC) is of a slightly different character. For more than three decades the Greek world had experienced continual war, and with it the incongruity of the joyful celebrations for a victorious battle with the grief for those who were killed. I assume that it was for this reason that the funerary rites for the war-dead were modified. The families of the war-dead were forbidden to wear on their clothes signs of mourning (*penthikon*) for longer than five days (Sokolowski 1962: no. 64; cf. Parker 1983: 43). In these cases new or modified norms aimed at preventing emotions that had been observed in the past.

Emotional reactions observed in a very specific historical situation could also create a new ritual or modify an existing one. In the late first or early second century AD, a woman of good family died in Knidos (Blümel 1992: no. 71; Bielman and Frei-Stolba 1998). We do not know her name, because the inscription is broken, but we know that she was a descendant of a benefactor, who had achieved for his fatherland liberty and exemption from taxes. As the woman's death became known, 'the people were shocked beyond measure because of her virtue and her reputation.' A decree, passed while the funerary ceremony was still in progress, gives us a direct impression of the emotions. The people 'assembled with great zeal in the theatre [lacuna], while her corpse was being carried out.' According to the norms, the funeral procession had been organised exclusively by her family. But as the funeral procession passed near the theatre, 'the people seized her body and then unanimously demanded that they may bury her with the participation of the entire people; they manifested through acclamations her virtue, in order that she receive also after her death the appropriate honours'. Here, a private funerary ceremony was interrupted by a demonstration of the masses and was transformed from a family affair to a public ritual with the participation of the entire community. The emotions undermined the norms and modified the ritual. If this had occurred only in this one instance, it would resemble the spontaneous decision of Queen Elizabeth to bow in front of Diana's coffin, breaking a rule under the influence not of her own emotions, but of those of her subjects. But the funeral of Knidos — or perhaps an unknown predecessor — became a trendsetter (Jones 1999; Chaniotis 2006: 224–6). A few years later, something similar occurred in another Karian city, in Aphrodisias (Reynolds and Roueché 1992). The relevant decree concerns again a woman, Tatia Attalis, again the descendant of a great benefactor. The inscription is, again, fragmentary: 'since she has now reached the end of her life, sooner than the destined time, for this reason the city has publicly [lacuna], and everybody unanimously seized her corpse [lacuna].' Here, too, the people interrupted the family funeral and carried the corpse away in order to bury it in a public ceremony. In AD 177, similar scenes occurred in Athens, during the funeral of Herodes Atticus, the teacher of Emperor Hadrian and the wealthiest man of the Roman East (Philostratos, *Lives of the Sophists* 14.20). The burial which was being performed by his freedmen — his *familia* in the legal sense — in Marathon was interrupted by the Athenian *ephebes*, who marched from Athens to Marathon, 'seized the body with their own hands,' brought it back to Athens in procession, and buried it there. All the Athenians attended the funeral lamenting the death of their benefactor 'like children who have lost a good father.' The immediate aim of these actions was to transform a family ritual into a public ritual (Chaniotis 2006: 226). The participation of the entire community at the funeral, in other words the incorporation of the community into a family ritual, created the fiction of the orphaned people. A ritual was interrupted and transformed into a ritual of togetherness. The fact that these decrees concerning the participation of the entire people in the funeral were inscribed guaranteed that these rituals were not forgotten. The inscription preserved the memory of the unique event that had bound the entire community into a virtual family.

From an Emotional Experience to a Binding Norm

A decree from the Sicilian city of Nakona elucidates how a unique emotional experience led to the creation of a new ritual. A civil war had divided this community in the third century BC. Peace could be established, but genuine reconciliation was hard to achieve. Amnesty, in such a case, may forbid the prosecution of past acts of violence, but it cannot eliminate the hatred. So the Nakonians decided to take a far more radical measure: they abolished the existing family bonds and created entirely new families, making the former enemies brothers (Dössel 2003: 235–47; Eich 2004: 95–8):

> Whereas fortune has taken a favorable course and order has been restored to the public affairs of the Nakonians and it is fit for them to govern themselves harmoniously in the future [...] let it be decided to call an assembly of the citizens on the 4th Adonios and to summon to the assembly all those citizens among whom the conflict arose as they were fighting (against one another) over the public affairs so that they put an end to hostilities among them, the two factions having each presented a list of thirty names of members of the other. Those who have previously been enemies shall write their names, each the names of their enemies. The magistrates shall transcribe the names of each faction separately on ballots, put them into vases, and choose by lot one member of each faction. They shall then choose by lot three men from the rest of the citizens in addition to the former two, avoiding relationships as defined by law. Those united into the same group shall live as elective brothers with each other harmoniously in full justice and friendship. When all sixty ballots have been drawn and those united by lot in addition to them, the magistrates shall allot all the rest of the citizens into groups of five, avoiding in the allotment the relationships as has been written above. Those united by lot into the same group shall also live as brothers like the former ones (Lupu 2005: 347–58 no. 26).

This measure was sealed with the sacrifice of a white goat. The selection of the victim corresponded to already existing ritual traditions. Goats are usually sacrificed to powers of the underworld, in this case to the ancestors, whose approval was necessary for such a decision that had abolished the established families

(Chaniotis 1991: 135). More interesting is the establishment of a new ritual. Nakone connected a new commemorative anniversary with the cult of the ancestors and the cult of an abstract idea, the idea of the Concord (Ibid.: 127, 135).

> The hieromnamones ['those who remember the sacred things'] shall sacrifice a white goat and the treasurer shall provide whatever is needed for the sacrifice. Similarly all subsequent magistrates shall sacrifice each year on the same day to the ancestors and to Homonoia [the goddess of Concord] a victim for each whichever they have found suitable, and all the citizens shall celebrate among themselves according to the created brotherhoods.

In Nakone, the emotion of hatred was expelled with the ritualised commemoration of reconciliation. An emotional experience justified the introduction of a new ritual norm (the commemorative festival), which in its turn was expected to be stronger than emotions. A similar interplay of emotions and new ritual can be observed in the establishment of the cult of king Antiochos III in Teos in 203 BC, after the king had freed the city from the payment of tribute and recognised it as inviolable (Chaniotis 2005, 2007). The inhabitants rejoiced and transformed their momentary feelings of joy and gratitude into an eternal festival of grateful memory, the central figures of which were the king, his wife and the deified personifications of Charis (Gratitude) and Mneme (Remembrance). I select only a few passages describing the newly established rituals:

> In order that the place where King Antiochos the Great made some of his benefactions and promised others, which he later fulfilled, be consecrated to him, we shall dedicate a bronze statue of the king, as beautiful as possible, in the town-hall; every year, on the first day of the month Leukatheon, the boards of magistrates, together with the priest of Antiochos and the president of the council, shall offer a sacrifice to the king, to the Charites [the personifications of grace and gratitude] and to Mneme [Remembrance] on the joint altar of the city, inaugurating with this sacrifice their term in office, so that they may have a good start in their office. And the ephebes who finish their training shall offer a sacrifice on the same day together with the director of the gymnasium, so that they not begin any public activity without first having expressed their gratitude to the benefactors and so that also our descendants accustom themselves

to regard everything else as secondary and unimportant and give the expression of gratitude the greatest priority [...]

One may argue whether we are dealing with genuine feelings of gratitude or calculated demonstration thereof, but the result of the genuine joy of the Teians at their liberation from taxes resulted into a radical transformation of the new year's festival, the festival during which the magistrates entered office and the *ephebes* were accepted into the citizen-body, into a festival of the royal family and two personifications.

Emotional Background of Private Cult Foundations

In the aforementioned cases I have treated normative interventions approved by communities, after taking into consideration 'the public feeling'. The Greek sacred laws include, however, also norms introduced by individual cult founders. Is it possible that personal experiences and emotions played a role in the norms they established? Can we recognise if a personal emotional experience has influenced the norm?

The individuality of a sacred law and its deviation from a stereotypical content and a formulaic language may hint to a particular experience, collective or individual, which had caused the divergence. Prohibitions against entering a sanctuary provide a good example exactly because they are numerous and rather formulaic; they usually forbid impure persons to enter a sanctuary, envisaging, in principle, two forms of impurity: the impurity of the body and the impurity of the mind (Parker 1983; Chaniotis 1997; Lupu 2005: 14–18). A Lindian sacred law (third century AD) exemplifies the content of such regulations (Sokolowski 1962: no. 91):

> It is pious to pass the lustral basin and the gates of the temple being clean and pure [...], cleaned not only in the body, but also in the soul. Whoever enters the sanctuary must be unarmed. He shall have clean clothes; he shall wear no band on the head; he shall wear either white shoes, which are not made of goat-skin, or no shoes at all. He shall have nothing made of goat-skin. His belt shall be without a knot. Entrance in the sanctuary is allowed

> forty days after the miscarriage of a woman, a dog, or a donkey; forty one days after sexual intercourse with a virgin; forty one days after death in the family; seven days after washing a corpse; three days after entering [the house where death occurred?]; three days after coming into contact with a woman in childbed; a woman in childbed twenty one days; [...] after sexual intercourse (enter) after washing yourself and performing the purification ritual, thirty days after sexual intercourse with a prostitute. From the unlawful things you are never clean.

At first sight, an analogous regulation from Eresos on Lesbos (second century BC), seems to follow this general pattern (Sokolowski 1969: no. 124): 'Only the pious are allowed to enter the sanctuary.' Then the law excludes all the 'usual suspects': individuals, who had come in contact with the dead, with birth, with menstrual blood, sexual intercourse, et cetera. But then we find a unique formulation: 'also traitors are not allowed to enter.' Traitors could be regarded as impure (*miaroi*; Parker 1983: 5: "because it is shamelessness that causes them to disregard normal constraints"), and the killing of a traitor was not regarded as causing pollution (Knoepfler 2001: 238). No other sacred regulation, however, specifically excludes traitors from cult. It is tempting to assume that the presence of a traitor was undesired because of the indignation it would cause among the participants. That this particular crime is highlighted — and not any other of the innumerable crimes that humans are capable in committing — can be best explained if we assume that the author of the regulation had a very particular event in mind. This assumption finds support in the fact that Eresos is known to have experienced decades of civil strife in the late fourth century (e.g., Bencivenni 2003: 55–77).

The sacred regulation of a private cult association at Philadelpheia (late second/early first century BC) sets the requirements for participation in the mystery cult. We know its author: a certain Dionysios, who claimed that he had received the instructions from Zeus in his sleep (Sokolowski 1955: no. 20; Barton and Horsley 1981; Chaniotis 1997: 159–62; Petzl 2003: 93–4):

> For health and common salvation and the finest reputation the ordinances given to Dionysios in his sleep were written up, giving access into his House to men and women, free people and slaves [...] To this man Zeus has given ordinances for the performance of

> the purifications, the cleansings, and the mysteries, in accordance with ancestral custom and as has now been written. When coming into this House, let men and women, free people and slaves, swear by all the gods neither to know nor make use wittingly of any deceit against a man or a woman, neither poison harmful to men nor harmful spells. They are not themselves to make use of a love potion, abortifacient, contraceptive, or any other thing fatal to children; nor are they to recommend it to, nor connive at it with, another. They are not to refrain in any respect from being well intentioned towards this House. If anyone performs or plots any of these things, they are neither to put up with it nor keep silent, but expose it and defend themselves. Apart from his own wife, a man is not to have sexual relations with another married woman, whether free or slave, nor with a boy nor a virgin girl; nor shall he recommend it to another. Should he connive at it with someone, they shall expose such a person, both the man and the woman, and not conceal it or keep silent about it. Whoever, woman and man, does any of the things written above, let him not enter this House. For great are the gods set up in it. They watch over these things, and will not tolerate those who transgress the ordinances.

This definition of guilt and sin is very interesting in itself, but in this context I am only concerned with an unusually long passage dedicated not to adultery in general, but very specifically to the adulteress:

> A free woman is to be chaste and shall not know the bed of, nor have sexual intercourse with, another man except her own husband. But if she does have such knowledge, such a woman is not chaste, but defiled and full of endemic pollution, and unworthy to reverence this god whose holy things these are that have been set up. She is not to be present at the sacrifices, not to offend the purifications and cleansings, not to see the mysteries being performed.

This passage is certainly connected with regulations concerning ritual purity. What we observe here, however, is not simply the exclusion of such a woman from the ritual but the moral condemnation of her behaviour with the use of a very strong language. This document treats the adulteress in a different way than all the other impure individuals. She is not only morally condemned; she is also condemned never to be purified for her sin, since she is forever excluded from purificatory rituals. What caused this different treatment? An adulteress is often, especially in small communities, the subject of gossip. One wonders whether it was her ritual impurity alone or also the indignation she provoked among the other participants that explain why her presence during the mysteries was felt to be the ultimate disturbance. Another thought comes to mind: What if the author of this regulation had himself been the victim of adultery condemning in the face of the anonymous, potential sinner his own treacherous wife? This hypothesis can never be proven — not even nearly — but the reason I dare mention it is quite simply in order to stress the fact that in Greece sacred regulations — even when they were presented as the result of revelation — were written by mortals, often by ordinary human beings with a particular interest in religion or with strong piety; even when they were (or presented themselves as) religious experts, they were still men (sometimes women) with individual experiences and emotions that always found ways to show through the cracks of the texts they wrote.

◈

Notes

1. Recent research on the role of emotions in Greek society: Foxhall (1998); Harris (2001); Braund and Most (eds) (2003); Gödde (2003); Konstan and Rutter (eds) (2003); Knuuttila (2004); Konstant (2006); Cairns (2008).
2. Social background of a *kanephoros* ('basket-bearer'): Brulé (1987: 302–05); Petrovic (2007: 66–70).
3. Position of victorious athletes in processions: Chaniotis (1995: 157 note 85).
4. Further examples: Sokolowski (1955: no. 15 [Pergamon, celebration concerning a treaty between Pergamon and Rome, 129 BC]); Sokolowski (1955: no. 33 [Magnesia on the Maeander, inauguration of the statue of Artemis, early second century BC]); Sokolowski (1962: no. 14 [Athens, cult of Apollo, 129 BC]; no. 69 [Thasos, no lawsuits during the major festivals, c. 300 BC]).
5. E.g., Sokolowski (1962: no. 32 [Arkadia, fifth century BC]: 'If a woman wears a garment decorated with embroideries, it shall become sacred property of Demeter Thesmophoros.' A cult regulation in Patrai [third century BC] forbids the female participants in a festival of Demeter to wear gold jewels with a weight of more than one obolos, colourful or purple garments, and make-up [Sokolowski 1962: no. 33]). Similar prohibitions against extravagant clothes, jewels, gold objects, and

make-up are quite common in sacred laws: Sokolowski (1955: no. 14 line 10) [Pergamon, Asklepios' cult]); Sokolowski (1969: no. 65 lines 15–26 and no. 94. Cf.). Chaniotis (2006: 236–7 and below note 6).

6. The sacred law of the mysteries of Andania contains a prohibition against see-through clothes (Sokolowski 1969: no. 65 line 16, first century AD). Cf. Deshours (2006, 102–06).
7. In Aristophanes' *Acharnians* (257–58), Dikaiopolis instructs his daughter, who bears the sacrificial basket in a procession: 'take care that no one steals your gold jewels unnoticed.' Sacred laws prohibit the carrying of jewels (Sokolowski 1969: no. 65 line 22) and money purses (Sokolowski 1962: no. 59).
8. E.g., Sokolowski (1962: no. 15 lines 27–9 [Athens, sacred law concerning the Eleusinian mysteries, first century BC]: 'and when the *mystagogoi* lead the procession of the initiates, they shall ensure that the procession takes place in an orderly and decent manner; the supervisors of the mysteries shall have the authority to punish those who behave in a disorderly manner or prevent others from marching, etc.'). Further examples: Sokolowski (1955: no. 9 lines 28–32); Sokolowski (1969: no. 33 B 33–5 and 83); Sokolowski (1962: no. 51). See also Wörrle (1988: 219–20); Breláz (2005: 174–46).
9. Prohibitions against the presence of foreigners are heterogeneous in origin; see, e.g., Sokolowski (1962: no. 49); Lupu (2005: 18–21). For women, see, e.g., Sokolowski (1962: no. 56, [Delos, cult of Egyptian deities, second century BC]: 'no one shall bring inside a woman'); cf. Sokolowski (1969: nos. 82 and 109).
10. Examples: Sokolowski (1955: no. 14 [incubation in the sanctuary of Asklepios in Pergamon, third century AD]: 'in white garments, crowned with pure wreaths made of olive branches, having neither a ring nor a belt nor gold jewels, having the hair unbound, without shoes'); Sokolowski (1969: no. 68 [cult of Despoina in Lykosoura, third century BC]: 'it is forbidden to enter the sanctuary of Despoina carrying gold objects other than those meant to be dedicated, or wearing purple, colorful, or black garments, shoes, or rings; they shall not have the hair bound or cover the head'); Sokolowski (1962: no. 59 [cult of Zeus Kynthios and Athena Kynthia, Delos, Imperial period]: prohibition against shoes, keys, iron rings, belts, purses, and weapons); Sokolowski (1962: no. 91 [Lindos, third century AD]: prohibition against weapons, head-gear, shoes, and bound belts); Sokolowski (1962: no. 60 [Amorgos, fifth or fourth century BC]: prohibition against iron objects).
11. A recent collection of most texts: Petzl (1994). The most recent relevant studies, in which the earlier bibliography can be found, are: Rostad (2002); Versnel (2002); Chaniotis (2004); Gordon (2004); Belayche (2006); Chaniotis (2009b).

References

Arnaoutoglou, I.N. 2003. *Thusias heneka kai sunousias: Private Religious Associations in Hellenistic Athens*. Athens: Academy of Athens.

Barton, S.C. and Horsley, G.H.R. 1981. 'A Hellenistic cult group and the New Testament church', *Jahrbuch für Antike und Christentum*, 24: 7–41.

Baslez, M.-F. 2004. 'Les notables entre eux. Recherches sur les associations d'Athènes à l'époque romaine', in S. Follet (ed.) *L'hellénisme d'époque romaine: Nouveaux documents, nouvelles approches (1er s. a.C. – IIIe s. p. C.). Actes du colloque international à la mémoire de Louis Robert, Paris, 7–8 juillet 2000*. Paris: De Boccard: 105–20.

Belayche, N. 2006. 'Les stèles dites de confession: une religiosité originale dans l'Anatolie impériale?', in L. de Blois – P. Funke – J. Hahn (eds), *The Impact of Imperial Rome on Religions, Ritual, and Religious Life in the Roman Empire*, pp. 66–81. Leiden: Brill.

Bencivenni, A. 2003. *Progetti di riforme costituzionali nelle epigrafi greche dei secoli IV-II a.C.*, Bologna: Lo Scarabeo.

Bielman, A. and Frei-Stolba, R. 1998. 'Femmes et funérailles publiques dans l'antiquité gréco–romaine', in *Études de Lettres. Revue de la Faculté des Lettres, Univ. de Lausanne*, Lausanne: 5–33.

Blümel, W. 1992. *Die Inschriften von Knidos. I*, Bonn: Habelt.

Brand, Helmut 2000. *Griechische Musikanten im Kult. Von der Frühzeit bis zum Beginn der Spätklassik*. Dettelbach: Röll.

Braund, S. and Most, G.W. (eds) 2003. *Ancient Anger: Perspectives from Homer to Galen*. Cambridge: Cambridge University Press.

Brélaz, C. 2005. *La sécurité publique en Asie Mineure sous le Principat (Ier–IIIème s. ap. J.-C.). Institutions municipales et institutions impériales dans l'Orient romain*. Basel: Schwabe.

Brulé, P. 1987. *La fille d'Athènes. La religion des filles à Athènes à l'époque classique. Mythes, cultes et société*. Paris: Les Belles Lettres.

Cairns, D. 2008. 'Look both ways: studying emotion in ancient Greek', *Critical Quarterly*, 50(4): 43–62.

Camp, J. McK. 2003. 'Notes for a philologist', in G.W. Bakewell and J.P. Sickinger (eds), *Gestures: Essays in Ancient History, Literature, and Philosophy Presented to Alan L. Boegehold on the Occasion of his Retirement and his Seventy-fifth Birthday*, pp. 183–7. Oxford: Oxbow.

Chaniotis, A. 1991. 'Gedenktage der Griechen: Ihre Bedeutung für das Geschichtsbewußtsein griechischer Poleis', in J. Assmann (ed.), *Das Fest und das Heilige. Religiöse Kontrapunkte zur Alltagswelt*, pp. 123–45. Gütersloh: Gütersloher Verlagshaus.

———. 1995. 'Sich selbst feiern? Die städtischen Feste des Hellenismus im Spannungsfeld zwischen Religion und Politik', in P. Zanker and M. Wörrle (eds) *Stadtbild und Bürgerbild im Hellenismus*, pp. 147–72. Munich: Beck.

Chaniotis, A. 1997. 'Reinheit des Körpers – Reinheit der Seele in den griechischen Kultgesetzen', in J. Assmann and T. Sundermeier (eds) *Schuld, Gewissen und Person*, pp. 142–79. Gütersloh: Gütersloher Verlagshaus.

——. 2004. 'Under the watchful eyes of the gods: aspects of divine justice in Hellenistic and Roman Asia Minor', in S. Colvin (ed.) *The Greco-Roman East: Politics, Culture, Society*, pp. 1–43. Cambridge: Cambridge University Press.

——. 2005. 'Akzeptanz von Herrschaft durch ritualisierte Dankbarkeit und Erinnerung', in C. Ambos et al. (eds) *Die Welt der Rituale. Von der Antike bis heute*, pp. 188–204. Darmstadt: Wissenschaftliche Buchgesellschaft.

——. 2006. 'Rituals between Norms and Emotions: Rituals as Shared Experience and Memory', in E. Stavrianopoulou (ed.), *Rituals and Communication in the Graeco-Roman World*, Liège: Centre International d'Étude de la Religion Grecque Antique: 211–38.

——. 2007. '*Isotheoi timai*: la divinité mortelle d'Antiochos III à Téos', *Kernos*, 20: 153–171.

——. 2009a. 'Acclamations as a form of religious communication', in H. Cancik and J. Rüpke (eds) Die Religion des Imperium Romanum: Koine and Konfrontationen, pp. 199–218. Tübingen: Mohr Siebeck.

——. 2009b. 'Ritual performances of divine justice: The epigraphy of confession, atonement, and exaltation in Roman Asia Minor', in H. Cotton et al. (eds), *From Hellenism to Islam: Cultural and Linguistic Change in the Roman Near East*. pp. 115–54. Cambridge: Cambridge University Press.

Deshours, N. 2006. *Les mystères d'Andania. Étude d'épigraphie et d'histoire religieuses*, Bordeaux: Ausonius.

Dössel, A. 2003. *Die Beilegung innerstaatlicher Konflikte in den griechischen Poleis vom 5.-3. Jahrhundert v. Chr.* Frankfurt: Lang.

Eich, A. 2004. 'Probleme der staatlichen Einheit in der griechischen Antike', *Zeitschrift für Papyrologie und Epigraphik* 149: 83–102.

Engels, J. 1998. *Funerum sepulcrorumque magnificentia. Begräbnis- und Grabluxusgesetze in der griechisch-römischen Welt*. Stuttgart: Steiner.

Foxhall, L. 1998. 'The politics of affection: emotional attachments in Athenian society', in P. Cartledge et al. (eds) *Kosmos: Essays in Order, Conflict and Community in Classical Athens*, pp. 52–67. Cambridge: Cambridge University Press.

Frisone, F. 2000. *Leggi e regolamenti funerari nel mondo greco. 1 Le fonti epigrafiche*. Galatina: Congedo.

——. 2004. 'Il rituale come campo di sperimentazione del "politico": l'esempio della normativa sul rituale funerario nella documentazione epigrafica greca', in S. Cataldi (ed.) *Poleis e politeiai. Esperienze politiche, tradizioni letterarie, proggetti costituzionalli*, pp. 369–84. Alessandria: Edizioni dell'Orso.

Gödde, S. 2003. 'Emotionale Verschiebungen. Zur Bedeutung der *euphemia* im griechischen Ritual', in A. Kneppe and D. Metzler (eds), *Die emotionale Dimension antiker Religiosität*, pp. 21–46. Münster: Ugarit.

Gordon, R. 2004. 'Raising a sceptre: confession-narratives from Lydia and Phrygia', *Journal of Roman Archaeology*, 17: 177–96.

Graf, F. 1996. *Gottesnähe und Schadenzauber. Die Magie in der griechisch-römischen Antike*. Munich: Beck.

Graham, A.J. 1998. 'The woman at the window: Observations on the "Stele from the Harbour" of Thasos', *Journal of Hellenic Studies*, 118: 22–40 .

Hallof, K. and Stroszeck, J. 2002. 'Eine neue Schauspielerstele vom Kerameikos', *Mitteilungen des Deutschen Archäologischen Instituts (Athener Abteilung)*, 117: 115–31.

Henry, A. 2002. 'Hookers and lookers: prostitution and soliciting in late Archaic Thasos', *Annual of the British School at Athens*, 97: 217–21.

Harris, W.V. 2001. *Restraining Rage: the Ideology of Anger Control in Classical Antiquity*. Cambridge Ma.: Harvard University Press.

Hotz, S. 2005a. 'Delphi: Eine störrische Ziege und Priester', in C. Ambos et al. (eds) *Die Welt der Rituale. Von der Antike bis heute*, pp. 102–5. Darmstadt: Wissenschaftliche Buchgesellschaft.

———. 2005b. 'Bigger, Better, More. Die Kleinstadt Bargylia im Bann eines Festes', in C. Ambos et al. (eds) *Die Welt der Rituale. Von der Antike bis heute*, pp. 59–65. Darmstadt: Wissenschaftliche Buchgesellschaft.

Inscriptiones Graecae (*IG*), Berlin 1873–.

Jones, C. 1999. 'Interrupted funerals', *Proceedings of the American Philosophical Association*, 143: 588–600.

Jordan, D.R. 2004. 'Magia nilotica sulle rive del Tevere', *Mediterraneo antico*, 7(2) 693–710.

Kavoulaki, A. 2005. 'Crossing communal space: the classical ekphora, public and private', in V. Dasen and M. Piérart (eds) *Idia kai demosia. Les cadres "privés" et "publics" de la religion grecque antique*, pp. 129–45. Liège: Centre International d'Étude de la Religion Grecque Antique.

Knoepfler, D. 2001. 'Loi d'Érétrie contre la tyrannie et l'oligarchie', *Bulletin de Correspondance Hellénique*, 125: 195–238.

Knuuttila, S. 2004. *Emotions in Ancient and Medieval Philosophy*. Oxford: Oxford University Press.

Konstan, D. 2006. *The Emotions of the Ancient Greeks: Studies in Aristotle and Greek Literature* Toronto: University of Toronto Press.

Konstan, D. and Rutter, K.N. (eds) 2003. *Envy, Spite and Jealousy: The Rivalrous Emotions in Ancient Greece*. Edinburgh: Edinburgh University Press.

Lupu, E. 2005. *Greek Sacred Law: A Collection of New Documents*. Leiden: Brill.
Marek, C. 2000. 'Der höchste, beste, größte, allmächtige Gott. Inschriften aus Nordkleinasien', *Epigraphica Anatolica*, 32: 137–46.
Muellner, L. 1996. *The Anger of Achilles: Menis in Greek Epic*. Ithaca: Cornell University Press.
Nordquist, G.C. 1994. 'Some notes on musicians in Greek cult', in R. Hägg (ed.) *Ancient Greek Cult Practice from the Epigraphical Evidence. Proceedings of the Second International Seminar on Ancient Greek Cult, Organised by the Swedish Institute at Athens, 22–24 November 1991*, Stockholm: Paul Aström: 81–93.
Parker, R. 1983. *Miasma. Pollution and Purification in Early Greek Religion*. Oxford: Oxford University Press.
Petrovic, I. 2007. *Von den Toren des Hades zu den Hallen des Olymp. Artemiskult bei Theokrit und Kallimachos*. Leiden–Boston: Brill.
Petzl, G. 1994. *Die Beichtinschriften Westkleinasiens*. Bonn: Habelt.
———. 2003. 'Zum religiösen Leben im westlichen Kleinasien: Einflüsse und Wechselwirkungen', in E. Schwertheim and E. Winter (eds) *Religion und Region. Götter und Kulte aus dem östlichen Mittelmeerraum*, pp. 94–101. Bonn: Habelt.
Reynolds, J. and Roueché, C. 1992. 'The funeral of Tatia Attalis at Aphrodisias', *Ktema*, 17: 153–60.
Rostad, A. 2002. 'Confession or reconciliation? The narrative structure of the Lydian and Phrygian "confession inscriptions"', *Symbolae Osloenses* 77: 145–64.
Rougemont, G. 1977. *Corpus des inscriptions de Delphes. Tome I. Lois sacrées et règlements religieux*. Paris: De Boccard.
Supplementum Epigraphicum Graecum (*SEG*), Leiden 1923–.
Sokolowski, F. 1955. *Lois sacrées de l'Asie Mineure*. Paris: De Boccard.
———.1962 *Lois sacrées des cités grecques. Supplément*. Paris: De Boccard.
———. 1969. *Lois sacrées des cités grecques*. Paris: De Boccard.
Stavrianopoulou, E. 2005. 'Die "gefahrvolle" Bestattung von Gambreion', in C. Ambos et al. (eds) *Die Welt der Rituale von der Antike bis heute*, pp. 24–37. Darmstadt: Wissenschaftliche Buchgesellschaft.
Stehle, E. 2004. 'Choral prayer in Greek tragedy: euphemia or aischrologia?', in P. Murray and P. Wilson (eds) *Music and the Muses: The Culture of Mousike in the Classical Athenian City*, pp. 121–55. Oxford: Oxford University Press.
Taylor, M.W. 1992. *The Tyrant Slayers: The Heroic Image in Fifth Century BC Athenian Art and Politics*. Salem: Ayer Company.
Versnel, H.S. 1994. *Inconsistencies in Greek and Roman Religion. 2. Transition and Reversal in Myth and Ritual*. Leiden: Brill.
———. 2002. 'Writing Mortals and Reading Gods. Appeal to the Gods as a Strategy in Social Control', in D. Cohen (ed.) *Demokratie, Recht und soziale Kontrolle im klassischen Athen*, pp. 37–76. Munich: Oldenburg.

West, M.L. 1993. Greek Lyric Poetry. Oxford: Oxford University Press.
Wörrle, M. 1988. *Stadt und Fest im kaiserzeitlichen Kleinasien. Studien zu einer agonistischen Stiftung aus Oinoanda*. Munich: Beck.
Zimmermann, M. 2000. 'Späthellenistische Kultpraxis in einer karischen Kleinstadt. Eine lex sacra aus Bargylia', *Chiron*, 30: 451–85.

10

Rituals of Possession

William Sax and Jan Weinhold

Introduction

For people from Europe or North America, spirit possession represents an alien and 'exotic' practice. But in the context of the world's cultures it is one of the most common techniques of ritual healing, and is moreover of great interest for scientific disciplines both within and without the field of ritual studies. As Janice Boddy (1994) points out, possession is a broad term that addresses issues of spirit and matter, power and corporeal reality, and the boundaries between individual and environment. It has been considered from various theoretical angles in several disciplines including religious studies, cultural anthropology, psychiatry and psychology. Questions of belief and behaviour, personhood and agency, gender, pathology, therapy and religion are all relevant to the study of possession (see also Klass 2003, Lewis 1989, Lynn and Rhue 1994). Likewise, the different approaches to and theories of dissociation are as wide-ranging as the phenomenon itself, and require interdisciplinary inquiry. Hence, one aim of this essay is to re-associate the 'dissociation' between anthropology and psychology, and to take a few steps towards bridging the gap between the two disciplines in research concerning the phenomena referred to by the term 'spirit possession' and 'dissociation'. A further aim is to address the role of spirit possession in relation to the notion of agency, and to raise the question of the efficacy of healing rituals. In the first part of the essay we set the theoretical frame by taking possession/dissociation out of the realm of (psycho)-pathology. Instead, we locate it in the framework of Complementary and Alternative Medicine (CAM), seeing it not as pathological but rather as an essential part of many healing rituals. Nonpathological models of dissociation from anthropological and psychological writings are introduced to chart the territory in an interdisciplinary manner. To support our theoretical claims, we will introduce ethnographic material in the second part of the essay, based on field-research conducted by us in 2006 in the North Indian healing and pilgrimage site Balaji (Mehndipur) in Rajasthan. In the third part, we challenge the (still common) assumption that spirit possession is to be understood primarily as a cognitive phenomenon, and focus instead on embodiment.

Spirit Possession between Pathology and Therapy

Within the disciplines of psychology, medicine and anthropology, dissociation/spirit possession has been often linked to notions of psychological disorder or mental illness (Klass 2003: 43, Wright 1997). Some anthropological accounts employ a psychoanalytic theory of spirit possession as culturally-shaped hysteria (Castillo 1994: 1, Jizek 1971, Klass 2003: 43). But the general consensus in anthropological field studies nowadays is that with some exceptions, possessed persons are usually not psychologically disordered. Because many mediums or other 'possessed' ritual specialists are highly valued within their particular socio-cultural contexts, e.g., as healers or oracles, spirit possession is viewed as an integral part of local cultural techniques that are functional for local medical and religious systems, as well as regulators of social power relations (Boddy 1994). In the twentieth century, the concept of dissociation did not play a significant role in psychiatric and psychotherapeutic models, mostly because of the predominance of psychoanalysis until the 1970s. Since then, various theoretical and clinical issues have led to a revival of interest in the topic, especially the discussions of Multiple Personality Disorder and trauma-related dissociative states, as in Posttraumatic Stress Disorder (Wright 1997: 50). In the medical literature, dissociation is usually understood to encompass some degree of pathological loss of consciousness and identity. In the *Diagnostic and Statistical Manual of Mental Disorders*, fourth edition (DSM-IV), 'Dissociative

Disorders' are seen as psychopathological phenomena, viz., 'disruption[s] in the usually integrated functions of consciousness, memory, identity, or perception of the environment' (American Psychiatric Association 1994: 477).

In the fields of clinical and personality psychology, the term 'dissociation' lost some of its stigma by its extension and application to various nonpathological areas. It has become an umbrella term, covering several different phenomena, including hypnotic processes, automatic behaviour, implicit memory, psychopathological states, trauma-responses and aspects of neurological syndromes (Cardeña 1994). This broader understanding of dissociation shows that many nonpathological aspects of human behaviour are basically dissociative. One illustrative example is automatic motor behaviour that occurs outside of conscious awareness, e.g., shifting gears while simultaneously maintaining a conversation in a car. Cardeña therefore criticises what he regards as the overextension of the term:

> Were we to accept every instance of unawareness, purposeful automatic behaviour, or divided attention as an example of dissociation, we would have to conclude that we live our lives in perpetual dissociation, as there are always some stimuli that have a demonstrable effect on us or behaviors that we are not reflectively aware of, but which we nonetheless enact (1994: 18).

Even if the realms of dissociation and spirit possession are more fuzzy than clear-cut, it is relevant for this essay to repeat that in our view, spirit possession is not necessarily pathological. On the contrary, many kinds of spirit possession are actually beneficial or therapeutic (e.g., Bourguignon 1973). While in some cases spirit possession may bring about distress and maladjustment, in many others spirit possession episodes are used therapeutically, either for a client, a family or a community. To differentiate dissociative experiences and behaviours, Krippner (1997b: 337) suggests a dynamic model for cross-cultural comparison with the following three dimensions: awareness versus dissociation (e.g., memory of the event versus amnesia), control versus lack of control over the beginning and the end of a dissociative state, and life-potentiation versus life-depotentiation (e.g., therapeutic versus pathological character of dissociation). According to this model, and depending on the particular cultural context, dissociative experiences can be culturally adaptive or maladaptive, positive or negative, therapeutic or pathological. The term dissociation then needs no longer to be pathologised, and western diagnostic categories can be modified or abandoned.

What do we Understand as 'Spirit Possession'?

Because of the semantic openness of the term, and the multifaceted nature of 'dissociation', we will narrow the focus of this paper by applying Krippner's descriptive definition:

> Dissociative is an English language adjective that attempts to describe reported experiences and observed behaviours that seem to exist apart from, or appear to have been disconnected from, the mainstream, or flow, of one's conscious awareness, behavioral repertoire, and/or self-identity (1997a: 8).

Consequently, dissociation is 'a noun used to describe a person's involvement in these reported dissociative experiences or observed dissociative behaviors' (ibid.). Spirit possession can be conceptualised as one specific form of dissociation among many. In his attempt to establish a typology of different dissociative phenomena, Klass (2003: 118) categorises spirit possession together with Dissociative Identity Disorder[1] (DID) under the category Dissociative Identity Phenomena (DIP). He characterises DIP as human experiences in which consciousness is not only significantly altered, but is also manifest in one or more alternative identities. In contrast to other states where, upon resuming self-consciousness, the individual may report encounters with other entities (e.g., shamanic power animals), DIP are characterised not only by encounters but by the manifestation of alternative identities. In the same category, but opposed to DID, Klass establishes the term 'Patterned Dissociative Identity' (PDI). 'Nota disorder, this category encompasses "spirit possession" and related phenomena and is proposed as a replacement for that term' (2003: 119). But even when DID and spirit possession — or PID — are categorised under the rubric of DIP, Klass is far from regarding Spirit Possession as a disorder.

> If we conclude, as anthropologists have, that spirit possession is not a 'disorder', it is therefore no more like DID than *normal sleep* is like a sleep disorder. Just as a sleep disorder is a malformation, or illness variant, of normal sleep [...] the dissociative disorders studied and treated by psychopathologists are illness variants of a normal (that is, a *nondisorder*), capacity of humans to dissociate, by either external or internal suggestion (2003: 115).

Individuals exhibiting PDI present alternative identities that are recognisable as entities of the specific culture. Spirits, demons, divinities, ancestors and so forth communicate and act in known and recognisable ways. The anthropological literature is particularly rich in descriptions of a variety of PIDs, which may be viewed as positive, benevolent or empowering (e.g., local gods incorporated for healing rituals), or as negative, malevolent and threatening (e.g., intrusive demons or angry ancestral spirits). But whether malevolent or beneficial, if the alternate personality is 'patterned' and is not viewed as constituting mental illness by members of the society, then we see no reason to classify it as a 'disorder'. Hence, spirit possession differs from DID in three significant aspects (Klass 2003: 115). First, while clients with DID suffer due to the alternation of two or more distinct personality states, possessed mediums are not necessarily under psychological or physical strain during or after possession. Second, for patients with DID the change in identities occurs involuntarily and against their wishes. In cases of PDI, the change in identity is actively sought by patients and their support groups in rituals where spirit possession plays an important role. Third, the alternative identities presented by the DID clients are idiosyncratic and highly variable, while in the case of spirit possession the 'new' identities are known by, and accepted as part of, the culture. These include deceased members of the family, gods or goddesses, guardian spirits, threatening demons and others. Unlike DID, in spirit possession the emerging identities are recognisable within the given cultural context and are not at all idiosyncratic. This is true even of undesired entities, e.g., in the case of 'demonic' spirit possession[2]. Empirical support for this theory can be found in ethnographic accounts, where local members of the community can clearly differentiate between unidentifiable entities — where mediums are sometimes considered to be in a pathological state — and individuals who are regularly possessed by the particular culturally-known entity (e.g., Mischel and Mischel 1958). This typology reflects current attempts to reintegrate the analysis of spirit possession into its various cultural contexts, and to take dissociation out of the frame of psychopathology.

States of PDI embedded within healing rituals often involve controlled and therapeutic spirit possession, and clearly seek the patients' recovery and/or the reordering of family, community or social structures. Not only do such rituals provide a background for the interpretation of the dissociative episodes, they also provide a method for inducing possession-phenomena as a structured and controllable form of dissociation. Hence, when we write of possession rituals in this essay, we do not mean spontaneous forms of possession, but rather rituals that cause external beings to temporarily inhabit a human body in order to give blessings, tell the future, reveal the causes of problems or help with the exorcism of negative spirits. Rituals of this type cause possession by means of techniques associated with rhythm: drumming, swaying, dancing, repeating certain sounds and the like (e.g., Needham 1997, Rouget 1985). In Klass's typology (2003), rituals of possession can be conceptualised as structured and performative forms for the temporary induction of PDIs that are culturally adaptive and therapeutic.

Rituals of Possession and the Body-mind System

Alert readers would have noticed that we have avoided the phrase 'altered states of consciousness'. Even though — as Krippner's definition allows — dissociative episodes are experienced by the mediums as a change in conscious experience and identity, and even though states of consciousness can be analysed with cognitive concepts, in our view the term 'altered states of consciousness' is not appropriate for the analysis of possession rituals because it focuses too much on 'consciousness' and not enough on the body. Possession rituals, however, do not only affect the conscious mind; they also affect and are expressed by the body[3]. Nor are we satisfied by purely neurobiological attempts to explain the causes of dissociation without reference to culture or mind (e.g., Brown 1994). As we see it, possession rituals affect both body and mind, or, as we would prefer to put it, they cause changes in the body-mind system and find their expressions with the bodies of the possessed.

Our attempt to transcend the old Western mind-body dichotomy is influenced by both Foucault (1975) and Bourdieu (1977, 1990) who, in their different ways, demonstrate the intimate connection between embodied practice and human subjectivity.[4] It is also influenced by much recent work in psychology and medical anthropology, which emphasises the importance of 'embodied' (as opposed to purely cognitive) knowledge.[5] Most importantly, we contend that the efficacy of such rituals is not simply a matter of changing the patient's beliefs or perceptions, as for example in the various forms of verbal psychotherapy that are based on a dialogue between client and therapist, but also of changing the form of their embodiment.

It has often been noted that rituals address all of the senses, through the media of food, drink, dance, music, et cetera (e.g., Tambiah 1979, Turner 1974). They are thus not solely or even primarily cognitive, and it is problematic to analyse them in purely semiotic or symbolic terms, unless our notions of 'cognition', 'symbolism' and 'semiosis' are broadened so as to take account of their embodied aspects (Jackson 1983). Possession rituals make this somatic dimension abundantly clear, since they are intended to produce certain kind of transformations in the body-mind system, transformations that are normally signalled and evaluated in somatic terms.

Not only do such rituals induce possession by working on the body, but the efficacy of the ritual is evaluated — at least by those who participate in it — primarily by means of bodily indicators. The signs of a successful ritual are somatic, e.g., the posture of the body and the quality of the voice change, thus indicating the presence of an external being in the body of the oracle or of the patient. This somatic aspect derives from the logic of a possession ritual: the goddess must appear to give her blessing; the ghost must appear and be identified before it can be exorcised. The embodiment of the god or the ghost is the point of the possession ritual, which is often only one in a series of rituals that eventually lead to healing. However, in our case study, as in many other examples of therapeutic possession, the healing is not believed to be the direct effect of ritual, but rather to lie in God's hands.

Possession Rituals at Balaji

Let us turn to our case study: therapeutic possession at the healing temple of Balaji, some seven hours south of Delhi and about an hour from the city of Jaipur in the North Indian state of Rajasthan, which we visited, together with Johannes Quack,[6] in October 2006. It is one of the best-known healing temples in India, specialising in the treatment of mental illness, mostly under the rubric of ghost possession.[7] The presiding deity of the temple is Balaji, the child-form of the monkey-god Hanuman. In Hindu mythology, Hanuman is the loyal follower of Rama, an incarnation of the god Vishnu, and is associated with physical strength and celibacy, along with abstinence from meat, alcohol and other intoxicants. His deep associations with virile masculinity and celibacy make him the favourite god of wrestlers (Alter 1992) and childless women (Lutgendorf 2006). At his temple, Balaji is accompanied by Pret-Raj, the 'king of ghosts', a powerful local demon who was converted into a follower of Balaji and who helps in driving out unwanted ghosts and other spirits. Another important personality from the area is Ganeshpuri, a local religious figure who, according to the literature produced by the shrine, was instrumental in initiating the exorcism of ghosts there, and later became the *mahant* or abbot of a prominent local temple.

Treatment in Balaji is essentially family-centred, with clients visiting the temple in the company of spouses, relatives and larger communities (cf. Pakaslahti 1998; Sax 2009; Sax, Weinhold and Schweitzer forthcoming). During our stay in Balaji we met several groups of pilgrims and afflicted persons who had come considerable distances along with their relatives. The majority came from outside Rajasthan, mostly from the neighbouring state of Haryana, although a large proportion come from Delhi as well, and some from as far away as Nepal, Assam or Karnataka. The clients' background is diverse. Relying on a sample of more than 700 persons, Dwyer (2003: 159) shows that visitors to Balaji range from illiterates to postgraduates, running through all age-groups, with an equal gender distribution. Interestingly, 80–90 per cent of help-seekers have searched for biomedical treatment before visiting Balaji and the common reason for this 'alternative' treatment is the failure of previous medical attempts (ibid.: 132). The main 'indications' — to use a Western framework — are mental illnesses and psychosomatic disturbances, although local persons do not necessarily distinguish between psychological disturbances, social problems and misfortune. The most common 'diagnosis' is spirit affliction. Pakaslahti (ibid.) points out that the characteristics of help-seekers in Balaji are not meaningfully correlated with illiteracy, lack of education, low social or economic status or rural versus urban background.

The temple of Balaji is conceptualised as a kind of court: afflicted persons file their case and obtain a hearing and then a trial, in which Balaji acts as judge and the afflicting ghost is condemned and sentenced.[8] The first step towards healing is to give a small offering, called *darkhast,* which is followed by a larger *arzi* offering. As Pakaslahti (1998) points out, both of these Urdu words refer to 'petitions' that are filed in court. An afflicted person may make a number of such offerings during his or her stay in Mehndipur. The next stage is called *peshi,* a term that refers to the actual court hearing. This stage is characterised by dramatic possession, and will be discussed below at length. According to the persons with whom we spoke, a ghost who is 'convicted' and 'sentenced' during this period must leave the body of his victim, and is then given a choice: he can be liberated and move on to his next life, or he can continue to function as Balaji's assistant, helping to drive away other ghosts. The third step is *parhez,* a period of moderation and abstinence following a successful 'hearing', in which the patient should go home and live a religiously disciplined life, abstaining from alcohol and non-vegetarian food, and worshiping Balaji as well as his own personal and family gods.

Here we concentrate on *peshi,* the second stage, the 'court hearing' during which afflicted persons exhibit dramatic forms of possession. Mornings and evenings near the main temple, one can observe a large number of people in possession during the *arati* ceremonies. *Arati* is the central ritual in any Hindu temple, the illumination of the god's image with lit lamps. The Balaji temple is so crowded that not all the devotees can fit inside, and so this ceremony is shown on video monitors outside the shrine. During the *arati* ceremonies, one sees a large number of people standing outside the temple and swaying, spinning or pounding their heads against the temple or the railings surrounding it. These people have successfully made their 'petition' to the court, so that Balaji is punishing the ghosts that possess them. The dramatic physical movements associated with *peshi* are evidence of the fact that

Balaji is actively working to drive them out. As Kakar (1982) and Pakaslahti (1998) have noted, the dramatic motions associated with possession are examples of learned behaviour. Through mimesis, new 'patients' at the temple — even very young ones — quickly learn to perform them. Typical behaviours involve rotating one's head very rapidly to the sound of music, which is particularly striking when women unbind their hair, so that it whips round and round[9]; rocking back and forth while sitting on the ground; spinning; rolling on the ground and beating one's head against a wall or against the ground. When a 'patient' reaches the temple at Balaji, he or she sees other afflicted persons performing such actions and quickly learns to imitate them. One of the distinctive characteristics of the temple is the fact that afflicted persons are encouraged to share their stories (thus constituting an ideal situation for the fieldworker!) and to engage publicly in possession behaviour. Afflicted persons should hold back nothing; they should not attempt to hide their condition. They are reassured that in the pervasive atmosphere of love and support at Balaji, their problems will soon be resolved. The ritual of possession called *peshi* is thus the most dramatic step of the healing process and is characterised by bodily movements of the patient. The ghost must be made to become physically present in the afflicted person's body, otherwise it cannot be identified and driven out. *Peshi* is therefore a necessary step in the therapeutic process, but it is not a sufficient one, because ghosts tend to lie and deceive, sometimes even afflicting an entire family over generations, so that every family member must be exorcised — a process that can be very lengthy.

During our visit to Balaji we were able to observe one case at length, that of Sanjay (a pseudonym), a young man in his mid-twenties who was visiting Balaji with his father. The father was an ex-soldier who had been able, several years earlier, to get over his drinking problem with the help of Balaji. Since then he had become a regular visitor to the temple, and was representative of a certain type of person for whom the paradigm of spirit possession and the healing power of Balaji become central orienting principles. This man had brought his son Sanjay to the temple for a visit, and soon after his arrival the young man began to exhibit signs of possession. He told us that he had never experienced any particular troubles or difficulties while at home, and that the symptoms of possession appeared only after he came to Balaji. He offered *arzi* and *darkhast*, and soon he could be seen several times a day at the *samadhi-sthal* (discussed later) along with a group of fellow-villagers from Haryana, exhibiting typical signs of possession: shaking and trembling, kneeling on the ground, rotating his head rapidly and the like. This was *peshi*, and it was positively regarded, since it indicated that Balaji was actively seeking to drive out the afflicting spirit. While we were there, the ghost identified itself as that of Kusum, a girl from Madras who had fallen in love with a young man who was subsequently compelled by his parents to marry someone else. Kusum committed suicide, and as a ghost she delighted in afflicting young men.

But according to local *bhagats* (healers) ghosts are deceptive and sometimes lie about their identities. Therefore, they must be compelled to confirm their identities several times, before attempting to drive them out. However, when Sanjay's healer attempted to make the ghost confirm its identity as Kusum, he was unsuccessful, because Sanjay was unable to speak. The healer tried over and over to compel the afflicting spirit to confirm that it was indeed Kusum. He used his powers of persuasion as well as a number of mantras, but when Sanjay opened his mouth, all that came out was an alarming screech, rather like high-pitched radio static. The villagers accompanying him advanced several theories to explain Kusum's failure to confirm her identity: perhaps another spirit was interfering, keeping her from doing so, or perhaps she was simply being deceitful. After several days they asked the ghost to draw on the ground with a stick, and this she did easily, writing 'Kusum' in the sacred earth of Balaji. When we left, Sanjay and his father were feeling quite optimistic that his therapy would soon be complete.

One of the most important ritual sites at the Balaji temple is the *samadhi-sthal*, a large field perhaps 150 metres long and 40 metres wide, where Ganeshpuri (the holy man who is said to have initiated practices of ghost exorcism in the nineteenth century) is entombed, and where most of the possession occurs. Upon arriving at the field, devotees circle the holy man's *samadhi* seven times. Many of them subsequently go into possession, sitting on the ground in front of the *samadhi* and swaying, or rolling on the ground or moving in various violent and dramatic ways. Friends and family actively participate by singing, clapping and playing musical instruments. They attempt to increase the intensity of the possession, to torment the ghost who cannot bear to hear them sing the praises of Balaji, and to drive him toward the *samadhi*, where he will beg to be released. Success is however difficult to obtain because often the ghosts do not reveal their true identities, or they afflict the entire family, so that repeat visits are necessary. Nevertheless, families try to persuade the reluctant ghost to go to the temple and beg for release.

Upon reaching the *samadhi-sthal*, one sees different kinds of groups assembled. During our visit, the largest of these groups were centred on portable stereos playing a kind of 'disco *peshi*' music. In the centre of the crowd were a dozen or more people in various states of possession, with onlookers standing in a circle around them, but such groups were so popular that it was difficult to get a glimpse over the onlookers' shoulders and see what was going on inside the circle. Other groups were led by singers who did not use electronic amplification, and sometimes the performers were very good indeed. Still other groups came from villages throughout the nearby states of Rajasthan, Haryana and Uttar Pradesh. These groups were guided by rural healers, *bhagat*s or *tantrik*s, who often led their followers in musical activity intended to initiate, or strengthen, the *peshi* of the afflicted persons in the group. We also saw a few solitary individuals doing *peshi* without the support of a group, but the pilgrims, healers and local residents with whom we spoke almost unanimously regarded such persons with pity. They felt that without communal support, the chances of such persons being healed were minimal.

Conclusion

In writing this essay we have confronted an old problem in philosophy, social thought and ritual theory: the mind/body problem, which takes a particularly sharp form with respect to 'possession' rituals. Clearly, such rituals work through the body and on the body, by facilitating its 'possession' by an alien spirit. However, they are usually just one step in a series of rituals or other procedures whose goal is to heal or restore the entire system, not just the body but also the mind. Matters are complicated even further because in many such rituals, one is confronted, not with just one alien being, but rather with multiple identities or 'minds' inhabiting single bodies. Because we as Western scholars are also afflicted by the mind/body problem, we tend to formulate our questions in its terms: either the ritual is efficacious because it works on the mind and consciousness, or it is efficacious for some purely material, non-psychological reason. But as we stated earlier, neither of these approaches seems adequate to us. On the one hand, 'symbolic' or 'semiotic' approaches to such questions are unsatisfying because what is happening here is not an act of speech; not a matter of 'representing' social relations or mental problems. Nor do we feel that a materialist, culture-free approach — that of the ethologists' for example, or the neuroscientists' — can adequately deal with the questions of meaning that are so evidently central to this kind of ritual therapy. We have attempted to overcome this problem by speaking of a single body-mind system. But the problem with such language is that it tends to reinforce the very dichotomy that we wish to transcend.

One way of overcoming this problem is suggested by practice theory, especially as developed by Bourdieu (1977, 1990). It seems to us that practice theory successfully avoids the body-mind dichotomy by firmly locating culture in a set of strategic, embodied practices (including ritual practices) that are shared and transmitted by groups, who are in turn defined in terms of their competition for various material and non-material resources. This implies a concept of culture that is neither mentalistic (culture as a set of ideas) nor linguistic (language as the key to culture), and which does not reduce practices to material or quasi-material determinants in the manner of evolutionary biology or ethology. 'Practice has its own logic,' writes Bourdieu, but this is not the logic of language, and it is certainly not the logic of 'belief' as expressed in a set of propositional statements. When we look at ritual as forms of practice we can clearly see that it is not intended to change personal beliefs but rather to alter, at least temporarily, a person's way of inhabiting their body, what Bourdieu would call their *hexis*. This is especially and dramatically true for possession rituals like those we observed at Balaji, where a dramatic change in bodily *hexis* is both a sign and a means of successful ritual therapy. Irrespective of the beliefs that may or may not be held by an afflicted person who visits Balaji, she or he must adjust to the local practice of *peshi*. She or he must articulate her or his distress in terms of its body practices, otherwise the rituals of possession will not be effective. The relevant logic is the logic of a particular practice in a specific social and historical context. Practice comes first, and belief must conform to it. As Bourdieu puts it, 'Belief is a state of the body.'

Rituals of possession also have important implications for a theory of ritual agency. A successful possession ritual involves the surrender of personal agency to an external being, and this surrendering of agency takes an extreme form: the external being takes over the body of the oracle, or afflicted person. It has often been noted in the literature on possession that this negation of personal agency involves release from personal guilt and responsibility. All of this is reminiscent of Humphrey and Laidlaw's notion of 'ritual commitment' (1994: 88), which we would prefer to describe as the attenuation or limitation of individual agency. But Humphrey and Laidlaw formulate their hypothesis in terms of a theory of social action that commits them to a notion of individual intentionality, rather like one of the ghosts at Balaji who refuses to leave the body of a suffering person. In order to achieve a cure, Humphrey and Laidlaw, along with the rest of us ritual theorists, would benefit from a strong dose of practice theory.

◈

Notes

1. In Western psychiatry the mental disorder called Dissociative Identity Disorder (DID) — formerly known as Multiple Personality Disorder — has the following diagnostic criteria according to DSM-IV: (*i*) The presence of two or more distinct identities or personality states (each with its own relatively enduring pattern of perceiving, relating to, and thinking about the environment and self). (*ii*) At least two of these identities or personality states recurrently take control of the person's behaviour. (*iii*) The inability to recall important personal information that is too extensive to be explained by ordinary forgetfulness. (*iv*) The disturbance is not due to the direct physiological effects of a substance (e.g., blackouts or chaotic behaviour during Alcohol Intoxication) or a general medical condition (e.g., complex partial seizures). (APA: 1994)
2. Klass's (2003) main point is that PDI is different than DID, even though some undesired forms of dissociation are perceived as negative or even pathological within the given cultural context. For a discussion

of positive and negative possession in India, see Schömbucher (2006). For classic discussions of possession in India, see Hitchcock and Jones (1976).

3. Within the last years, cognitive psychology has emphasised the inseparability of somatic and psychological processes and shifted from metaphors of computer science to concepts of embodiment (e.g., Damasio 1994, Storch et al. 2006). However, the notion of 'consciousness' — mirroring the Cartesian separation between body and mind — still evokes associations of 'purely' psychological states and symbolic processes that are not connected with somatic aspects.
4. See Bourdieu (1977, 1990) and Foucault (1975).
5. See especially Connerton (1999), Jackson (1983), Locke and Scheper-Hughes (1987), and Strathern (1996).
6. We thank Johannes Quack for helping us to think through some of the issues presented here.
7. The Balaji temple has been written about by psychiatrists Sudhir Kakar (1982) and Antti Pakaslahti (1998), by the English anthropologist Dwyer (2003), and by the American Indologist Fred Smith (2006).
8. The following discussion is based on Pakaslahti (1998).
9. The significance in South Asia of unbound long hair has often been discussed in the anthropological literature (Hiltebeitel 1981, Obeyesekare 1984). For the association of unbound hair with female possession in North India, see Erndl (1992).

References

Alter, J.S. 1992. *The Wrestler's Body: Identity and Ideology in North India.* Berkeley: University of California Press.

American Psychiatric Association. 1994. *Diagnostic and Statistical Manual of Mental Disorders — fourth edition.* Washington, DC: American Psychiatric Association.

Boddy, J. 1994. 'Spirit Possession Revisited: Beyond Instrumentality', *Annual Review of Anthropology,* 23: 407–34.

Bourdieu, P. 1977. *Outline of a Theory of Practice,* trans. R. Nice. Cambridge: Cambridge University Press.

———. 1990. *The Logic of Practice,* trans. R. Nice. Stanford: Stanford University Press.

Bourguignon, E. 1973. *Religion, Altered States of Consciousness, and Social Change.* Columbus: Ohio State University Press.

Brown, P. 1994. 'Toward a Psychobiological Model of Dissociation and Post-Traumatic Stress Disorder', in S.J. Lynn and J. Rhue (eds) *Dissociation: Clinical and Theoretical Perspectives,* pp. 94–122. New York: Guilford.

Castillo, R.J. 1994. 'Spirit Possession in South Asia: Dissociation or Hysteria? (Parts 1 and 2)', *Culture, Medicine and Psychiatry*, 18: 1–21, 141–62.

Cardeña, E. 1994. 'The Domain of Dissociation', in S.J. Lynn and J. Rhue (eds) *Dissociation: Clinical and Theoretical Perspectives*, pp. 15–31. New York: Guilford.

Connerton, P. 1999. *How Societies Remember*. Cambridge: Cambridge University Press.

Damasio, A.R. 1994. *Descartes' Error: Emotion, Reason, and the Human Brain.* New York: Avon Books.

Dwyer, G. 2003. *The Divine and the Demonic: Supernatural Affliction and its Treatment in North India.* London: RoutledgeCurzon.

Erndl, K.M. 1992. *Victory to the Mother: The Hindu Goddess of Northwest India in Myth, Ritual, and Symbol.* New York: Oxford University Press.

Foucault, M. 1975. *Discipline and Punish: The Birth of the Prison.* New York: Random House.

Hiltebeitel, A. 1981. *Draupadi's Hair, Purusartha* 5: 179–214.

Hitchcock, John T. and Jones, Rex, L. (eds) 1976. *Spirit Possession in the Nepal Himalayas*. Warminster: Aris & Phillips.

Humphrey, Caroline and Laidlaw, James 1994. *The Archetypal Actions of Ritual: A Theory of Ritual illustrated by the Jain Rite of Worship:* Oxford: Clarendon Press.

Jackson, M. 1983. 'Knowledge of the Body', *Man* 18 (2): 327–45.

Jizek, W.G. 1971. 'From Crazy Witch Doctor to Auxiliary Psychotherapist — The Changing Image of the Medicine Man, *Psychiatria Clinica* 4: 200–20.

Kakar, Sudhir 1982. *Shamans, Mystics, and Doctors: A Psychological Inquiry into India and its Healing Traditions.* London: Unwin.

Klass, M. 2003. *Mind over Mind: The Anthropology and Psychology of Spirit Possession.* Oxford: Rowman & Littlefield.

Krippner, St. 1997a. 'Dissociation in Many Places and Times', in S. Krippner and S. Powers (eds) *Broken Images, Broken Selves: Dissociative Narratives in Clinical Practice*, pp. 3–40. Washington & Bristol: Brunner/Mazel.

———. 1997b. 'The Varieties of Dissociative Experience', in S. Krippner and S. Powers (eds) *Broken Images, Broken Selves: Dissociative Narratives in Clinical Practice*, pp. 336–61. Washington & Bristol: Brunner/Mazel.

Lewis, I.M. 1989. *Ecstatic Religion: A Study of Shamanism and Spirit Possession.* London and New York: Routledge.

Locke, M. and Scheper-Hughes, N. 1987. 'The Mindful Body: A Prolegomenon to Future Work in Medical Anthropology', *Medical Anthropology Quarterly* 1 (1): 6–41.

Lutgendorf, P. 2006. *Hanuman's Tale: The Messages of a Divine Monkey.* New York: Oxford University Press.

Lynn, St. Jay and Rhue, Judith W. 1994. *Dissociation: Clinical and Theoretical Perspectives*. New York: Guilford.
Mischel, W. and Mischel, F. 1958. 'Psychological Aspects of Spirit Possession', *American Anthropologist*, 60: 249–60.
Needham, R. 1997. 'Percussion and Transition', in W.A. Lessa and E.Z. Vogt (eds) *Reader in Comparative Religion: An Anthropological Approach* (fourth edition), pp. 311–17. New York: Harper & Row.
Obeyesekere, G. 1984. *Medusa's Hair: An Essay on Personal Symbols and Religious Experience*. Chicago, London: University of Chicago Press.
Pakaslahti, A. 1998. 'Family-centered Treatment of Mental Health Problems at the Balaji Temple in Rajasthan', in A. Parpola and S. Tenhunen (eds) *Changing Patterns of Family and Kinship in South Asia*, pp. 129–66. Helsinki: Studia Orientalia.
Rouget, G. 1985. *Music and Trance: A Theory of the Relations between Music and Possession*. Chicago: The University Press.
Sax, William S. 2009. *God of Justice: Ritual Healing and Social Justice in the Central Himalayas*. New York: Oxford University Press.
Sax, William S., Weinhold, Jan and Schweitzer, Jochen. Forthcoming. 'Ritual Healing East and West: A Comparison of Ritual Healing in the Garhwal Himalayas and Family Constellation in Germany.' In Sax, William S. and Omack, Johannes, (eds). How Rituals Work. Special issue of *Journal of Ritual Studies* (scheduled publication for 2010).
Schömbucher, E. 2006. *Wo Götter durch Menschen sprechen: Besessenheit in Indien*. Berlin: Reimer.
Smith, F. 2006. *The Self Possessed: Deity and Spirit Possession in South Asian Literature and Civilization*. New York: Columbia University Press.
Storch, M., Cantieni, B., Hüther, G. and Tschacher, W. 2006. *Embodiment: Die Wechselwirkung von Körper und Psyche verstehen und nutzen*. Bern: Huber.
Strathern, A. J. 1996. *Body Thoughts*. Ann Arbor: University of Michigan Press.
Tambiah, St. J. 1979. 'A Performative Approach to Ritual', *Proceedings of the British Academy*, 65: 113–69.
Turner, V. 1974. *The Forest of Symbols: Aspects of Ndembu Ritual*. Ithaca/New York: Cornell University Press.
Wright, P.A. 1997. 'History of Dissociation in Western Psychology', in S. Krippner and S. Powers (eds) *Broken Images, Broken Selves: Dissociative Narratives in Clinical Practice*, pp. 41–60. Washington, Bristol: Brunner/Mazel.

11

Regarding Ritual Motivation Matters

Agency Concealed or Revealed

Fletcher DuBois, Rolf Verres and Jan Weinhold

Introduction

While being engaged in a highly interdisciplinary research centre for the study of ritual dynamics, we have come to see that psychology — and motivational psychology in particular — has its place at the research table along with anthropological, sociological, linguistic, historical and other area-specific disciplines. We all benefit from each other's expertise and exchange ideas as we try to understand the elusive nature of ritual over space and time.

In this essay we would like to share some of the ways in which motivational psychology can be used as a lens to view how individuals respond to, and act within a ritual context. This lens may help in gaining a more inclusive notion of the complexities of ritual behaviour. But even here at the outset our use of the metaphor 'lens' accents notions of what is (or is intended to be) known as being what should be (individually) seen. Why don't we refer to theory (in this case regarding motivation and its application to and relevance for ritual) as offering a possibility for amplification (e.g., by being like a loud speaker)? The auditory and group aspect would then come to the fore rather than the more common visual and more individualistic metaphor. What difference would that make and what implications would it carry with it?

Should visual metaphors really continue to be so much more central than aural or tactile or even gustatory ones (e.g., 'I want it so much I can taste it') within academic discourse about rituals? Recently, Ronald Grimes, a leading figure in ritual research, posed similar questions about sensory aspects of theorising ritual in a guest lecture given at a meeting of our ritual dynamic research area. Similarly one can ask about how motivation is presented sensuously (as something to be observed, heard, felt or to be touched by). According to the traditional emphasis of motivational psychology we will focus, for the most part, on the individual and her or his commencing upon, and maintaining, goal-oriented activity in rituals. Furthermore, we will focus on factors which can influence those actions and how individuals perceive and value them. But in the closing sections we will also consider critiques which call for more cross-cultural sensitivity and socio-cultural relevance in how motivation is conceived and how research is conducted making a case for agency being a construct that is not only related to internal processes of person seen as individuals, but also as group members and participants in a culture or cultures.

We will centre in on just a few aspects using two scenarios about adolescents in present day Germany taking part in either a ritualised setting of drug-consumption or in a religious ritual called 'confirmation' and the festivities that follow it. How can we understand what motivates a youngster to take part or not take part? If attendance and participation are mandatory or considered self-evidently necessary, how do young people respond inwardly to the external events in which they are involved? What we present here is an introduction to this form of psychological research, and an answer to the question, which motivational theories might contribute to our understanding of the thoughts and actions of these adolescents. We also come with a number of questions, for example, to what extent do the scenarios and theories to be discussed here make sense or relate to better understanding the dynamics of non-Western rituals?

Scenario 1: Cannabis-circle

Our first scene is a ritualistic setting and it is connected to the long-term research we have been engaged in, where we focus on young people's use and abuse of psychoactive substances and the possible protective or negative role of ritual. The scene we will consider is that of a group of young people after school, gathered in a secluded place. After some conversation and mingling the group is beginning to sit down in a circle so they can pass a joint, 'a marijuana cigarette', around. No adults are present but there is a new student who has been invited by one of the participants to join them. This new student struggles inwardly with the decision 'Should I join the circle? And if I do what should I do when my turn to smoke comes? Should I refuse, and if so how can I do this and still be accepted by the group which includes newly-made friends?' This is not simply a spontaneous gathering and there are certain actions that go along with smoking the marijuana. Music is played in the background and precautions are taken so they will not be disturbed. The 'joint' is not passed at random. The person who invited the new student to join seems to have some kind of leadership role or at least a higher status in the group. The invitation was not specific about exactly what would happen. So the new student is confronted with the necessity of choosing to participate fully, partly, or not at all in this ritualised event.

Research Questions

To understand the inner ambivalence of the new student and the impending decision one could analyse the inner state of that person in terms of

(*i*) approach avoidance conflict, or as
(*ii*) a conflict between two desirables (an approach — approach conflict) or as
(*iii*) the conflict between two undesirables (avoidance — avoidance conflict).

What applies can only be ascertained by knowing the subjective expectations and values that guide the young student's decision. Is it about being accepted by the group as opposed to maintaining an abstinence towards drugs that the student values? Or are the relevant factors a fear of exclusion versus a fear of having a 'bad trip' on the drug? Other questions relevant to ascertaining the motivational make-up of the student might be: has the student already smoked marijuana and does he or she have a self image of being knowledgeable about the drug and what constitutes safe use? Or is it rather the risk involved in trying something new and not approved by one's elders, which seems attractive? These kinds of questions are relevant to understanding this ritualised setting as well as the individual motives of the student.

Lewin's Field Theory

Kurt Lewin's classical but still relevant field theory (1951) can help to capture the complexity of the situation. This ecological-psychological approach would look at the life-space, the needs, goals, and the cognitive structure of the student — as they are connected to the external forces in the field (both attracting and repelling much like what occurs in a magnetic field). Kurt Lewin speaks of 'vectors' to make clear, that the energies in a magnetic field are directions. So now we are not only seeing the doubts and deliberations of the student but the configuration of the particular group of students: the inclusiveness or rejection in the ritualised action. Further, one would have to take into account the particular relevant laws concerning cannabis, and whether the student is aware of them or anxious about not knowing enough about them. The influence of possible reactions of significant others if participation in the event became known to them and one's own ability to situate one's participation within a framework of personal meaning, all these are relevant to the onset and continuation of motivation to participate or not.

The present situation of the subject is also influenced by goals and needs as they relate to the past and future. Lewin's notion of needs, quasi-needs (intentions) and the valence of activity are highly refined. Important are not simply needs or values as seen individually but more how they are interrelated, finding out which have proximity and relevance to other elements in the field. What Lewin noted more than a half century ago is relevant to our first scenario: 'Frequently "learning" to like or dislike certain activities is the result of long range change of needs which takes place during development and seems particularly marked during the so called crises, such as adolescence'. (Lewin 1951: 79)

Currently in motivational psychology the importance of the contextual factors of behaviour seems to be on the rise along with cognitive approaches going along with a concomitant decline in the importance of more classically behavioural models. Thus, Lewin's work is much more than of historical interest. (see Pintrich and Schunk 1996)

Methodology

How can knowledge about motivational aspects of ritual behaviour be obtained? Qualitative in-depth interviews can help to reveal unexpected factors which are motivationally relevant. In our longitudinal research, interviews with about sixty students, now aged sixteen, have been conducted once a year over the course, so far, of four years. Which answers did and do come up? For example, the new student might find him-or her-self especially attracted to one particular participant in the group. Will this emotional vector be even more important than the vector which is relevant for group acceptance? Or to take another possibility, what if this student is familiar with someone else who seems to be addicted to drugs and is having great trouble both personally and academically due to being 'high' so often? Will that acquaintance and knowledge of those circumstances be a force to pull away from participation or — on the contrary — could it promote participation in a structured event with the reasoning 'I will only participate in using cannabis with others in a circle like this since that is not such a common occurrence. I won't smoke it alone'. Initial self-report could help the researcher to first pose and then clarify these kinds of questions in interviews or focus-group discussions.

Further methods: through sociograms (*Soziogramme*) the interpersonal relationships between the student and other members of his class or peer-group can be pictured and interpreted within Lewin's theory as positive, neutral or negative vectors. Surveys or questionnaires would help to generate statements about trends concerning the likelihood of substance use, consumption patterns and possible positive or negative consequences for a group. Such seemingly simplifying and reductionist methods may not fully capture individual motives, however, they can give fruitful information about the 'whys' and 'wherefores' of the behaviour in groups and subgroups, e.g., with regard to the question of gender-differences.

Scenario 2 — Confirmation and First Communion

If we return to the first scenario: the new student chooses to join the group and has never smoked marijuana before. This event can be interpreted as a kind of initiation into that activity but was not planned as an initiation-ritual as such. But in the second scenario of 'confirmation', ritual initiation is often intended on the part of those officiating at the ritual. The ritual of confirmation has its own complex and dynamic history as Ronald Grimes notes in his excellent recent work on rites of passage, called *Deeply into the Bone* (2000).

Imagine a brother and sister both in their early teens preparing to be confirmed in a Protestant Church. They attend confirmation classes for a significant amount of time. On the Sunday when they are finally to be confirmed and take their first communion, a ritual is performed in which the minister (or in some denominations the bishop) lays his hands on the head of each person waiting to be confirmed and says the necessary words to make them full members of their church enabling them to take part in the communion ritual (the Lord's supper) from now on. The Catholic Church's confirmation is significantly different in a number of ways, not the least of which is that the first communion precedes it by several years. Here we will take the Protestant example as studies have been done of this ritual recently with the emphasis on how the participants experienced both the service in the church and the festivities afterwards with their relatives and friends. (see Tervooren 2004 on the former, and Audehm 2004 on the latter)

Subjective Theories

The preparation for the ritual and the actual ritual performance itself can be experienced differently by the siblings and the other members of their confirmation class. When interviewed they may perhaps not be able to articulate why they decided to be confirmed. It can often simply be an implicit understanding that this is what is to be done at this time; it is just expected of them in their particular family context. Although they may know many peers of their own age without any religious affiliation, they decide not only to be confirmed but where they will be confirmed. To answer the key questions of motivational psychology — *'what for?'* or *'to what end?'*, it would be helpful to understand the siblings' own 'subjective theories'. By 'subjective theories' we mean psychological concepts which describe implicit cognitive and emotional assumptions about the interrelatedness of concepts connected to a topic, in this case confirmation.

Research Questions

Pragmatic issues about getting to the confirmation class but also possible group affiliation and friendship ties can all play a role in that choice. The motivation to embark on and stay the course of confirmation studies seems relevant as well. A group can be highly critical of others who drop out of the confirmation class before confirmation.

(*i*) Do the youngsters see confirmation as a chance to learn more about their religion and become more active in their religious community afterwards?

(*ii*) Or do they see the learning as a necessary but boring part of an event which is a non-negotiable expectation on the part of their parents or guardians?

(*iii*) Do they understand the entire ritual — what leads up to it and follows it — more as social event connecting with peers and with their family than as a religious occasion?

(*iv*) Is the actual ritual of confirmation being understood as connected to what they were expected to learn, or is it the mere act of attending and sitting there which serves as proof of their worthiness to receive confirmation?

(*v*) Does the ritual mark a new intensified engagement in the church community or quite the opposite; does the ritual after its completion provide the permission to leave that community? Some parents, for example, withdraw from the church after their children have been confirmed. Is a major expectation on the part of the youngsters a material one of what presents one will receive, or do these gifts play only a minor role (and does that in turn have to do with what is actually given)? Is there intensive expectations of spiritual (hence invisible) experience at the moment of confirmation (the laying on of hands and ritual pronouncement) or is the major concern that this moment of being confirmed be visibly documented (by photograph or video) to prove to others later that they have indeed been confirmed and what the event looked like at the moment of their own confirmation?

All of these questions are relevant to understand motivation with regard to ritual behaviour. So is the possible attitude of disengagement — that the ritual has to be endured, that it was more or less meaningless but had to be done to appease parental expectations. Here 'parental' need not imply both parents. Often it is the wishes of only one parent that is decisive. To know how an individual youngster experiences the involved preparation for the ritual, the ritual itself (the service), and the festivities that follow, one needs to know about that person's religious history. What meaning does the service have for her or him? Does the person feel simply as having no input at all in what is done — simply being a 'pawn' as opposed to an 'origin' of action to use DeCharms's terms (1968)? How much does religious ritual allow for a sense of self-efficacy and to what extent can one feel motivated to be a creative actor in a ritual event? This latter question is most relevant for our research-group with regard to ritual-dynamics.

One social goal of confirmation is to strengthen the engagement of the young person in her or his conducting a life that is in touch with the expectations of the religious community. The question at this point is one of moral motivation. Does the ritual play a part in strengthening moral motivation? Recent research at the Max Planck Institute for Human Cognitive and Brain Sciences in Munich, done by Gertrud Nunner-Winkler and her colleagues points to the importance and complexity of moral motivation in a pluralistic society. In terms of learning not only to make moral judgments but to carry those judgments out in action under duress they have found that although there are a number of learning factors involved, 'For the constitution of moral motivation the most decisive learning mechanism is that of biographical experimental learning'[1] (Nunner-Winkler, Meyer-Nikele, Wohlrab 2006: 43). If we assume that the formative years of adolescence — with conflicts, identity-building and search for meaningfulness in life beyond the own person, family, or peer group — go along with a latent need for 'spirituality', then we can also ask, how such a latent motivation interrelates to expectations and participation in such rituals as the 'confirmation'.

In interviews with recently-confirmed girls in Berlin, Anja Tervooren found that there was wide-spread dissatisfaction with how the actual service was conducted. The participants wished to have more influence on how the ritual was actually organised. In short, they felt they were too passive (pawns) with regard to certain aspects although they were involved with reading passages from the gospel and sang a confirmation song.

When making sense of ritual and determining if one will participate and, if it is not a one time ritual, continue to take part, the placing of the ritual within a framework of moral meaning can be quite influential where that meaning does not refer only to judgment but to emotive and cognitive components as well. Different institutions which help shape moral judgements — parents, peers, media — along with biographical experiences can be seen as vectors in Lewin's theory: influences, which shape the individual motivation for ritual participation and for moral action outside the ritual performances.

Interim Conclusion

We've argued so far that differing individual motives can play a significant role related to the question of whether to attend or not to attend a ritualised setting, as shown in the first example with the 'Cannabis' group. We have furthermore shown that the degree of engagement and commitment within rituals depends on a variety of aspects, or vectors in terms of Lewin's field theory.

Especially this last point — the relationship between individual motives and the degree of participation — seems to point out a promising research direction. How are different motives for the optional attending of certain rituals related with the 'experiential depth' of these rituals? Are there differences in the degree of involvement — or alternatively absorption or identification — by the ritual scenario, when different individual motives are prevailing?

In *The Archetypical Actions of Ritual,* Caroline Humphrey and James Laidlaw have encouraged fruitful discussion with their contention that ritual behaviour is 'intentional unintentional' (Humphrey and Laidlaw 1994). However, individual motives to engage and participate in such actions as well as subjective experiences are hardly included within the analyses of ritual performances as such. There is a rich tradition of theory-building regarding motivation in psychology that is relevant to the study of ritual which one of us has explicated elsewhere (Verres 2006). In this essay we have tried to offer some questions which may be important for an understanding of why young people engage in certain rituals or ritualistic settings and how they evaluate their participation in or distance from those events.

Having said this we need to note that the examples we h[illegible]ven [illegible] from recent research done in Germany and [illegible]ries [illegible]risen out of particular (Western) acade[illegible]ngs.

There has been of late a real impetus to demand giving attention to cross-cultural and socio-cultural aspects of motivation and concepts of agency. Though motivation is eminently about motives and valuing and their translation into action, how individuals understand agency can vary widely both within a geographical area (e.g., class differences) and cross-culturally.

Two recent volumes have called for and been engaged in an expansion or revision of psychological research on motivation to include new understandings of agency and the importance of taking socio-cultural contexts into account.

The 49th volume of the Nebraska Symposium on Motivation (2003) is titled *Cross-Cultural Differences in Perspectives on the Self* and includes essays that look at the impact of reconfiguring what counts as agency for psychological theories of motivation. Joan G. Miller advises

> to go beyond the stereotypical views of culture embodied in certain approaches within the individualism/collectivism tradition as well as to develop more dynamic views of culture and psychology. This means giving greater attention to cultural practices rather than focusing merely on ideational aspects of culture as well as recognising the contextual dependence of psychological processes. (in 'Culture and Agency: Implications for Psychological Theories of Motivation and Social development': 59–100).

Her call to develop more dynamic views squares nicely with the intentions and now also the ongoing results of our research area on ritual dynamics. The recognition of change processes that have been formerly overlooked is a key element both in our study of rituals but can also be applied to studying motivation. Hazel Rose Markus and Shinobu Kitayama in the same volume (2003: 15; in 'Models of Agency: Sociocultural Diversity in the Construction of Action', pp. 1–58), note that it makes a difference if agency is conceptualised as belonging to the individual who is the source of action or if it is (also) seen as a property of the group. A recurrent issue in some of our research area's discussions has also been about the locus of agency. Who or what is conceived as the source of an action and the results of that action? This is not easily answered particularly in the case of rituals. In turn t[illegible] can have consequences for our understanding of motiva[illegible] carrying out one's duty may be the way to be par[illegible] much larger than oneself and a source of satisfaction that is not perceived as being located solely within the individual.

Because of the growing perception that earlier theories of motivation have centred too exclusively on the (middle-class European American) individual as subject, Dennis M. McInerney and Shawn Van Etten asked a number of very prominent theorists to review their long-standing work on the psychology of motivation, and to respond to a challenge which 'was for the authors to address the issue of whether or not their theoretical perspectives was developed in a socio-cultural vacuum' (McInerney and Van Etten 2004: 2)

Thus theories that have been quite influential (e.g., Attribution, Self Determination, Self Efficacy, and Expectancy Value Theory) are all presented including how socio-cultural issues have been or are being addressed.

Just to take one example, Deci and Ryan (in Miller 2003) maintain that their Self Determination theory (which for example Miller, mentioned above, singled out for critique) has been misinterpreted as being individualistic. Their triad of universal needs of autonomy, competence and relatedness which they postulate as being universal needs which are at the core of motivation allows for introjections processes that explain how autonomy need not necessarily be equivalent with individualistic and independence motives. And they cite intercultural research to show that this is not the case. Markus and Kitayama, however, though aware of Deci and Ryan's position still see their theory as belonging to those they categorise as 'disjoint' (as opposed to 'conjoint') models of agency (2003: 7).

In the afore-mentioned article by Miller, Deci and Ryan's definition of agency is given as: 'In our theory, the term human agency refers to those motivated behaviours that emanate from one's integrated self. To be agentic is thus to be self-determined (Deci & Ryan 1995: 35, quoted in Miller 2003: 65).'

Yet here we see just how intertwined agency, motivation and the conception of self can be. What do we do when rituals are built upon notions (for example) of possession and thus a plurality of selves?

It seems that the conversation about how motivation is situated in cross-cultural and or socio-cultural contexts is well under way and this parallels some of the interdisciplinary discussions we have been engaged in.

A challenge here is to maintain what psychology and specifically motivation psychology can contribute which includes looking at individuals and how they conceive of and understand their participation in and experiences of ritual while not engaging in a culturally bound and restrictive notion of agency or what can be considered a motive. Psychology does not have to be sociology or anthropology to acknowledge the power of groups and the diversity of ways that human beings perceive and experience the world(s) around and within them.

Our title echoes that of the volume in which it appears. The double meaning of matters has been used much of late. It is particularly fitting in connection with motivation. If something is considered 'not to matter' then it probably functions as what is not to be chosen over what is deemed to 'matter'. What matters is 'what is' and is also worthy of being considered (either for its positive or its negative value and or consequences).

The two scenarios we have presented here in terms of concealed or revealed agency and how that matters with regard to motivation can be reprised as follows. For those in the circle of young people 'passing the joint' the good feeling or high that is expected may be seen as the result of what the group has done (the agency there being in the group's activity which includes but is not solely confined to the taking of the drug). Here the agency is revealed to the participants through the participation in the 'ritual' yet this agency and their part in it is something that is to be concealed from, for example, the authorities or most likely also their parents. The young person deciding to join the circle may have a very different notion of agency, namely her or his own decision representing a choice but this is not necessarily the case. If the participation feels like something that has been forced upon the novitiate then agency may be perceived to be external.

In the second scenario, agency can be construed in numerous ways. The minister officiating most likely has a very different notion of what is agentic in the ceremony being performed than the girls participating in the confirmation. For the latter the importance of being videoed at the moment of confirmation might imply that the media provides not only proof of the event but is involved in some agentic way allowing what has happened to be seen by others not present at the ceremony as well to serve as an audio-visual external memory of the event. Certainly their own attempts to have this video taken at what they considered the appropriate time were thwarted since what mattered to them (to be filmed at precisely that moment) collide with the minister's perception that having that take place would take away from what really mattered, namely the laying on of hands and the actual act of being confirmed. There are levels of agency here where full agency can not be conceived of without the spiritual dimension that is involved.

In his article 'The Person', the philosopher Charles Taylor at the outset clarifies that '[...] an agent is a being to whom things matter.' (Taylor 1985). This is done to rule out appliances and other objects having agency. But being a person rather than say a wolf entails what he calls 'agency Plus' and that 'plus' is the capacity to reflect on what is chosen (not just to choose or be moved to choose). This self-interpretation is essential and is the result of being born into social arrangements and having language. He draws distinctions, for example, between 'anger' and 'indignation'. The social, the valuing, the creating of life plans are all part of what we can consider relevant to a non-reductionist view of motivation. The social space necessary for the emergence of such 'agency plus' in turn brings us to a point where the isolated individual and her or his presumed representations and drives is not enough. A person's motivation is not to be reduced to some materialistic level. It seems that motivation matters because a person's motivation is part and parcel of being able to interpret oneself. And that takes place not just alone but in conversation (Taylor's term) with others.

Understanding the person — an eminently appropriate undertaking for the discipline of psychology — can not be done, it seems, without according 'the social' its due, both contextually and theoretically. By looking at motivation and its role in ritual we may be helping to move away from the over emphasis on individual processes cut off from their surroundings and cultural contexts. Stressing only contexts and group agency, however, without individuals and their own life plans and valuing, would be a pendulum swing going much too far in the other direction.

Conceptions of agency connect to how people perceive what makes what happen. That is, notions of causality are involved. And when what happens matters — is valued, feared hoped for, expected or longed for — then we have a setting ripe for investigation regarding motivation. When that setting is a ritual or contains ritualistic elements then we are right where our title intended us to be — 'regarding ritual motivation matters'. When a comma is placed after 'ritual' then what we maintain is reiterated. Motivation does matter! There is much to be done in this arca. This is just a start. For example, research on young people's subjective theories about substance-induced altered states of consciousness and connections to moral decision-making as well as recent investigations of the role of 'resonance' — another highly interdisciplinary concept — in ritualistic settings are all avenues we intend to continue to explore.

◈

Note

1. 'Für den Aufbau moralischer Motivation ist also biographisches Erfahrungslernen der entscheidende Lernmechanismus.'

References

Audehm, K. 2004. 'Familienfest zwischen Glauben, Wissen und Können', in Ch. Wulf (ed.) *Bildung im Ritual: Schule, Familie, Jugend, Medien*, pp. 211–40. Wiesbaden: Verlag für Sozialwissenschaften.

Grimes, R.L. 2000. *Deeply into the Bone: Re-inventing Rites of Passage*. Berkeley: University of California Press.

DeCharms, R. 1968. *Personal Causation: The International Affective Determinations of Behavior*. New York et al.: Academic Press.

Humphrey, C. and Laidlaw, J. 1994. *The Archetypical Actions of Ritual: A Theory of Ritual Illustrated by the Jain Rite of Worship*. Oxford: Clarendon Press.

Lewin, Kurt. 1951. 'Field Theory and Learning', in K. Lewin *Field Theory in Social Science: Selected Theoretical Papers*, ed. by Dorwin Cartwright, New York: Harper.

Markus, H.R. and Kitayoma, S. 2003. 'Models of Agency: Sociocultural Diversity in the Construction of Action', in Nebraska Symposium on Motivation (ed.) *Cross-Cultural Differences in Perspectives on the Self* (Current Theory and Research in Motivation, vol. 49: 1–58. Lincoln, London: University of Nebraska Press.

McInerney, Dennis and Van Etten, S. (eds) 2004. 'Research on Sociocultural Influences on Motivation and Learning', in *Big Theories Revisited*, vol. 4, Greenwich, Conn.: IAP.

Miller, J. 2003. 'Cross-Cultural diffrences in Perspectives on the Self', in Nebraska Symposium on Motivation (ed.) *Cross-Cultural Differences in Perspectives on the Self*, (Current Theory and Research in Motivation, vol. 49: 59–100. Lincoln, London: University of Nebraska Press.

Nunner-Winkler, G., Meyer-Nikele, M. and Wohlrab, D. 2006. *Integration durch Moral: moralische Motivation und Ziviltugenden Jugendlicher*. Wiesbaden: Verlag für Sozialwissenschaften.

Pintrich, P.R. and Schunk, D.H. 1996. *Motivation in Education: Theory, Research, and Applications*. New Jersey: Prentice-Hall.

Taylor, C. 1985. 'The Person', in M. Carrithers, St. Collins, St. Lukes (eds) *The Category of the Person: Anthropology, Philosophy, History*. Cambridge: Cambridge University Press.

Tervooren, A. 2004. 'Ent/ bindende Rituale. Die Konfirmation als Ereignis', in Ch. Wulf (ed.) *Bildung im Ritual: Schule, Familie, Jugend, Medien*, pp. 173–210. Wiesbaden: Verlag für Sozialwissenschaften.

Verres, R. 2006. 'Was macht Rituale attraktiv? Eine motivationspsychologische Analyse', in H. Jungaberle, Verres, R., Dubois F. (eds) *Rituale erneuern: Ritualdynamik und Grenzerfahrung aus interdisziplinärer Perspektive*. Gießen: Psychosozial-Verlag.

Part III
Ritual Economy Beyond the Ritual Frame

12

The Power of Ritual in Marriage

A Daughter's Wedding in North-west India

Tulsi Patel

'*Beta ho to taliyan, beti ho to galiyan*'[1]: This is the most common saying describing the difference between the sex of offspring encountered by a mother in Bundelkhand region in central India. A daughter is '*parayo dhan*' (others' property) or '*ukkaro dhan*' (garbage wealth, in Rajasthan; it is ... wealth and not waste, ironically called wealth). She is an inferior kind of wealth or an indirect form of wealth which is deployed to generate wealth; *ukkaro* is literally the heap of garbage which is collected in the cowshed. Though it has no use in the house, it is valuable when it is spread in the fields as bio-manure for the crops. The garbage heap has a special value for the fertility of the household's agricultural fields as is a daughter's fertility for some family other than the natal one. These adjectives for a daughter imply that like a rubbish heap she grows up fairly quickly and has to be married off. Marriage and dowry frequently crop up in the conversation right after and subsequently following a daughter's birth, but never upon the birth of a son, though marriage of sons is no less obligatory. A son lives in the family, while a daughter leaves the family upon marriage; in that sense she is viewed also as an avoidable burden raised for another family. People commonly view a daughter as a complex bundle comprising emotions, a responsibility to be cared for as someone else's property, protected sexually and handed over in marriage to chosen

* I have benefited from the comments made by Axel Michaels, Christiane Brosius, Ute Hüsken, Amit Chaturvedi, Anuja Agrawal, Sudha Wasan, Roma Chatterji, Patricia Uberoi, Ursula Sharma and Deepak Mehta. I thank them all.

ones for reproductive and fruitful family regeneration and establishment of affinal ties with other families. In this light, her birth signifies her future role of a wife and mother along with that of her parental family's role as her custodians. The juxtaposition between her birth and her marriage is cryptically communicated in several ways. For instance, a mother after she delivers a daughter is often told that she may not wear the best dresses, the implication being she has to begin collecting items for the daughter's trousseau rather than splurging on her own clothes. A newborn daughter's wedding is foregrounded at once upon her birth, i.e., she is perceived as a daughter (and a female). Marriage in Indian society is one of the most important life-cycle rituals, and is of critical importance across all castes. It is the fountainhead of the family, a preponderant social institution of Indian society that enables it to replenish the human capital from generation to generation. In the Indian context, while replenishment of the human capital across generations takes place through the family-household, the onus of the marriage of children rests with the family elders, especially the parents. The most important and often reiterated social and religious duty of parents, especially that of a father, is to give away his virgin daughter as a gift in marriage to a suitable groom (*'kanya daan'*). The word gift is a poor substitute for the word *daan* in the Indian context, as we shall see shortly. Finding a suitable groom for one's daughter is a major preoccupation and is the subject of popular discourse not only in the family circle but also among a wider circle of relatives as well as acquaintances, with varying intensity, right from birth until a girl's much relieving betrothal. It is strikingly different in the case of a son whose marriage is also the 'father's responsibility' despite the fact that a son's marriage is critical for the continuity of the lineage. A father, and by implication also the family's seniors is described as having had a heavy burden removed from his shoulders, shortly after his daughter's wedding is over.

Methods

The sources of data for this paper are varied. Data was collected through unstructured interviews and observations during the intermittent visits to towns and cities in Rajasthan ranging over a few weeks to a few months between 1980 and 2008. Participation and observation during scores of wedding rituals and ceremonies have provided ethnographic data during this period. Insights from earlier fieldwork in the early and mid-1980s and more recently with non-governmental organisations (NGOs) in Bundelkhand have been of cumulative worth. Unstructured interviews in Delhi over the past two decades have embellished data on rural as well as urban north-west India. Empirical data have also been extracted from mass media, both print and audio-visual, including wedding and related advertisements, television soaps and news coverage of celebrity wedding events and Bollywood films in tracing the transformation in the wedding ritual for over a decade and a half. The essay draws on the Indian census data on sex ratios (female to male ratio) for the age group of zero to six years in the last two decades of the twentieth century. As this ratio is worse in the north-west compared with other parts of India, the essay limits itself to upper castes and particularly the other intermediary castes who form the middle classes[2] from cities and towns, and those who aspire to belong to the middle classes in north-western India and are actively limiting their family size and are known for curtailing the births of daughters. It is not the aim of this essay to labour the increasing intensity of discrimination against daughters practised through female selective abortions in this section of the Indian society. Thus, the essay restricts itself to the upwardly mobile among the intermediary and lower castes. These socially and ritually lower-caste groups (i.e., the intermediary and lower castes, especially those who have practised agriculture, animal husbandry and artisanship as their traditional occupations) have been taking after the upper castes and claim to have been practicing dowry[3]. In other words, they are becoming gentrified through the practice of dowry. Dowry is also believed to be a means of intra-caste hypergamy, a sign of the people with social status and means. The upwardly-mobile among these caste groups are increasingly emulating rituals indicating status difference between the families of wife-givers and wife-receivers, as an unintended gender consequence of Sanskritisation[4].

Wedding Rituals and Daughter Devaluing Syndrome

This essay discusses the discourse connected with the birth of a daughter, the burdensome responsibility of arranging her wedding, and the changes in the wedding rites accompanied with dowry, which reinforce the mindset that devalues a daughter. The essay later argues how the upwardly-mobile Sanskritising castes are giving up the customs associated with the erstwhile practice of bride price, organising a common wedding ceremony for all the family's daughters at one time, sister and/or aunt-niece exchange marriages and the practice of *ghar–jamai*, and adopting the rituals of *kanya daan* with dowry which are instrumental in constituting the daughter-devaluing syndrome. Shah (1988) and Vishwanath (2000) have analysed the relationship between hypergamous marriage and dowry among the landed in north and north-west India. The preferred hypergamous marriage in the north Indian kinship situates a daughter's natal family at a socially lower status *vis-à-vis* that of her spouse's, i.e., as wife-giving *vis-à-vis* wife-receiving households. Daughters, especially more than one, are disliked by the upwardly-mobile caste groups in north India. Ultrasonography and female abortion following ultrasonography are public secrets, information about which is readily offered only in close family circles. Intimate family members and relatives often forward confidential strategic suggestions to pregnant women for having at least one son rather than continue to have daughters until a son arrives (See Patel, 2007b for informal social networks). They are also informed about where to find technological aid in their pursuit to have a son. Technological mapping of the pregnant body, i.e., ultrasonographic screening provides information about the sex of the foetus, which in turn allows mediation through contemplation and planning of sex-selective abortion. It is promoted and in turn promotes the ideology of the small family, while maintaining its continuity through a son as well as the family's material prosperity (in north India). With respect to the dynamics of ritual, the key question is how this selective abortion relates to the ritual of *kanya daan*. Let us see how the dynamic of the rituals of wedding, dowry and hypergamous inequality between the families of wife-givers and wife-receivers creates and sustains what may be called the perception that one daughter is too many, i.e., a daughter-dislike syndrome. The race for material prosperity and gentrification through marrying a daughter upward in the social ladder through giving large dowries is considered to be means to improve the status of the family-household.

Honour Through *Kanya daan*

The gift of the virgin daughter, literally *kanya daan*, is not just a pious duty of a father. It also brings him *punya* (religious merit). In this spirit of earning *punya, kanya daan* is popularly described in social-anthropological, especially kinship studies, as a gift in the sense of Marcel Mauss (1966)[5]. The difficulty of applying the Maussian principle of exchange in the gift theory is raised by Jonathan Parry (1986), who finds the absence of a return gift to be a unique marker of the 'Indian gift'. Quite like Mauss, he considers the giving of the gift as the attribution of reward. While the social status of the gift-giver is enhanced, any return would wipe out or at least diminish the merit once earned through the gift-given. The receiver of the gift, in the very act of receiving it, is understood to extend a favour to the gift-giver, who is then indebted to the receiver of the gift. In other words, debt is built into the idea of gift of the virgin through the institution of marriage. While agreeing with Parry, this essay finds further complexity in the case of *kanya daan* within the larger rubric of the gift theory. In the *Kanya daan* ideology the gift is *par excellence* and is more like an offering, in the sense Firth (1963) argues. *Kanya daan* is a religious endeavour and characteristic of the religious gift like in other Hindu religious sacrificial offerings. Making a sacrificial offering brings religious merit to the offerer. In the same way, giving a daughter in marriage is symbolic of a sacrificial offering. It involves a series of conceptions of transfer (i.e., offering) of a daughter from one person to another person without direct or immediate counter-transfer of any visible equivalent. The giving (*daan*) of a daughter is etymologically related to the Hindi verb *dena* (to give; Sanskrit: *daa*) and *dhamna/dhami*[6] and thus signifies that the daughter is offered in marriage. This implies that she is the giver's own property over which he has rights of alienation. She has some value to the parents (who hand her over) and is transferred with an emotional element, a notion of respect and voluntary initiative.

The demeanour of a humble host before superior guests (e.g., when a large group of people accompanying the groom, called *barat* or *jaan* arrive at the bride's house for a wedding) is a palpable constant at Indian weddings. The bowed head of the bride-giver and his family continues to be a key symbol of an unequal relationship between bride-givers and bride-receivers. In the Bundelkhand region, a groom's kin are referred to as *manya* (valued/honoured) *vis-à-vis* the bride's kin. They have an asymmetrical status relationship, a subordination of sorts on the part of a bride's kin, and a superiority on the part of the recipients to whom the bride is offered. The mild and humble comportment before the groom's party at a wedding signifies a status difference; it is a means of social distinction. Efforts are in fact made to maintain such an asymmetry through intra-caste hypergamy by finding a groom who is an edge above one's daughter. In other words, a more qualified, wealthier and higher salaried boy from a family having high social esteem is desired and sought, preferably from within the same caste. If the prospective groom happens to be professionally equal to one's daughter, his family should at least be better off with property or cash and contacts. Thus, what is symbolically an unequal relationship is sustained socially as well. The status asymmetry between the bride-giving and receiving families is mediated through recognisable practices of preferential treatment in language, rites and recurrent discourses on the relationship between two affinal families. The moral virtue attached to giving a daughter to honourable affines is an end in itself. This is materially expressed through the flow of gifts along with the bride from her natal to her affinal family even before, and continues well after, the wedding ceremony. In this context, the bride-givers regard the satisfaction arising from the attainment of the moral virtue of bride giving in itself as more than compensation. When faced with the question, 'What do you get from giving a bride with a trail of gifts?', several young and old respondents in Bundelkhand promptly replied 'We get *maan*' (literally, honour). However, this statement did not come forth without a direct question. As stated above, bride-receivers are occasionally referred as '*manya*' (honourable).

As a rite of passage, wedding rituals have their typical symbolic value in that they unite the bride and the groom. Besides the *kanya daan* and associated rituals, the partaking of the meal brings the two affinal families and their kin closer. Nevertheless, a subtle asymmetry remains between the two families. And, a higher pressing claim of proximity with the more honourable family *in lieu* of surrendering one's rights over a virgin daughter by giving her to a socially more honourable lot in the community is the norm, often earnestly attempted.

Kanya Daan and Female Foeticide

The *barat* reaches the bride's house or the wedding site amidst much fanfare and dancing. Upon their arrival, the awaiting hosts perform rituals to receive and usher them in with warmth and respect. As already stated, in this honouring lies the honour of the bride's kin. If marrying away a daughter is a religiously meritorious act, and it also links the family to other families in the social group, then why is the daughter a less desired offspring? This dilemma turns on its head Levi-Strauss's (1969) thesis that sees women as a scarce resource, and alliance as a means to establish relations within endogamous social groups outside the incest circle. If marriage alliance is a means to create link with others in society, why should daughters be seen as undesirable? And why have daughters between the ages of zero and six been rapidly disappearing in recent times, especially since the 1991 census? A daughter's marriage enables one to earn religious merit and attain social honour. This religious merit is enhanced further through economic means, i.e., by organising extravagant weddings and giving large dowries as already discussed in the previous section. Thus, the religious ideology and its mundane dimension are closely juxtaposed with each other. On the other hand, while prayers and rituals to fulfil the desire for a son's birth are performed and good wishes are often expressed in anticipation of a son's birth, there is no such ritual meant to express the desire for a daughter's birth. Yet, once born, raising her and finding a suitable groom for her is viewed as a moral as well as a social responsibility of the parents. So, if marrying off a daughter is morally virtuous in itself why is female foeticide resorted to? Furthermore, why are castes other than those historically notorious for female infanticide adopting the practice of wiping out second and subsequent daughters even before they are born? The depleting proportion of the population of girls up to the age of six is indicative of something amiss. There is a rise in frequency of ultrasound tests during pregnancy as part of routine ante-natal check-ups in hospitals and maternity homes. Easily detectable foetal sex technology has gone hand-in-hand with ante-natal check-ups in India over the last two decades of the twentieth century. Besides, an association is found between the wealthy, dominant landowning castes who practised female infanticide and hypergamy in Gujarat, Rajasthan, Punjab and the central provinces in the late-nineteenth and early-twentieth centuries and the upwardly-mobile middle classes of present day north-west India in their efforts and intent to eliminate daughters even before they are born. The historically supported explanation is that they sustain their socio-economic dominance and influence by having no daughters or at the most one daughter. Vishwanath's (2007) study also shows the role of land tenure and taxation policies of the British in eliminating daughters by the landed elite castes to retain social esteem and large properties.

The female to male sex ratio in India for all ages was 935 in 1981 and declined to 933 in 2001. Over the same period the female to male sex ratio for children (zero to six years) declined from 971 in 1981 to 927 in 2001. Punjab and Haryana are both states with a high level of development. Yet they stand out among states and union territories for deficit of girls in their population. While Punjab shows a decline in child female to male sex ratio from 908 in 1981 to 793 in 2001, Haryana comes a close second with the figures of 902 in 1981 to 820 in 2001 (Census of India 2001). Other states that have caught up with Punjab and Haryana during this period are Himachal Pradesh, Gujarat, Rajasthan and Maharashtra. Visaria's (2007) study of Gujarat villages shows a progressive deficit of females by birth order of live births. She found that the decline of female births was inversely related with caste status (2007). Punjab, Haryana, Maharashtra, Gujarat and Rajasthan have shown a rise in per capita income during the decade of 1991–2001 and also a decline in the proportion of girls aged zero to six years over the same period. North-western India is also known for being gender discriminatory and has shown higher female infant and child mortality than their male counterparts. But difference in mortality is not sufficient to explain the deficit in the proportion of girls in India.

Though I (Patel 2007) found little upfront admission by women or parents who aborted foetuses after discovering that they carried female foetuses, almost all of the fourteen NGOs and their federation in Bundelkhand recounted cases of encounters with ultrasound tests to detect foetal sex before deciding on abortion. In this study, I corroborated other evidence showing decline in proportion of girl children in an overall ethos of the small family norms perpetuated and pushed down by the Family Welfare Department of the Indian Government since 1951. While attempts have been made since 1951 to modernise Indians through planning families, abortion was legalised in 1971 and couples accepted sterilisation to prevent further births. Many parents now find body mapping technology of ultrasonography and pre-birth elimination of female foetuses a yet smarter way of planning families.

Why female foeticide has been on the rise in India is a question that has attracted a great deal of feminist, demographic and government attention, especially since the decennial census of 2001 in India. It is common to find mass media and other such reports attributing the cause of lowered female to male sex ratio up to six years to rising dowries. This essay considers this view as simplistic, especially when analysed in terms of the relations between the two processes of birth and marriage of daughters and in the sentimental relationship between parents and daughters. However, it acknowledges that dowry is indeed frequently stated to be a cause for the rise in female foeticide in north-west India. Yet, while marriage is crucial to organising family life in India, arranging an extravagant wedding of one's daughter, more than that of one's son, is of critical significance to the parents, the family and the circle of kin. Demonstration of taste and heavy expenses at a wedding is part of the responsibilities of an Indian family. Accordingly, a daughter's wedding is organised on a grand scale, especially among the middle classes in north India. Loans are often taken out of one's provident fund or from banks towards arranging a daughter's wedding. Here lies a great deal of emotion and sentiment, over and above the economic standing of the parents, in offering a girl to a suitable match, for him to keep for life. Parents suppose that by relinquishing their alleged domain over her, they perform a moral duty, irrespective of economic resources. Nevertheless, while concepts of ritual cannot be reduced to economic calculus, people's ideas about their control over economic resources may influence their style and frequency of rituals. We shall see later how parents of daughters feel pulled in opposite directions in performing the religiously meritorious ritual of *kanya daan* and having to do this through accumulating and spending enormously large amounts of resources at each such ritual. The arduous and emotionally taxing clamber by the upwardly-mobile parents in the middle classes makes them curtail their family size through avoiding the birth of more than one daughter. As a daughter's parents are obliged to search for a suitable match (one who is preferably of the same caste — to keep with the popular rule of endogamy — and of somewhat better socio-economic standing than one's own, i.e., the practice of intra-caste hypergamy) to whom she can be given away once and for all, they feel she is a heavy burden on their shoulders. After marriage she is welcome only as a guest in her parental home. Thus a daughter's family tries to arrange her wedding with all those material resources that are in vogue and don an appropriately humble comportment as these are thought to keep her happy in her conjugal home where she is to live for life. In a way, she is a ritual commodity whose custodians hand her over to the son-in-law, her rightful owner, and thereby lose all authority over her person (in the spirit of an ideal *daan*). A daughter's birth is a sort of a setback, but her parents are not deterred by it. They try harder as a daughter's parents to sustain and even enhance their social status through offering her in marriage to a groom who has an edge over them in social prestige and economic prosperity. They would rather have a lavish wedding ceremony for an only daughter than have their resources split among the wedding ceremonies of more than one daughter.

Culture Industry and the Indian Wedding

If marriage remains a critical life-cycle ritual in India and is nearly universal, organisation of the elaborate wedding ceremony (of which *kanya daan* is an integral part) is a socio-religious occasion that combines morality and religiosity with ostentatious festivity and social celebration. As mentioned earlier, weddings can be observed as enthusiastic attempts at gentrification and Sanskritisation. The simultaneously commercialised services provide a rich view of the glitter and grandeur associated with Indian weddings. Ostentation in costume, cuisine and decor for a wedding is on the rise, more so since India's economic liberalisation in the early 1990s. The Indian wedding industry has grown by 25 per cent, i.e., over three times the 8 per cent growth rate of the economy (2008). Simultaneous processes have been at work to make and mark the event as a memorable one. The festivity in a way overwhelms and overshadows the critical significance of the rituals of *homa*, *phera* (the circumambulations around the sacred fire) and the rite of *kanya daan* as parts of a wedding ceremony. The ritual gets shrouded in the competition and comparison its festive organisation invokes. This seems to resonate with Durkheim's (1976 [1912]) observation that unthinking reenactment of ritual and belief become like mundane parts of everyday world and lose the element of critical edge of its sacredness. The edge of religious merit is somewhat overshadowed under the pressure which many upwardly-mobile groups are coming under in recent times in organising ostentatious weddings. The increasingly expenses incurred by parents on a daughter's wedding over the last decade are enormously large compared with the expenses during their own weddings, a generation ago. The discourse recognises that with a daughter's wedding the moral burden of the parents is over, but the recurrent accounts of the material expenses and tasteful organisation of a wedding ceremony and the cost incurred by the parents is outlasting.

Preparations for a wedding begin several months in advance. Besides the bride and the groom, the family and friends participate in various plans for the organisation of the event for varying periods of time before the wedding day. While a mother might have had a marginal say in deciding her wedding location, cuisine, et cetera, her young daughter today has a large range of choices available to decide from. While the ritual may take place in the house or the street in rural areas, among the urban middle classes of Delhi it is organised in a large temple, community hall, hotel, high-end club, farm house or a resort, several of which are available on hire in and on the outskirts of Delhi with lush green lawns and facilities in toe for much fanfare and attendant ambience. The private ceremony performed at home amidst a large group of people has moved into public space. The cherished desire to perform the *kanya daan* ritual of one's daughter in one's courtyard (*aangano*) is increasingly fading away as one moves to larger cities with little room for large courtyards. The craving to have the honour to consecrate a family's courtyard through a daughter's wedding ritual for each generation of parents is giving way to public places, such as those mentioned above.

Just as hotels, farm houses and resorts are replacing the house as a wedding location, an industry of service organisers for cuisine, costume and décor is replacing individual family's efforts to arrange them. Throughout India, special cuisine/dishes at weddings has/have assumed a new incarnation. To have a range of fast foods from various regions of India and the West, such as *paani puri*, pizza and cocktail/button *idli,* spring rolls, roasted chicken and grilled cheese as starters is common. Besides, the main meal easily combines Kashmiri saffron *biriyani* with Punjabi *chole,* South Indian *sambhar* and Chinese chow-mein or Italian pasta. The range of sweets is similarly large. Coffee and *paan* (betel leaf or some mouth-freshening herbs) go together to end the meal. The typical Karnatak wedding meal, (*oota*) is turning haute, claimed the Bangalore editorial of *Indian Express* (2007). In north India, I was told about a couple of rather modest means who migrated to Hubli in South India from rural Rajasthan a few decades ago. Recently they returned to their village to organise their daughter's wedding and made a record of sorts. No item on their menu was repeated over the three days of the wedding ceremony. The amazing wedding was recalled with an element of awe even a few months after it was over, when it was reported to me by unrelated caste members who were visiting us in Delhi and knew the bride's parents. Interestingly, my family did not know the bride's parents, but this was recounted as a sign of success of the migrant family and their business in Hubli. '*Nit nava jeeman, nit nava jeeman*'; literally, there were new dishes every single day.

The rapid rise in hotel industry and the coverage of cuisine and restaurants in weekend or pull-out sections of newspapers, television programmes as well as television advertisements are attempts to dangle the Pavlovian bell. Theme weddings (not restricted to India and Indians alone) are set up by event managers for those who can afford. Liz Hurley and Arun Nayar's wedding in early 2007 in Jodhpur district in Rajasthan is an example of a Rajasthani theme wedding.

The systemic evolution of services geared to complement and cater to the culturally-rooted wedding niche is palpable in the mushrooming of complementary enhancing affectations. The range traversed by the textile industry is impressive. The advent and spread of fashion technology institutes, garment industry and designer wear, exclusive boutiques for weddings and theme exhibitions present in all metropolitan cities of India beckon the would-be weds. The range of designer bridal trousseau is readily arranged to suit the well-lined pockets. Exquisite *lehengas* for women and *kurtas* with *dupattas* for men are in vogue in place of saris and men's suits. The garments and jewellry to be presented to a groom and his kin are similarly of a wide range in terms of expenses. For shallow purses, textile and garments imitating the grand designers from India and abroad are found in parallel markets. Besides exclusive show rooms and designer advertisements for bridal and groom wear, jewellry and accessories, five star hotels in metro cities put up *vivah* (wedding) exhibitions for three to five days every few months with full page newspaper advertisements before and during each day of the exhibition. *The Hindustan Times* (2008) correctly reported that the Indian marriage has assumed the role of an industry and is increasing its turnover.

Young girls in Delhi, Rajasthan and parts of Bundelkhand were invariably excited about acquiring expensive designer garments and other items on the occasion of their wedding. Most of the women working in the fourteen NGOs in Bundelkhand held the view that their wedding is the only time when their parents would be willing to spend on them even beyond their means. 'Later the expenditure on us [daughters] is never so high nor do we get property. Why not have a snazzy and extravagant wedding at least? This is a once in life time opportunity to feel like a queen', said one NGO staff. A rough and ready estimate of expenditure on costume and cuisine is equivalent to nearly two years of a middle-class, say a university professor's, income. Gold and silver jewellry and cash offered to the groom and/or given to a daughter amounts to another one or two years of a family's income. A girl's parents are preoccupied with acquiring and accumulating for her wedding throughout her growing years.

Exclusive and designer jewellry with latest and seasonal fashions invades the Indian market pushing out old-fashioned jewellry, which used to be passed down from senior kin and relatives to the younger ones. It is considered cool to buy the latest jewellry in fashion, especially at a wedding. Accessories, such as footwear, hand bags, trinkets, vanity items and other embellishing affects enhance expenses on weddings. Designer garment outlets may have exclusive designer jewellry to match with dresses and different ritual performances for the occasion.

Furthermore, event management has made its mark on the Indian scene in the globalising era. Professionally-trained event managers advertise their services through newspapers, magazines, radio channels, internet websites and word of mouth. Advertisements and features covering leading event managers are found in newspapers and other magazines. They also find mention on the plethora of disc jockey programmes aired on radio channels. From the earlier practice of each family having a member, relative or friend specialising in some aspect of the organisation of the wedding ceremonies and festivities, professional event managers have increasingly taken over to care for the last detail for a big fee.

The mass media industry's expansion, with over 500 television channels in India, has spread the reach of event-managed spectacles far and wide among the middle class and the aspiring-to-be middle class. Mass media has informed and also created a desire for the value addition idea through professional event managers in the organisation of weddings.

The beauty industry supported by indigenous and exclusive herbal and other cosmetic industry has not only brought in a 'feel good, look beautiful' perception, it has also found a favourite clientele on the wedding scene. Almost any one who can scrape to arrange a payment goes to a beauty parlour for one's own or to attend someone else's wedding. Bridal make-up costs any where from a few thousand to several thousand rupees. Beauty parlours are found almost on all streets in the cities. They cater to a range of different payment capacities of patrons, and the trend is spreading to lower socio-economic sections of the society as well. Television soaps and Bollywood film scenes of various wedding rituals are not only setting standards for the audiences to follow, they are also demonstrating the finer details of how to follow these Sanskritic (upper-caste ritual practices) as well as consumer standards. Television soaps, which people watch, keep track of and also discuss in buses, cars, trains, parks and on walks, are often ideal type images for audiences to emulate[7]. Shopkeepers in Delhi markets like Chandni Chowk have been overjoyed by the massive revival of the designer sari industry through television soaps. Sari as women's wear had been on the decline, especially for everyday use among middle-class urban Indians; it got a shot in the arm with television family soaps where women wear designer saris and expensive jewellry even at home. Imitation of these soaps and films has led to a rise in demand and supply of saris, matching jewellry and cosmetics. Many tie-and-dye sari houses in Jodhpur (Rajasthan) send complimentary saris to Ekta Kapoor (a film and television soap producer and co-producer whose serials have captured TRP ratings for over eight years; besides, she has also produced Bollywood films) hoping her actresses in the soaps would wear them to rake in huge business. Once people see a sari they try to acquire one like that. Customers ask for saris worn by Rani Mukherjee (a leading Bollywood actress) in films like *Paheli*

(2005 film starring Shahrukh Khan and Rani Mukherjee, directed by Amol Palekar) and *Vivah* (2006 film written and directed by Sooraj Barjatya of *Hum Aapke Hain Kaun* (HAHK) fame, starring Shahid Kapur and Amrita Rao; the film literally means wedding. It deals with the most intense journey from engagement to marriage in the life of a couple and domestic courtship). Like saris, accessorising has become popular, and a wide range of brand names and their fakes are easily available in the market to suit different pockets. Bollywood films like *Dilwale Dulhaniya le Jayenge* (DDLJ, a film released in 1995, screenplay written by Aditya Chopra, also its director, dialogues by Javed Siddiqui, starring Shahrukh Khan and Kajol, and HAHK are reference points many among the middle-class Indians aspire for. HAHK is a 1994 released film, directed by Sooraj Barjatya, with the depiction of lavish Indian wedding ceremonies and relationships between modern Indian families, starring Salman Khan and Madhuri Dixit. It was the biggest grosser ever of Indian film industry until 2001. Made on a budget of around 60 million Indian Rupees, i.e., 11 million Euros, it went on to collect over 650 million rupees (over 120 million Euros) in India and over 150 million rupees (30 million Euros) overseas. The film was dubbed in regional languages such as Telegu (*Premalayam*) and became silver jubilee (175 days) film in Tollywood, i.e., Andhra Pradesh's Telegu film industry. Films such as these are emulated for organsing weddings even by non-resident Indians in the United Kingdom and The United States (personal communication with Leela Dube[8]). Patricia Uberoi's (2006) work on the imagination of the family through film viewing based on the latter films support the case of viewers emulating lavish weddings. Indian dresses and appearances are on public display through a wedding ceremony. Uberoi's analysis of the films DDLJ and HAHK deals with how these two films appeal to Indians in the diaspora. These films serve as models for Indians in exile and also have a demonstration effect on them. The actors are seen as Indians who behave as Indians and those who imitate the *filmy* ceremonial practices are seen as Indians by themselves and by other Indians. Closer, at home in urban India, the middle classes are increasingly taking the upper-caste north Indian homogenising of rituals and ceremonies in television soaps as models worth emulating. Adopting ceremonial and ritual practices from these soaps is seen as a marker of being trendy and in tune with the times.

Each wedding among the middle classes and aspiring to be middle-class sections I attended during the last two decades in Delhi (since the early 1990s), remained a point for repeated conversation for several days or weeks after the event was over. Conversations of the weddings took place in homes, parks, temples, housing society complexes and such other places where people met. It is common to find people recounting the happenings of the latest wedding in the family or that one was invited to as a relative, friend or colleague. 'The farm house was so beautifully decorated, the grass was lush green, there was a large enough space for two weddings, the dance floor with music in tune, the food was delicious, the variety in the menu was so large it was not possible even to try all the items.' The bride's dress, her neck choker, her hair-do, et cetera are admired and similarly an evaluation of the groom's appearance is made. 'A family in Aakash Deep, a multi-storey housing apartment in east Delhi spent rupees 1.25 crore (i.e., ten million) for their daughter's wedding. It was lower than they expected because the girl is very beautiful. Had she been of average looks the expenses would be higher', reported a young anesthetist (who had been to the wedding) while we were taking a walk in Ekta Gardens, near the Aakash Deep complex.

Television soaps and Bollywood films have introduced newer and transformed simple regional and caste-specific rituals into more elaborate and glossy ones with attendant festivity and expenses. One example is the *mehndi* (henna) ritual which has become a lot more festive an occasion prior to the day of the wedding, especially in north India. Each wedding is organised as a memorable event with an element of competition that sets off and lasts until long after it is over. The wedding of Abhishek Bachchan (a film star from a film star family) with Aishwarya Rai (a film actress and former Miss World) preoccupied the Indian media for over a month. There were hopeful rumours of video discs likely to be available for watching their wedding ceremony at home (which did not happen though Youtube has clippings of the wedding which attracts thousands of hits). Video coverage of weddings too, is a done thing in the middle-class weddings these days.

The impact of television soaps and Bollywood films on audiences, including the attendant priests seem to be on the rise, as is the homogenisation of rituals at a wedding, i.e., people of lower castes adopting new rituals shown by the audio-visual media. The emulatory performances by audiences is also contributing towards Sanskritisation of the wedding ritual. The Sanskritic way of performing the *Kanya daan* rite is perceived as an ideal typical ritual for a wedding. On the whole, as far as the costume, cuisine, décor and ritual are concerned, the middle-class wedding is getting increasingly homogenised. Of course, some aspects of the rituals, such as a specific folk song or the manner of introducing the bride's and the groom's people to one another, may still convey the ethnic and community or region-specific context of the people concerned during the wedding.

Several OBC (a formal category of Other Backward Classes consisting of castes considered backward are categorised as such by the State for positive discrimination) castes, such as Jats, Patels, Gujjars, Raikas in Rajasthan had been traditionally practising bride price and remarriage of widows and divorcees until a few years ago. They also practised group weddings, i.e, weddings of several daughters of a family at a time. Weddings of a household's or a family's daughters were held together when the eldest daughter reached marriageable age or on the day of the death feast of an elderly parent. They also practised sister-exchange and sister-niece exchange marriages (Patel 1982 and 1994). Over the last few years, both these occasions for clubbed weddings are being discarded by many middle-class urban OBC families. In the manner of disowning the above stated marriage practices and adoption of the wedding ceremony for one daughter at a time, there is evidence of emulation of upper-caste customs and thus of Sanskritisation. However, emulating the consumer wedding of television soaps and Bollywood films may not be seen as Sanskritisation, it is more of an attempt at gentrification. Avid watching of television soaps and films are drawing the aspiring middle classes towards rituals they never performed before. Standardisation of wedding rituals as a consequence of emulating electronic media and films is attempted by an ever-rising number of people. The overall effect of following the ideal typical wedding has by and large been towards a homogenisation of the ritual across castes among the middle classes. The differences in ritual details across time, region and caste is undergoing change, and its homogenising direction (towards north-Indian upper-caste ritual and customary events) finds further support through the demonstration effect of the mass media, simultaneously commercialised by the liberalised market and supported by professional service industry.

The event management industry and the large resources steered towards each wedding by the family signify the organisational enormity involved in the performance of the ritual. The material and the mundane aspects of a wedding are as significant as the rites. In fact, for most of the guests other than the family, close kin and close friends, the festive feast (called reception) is the main event during a wedding. The specific rituals of the *phera* and *kanya daan* are increasingly becoming a family affair, especially in middle-class Delhi weddings. The sentiment behind the sacrament and its organisational location in this world go hand-in-hand with the norms. The ritual ideals are found somewhat modulated and fine tuned in actual performance. The economic and social burden of organising a daughter's wedding is a scary and overwhelming thought for the parents, so much so that the notion of earning religious merit through recurrent *kanya daan* for more than one daughter does not seem to be meaningful. The frequency with which a *kanya daan* is organised, invariably with all the organisational paraphernalia described above alongside a continuous bowing down of the bride-givers' head before the bride-receivers', makes a case against daughters being desirable and for accepting one only if she happens to come by. Once she is born, they cherish a dream for organising a grand wedding for their daughter after striking an alliance with a family of better status but would rather not have to do it more than once. Also, it is noteworthy that giving to a daughter and her marital family is continual, and does not end at her wedding. Wedding happens to be the most expensive among the occasions of gift giving to a daughter but gifts in cash and kind given to a middle-class daughter at her wedding are not on public display for fear of conviction under the anti-dowry law of 1961.

Conclusion

Religious and social obligation, as in the case of *kanya daan* is performed by all parents irrespective of the economic situation, but the scale of the wedding celebrations is extensive among the aspiring middle-class Indians. In other words, even poor parents organise the wedding of their daughter(s), even if they have to keep them as low-key affairs, not for want of efforts, including indebtedness.

television soaps is they show middle-class dressy women in make-up in well-kept homes, but who do little household work.

8. Leela Dube is an Indian anthropologist with expertise on gender studies and kinship.

References

Census of India. 2001. *Provisional Population Total, Series 1, Paper 1*. New Delhi: Registrar General of India.

Durkeheim, E. 1976 [1912], *The Elementary Farms of Religious Life*. London: George Allen and Unwin Ltd.

Firth, R. 1963. 'Offering and sacrifice: problems of organization', *Journal of the Royal Anthropological Institute,* XCIII: 12–24.

Hindustan Times. 2008. (a news report on growth rate in the Indian marriage industry), 14 December.

Indian Express. 2007. 'Oota goes haute', 28 August.

Levi-Strauss, C. 1969. *The Elementary Structures of Kinship*. London: Eyre and Spotiswoode.

Mauss, M. 1966. *The Gift: forms and functions of exchange in archaic societies.* London: Cohen & West.

Porry, J. 1986. 'The Gift, the Indian Gift and the "Indian Gift"', *Man,* NS, 21 (3): 453–73.

Patel, T. 1982. 'Domestic Group, Status of Women, and Fertility', *Social Action,* 32 (4): 363–67.

———. 1994. *Fertility Behaviour: Population and Society in a Rajasthan Village.* Delhi: Oxford University Press.

———. 2007. 'The mindset behind eliminating the female foetus', *in* T. Patel (ed.) *Sex Selective Abortion in India: Gender, Society and New Reproducitve Technologies*, pp. 135–74. New Delhi: Sage Publications.

———. 2007b. 'Informal Social Networks: Sonography and Female Foeticide in India', *Sociological Bulletin*, 56 (2): 243–62.

Shah, A.M. and Desai. I.P. 1988. *Division and Hierarchy: An Overview of Caste in Gujarat*. Delhi: Hindustan.

Srinivas, M.N. 1956. 'A Note on Sanskritization and Westernization', *Far Eastern Anthropologist*, xv (4): 481–96.

Uberoi, P. 2006. *Freedom and Destiny: Gender Family and Popular Culture in India*. Oxford University Press, Delhi. (See especially the following two sections: 'Imagining the Family: An Ethnography of viewing Hum Aapке Hain Kaun ...!' (138–79), and 'The Diaspora Comes Home: Disciplining Desire in the DDLJ, (180–216).

Visaria, L. 2007. 'Deficit of girls in India: Can it be attributed to female selective abortion', *in* T. Patel (ed.) *Sex Selective Abortion in India: Gender,*

Society and New Reproducitve Technologies, pp. 61–79. New Delhi: Sage Publications.

Vishwanath, L.S. 2000. *Female Infanticide and Social Structure*. Delhi: Hindustan.

———. 2007. 'Female infanticide, property and the colonial state', *in* T. Patel (ed.) *Sex Selective Abortion in India: Gender, Society and New Reproducitve Technologies*, pp. 269–85. New Delhi: Sage Publications.

Yalman, N. 1967. *Under the Bo Tree*. California: California University Press.

13

Ritual Economy and South Indian Ritual Practice[1]

Ute Hüsken and K.K.A. *Venkatachari*

As an Indologist who was rather inexperienced in field research, I entered the field (the South Indian temple town Kāñcipuram) with some Deutsche Forschungsgemeinschaft (DFG) money in my pocket — but suddenly found myself having many expenses for ritual gifts I could not reimburse with the DFG. Thus, saris, dhotis, fruits etc., had to be brought along with my visits and requests for interviews to the diverse ritual specialists I met. Retrospectively I also discovered that my *vastradāna* (giving traditional clothes) to all the employees and hereditary office holders in the Varadarāja temple had opened many doors which would have remained locked for a long time otherwise. At the same time, I myself was also showered with saris, blouse pieces, *mañjanam*, and other items suitable to be given as token of respect to a married woman. This way I was first personally confronted with a South Indian system of ritual economy, and then with the difficulties of translating this into a Western research grant economy, which had allowed me to do my research in Kāñcipuram. *UH*

This tricky situation quickened the interest of the first author Ute Hüsken of this essay. Further discussions with the other author, K.K.A. Venkatachari, Hüsken's long-term teacher and friend in South India, made them work more systematically on the issue of ritual economy.[2] 'The importance of this kind of ritual distribution lies rather in expressing and negotiating the statuses and self-identities of the recipients. It thus goes far beyond their monetarian and utilitarian value' (Good 2004: 22). Taking this as their starting point, the authors present here some thoughts on why the notion of 'economy' should be explored further for ritual studies.

In this essay, they deal with two sets of Brahmanic rituals: domestic rituals, and those performed in public. Change can be observed in public temple rituals as well as in domestic rituals, there is no stagnation in their form. What is common to both, although ideally following a set of rules,[3] and based on norms and conventions, is that their scale and elaborateness depends partly on the economic conditions of the performers. However, it is also argued here that the impact and effect of monetarian issues is different in both sets of rituals.

Domestic Rituals

Domestic rituals are those rituals performed by a Hindu householder for his family, usually with the help of a ritual specialist, the priest. Most of them can be labelled as rites of passages or life-cycle rituals. Nowadays, the most important of the twenty-four life-cycle rituals (*saṃskāra*) prescribed, for example, by the *Apastambhagṛhyasūtra*[4] are those connected with wedding (the making of a bachelor into a householder, and a woman into a wife), and those connected with death. If performed at all, usually the prenatal, the childhood and the adulthood rituals are enacted together, along with the corresponding atonement ritual (*prāyaścitta*) for 'not performing them at the right time'.[5] This is also due to the extensive expenses of such a ritual, if performed properly: the more people attend these rituals and bless the occasion with their presence, the more auspicious they are. Thus, many relatives and friends have to be invited, and to be entertained with food and presents, the priest's fees (*dakṣiṇā*) have to be paid, the ritual materials have to be purchased, et cetera. Here, the rituals are an expression of the performers' status, and at the same time they create the performers' status anew. However, death rituals seem to be an entirely different issue. Death, and the rituals connected with it, are inauspicious, and partly also polluting for the participants. The main motivation to perform these rituals as close to the rules as possible is the concern for the afterlife of the deceased on the one hand, and on the other the fear of the return of the deceased, who might, if not ritually taken care of properly, cause harm to the living.[6] Part of it is sometimes the pilgrimage to places which are connected to death and afterlife, like Benares. There, a special caste of priests performs the death rituals. But for their performances, too, the affluence of the performers determines the scale of the ritual, which may take one to two days but might also take just one or two hours.[7] For instance, if the performers lack the means to go to Benares for these rituals, they enact them at their own places with the help of a priest.

Temple Rituals

The situation is different in public rituals such as temple festivals. Good (2004: 21) states: 'South Indian temples are certainly major economic enterprises, but to analyse them purely in terms of secular economics would clearly miss the point.' He emphasises that 'the material results are not to be confused with the ultimate purpose. Public display, assertion of hereditary rights and obligations, and devotionalism (*bhakti*) are far more important than economic rationality, or the maximisation of material outcome' (ibid.: 21). Although, as we would like to add, in the end, they might again find expression in economic terms. The South Indian temple is in fact of great importance to the local economy — as an employer, a centre for market activities and a consumer. Nevertheless, the situation is more complex than it might seem at first sight. Ritual and economy in South Indian temples are not independent and autonomous domains. We argue here that in this context rituals — or shares in rituals — are first of all themselves values, and, as such, property.

The case serving as a base of our considerations is a large Viṣṇu temple in the South Indian town Kāñcipuram. The main deity housed in this temple is a form of Viṣṇu called Varadarāja, hence the name of the temple, Varadarāja temple. Apart from Varadarāja there are also Yoga-Narasiṃha and Lakṣmīdevī (Tamiḷ: Tāyār, or Peruntēvi), Varadarāja's consort, hosted in separate shrines. The temple's rituals are performed according to the Pāñcarātra mode of worship. This implies, for example, that the three main images of the temple may only be touched by initiated male members of six hereditary families of temple priests (Skt. *arcaka*). But there are many more groups involved in the temple activities. Some of them have hereditary rights and duties, and some are appointed by the temple management (Devasthānam board). The groups and individuals involved are, for example, the temple-cooks, the *Paricārakas* who help the priests during worship but who do not touch the images of the gods, watchmen, those who carry the god during processions, those who care for the activities outside the temple such as selling tickets for worship (*pūjā*), the women who clean the floor, a group of musicians, the members of the Tātācārya families who hold certain rights during most ritual performances, members of the Vaṭakalai sect who chant the Vedas and other Sanskrit texts during the rituals, members of the Teṉkalai sect who recite the Tamiḷ Tivyapirapantams, and many more. The number of individuals involved in daily and festival worship is vast, and the ritual schedule of the Varadarāja temple is a very tight one: six times a day regular worship takes place in the *sanctum sanctorum*, and at an average every alternate day a small or big temple festival is performed.

For these temple rituals, depending of course on their scale, considerable manpower and material resources are mobilised. Huge amounts of flowers are needed every day as decoration for the gods, the food for the gods (*naivetiyam*) is cooked in the temple kitchen, the immovable images of the gods are frequently bathed with milk, honey and other expensive substances, in the kitchen a lot of fire wood is needed, and additionally there are the salaries of the temple employees. Moreover, many devotees give huge sums of money to the temple: they donate expensive clothing and jewellery for the gods, and contribute towards renovations and maintenance of the diverse shrines in the temple. The acts of worship (especially festivals) are sustained by pooling independent[8] sets of resources and materials, and of services.

The Economy of Ritual Shares

Thus, for the festival performed during Kṛṣṇajayanti, one specific donor provides flowers, butter, rice grains, wood for cooking, incense, fruits, coconuts, vermilion powder, sandal paste, saffron, gingilee oil, milk and so on. The acting priest provides his service, like 'offering śaṅku pāl', the *Paricāraka* provides his services (handing over the required utensils to the officiating priest), the office holder Varadan Kattiyam announces the ritual acts, the members of the Tātācārya families recite the Mantrapuṣpa verses, and so on. Such a pooling of resources generates a set of prestational and honour distributions. Receiving shares of materials that were in physical contact with the god (a sip of water [*tīrtam*] that was used for bathing the god, a part of the basil-leaf garland that hung around the god's neck, etc.) and also the sequence of being touched by the *catāri* (a metal bowl symbolising the feet of the god) are such honours. Because the contributions of the diverse participants are independent from each other but at the same time relate to the same ritual event, conflict and competition over these honours frequently arise between participant groups or their representatives, which leads to change in some cases, and to a reinforcement of existing arrangements in others (see also Appadurai & Breckenridge 1976: 201–04).

Thus, in the Varadarāja temple a material expression of temple honours is the food (*naivetiyam*) consumed by the god, which is distributed after the ritual performance among the devotees. There are several schemes (differing considerably depending on the ritual occasion) according to which certain participants have the right to a specified amount of the food after the god has consumed it. The person in charge of distributing the food describes this task as very delicate. His father taught him the diverse schemes. However, even then, initially, when he himself started distributing *naivetiyam*, he made many mistakes. In such instances, and in order to prevent a dispute or even a court case, he immediately had to apologise to those who did not receive their proper share. Now he is familiar with the diverse schemes of distribution but still he describes his task as very difficult. Even if this food is nowadays not always consumed by the recipients — in fact it is frequently immediately given away — the share-holders insist on being allotted the proper amount.

The importance of the right to receive the materials used during worship refers even to the flower garlands, worn by the god and given to the donors after the ritual. A donor reports:

> The Ceṉai Mutaṉmaiyār festival took place, and I was the donor. During this festival the god Ceṉai Mutaṉmaiyār goes to the hill, Perumāḷ [the main deity Varadarāja] is invoked, and a turban and a flower garland is brought from Perumāḷ to Ceṉai Mutaṉmaiyār. With that turban and garland he comes straight to the Nammālvār shrine. There the garland which was taken from Perumāḷ and then was put on Ceṉai Mutaṉmaiyār is taken and put on [the image of the Vaiṣṇava saint] Nammālvār. Ceṉai Mutaṉmaiyār then returns to his shrine without garland. That garland has to be given to the donor, that is to me. [...] They [the priests] should give the garland to me also automatically, without any request, without any court order. The garland which goes from the main deity to the sub

> deity should be given to me. But they don't give it to me. What I am asking the temple administration is, the garland that is coming from Perumāḷ to Ceṉai Mutaṉmaiyār and from him coming to Nammālvār, I want the garland pertaining to Perumāḷ. Even if the garland is dry it is alright, even if it is leaf alright, lastly if it had become sand also it is alright, I want it, at least the sand of the garland pertaining to Perumāḷ.'[9]

The perceived right of this donor refers explicitly not to the material value of the garland.

Not only are the form and content of the honours important, but also the sequence of their distribution. Although even in sponsored festivals everybody present receives the material benefits of worship, the sponsors should receive it first. The public nature of the temple rituals makes their respective role in the ritual visible through the sequence of distribution. The importance of this sequence is, for example, expressed by certain honorary (and hereditary) offices, called *tīrtakārar*. After worship the water used for washing the god (*tīrtam*) is distributed as *prasādam* (divine blessing) among the persons present. Since at least one century the right to the first ten portions of this water is held by certain *tīrtakārar* families, hailing from Kāñcipuram. This right, however, is also a duty. In order to maintain it, one regularly has to show up and collect the *tīrtam*. Since many of these families do not live in Kāñcipuram any more, they have appointed deputies, who collect the *tīrtam* on their behalf. Meanwhile even this deputyship has become a hereditary right, and people fight for it in court.

As we could see, the donor of a specific festival is usually entitled to receive the garland which was worn by the god during worship. However, in many rituals other participants are also entitled to a garland or parts of it, for instance, a representative of the Tātācārya families. They receive a garland not for the material they provide, but for their service, such as fanning the god during worship. In one case, a donor wanted his independent contribution to the ritual, the material, to be rewarded with identical honours as the honours given to the Tātācāryas for their service, the fanning and chanting of mantras. This created a dispute as to who should get the garland first, a conflict derived from this pooling of independent ritual shares. One member of the temple staff relates:

'For the Pallava festival there is a certain donor. He pays for everything from A to Z, for all the expenses. However, once the function was over, the garland which was put on the god is put on one representative of the Tātācārya family, and then only it is given to others. But the donor wanted the garland to be given straight away to him, and not via the Tātācārya. He sought a solution and proposed that he would provide for three garlands, so that the Tātācārya could retain their hereditary right to receive a garland, one should be for the EO [the Executive Officer of the temple] or another representative of the administration, and one should go directly to him. All three garlands should be handed over directly to the concerned persons. In 2004 he went to the court, but the Commission Officer decided that the "usage and custom" of the temple should be followed, so it should be done as before without alteration.Then the donor went to the High Court. There it was decided that the option given by the donor should be followed.'[10]

These court procedures, which are common means to ensure or enforce ritual honours, can also be seen as a kind of 'investment' because they cost a lot of money and effort, while the material fought for might be, as in this example, 'just' a garland or rather the sequence of being in contact with the garland.

Considering the public nature of temple rituals, the temple festivals have a crucial position because during these occasions the diverse participants publicly display their status and their relation to each other and to the main deity. During these festivals the value of participation in the temple rituals becomes evident — not only for those who have a claim to a share of the temple honours, but to all the local inhabitants 'as a symbol of their collective religious and social identity' (Mukund 2005: 65). Temple festivals are public events. Their performance includes the deity's processions through the streets of the town which are of great significance to the general public, since it essentially signifies that the god as paradigmatic sovereign leaves his privileged seclusion of the temple and approaches the people, to mingle with them and to be accessible in public space. In general perception these processions signify a properly functioning government, public order and stability. However, many internal disputes regarding ritual matters are strategically enacted and negotiated at the time of these festivals and especially during these processions through town. The 'ordinary' devotees are then spectators and participants on the one hand, but on the other they become judges of conflicts between the two parties. In Kāñcipuram, the god Varadarāja's processions are accompanied by two groups: the Vaṭakalais recite the Veda and walk behind the deity,[11] the Teṉkalais recite the Tamiḻ hymns and walk in front of the deity. This spatial separation is itself the result of the conflict between the two groups and visibly attests to it. On these occasions there is a high risk that members of the two sects try to sneak into the 'ritual space' of the other group and take over at least part of it. Such occurrences can be witnessed during several temple festivals, for example, when the members of one sect suddenly infiltrate the rows reserved for the other sect. The situations sometimes even end in an abrupt termination of the ritual because of the scuffle ensuing from this transgression. Therefore, many policemen are usually present during these festivals in order to 'maintain law and order'.

The examples given above underpin Appadurai's and Breckenridge's (1976) argument that South Indian temples constitute the frame in which individuals and groups participate in a dynamic redistributive process, considered immensely important by the participants. However, they not only include the redistribution of material resources into their considerations, but explicitly also refer to 'shares' (*paṅku*) and honours (*mariyāṭai*) in the temple rituals. The specific participation of the diverse groups and individuals in the ritual processes is therefore labelled by Appadurai and Breckenridge as 'ritual share'. Depending on the context,

> '[...] one's share in the ritual process has a different concrete content. But the sum of one's rights, over time, constitutes one's share in the ritual and redistributive process of the temple. This share is given public expression and authoritative constitution by some combination of a finite set of substances transvalued by association with the deity, which are referred to as "honours". (Appadurai & Breckenridge 1976: 198).

In this sense, the diverse individuals and groups involved in the temple rituals just mentioned perceive their role as a specialist role: all participants involved are 'specialists'[12] and from this 'specialisation' a kind of autonomy of their role is derived. The participants in the diverse rituals, from the 'ordinary' devotee to the temple priests, each claim a unique and individual relationship to the deity. This relationship is expressed through separate and autonomous shares in the ritual and through economic advantages received (see Appadurai & Breckenridge 1976: 198f.).

Ritual Shares in the Varadarāja Temple

We want to illustrate now what concrete issues in the South Indian temple context are perceived as 'ritual share.' As we have seen, not only are the main donors (sponsors) of a specific ritual event rewarded by the public distribution of material and honours, but the other specialists (participants) involved also get their share. This share can also be cash or a fixed sum, however nominal. Thus, the leader of the group of temple musicians receives 50 paisa per day of the temple festival Brāhmotsava for walking with his drum during the entire procession in front of the god.[13] Here, as in the context of salary, it is frequently stated: 'it is not a payment but a right'. These rights, it seems, are an important basis of the ritual economy of South Indian Hindu temples.

The perception that doing service in a temple ritual is an honour as well as a right is also expressed by the distinction of salaried and hereditary temple staff. It is striking that those who are not salaried for their regular services by the temple administration but claim to occupy a hereditary post explicitly insist on this fact and refuse to accept salary. Thus, the members of the six priestly families are not paid by the Devasthānam office. Instead, they receive certain fixed shares of *pūjā* ticket and a share from the plate, on which additional contributions of the worshippers are collected. Here, as in other cases, the insistence on the hereditary nature of their office is closely related to their desire to preserve the special link with the local god. A hereditary right to ritual shares cannot be dismissed by the administration, and the office holder can permanently enjoy the honours and status associated with the hereditary office (Good 2004: 161). They inherit the required qualities to perform their respective ritual tasks. All this emphasises the indispensability of one's service. Thus, those holding rights in some aspect of temple activity enjoy a kind of 'ownership': individuals or families own the right to participate, to perform, to supply and so on.[14]

Therefore, offices and individual rights to offer certain services to the deity are ardently defended. One of the office-holders, for example, is in charge of fetching the water from the well inside the temple for the daily worship of the main image of the deity. He inherited this right from his father. Now, however, he has serious health problems and the strenuous task of carrying many buckets of water up the hill is difficult for him to perform. Nevertheless, he refuses to allow others to assume this duty. He openly fears that his family would lose this right permanently if he temporarily handed it over to some unrelated person.

It is evident that for donors, for recipients of ritual prestations and for owners of ritual rights social status and prestige loom at least as large as economic motivations. People did and do spend enormous sums for the 'mere dignity of holding some *mirasi* [hereditary] office in the temple' (Good 2004: 163). This 'mere dignity' seems to be the heart of all ritual activity in the temple. There is a severe competition about this dignity — that is about the ritual honours distributed in the temple — which makes scholars dealing with South Indian temples inadvertently mention that these institutions are well known for their litigations and for the fact that the people involved tend to fight for the smallest issues in court. This holds especially true for the Varadarāja temple. Many employees of this temple (only half-jokingly) say that the rituals in the temple are nowadays regulated by court orders rather than by the relevant prescriptions of the Sanskrit ritual texts (*āgama*). They seem to be largely right. The privileges of offering service to the deity, of receiving honours in front of the deity, evidently have great value for the participants. Thus Good (2004: 19) says:

> In any case, there exists an intense desire to receive prestations to which one believes is entitled. If this perceived right is threatened, this can lead to ruinously expensive legal actions or extreme forms of interpersonal violence, even though most such honours have little value in any conventional economic sense. They have in fact far more to do with recognising the recipients' specialised and hence indispensable contribution to the temple's complex liturgical cycles.'

The fact that secular courts are resorted to in these conflicts is the result of a historical development, as Mukund argues (2005). Hindu kings built and endowed temples and had the duty to protect them, but they also maintained administrative departments for temple supervision and control. At first the East India Company followed suit, but then the British were forced to withdraw in the mid-nineteenth century (1863 CE) from participation and donations to rituals. The management of temples was then handed over to trustees who thus had unrestricted control over temple assets. Due to this process, law courts became the only source for redress for the priests, temple staff and devotees. However, while the former kingly function was administrative rather than legislative, and while royal commands were rather pragmatic responses to particular circumstances affecting specific groups than statements of principle, the colonial and postcolonial administrations demanded rules rather than commands, specifically rules of general and permanent applicability. Moreover, temples were classified as religious rather than secular institutions. This was an important distinction because it implied that economic, social and political aspects were not considered valid in the temple context. In addition, the government increasingly came to see temples as public institutions in the sense of being part of Tamil cultural heritage. The decisions made by the legal bureaucrats were and are therefore based on the one or other representation of past, the so-called 'custom and usage'. Mukund says: 'the English administrators in India had a deep-rooted belief that following old usage and precedent was the only way to preserve societal stability and tranquillity, with the added rider that Indian society was timeless and unchanging' (2005: 68).[15] However, this attitude was also supported by the local petitioners themselves. 'Custom — more often the term used was mamūl — was claimed to have overriding legitimacy and authority and any innovation was inherently neither legitimate nor acceptable' (Mukund 2005: 68). In this process, 'custom' is in fact frequently reinvented to suit the interest of any concerned party.[16] 'The reinvented history created by the petitioners now became official history validated by the state' (Mukund 2005: 68).[17]

There are, of course, attempts to avoid the outbreak of conflicts, and to settle disputes about ritual shares before the concerned parties go to court. The mentioned police presence is one method; and before courts are resorted to, in this specific temple one person is in charge of solving the problems. The holder of the so-called Maṇiyakkāraṉ ('superintendent') office specifically has to keep an eye on the performers of the rituals and has to ensure that they follow the rules. The Maṇiyakkāraṉ is present in the temple all the time, in order to make sure that things are done according to the rules and to settle disputes. Only when he is not able to get the participants involved to do what is 'proper', does he go back to his superior for mediation, to the Executive Officer who is in charge of the temple. As preventing conflicts is one of the main duties of the Maṇiyakkāraṉ he, therefore, is competent in the daily ritual practice, and also knows the legal history of the temple. In order to be able to solve the conflicts he has to know the former legal cases and the court orders resulting from these disputes (see Hüsken 2006).

Ritual Shares as Property

South Indian temples are usually arenas of intense conflicts about ritual shares, because these shares are constitutive rather than merely denotative. 'They do not merely recognise the status of the recipient, but actively create and maintain it' (Good 2004: 19). The fragility of the consensus about who owns what kind of ritual share is the result of inevitable competition about status, furthered by the fact that each ritual consists of the pooling of shares which are independent from each other. Moreover, this instability is even further enhanced by the fact that there is no single authority or structure in a temple to orchestrate the diverse shares, but rather a 'logic of functional interdependence' as Appadurai (1981: 47) calls it, a shared orientation towards the deity, and a vague consensus on adherence to 'historical custom.' Only a few temples have individual authorities that are able to orchestrate the diverse ritual shares so as to keep the moral and economic cycle of temple-ritual going (Appadurai & Breckenridge 1976: 205).

The conflicts relating to individual or group participation in the temple rituals refer thus to the fact that in South Indian Hinduism the temples have a crucial role for assigning social status, for validating social leadership and authority (Mukund 2005: xii; references there). Therefore, we need to look more closely at the value system which forms the basis for the context at hand. Here, Simon Harrison's (1992) interpretation of 'ritual shares' as 'property' helps to understand the mechanisms involved. Harrison argues that even when ritual shares do not have any material expression they can be perceived as a form of property which he calls 'intellectual property'. According to him, ritual actions are 'luxury goods' which serve to signify social, especially political, relationships. While he discusses the existence of property rights in this context he is able to show that ritual shares as property can be understood as representations of persons. Participation in the redistribution of ritual shares is thus both a privilege of those in power and an instrument of status contests between them — or a means to acquire power and status. Thus, contests for the control of these high-status forms of property are in fact competition for prestige and legitimacy. The notion of ritual as property presupposes a common value system or shared comparable mental models: '[…] intellectual property presupposes a shared system of information and meaning, […] not only for its value, but also for its mere existence' (Harrison 1992: 235). As Harrison sees property as a (symbolic) representation of individuals or groups, the right in ritual is a piece of one's identity. He says: '[T]he performer of ritual […] is simultaneously projecting his identity into, and drawing identity from, a universe of social relations transcending his own time and place. Participation in this larger world is an important privilege, and the measure of a man's rank or status' (ibid.: 239). Only on the basis of this concept of 'ritual as intellectual property' and at the same time as an essential part of the participants' identity, are some features of the conflicts within South Indian temples — and especially in the Varadarāja temple — intelligible, which remain obscure if one presupposes a solely material notion of property (see also Appadurai & Breckenridge 1976: 205).

As ritual shares comprise both expression and constituent of identity, they also serve to demarcate separation and distinction. An independent value is attributed to them. Religion and ritual are not symbolic, but actively involved in contexts; they are active fields with often profound effects. At the same time these shares in ritual, the sources of status and prestige, are perceived as easily perishable and difficult to maintain. In contrast, as we argued at the beginning of this essay, the urge to perform ancestor rituals as close to the prescriptions — at any costs — as possible, seems to be derived from an entirely different motivation: it is the responsibility people feel for their deceased relatives, but also the fear that ancestors who have not been well or sufficiently provided for will cause harm to the living.

Accepting that ritual shares are 'luxury goods' also implies that it is the exchange and the challenge to ownership that actually creates and enhances their value, as Appadurai argues, based on Georg Simmel's thesis[18] that 'value is no inherent property of objects but is a judgement made about them by subjects'. Demand endows objects with value: 'exchange is not the by-product of the mutual valuation of objects, but its source' (Appadurai 1986: 4). Things — and rituals or ritual shares — are not commodities *per se*, but rather have commodity potential. Seen the other way round, valuables — and in this case ritual shares — do not simply reflect the high status of those who use them, but the use of these valuables is critical to shifts in status structure. Or, in the words of one temple employee: 'It is the prestige issue. Whether you are superior or we are superior. Whether you have got more rights or we have got more rights.'

◈

Notes

1. This paper developed from a presentation by Ute Hüsken 'Ritual and Exchange Relations' — a workshop held as part of the Sonderforschungsbereich 'Ritualdynamik', Heidelberg, 18th and 19th April 2007, and the presentation 'Rituals and Economic Conditions' by K.K.A. Venkatachari during the conference 'Change and Stability in Rituals', held from October 12th to 14th 2006 at the Max Müller Bhavan, Delhi.
2. We wish to thank the Deutsche Forschungsgemeinschaft and the Sonderforschungsbereich Ritualdynamik (SFB 619, Heidelberg) for funding Hüsken's research in Kāñcipuram, and for enabling both authors to discuss their ideas at the conferences in Leiden and Delhi.
3. The relevant rules are codified in the case of domestic rituals in the diverse *Gṛhyasūtras* and subsequently written Prayoga texts, and in the case of the temple rituals dealt with here, in the so-called *Pāñcarātrāgamas*.
4. There are many *Gṛhyasūtras*, belonging to the diverse Vedic 'branches' (*śākhā*), some of which have been composed considerably before the beginning of the Christian Era. *Apastambha* is the tradition most commonly followed in South India nowadays.
5. Thus, for example, the prenatal life-cycle ritual *puṃsavana*, the 'making of a male child', which is supposed to be performed during the second or third month of pregnancy, is nowadays usually performed together with *sīmanta*, a ritual enabling an easy delivery, in the eighth month of pregnancy, together with the relevant atonement rituals (see also Hüsken 2009: 2.2.1).

6. See Buss (2005) and Gutschow & Michaels (2005).
7. For a detailed study see Parry (1993).
8. These are independent insofar as they are from different donors or participants and are assigned for this specific occasion only.
9. Interview conducted by Hüsken with the then incumbent Arcaka of the Nammālvār shrine in the Varadarāja temple on 10.9.2006.
10. Interview conducted by Hüsken with a former Maṇiyakkāraṉ of the temple, conducted on 25 May 2006.
11. As per court order, only the Vaṭakalais hold the right in the Varadarāja Perumāḷ temple to chant the Vedas.
12. This does, however, not only refer to hereditary caste specialism, for in this context donors, too, are specialists insofar as their role is indispensable for the ritual performance.
13. During this festival the god is carried twice a day along a ca. 10 km long route. The musicians walk along with the god, barefoot, sometimes in the hot burning midday sun.
14. This holds true for some of the salaried staff, too. The basic salary is supplemented at diverse occasions to some extent by ritual prestations. Although the amounts of these prestations are also rather nominal, the honour and prestige involved are seen by many (literally) worth fighting for. Temple staff — in spite of the seemingly insignificant rewards for their services — stress their intimate relationship with divinity, and, if possible, the hereditary character of the honours they receive, if not of their office.
15. This perception is based on the Orientalist construction of India as a timeless society whose norms do not change, such that 'custom' was allowed to become the main governing principle in the legal system (see Mukund 2005: 4).
16. Dirks (1987: 290) even says that temples were 'reinvented' as a means to secure social and economical supremacy, not only from the colonisers' side, but as a dialogic process furthered by both, local groups and colonials (see also Irschick 1994: 4–7).
17. Fuller (1984: 110) therefore convincingly argues that the transition from a system resting on the authority of the king to one based on legality and the courts led to greater codification in the sphere of property succession and may have actually contributed 'to a greater stress on the hereditary nature for example, of priestly office'. This, Fuller postulates, was reinforced by the tendencies of nineteenth century British administrators to exaggerate the salience of heredity in respect of rights perceived as 'traditional', an exaggeration which quickly became a self-fulfilling prophecy.
18. In *The Philospphy of Money* (dt. 1907), engl. 1978: 73.

References

Appadurai, A. 1981. *Worship and Conflict under Colonial Rule: A South Indian Case.* Cambridge: Cambridge University Press.

———. 1986. 'Introduction: Commodities and the Politics of Value', in A. Appadurai (ed.) *The Social Life of Things: Commodities in Cultural Perspective.* pp. 3–63. Cambridge: Cambridge University Press.

Appadurai, A. and Breckenridge, C. 1976. 'The South Indian Temple: Authority, Honor and Redistribution', *Contributions to Indian Sociology (NS)*, 10 (2) (Dec. 1976): 187–211

Buss, J. 2005. 'Gieriger Geist oder verehrter Vorfahr? Das Doppelleben der Verstorbenen im newarischen Totenritual', in J. Assmann, F. Maciejewski and A. Michaels (eds) *Der Abschied von den Toten. Trauerrituale im Kulturvergleich.* pp. 181–98. Göttingen: Wallstein.

Dirks, N.B. 1987. *The Hollow Crown: Ethnohistory of an Indian Kingdom.* Cambridge : Cambridge University Press (Cambridge South Asian Studies).

Fuller, C.J. 1984. *Servants of the Goddess: The Priests of a South Indian Temple.* Cambridge et al.: Cambridge University Press.

Good, A. 2004. *Worship and the Ceremonial Economy of a Royal South Indian Temple.* Lewiston, N.Y.: Edwin Mellen Press.

Gutschow, N. and Michaels, A. 2005. *Handling Death: The Dynamics of Death and Ancenstor Rituals Among the Newars of Bhaktapur, Nepal.* Wiesbaden: Harrassowitz Verlag.

Harrison, S. 1992. 'Ritual as Intellectual Property', *Man* (New Series) 27 (2): 225–44.

Hüsken, U. 2006. 'Pavitrotsava: Rectifying Ritual Lapses', in U. Hüsken, P. Kieffer-Pülz and A. Peters (eds) *Jaina-Itihāsa-Ratna: Festschrift für Gustav Roth zum 90. Geburtstag,* (Indica et Tibetica 47), pp. 265–81. Marburg: Indica et Tibetica Verlag.

———. 2009. *Viṣṇu's Children. Prenatal Life-cycle Rituals in South India.* (Ethno-Indology. Heidelberg Studies in South Asian Rituals 9.) Translated from German by Will Sweetman. Wiesbaden: Harrassowitz.

Irschick, E.F. 1994. *Dialogue and History: Constructing South India, 1795–1895.* Delhi: Oxford University Press.

Mukund, K. 2005. *The View From Below: Indigeneous Society, Temples and the Early Colonial State in Tamil Nadu, 1700–1835*, New Delhi: Orient Longman.

Parry, J. 1993. *Death in Banaras.* Cambridge: Cambridge University Press.

Simmel, Georg. 1978. *The Philosophy of Money.* Translated by Tom Bottomore and David Frisby. London: Routledge & Kegan Paul.

Part IV

Media and Sensual Dimensions of Ritual Action

14

Ritual Differs

Beyond Fixity and Flexibility in South Indian Hindu Ritual

Saskia Kersenboom

On 30 September 1982, T. Sankaran interviewed in Tamil, T. Natarajasundara Pillai, one of the great *nagasvaram* players of the Shri Tyagarajasvami temple at Tiruvarur, for All India Radio. One of his questions concerned the issue of change in the tradition of ritual performing arts. Problems of change and continuity cut deep into the heart of the hereditary community of ritual artists (Ta. *melakkarans*). Both music and dance are part of South Indian, Karnatic tradition. The male colleagues of the late T. Natarajasundara Pillai continue their ritual labour up to this day in South Indian Hindu temples and in social rites of passage; their instrument, the *nagasvaram* 'sound of the snake', marks them as members of the *periya melam,* or, 'big band'. In contrast, the 'small band' of female dancers, (Ta. *cinna melam),* was ousted by law (1947 Devadasi Act) from its ritual tasks. (Kersenboom 1987: xxi) Taking this drastic verdict into consideration, T. Natarajasundara Pillai's answer to the problem of 'change' is amazing: *'marapu marutal alla'*. What does this mean? Tamil is a very flexible language, capable of expressing concepts that are broader and more sensitive than simple black-or-white contrasts. In this case the choice of *'alla'* is crucially revealing. On close scrutiny, the verb 'to be' offers three, not two variants; instead of opting for a 'yes' employing the verb 'to be' (Ta. *ul, untu*) or for a 'no', using 'not to be' (Ta. *il, illatu*), T. Natarajasundara Pillai chose *'al, allatu'*, that is, 'to be different'. In other words, tradition (Ta. *marapu*) cannot be defined conclusively in terms of 'continuity' or 'change' (Ta. *marutal*); they are 'different' (Ta. *allatu*), different from *stasis* and different from change: changing and not changing at the same time. Something else is at work. It is this 'difference-at-work' that is central to this essay.

The issue of 'change-versus-not-change' is basically a comparative, historical question. Instead, I would rather like to interpret '*marapu marutal alla*' as 'tradition facilitates'. Tradition has a broad capacity to facilitate a number of flexible possibilities that are realised in the course of performance according to the coordinates of space and time, and the perspective of senders and receivers. This interpretation poses its own questions; it does not aim to delineate a historical development, nor a definition of what tradition '*is*' in a descriptive manner nor what tradition '*should be*' in a prescriptive manner. It rather tries to throw light on how tradition '*works*' in terms of its rituals, its relevance to its users, its tenacity and vitality; how does it refresh itself and from where does it draw that potential? An inherent flexibility that generates identification and commitment seems crucial for its own survival. *Alla* inheres this general potential that is exemplified by the rituals performed in South Indian Hindu temples.

ALLA — Difference

The attempt to articulate this 'difference' may draw from both Indian and Western discourse. On the one hand, the Karnatic field of cultural production can be understood in general terms of Bourdieu's *habitus* (1990a: 78). His analysis of structuring structures, structured structures and generative principles offers flexibility in short, middle and long term transformations that rituals seem to go through. Also it recognises the heterogeneous, multilayered character of the Karnatic tradition. On the other hand, we will approach this complex phenomenon through one specific example: ritual music performed by *nagasvaram* players of the Tyagarajasvami temple at Tiruvarur. Their repertoire, written down in a family manuscript, comes to life in their performance *praxis*. It projects musical tastes of roughly the last two centuries, still figuring several compositions for dance by their former collagues, the *devadasis*. At the same time its ritual context is rooted in earlier linguistic, literary and aesthetic conventions of Sanskrit and Tamil. Its cosmological orientations have been generative principles for almost two thousand years. Such cultural embeddedness is not necessarily at odds with history. However, it does not share the concerns of modernity. Here, the dimensions of space and time neither serve the agenda of historical data or authority, nor do they yield general, universal truths. On the contrary, as A.K. Ramanujan (2004: 426) remarks, they particularise: they work within a specific context of space, time and efficacy. In his informal essay 'Is there an Indian way of thinking?' he evokes his father, a south-Indian Brahmin gentleman who was both a mathematician and astronomer as well as a Sanskrit scholar and astrologer. Questioning him on this apparent inconsistency he received a simple answer: 'you make the necessary corrections, that is all', and, in another instance '[…] don't you know that the brain has two lobes?' Ramanujan's attempt at a formulation of this pragmatic, troublesome position is interesting for our discussion. In short, his argument is a linguistic one: continuity versus change, or, fixity versus flexibility is understood here in terms of 'context free' versus 'context sensitive' rules of grammar. The context sensitive ground provides a type of flexibility that Foucault traces back to the Stoics. Their philosophy of language recognises the relationship between form and content, sign and signified, as a ternary system. Meaning cannot be stabilised or fixed conclusively but depends on a third factor called 'conjuncture' (Gr. *tujchanon*). This ternary organisation will turn out to be our central key in identifying the 'different dynamics' of ritual. In *Les mots et les choses* he identifies this situatedness as *l'être du langage* (Foucault 1966: 57): the ancient, mutually interactive relationship of language with its organic, existential world. His use of *langage* instead of *langue* (language system) or *parole* (speech) is striking. *Langage* includes both the verbal and the non-verbal aspects of language, thereby it addresses 'both lobes' of the human brain and allows emotional and sensory affects to generate 'experiential meaning'. The ternary logic of *langage* continues well into the Renaissance. Binary equations emerge from the middle of the seventeenth century onwards in line with the classical grammars of Port Royal (ibid.: 78ff.). Here the relationship between form and content is understood as either 'natural', or as 'conventional', which means, arbitrary and depending on conceptual, shared consensus. The ternary ground of concrete realisation of the sign/signifier relationship recedes into the background of scholarly reflection for almost two centuries.

C.S. Peirce (1839–1914) proposed a dynamic, triadic sign system that interrelates three aspects of the sign/signifier relationship as *index, icon* and *symbol*. The earlier physical manifestation of signs is necessarily *performative* and rooted in context-based *practices* such as ritual recitation, music and dance. Their applications turn 'change' into pragmatic reasoning; the enigmatic *alla* works out its 'necessary corrections' in 'discursive action'. First and foremost, ritual expertise should 'work' in performance. 'Critical mass' here, means flexible *praxis*, not empirical truth, neither historical authenticity, nor theory; its vitality and survival depend rather on an embodied 'logic of practice' (cf. Bourdieu 1990b).

MARUTAL — Change

Grammar

In linguistic terms, we encounter continuity and change of *marapu* (Ta. 'tradition'), again, in a triadic relation. Here, the disciplines of 'form' and 'content' (Ta. *ilakkiyam* 'marked', 'sign' and *ilakkanam* 'marker', or, 'grammar') commit themselves to a third factor, namely, the situated event of application (Ta. *pirayokam*, Skt. *prayoga)*. Among these three, only the grammatical treatises on form and content are existent in written records and open to long-range, historical scrutiny. We will follow these on the use of the term *marapu* from its earliest mention in the Tamil grammar *Tolkappiyam* (ca. 100 BC–AD 400). Its three chapters constitute a grammar of pragmatic rules: *Eluttu atikaram* (Ta. 'chapter on graphemes') deals with the analysis and representation of sound, *Col atikaram* (Ta. 'chapter on utterance') analyses units of speech and *Porul atikaram* (Ta. 'chapter on reference') outlines semantic networks. At this point, the linguistic insights of Ramanujan reveal their full potential and unite terminology found in the ancient *Tolkappiyam* with contemporary philosophy on language and with artificial intelligence. Both linguistics and the study of ritual are deeply concerned with the nature of rules. Wittgenstein holds that prescriptive rules are not concepts but rather a 'set of activities that follow a rule' (1953: 201). Ritual is constituted by similar 'sets of activities', i.e., numerous practices that form together the *praxis* of Hindu worship. Artificial intelligence (Goeranzon 1988: 15) takes us one step further: it discerns two types of practice, namely, routine practice and development practice. In the first, rules are closed and can be described in a set of essential and sufficient conditions; these resemble Ramanujan's context-free rules. Development-based rules are open rules and allow a variety of meanings: they, in their turn, recall Ramanujan's context-sensitive logic. In *Tolkappiyam* we come across concepts, approaches and tools, that enable us, finally, to identify *alla*, the different workings of tradition. Its first two chapters on aspects of 'form' offer a combination of both closed rules (Ta. *marapu*, lit. 'usage') belonging to routine practices and open rules (Ta. *iyal* , lit. 'word', discourse') modifying development practices. They are employed together in strategic ways to ensure continued efficacy. The third chapter on 'referential meaning' consists of *iyal* 'open rules' only. Closed rules agree well to codification and inscription; however, their potential *stasis* is prevented by a constant updating through flexible application of open rules that are found in development practices. An example of such synergy is found in *Eluttu atikaram* stanza 33, where phonological problems of the lengthening of vowels and consonants are argued along a particular *logic of practice*, namely, that of the production of musical sound by stringed instruments. In a similar way the form of *marapu* does not change essentially, but due to its liaison with the 'open rules' of *praxis* it modifies back and forth in accordance with the needs of time. However, its networks of reference are fully embedded in processes of application, interaction and reception in performance; they are basically open ended and therefore more difficult to assess.

Sign

Col atikaram 152–3 expresses very powerfully the symbiotic relationship of the Tamil utterance (Ta. *col)* and its semantic reference (Ta. *porul*) to the Tamil *habitus*:

> *ellaccollum porul kurittanave//* 152/
> 'each utterance expresses reference matter'
> *porunmaiterintalum conmai terintalum collin akum enmanar pulavar//* 153/
> 'the knowing of the thing(ness), i.e., object, reference, and the knowing of the utterance(ness) come into existence in the act of speaking, so say the experts'.

Thus, the Tamil language is not only the rules of its grammar, it is also its very ground: it is Tamil Nadu, the Tamil country, the Tamil people, the Tamil gods. Its performative potential was conceptualised by Tirumular (sixth century AD) as *Muttamil*, the 'threefold Tamil'. Grammatical Tamil encompasses words (Ta. *iyal*), sounds (Ta. *icai*) and images (Ta. *natakam,* Skt. *nataka*). Its three disciplines of poetry, music and dance form the threads that have to be woven with great artisanal skill into a live 'sign' (Ta. *ilakkiyam,* Skt. *laksya*) regenerating the Tamil world.

This apparent self-enclosure is telling in the light of Foucault's interpretation of the spoken word as a 'sign' in a productive relation to its 'world'. In his 'archaeology of human sciences' he discerns two major ruptures in such relationship. (Foucault 1966: 13ff.) Until the first rupture, he distinguishes an 'ancient sign': merged with the organic world it can trace its concrete, physical emergence back to the Stoics. To utter the word is to enter the thing. Activated by the mysterious powers of language, the word opens up the very experiential reality it refers to. The first rupture takes place around the middle of the seventeenth century, and tears the word just a quarter away from its interactive relationship with the organic world. The new sign, called 'classical', observes nature, organises it findings by binary oppositions and strives to systematise and externalise these data in disembodied representations. The second rupture turns the human word onto its introspective self, shying away from the lived-in world. The doorstep of the nineteenth century heralds a new focal interest on 'mankind' as an independent species. Questions of 'origin', 'meaning' and 'identity' underlie the 'modern' sign/world relationship. These developments and their far-reaching consequences for the world of ritual and ritualists have been discussed by me elsewhere (Kersenboom 2008). However, here it is important to note that the 'dynamics' of Foucault's 'ancient sign' show great affinity with the Hindu position of verbal arts, and the rituals that emerge from them. We will follow this trajectory in a comparative perspective. In contrast to Foucault's observation that today such *'parole premiere'* is no longer extant. (ibid.: 59), we will argue that the three signs described in his *'Archaeologie'* continue to co-exist, even today. Whether productive or dormant, they are embedded in the soil of any cultural field, potentially manifesting themselves according to the *'conjuncture'* of the time, space and opportunity. Hindu temple ritual is only one such instance.

Victor Turner (1982: 86) presumes that the vitality of rituals is embedded in their reflexive activity which seeks to 'know' through narrative enactment; its generative and regenerative processes yield 'experiential knowledge'. This type of knowledge is derived from an ancient, wide-spread Indo-European root — *gna* — to be found in *gnosis* as just one example of metaphysical, yet embodied, experiential knowledge. The 'two lobes' hinted at by Ramanujan's father now emerge centre stage. Turner sees that both in the postmodern West, and in the postcolonial, industrial third world such subjunctive and cultural transformative modes play an important role. The former as a matter of return and rediscovery, setting remembering of such ancient past in a living relationship to the present; the latter as 'they have incorporated into their ritual performances many of the issues and problems of modern urban living and succeeded in giving them religious meaning'. In both cases — *gna* — struggles 'to know', fully, experientially with 'both lobes' at work. It is in this quest that tradition facilitates *alla:* 'experience' meandering between analysis (of continuity versus change), and, synthesis (of changed yet continuous). Its opposite, namely, externalisation of human knowledge, stored into static computerised data bases meets with enormous hurdles in the sphere of somatic and habitual knowledge. In trying to transfer this type of semantic information into analytic, programmatic and technological thought, artificial intelligence came to distinguish at least three categories of knowledge: (*i*) propositional or theoretical knowledge, (*ii*) skills, or practical knowledge, and (*iii*) knowledge of familiarity. The latter two are called 'tacit knowledge' and work in ways that are mostly 'implicit'. The first is conceptual knowledge that allows explicit articulation outside the human body in writing or other graphemes. (Goeranzon 1988: 17) These three modern categories echo the ancient self-definition of Tamil as threefold: (Ta. *iyal*) verbal and propositional; (Ta. *icai)* sound and performative, and therefore practical; plus (Ta. *natakam)* image as knowledge of memory and familiarity. They resemble the three aspects of the Peircean sign mentioned earlier: *icon, index* and *symbol.* The playground for the *alla* proves fertile indeed: *Muttamil* realises the *gna* factor only when the 'body' undergoes and testifies experiential meaning. This process of sensuous affect turning into psychosomatic effect, is termed *meypatu* (Ta. 'body affliction') and resonates with Sanskrit dramatic *poieisis* called *rasa* (Skt. 'tasting') to which we will return later.

MARAPU — The 'Prose of the World'

World

In 1991 I proposed a comparison of *Habitus* with the Hindu concept of *Dharma,* a term derived from the Sanskrit root *dhr-,* 'to hold, contain, maintain; possess, practice certain qualities'. This flexible coherence involves both a cosmology and cosmopraxis, branching out in many *svadharma,* that is, 'own *dharma*'; the Tamil *marapu* is understood here as one such 'situational *dharma*'. Bourdieu was delighted at the suggestion and answered that he had just returned from Japan where he proposed a similar position in the context of a lecture. This exchange supports the following working hypothesis, approaching *marapu* and its referential networks through Western and Indian linguistic methodologies, namely: *langage as praxis is habitus/marapu in practice*. Thus the practices of Hindu ritual articulate and regenerate the Tamil, Hindu *habitus* through the *langage* of *Muttamil* in 'words, sounds and images'. *Tolkappiyam* offers an analytical tool for its graded analysis. *Porulatikaram* sets out three basic parameters of reference: *mutal, karu* and *uri*: *mutal* — a 'first' demarcating the dimensions of 'space' and 'time'; *karu* — 'embryo' listing the phenomena born there; and *uri* — 'peel, skin, propriety' positioning its *dramatis personae* in a clear perspective. Hindu worship found in temples is a fully-fledged blend of Tamil and Sanskrit transmission. Both subdivide the dimensions of space and time, again, into three: the three worlds of gods, mortals and nether regions relate to the three times of *potentialis,* happening present, and past (Kersenboom 1989–90: 191–203). Worship is efficiently organised in cycles of the day, week, half months, seasons and year. These structures of ritual time correspond to structures of ritual space and can be considered the *structured structures* of Hindu cosmology, temple architecture and ritual agenda that is drawn according to a yearly horoscope. They form the framework for ritual worship and lead us to the ritual expertise of priests, singers, musicians, dancers and other servants who embody the *structuring structures* of ongoing temple worship that are laid down in temple manuals (Skt. *agama*, in free translation 'method') but transmitted by oral tradition. These experts mediate the coherence of the Tamil universe through a pragmatic *alchemia* of *mutal, karu* and *uri:* macro and micro cosmos, natural phenomena material, immaterial, elements subtle and gross, the five senses, body and consciousness — all mix and mingle through the ritual performances in words, sounds and images. Foucault has termed this type of performance dynamics '*la prose du monde*': its 'ancient' *langage* interlaces with the world as an embodied sign, inheres it and transcends it only to merge with it on another level (Foucault 1966: 32ff.). The three worlds and three times form a well-structured, dynamic texture that underlies human perception, stretching out as a fertile perennial presence. Restoring and restructuring the primordial tie of such 'words' and 'matter' is wholesome, yielding vitality as an embedded, generative principle. Direct access is opened up and mediated through significant 'resemblances' (Lat. *similitudo*). Out of the rich array that was in use during the sixteenth century, Foucault selected four major, powerful resemblances that activate the 'ancient sign': *Convenientia, aemulatio, analogia and (sym- or anti)pathos.* The first, *convenientia,* works on the basis of proximity, touch and the physical exchange of qualities. In Hindu ritual praxis this type of dynamic resemblance is considered extremely important; its immanent danger or hopeful expectation results in a great number of rules on ritual purity and impurity, and in elaborate pro-active or redressive behaviour. Ritual specialists like *gurukkal,* Brahmin officiating priests, are the only servants who can actually touch the divine image and thereby exchange substances directly without mediation. They are empowered by their physical, 'pure' birth, ritual initiation and codes of behaviour. *Convenientia* underlies both daily and festival worship; it enables devotees to offer and receive gifts in return in an act of mediated, mutual incorporation with their god or goddess. *Aemulatio* operates at a distance and discloses micro-macro cosmic relations on an accessible, synoptic scale: the layout of the temple ground, ritual diagrams and miniature *simulacra* provide a stage for the enactment of mythologies and legends of old. In *analogia,* the two resemblances of *convenientia* and *aemulatio* fall together: at that point gods descend into statues used for daily worship, circumambulate the temple, town and countryside in procession, or manifest themselves suddenly and spontaneously in random forms, most powerfully felt when bestowing 'grace' onto chosen devotees. *Sym-* and *antipathos* churn such fields of possible experiences into diametrically opposed directions. Their volatile forces have to be manipulated into centripetal (*sympathos)* or centrifugal (*antipathos)* transformations that manage and balance 'auspicousness' (Skt/Ta. *mangalam*) and 'inauspciousness' (Skt./Ta. *papam*). Here, the ancient sign, Tamil priests, musicians and dancers meet sharing an ancient *generative principle* of 'life over death'. We will follow their interactions closely and examine their ritual performances along the dynamics of these four, ancient resemblances.

Prose

Today only two *nagasvara* players continue to perform ritual music in the Shri Tyagarajasvami temple at Tiruvarur. Shri T.S. Celvakanapati and his son Shri T.C. Palani are the only local heirs of a heritage that goes back to Ramasvami Diksitar, the father of the great Karnatic classical composer Muttusvami Dikshitar (1775–1835). The art of the *nagasvaram* is basically an oral tradition, transmitted from father to son or other, adopted family members. Ramasvami Dikshitar developed a basic syllabus for training in *nagasvaram* while his son Muttusvami Dikshitar composed music for dance by *devadasis* as part of his large *oeuvre.* The Tiruvarur format of ritual music and dance serves as an example for the region and is copied by many temples. The hereditary right (Ta. *murai*) to study and perform this traditional repertoire belongs to the present family for many generations. Apart from the *nagasvaram* they also play other 'auspicious instruments' (Skt./Ta. *mangalavadyam*): the *tavil, kotukkotti* and *talam* percussion instruments are part of their professional identity as members of the 'big band' (Ta. *periya melam)*. Their music envelops both temple rituals and social rites-of-passage in 'auspicious sound'; thus the inauspicious 'evil eye' and other harmful, dark destructive forces are warded off. In the recent past, the *periya melam* was teaming up with the *cinna melam*, the small band of *devadasis*, female dancers and singers. Both bands can look back at antecedents mentioned in early Tamil poetry, contemporary with *Tolkappiyam*. Here, we encounter instrumentalists who play the 'big lute' (Ta. *perumpanar)* and others who play the 'small lute' (Ta. *cirumpanar)* travelling from court to court in search of patronage. Their musical, dramatic and dance performances were believed to fortify the king in both his private and public life (Kersenboom 1987: 3–16). In Tiruvarur, only a single *devadasi* exemplifies this continuum of the 'small band'. Smt. P.R. Tilakam is now over 80 years old and safeguards one hereditary right against the tide of the legal onslaughts: she partakes in the yearly procession of Shri Tyagarajasvami by offering him flowers as he sets out for his journey on his huge, wooden chariot. In return she receives a ritual head cloth and ritual food.

Many musical compositions of the 'big band' remind one of former participation by *devadasi*s and make the lack of interest in their disappearance all the more striking. We will have a look at two ritual music cycles performed in Tiruvarur and vestiges of *devadasi* music and dance therein. One cycle structures daily worship, the other cycle festival worship. The data are taken from interviews conducted between 1977 and 2007 with *nagasvara* players and *devadasi*s in Tiruvarur and other temples in Tamil Nadu (cf. Kersenboom 1987, 1991).

Nityaracana — Daily Ritual

According to *Ajitagama* Ch.XX.11.18 the number of daily (Skt. *nitya*) worship (Skt. *arcana*) is left to the discretion of each individual temple. However, a graded evaluation shows a scale from 'best of best' to 'lower of lower' ranging from four performances during daytime to four during the night, to 'no *linga* (Skt. '*index*': abstract representation of Shiva) to be seen'. Common practice observes at least three 'junctions' (Skt. *sandhi*) that mark the changing positions of the sun: from sunset, to noon, to dusk the gods are attended to by major and minor rites. The *nagasvaram* repertoire for daily worship lists twelve time slots for the performance appropriate *ragas* (Skt. 'melody scales'), spread over twenty-four hours. Nowadays only two time slots are attended to in ordinary, daily ritual. Around 6 p.m. Shri Tyagarajasvami is offered supper. The temple cook brings this dish into the temple shielded by a parasol and protected by the sound of the *nagasvaram*. The tune of *mallari* accompanied by the *tavil* drum operates on the level of *antipathos*: it wards off the possible attack of inimical forces like a wrestler (Ta. *malla*) by imitating the rhythmical supple movements of wrestlers in combat. This composition also figures right before the temple chariot is set into motion during the Car Festival. Earlier we saw how Smt. P. Tilakam is still officiating in this ritual passage. The ambivalent tension between the auspicious result and inauspicious danger recurs in the evening *sandhi.* Traditionally, it marks the 'inausipicious' transition from the brightness of daylight to the darkness of the night and requires teamwork by several specialists: the *nagasvaram* musicians, the *gurukkal* priests, the *otuvar* singer of Tamil hymns and ritual by *devadasi*s to achieve the powerful effect of *convenientia* 'proximity, touch', 'exchange of qualities'. Apart from the regular expertise of the *gurukkal* priests to cleanse, adorn and serve the deity his regular lustrations, the participation of *devadasi*s was crucial at this point of the day. In her role as synonym of the goddess through earlier rituals of *aemulatio,* she is understood as *nityasumangali* (Skt. 'ever auspicious one') and is believed to be the only human being capable of wiping off the effects of 'evil eye' that have accumulated during the daily interactions of the god and goddess with the outside world. This ritual act is one of transformation. The *Devadasi* dance, song and waving of several lamps rinse the image clean and peaceful, ready to enter the night. One lamp in particular is considered very powerful: the *kumbhadipa* (Skt. 'pot lamp') because its shape forms another *aemulatio* with the female womb and thereby evokes the fertile, life giving aspects of the goddess. Nowadays, the waving of these lamps, including the pot lamp is performed by priests. The evening *sandhi* continues to be the highlight of the day. It draws huge crowds of devotees who gather to exchange glances with the divine pair: peaceful, content and pleased with the offerings of food, flowers and all other royal services. The thrill of this 'encounter' (*darsanam:* Skt./Ta. 'eye contact', 'seeing') culminates in the force of *analogia* when for a moment god and devotee exchange substances through offer gifts (Skt./Ta. *prasadam* 'contentedness', 'gracefulness'). While applying holy Ash, *kumkumam* powder, holy water, milk, sandal or rose water that has touched the Lord earlier, or swallowing his left-over evening food, means nothing less than temporary, mutual incorporation and thereby transformation. This falling together (*analogia)* of proximity (*convenientia*) and distance (*aemulatio)* is a powerful experiential longing that craves to be refreshed every day. Data from Tiruttani suggest that dance by *devadasi*s and their erotic songs added to the sureness of the vigorous, vital and unblemished state of the divine. Nowadays these songs are not performed. Tiruvarur employed three groups of *devadasis* who followed their own routine along several routes spread out in the temple territory (Kersenboom, 1987, 113ff). Only a window in the wall of the inner shrine of Shri Tyagarajasvami bears testimony of their earlier presence. Tamil songs from *Tevaram*, the songs of the 63 poet-saints, by the *otuvar* have substituted this ritual slot, adding it to their own opportunities within daily worship.

Approximately at 10 p.m. *raga ananda bhairavi* and *raga nilambari* are played in front of the divine bedchamber. These two *ragas* were sung, accompanied by mimetic dance, by *devadasis* in Tiruttani while swinging the divine pair to sleep. All temple servants involved attempt to create an atmosphere of pleasant auspiciousness through strategic triggering of the forces of *sympathos*. Other compositions that both professional groups of *periya* and *cinna melam* share are the 'swing songs' *Unjal* and *Lali* and can be sung or played at this occasion. These form part of the processional repertoire as well when performed outdoors during large festivals. Alternatively, they can be added to the indoor programme of daily worship during special periods like auspicious months, or parts thereof. One example of such extension of daily rituals is the early morning *sandhi* during the Tamil month of *Markali* (from mid-December to mid-January). Again this period is experienced as ambivalent and dangerous. As the sun reaches its weakest and shortest presence, the need for music and dance intensifies. Thus, during *Markali* the gods are woken up by the sounds of morning hymns and encouraged to rise and resume their daylight splendour. Sanskrit *suprabhatam*, Tamil *tiruppaliyelucci*, or Telugu *melukolopu* were formerly performed by *devadasis;* now *otuvars* may add these to the hymns of poet-saint Manikkavacakar (ninth century AD) that they sing during this early morning hour. The next *sandhi* at noon is preceded by a small-scale circumambulation, wishing all the gods on the temple ground 'good luck' through *mangalam*, *curnikai* and *stotra* performed by *devadasis*. On such occasions the *nagasvaram* players join in with suitable compositions from their own repertoire. In Tiruvarur, the *nagasvaram* musicians know how to substitute for all missing colleagues: their repertoire contains *devadasi* song, music for *devadasi* dance and Tamil *Tevaram* that is normally rendered vocally exclusively by *otuvar*. Apart from their very specific domain that can be rendered only by *nagasvaram*, their repertoire is a veritable archaeology of the ritual performing arts in Hindu worship.

Naimittikarcana — Festival Ritual

Festival ritual is performed because of a 'special reason'. The Sanskrit *naimitta* relates to 'special signs'. These signs are embedded in the *structured structures* of the three times (Skt. *trikala*) and the three worlds (Skt. *triloka)* discussed earlier. They take a pressing physical shape only when their time is coming up. The twelve months of the year form a cycle known to human beings who inhabit *bhuloka,* the world where life enters birth (Skt. *bhu*) and therefore also death. Perhaps therefore this cycle knows two phases: an upward movement (Skt./Ta. *uttarayanam)* where life is gaining strength, vitality and brilliance not unlike the world of the gods (Skt. *devaloka*) and downward movement (Skt./Ta. *daksinayanam*) where life gradually dwindles, decays and the dark, chtonic forces who live under the earth (Skt. *patala loka)* threaten to take over. The latter period runs from middle of July to mid-January, the former from mid-January to mid-July. Major outdoor festivals are held during the bright part of the annual cycle, invoking divine agency through a complex play of resemblances. The famous *Brahmotsava* festival of Tiruvarur celebrates the establishment of the world of gods among mortals in the course of twenty-seven days. Stories from Hindu mythology usually provide resemblances at a remote distance, but during such festival days their *aemulatio* turns into *convenientia,* a close proximity that might well transform into straight *analogia,* an act of divine 'grace'. We will restrict ourselves to an analysis of this major festival as an example of the rich ritual play of resemblances and complementary collaboration of the big band of *nagasvaram* players and the small band of *devadasis*.

Before entering into details of music and dance, an outline of the *utsava* ritual offers a useful frame of reference and interpretation of the festival proceedings. *Kumaratantra* Ch.XXX 25–9 offers sixteen essential steps that mark the entire ritual. These steps can be glossed into eight progressive movements (Kersenboom 1987: 108): (*i*) Preparation of the site; (*ii*) starting signal; (*iii*) preparation of the god to be taken outside the temple; (*iv*) procession of the god surrounded by all pomp; (*v*) royal court — display of divine splendour for the benefit of the crowd of devotees;

(*vi*) purification of evil influences that have attached themselves to the god; (*vii*) withdrawal of the *utsava* into its source; and (*viii*) peaceful auspiciousness established. It is interesting to note that the first step of the first movement is 'sowing the seed' (Skt. *ankura*). And indeed, according to *Kumaratantra Skandotsavavidhi* 'anything that is begun without the sowing of seeds will be without fructification'. This rite sets the logic of the *utsava* that aims 'to go upwards', to cause 'blossoming' (Skt. *utsu-*). Music and dance are part of this agrarian logic that aims at growth, vitality and splendour as its generative principle; they play a crucial role in all eight movements. The end terms of an *utsava* are listed by *Kumaratantra* as 'merit', 'order', 'prosperity', 'wealth', 'eros', 'liberation'.

Roughly fifteen hours of *nagasvaram* music recorded in fieldwork contain seven *varnams* and eighteen *padams* that can be rendered instrumentally, vocally and in mimetic dance by *devadasis*. These compositions continue to be played on *nagasvaram* today even without *devadasi* participation. Two dance drama's (Ta. *prabandham)* that belong to the repertoire of Tiruvarur *devadasis* are now performed outside the temple as historical *curiosa*. Lack of space forces us here to return to our initial focus on the problems of 'continuity and change'. When approached from this angle, the gradual disappearance of *devadasis* from ritual participation is striking indeed. Their tasks were varied: from gesticulating the actions (Ta. *kaikattum murai)* of the officiating priest to the ever-recurring removal of evil eye, their artistic repertoire shows great inner diversification. On the one hand they sand lyrical and devotional poetry found in Sanskrit *astapadi*'s, Tamil *Tevaram* hymns, *varnams* and *padams*, on the other outspoken erotic songs where the god's unfaithfulness is apparent by the marks of the 'other woman's' teeth on his lips. In another *padam*, set in *raga etukulakambhoji* the god is rebuked with the words 'Take back your money — you sinner — leave me alone'. These songs figure in a context where the god and goddess quarrel only to make up happily which leads to the celebration to their yearly renewed marriage as guarantee for renewed fertility. In today's public awareness of temple dance this erotic past is obliterated by selective memory. Its prose has ceased to weave itself into the world of Hindu ritual and seems to have disappeared without a trace; which leads us back to our initial puzzle, the enigmatic *alla*.

Perspective

Tolkappiyam offers a third parameter of referential meaning, next to the dimensions 'space, time' and 'creation'; *uri* (Ta. 'peel', 'skin') a pragmatic version of our contemporary concepts of 'agency', or, 'perspective'. Questioning *devadasis* about the annihilation of their ritual rights and heritage would certainly not have resulted in '*marapu marutal alla*'. The 'rewriting' of their prose and transfer to other social strata of society is deeply political in terms of Hindu renaissance and nationalism, and has overlooked their interests completely (cf. Allen 1997). The careful choice of *alla* — 'not so' — by T. Natarajasundara Pillai makes sense only in his own situational and larger Hindu context. Seen from the angle of 'agency' and production of ritual, *alla* thus takes a negative, heartless connotation. Nevertheless, on the work floor and reception of tradition it works. How? Does *alla* voice a perspective that 'really matters' and that opens up perspectives that we may have overlooked?

We argued that 'tradition' offers a broad playground where the relationship between form and content is context sensitive. Closed and open rules provide a flexibility that guarantees continuity and change at the same time. Change turns out not to be a linear development but rather a matter of 'making the necessary corrections' and of employing 'both lobes of the brain' as part of an ongoing cultural praxis. On the one hand this results in a 'division of labour' where one group of ritualists substitutes another, rotating qualitative expertise back and forth. Flexibility allows quantitative variance too: rituals may flex from one to eight instances per day without threatening continuity. On the other hand, change facilitates ongoing transformation: on the larger plane, embedded in and attuned to the lived-in world, it refreshes the quality of life, while on the individual plane, it turns knowledge into experiential embodiment.

Richard Schechner observes that the phenomenon of 'Performance' is basically about 'Transformances'. The basic polarity within the field of performance is between *efficacy* and *entertainment* , not between ritual and theater (Schechner 2003: 130, italics mine). Throughout history these two have formed a *continuum* rather than irreconcilable polarities. In the case of Hindu temple ritual in Tamil Nadu these various perspectives blur, mix and separate themselves to gain autonomy. The fate of *devadasi* expertise is a point in case where *efficacy* is reconfigurated into *entertainment,* easily pointing back at an earlier, similar function at the royal courts. The crucial question here remains how the perspective of *alla* succeeds to obliterate this historical blind spot. The other pole of the continuum, namely *efficacy,* may offer keys. The notion of *efficacy* is intimately connected with the notion of 'success', a 'practice that works'. Bourdieu offers a 'logic of practice' that works in a shared cultural field, rooted in *structured structures* that are maintained through *structuring structures* and motivated by shared generative principles. His *habitus* resonates well with the Hindu *dharma* that operates along an agrarian logic of growth, fertility and vitality as a leading generative principle. The three worlds and three times that form the structured backdrop for ritual activity become meaningful only through embodiment by the concrete, Tamil world and its flourishing nature, and by the individual who 'melts with the divine' (Skt. *bhakti*) through devotional action. The *structuring structures* of ritual facilitate such experience; they serve the aim of transformation and do not form an aim in themselves. The perspective of *alla* works like a 'logic of practice' that attunes the situational perspective(s) (Ta. *uri*) to achieve realisation, embodied experience, transformative grasp of primordial space and time (Ta. *mutal*). What lies in-between is creation (Ta. *karu*) and all operational *structuring structures* that methodically open up such experience of reconnecting. In terms of Hindu temple ritual these are the *agamas* and their 'science of the concrete' (cf. Levi-Strauss 1966), in terms of Foucault these are the resemblances (Lat. *similitudo*) that integrate the world of mankind with the perennial texture of the cosmos. The *generative principle* in both cases is experiential knowledge, the *gna* factor that addresses 'both lobes', and that constantly makes the 'necessary corrections' in order to bear fruit; its transformative power supports the processes of life, of those of decay by its wholesome, continuous reconnecting. The critical mass of such knowledge is in the 'tasting' (Skt. *rasa*), and its most powerful form is *rasa,* or 'juice', that is saturated with the quality of 'beingness' itself (Skt. *sattva).* This type of knowledge becomes manifest through involuntary reactions like 'gooseflesh and tears' (*Natyasastra* Ch.XXIV 1–3). *Alla* operates on this middle ground of the utterly concrete, situational and somatic plane; it particularises each individual instance.

Talal Asad (1986: 141) warns us that languages are not equal: how can a 'strong language' like English accommodate a 'weaker language' like Tamil. He wonders how the notion of culture, and as a result the notion of cultural translation, was transformed from the processes of learning and social heredity into the notion of a text. Asad employs Luria's term '*synpraxic* speech' in order to bring out the fact that, while in the field, the process of translation, the grasping that precedes verbalisation, comes with learning to *live* a new mode of life not by learning *about* a mode of life (Ibid.: 159). This essay basically raises deep and far reaching problems of cultural translation that surface when the *verbum existentiae* takes on a third, 'different' modality. Grasping the ever flexible nature of ritual labour is one step, translating these insights into academic language seems still far off: not only do its idiom and mediality fall short, the biggest hurdle is to share the *perspective (uri)* of transformation.

◈

References

Primary Sources

Ajitagama (1964/67), Vol. I and II, edited by N.R. Bhatt, Pondicherry: Institut Francais d'Indologie.

Bharata Natyasastra (1967) Vol. I, edited by M. Ghosh, Calcutta: Granthayalaya.

Kumaratantra (1974), edited by E.M. Kandaaswami Sarma, Madras: The South Indian Archaka Association.

Tolkappiyam (1967), edited by K. Cuntaramurtti, with commentary by Naccinarkkiniyar, (1952; repr. 1974) Madras: The South Indian Saiva Siddhanta Works Publishing Company.

Tiruvarur sampradaya, nagasvaram paddhati, T.S. Celvaganapati, T.C. Palani, Tiruvarur, Sri Tyagarajasvami temple.

Secondary Sources

Allen, M. 1997. 'Rewriting the Script for South Indian Dance', in *TDR (The Drama Review), Journal of Performance Studies,* New York University T155, 41 (3): 63–100.

Asad, T. 1986. 'The Concept of Cultural Translation in British Social Anthropology', in J. Clifford and G.E. Marcus (eds) *Writing Culture: The Poetics and Politics of Ethnography*. London: University of California Press.

Bourdieu, P. 1990a. *Outline of a Theory of Practice*, Cambridge: Cambridge University Press, 7th ed.

———. 1990b. *The Logic of Practice*, Cambridge: Polity Press.

Foucault, M. 1966. *Les mots et les choses*: une archeologie des sciences humaines. Paris: Gallimard.

Goeranzon, B. 1988. in B. Goeranzon and I. Josefson (eds) *Knowledge, Skill and Artificial Intelligence*. Heidelberg: Springer Verlag.

Kersenboom, S.C. 1987. *Nityasumangali: Devadasi Tradition in South India*. Delhi: Motilal Banarsidass.

———. 1989–90. 'Natya — the Desi Yajna', in *Indologia Taurinensa*, Vol. xv–xvi, Turin: Universita Turino: 187–205.

———. 1991. 'The Repertoire of Tiruttani Temple Dancers', in J. Leslie (ed.) *Roles and Rituals for Hindu Women*. London: Pinter.

———. 1995. *Word, Sound, Image, the Life of the Tamil Text*. Oxford: Berg.

———. 2008, (forthc.). 'Mirrors, Frames, Reflections', in A. Hobart and B. Kapferer (eds) *The Human Interface*. Ascona: Centro d; Incontri Umani Series.

Levi-Strauss, C. 1966. *The Savage Mind*. Chicago: University of Chicago.

Ramanujan, A.K. 2004. 'Is There an Indian Way of Thinking? An Informal Essay', in A. Chaudhuri (ed.) *The Vintage Book of Modern Indian Literature*. New York: Vintage Books.

Schechner, R. 2003. *Performance Theory*. New York: Routledge.

Turner, V. 1982. *From Ritual to Theatre: The Human Seriousness of Play*. New York: Performing Arts Journal Publication.

Wittgenstein, L. 1953. *Philosophical Investigations*. Oxford: Blackwell.

15

'Wedding Design' Online
Transfer and Transformation of Ritual Elements in the Context of Wedding Rituals

Kerstin Radde-Antweiler

As Ronald Grimes stated in 2000, 'Weddings in North America, as in Europe, are *the* rites of passage' (Grimes 2000: 153). Interestingly, the so-called 'Online-Weddings' are also *the* rites of passage in online games and Virtual Worlds! But what can be deduced from such an observation when we look at weddings online or weddings in games, such as 'Massively Multiplayer Online Role-Playing Games' (the so-called MMORPGs)? Are they 'really' rituals or 'just' a game, a mere play or imitation of a wedding? What are the differences between an offline and an online wedding? Are there any? This essay presents the Virtual 3D Environment *Second Life* and Online-Weddings within this Virtual World and discusses them as new fields of ritual research and inquiry.

Second Life and its Meaning for Cultural Studies

> A new society, a new world, created by the resident.
> Explore a world of surprise and adventure.
> Create anything you can imagine.
> Compete for fame, fortune, or victory.
> Connect with new and exciting people.
> Your world. Your imagination. Second Life.[1]

The growing popularity of Virtual Worlds in the past years and the emergence and development of 'Online-Rituals' have opened up a new opportunity for experiences of all kinds — like the above-quoted official trailer that underlines self-assessment as an opportunity for a new and better world. Likewise, it has also established a completely new field of research for social and cultural studies in the context of religion and rituals. The distinction between 'Rituals Online' and 'Online Rituals' was developed in analogy to Helland's differentiation between 'Online Religion' and 'Religion Online' (Helland 2000).[2] In contrast to Rituals-Online, which means prescripts or communication about rituals, presented predominantly in Internet discussion forums, personal homepages, chats et cetera, an 'Online Ritual' can be described as a synchronous[3] form of interaction: the performers have the actual possibility to meet online and perform the ritual simultaneously as a group.

Virtual Worlds can be described as a special form of MMORPGS, which have become more important since the 1990s. In this context they can be described as 'sophisticated pieces of software that enable their users to project an identity into a generated three-dimensional reality through the use of advanced computer graphics and — through the eyes of this digital persona or avatar — interact with other players and wander through this generated reality' (Mayer-Schönberger and Crowley 2005: 6f). In contrast to the primarily two-dimensional context of the World Wide Web, virtual worlds constitute a growing three-dimensional area of the Internet in which each individual is represented by a so-called avatar[4] and can interact with each other. Online Rituals can be performed in a virtual space, irrespective of geographical or 'real-life' conditions. These rituals are in general similar to those known from the offline-areas, such as weddings and church services. But there is a multitude of rituals such as prayers, meditation and so on, which focus on individual persons.

Second Life represents the most well-known example of such Virtual 3D-Worlds.[5] Existing since 1998, it is a subscription-based application privately owned by the American company Linden Lab. The user can download the necessary client software from the website http://www.secondlife.com. By July 2007, over nine million users, called 'residents' from over eighty countries had been registered, and approximately 10,000 to 50,000 users are simultaneously online.[6] This world had primarily been dominated by the residents of the United States (US). But thanks to the immense global coverage on radio and television, *Second Life* has become famous in Europe and especially in Germany. As a result, there has been an increase of users from the European community in the past months.[7] According to demographical data, Virtual Worlds like *Second Life* are not typical 'youth games'. They are predominantly used by middle-aged persons with higher education: 'Demographically, 60% are men, 40% are women and they span in age from 18–85. They are gamers, housewives, artists, musicians, programmers, lawyers, firemen, political activists, college students, business owners, active duty military overseas, architects, and medical doctors, to name just a few'.[8]

In contrast to conventional online computer games, *Second Life* does not pursue a given or specific goal. It allows the resident the greatest latitude in creating his/her own content of meaning. Another difference is the litigable ownership: the user, called the resident, is acknowledged as the owner of the virtual things he creates, for instance houses, objects, clothes and so forth. This means that s/he can sell them to other residents and earn virtual money. This currency, the Linden Dollars, can be converted into real US Dollars via a stock market system and vice versa. The world of *Second Life* depends on the creativity of the residents. Linden Lab, thereby modelled a world with an appearance that is very similar to modern Earth.

Figure 1: *Second Life* — Replication of the City of Amsterdam.
Source: All images © author.

In addition to replicas of real — offline — cities, different landscapes and buildings have been created as well as religious and ritual rooms and spaces that are generally open to the public. A lot of religious offline-groups use *Second Life* to launch a communication platform. For instance, a lot of churches were built in 2006, providing weekly public services, group-meetings with different religious lectures and prayer possibilities. Earlier studies have pointed out that *Second Life* is more than a virtual playground, and that it can be considered to be an enhancement of real-life possibilities regarding economic, social and also religious aspects (Quandt et al. 2008). Jakobsson's qualitative survey for example questions Sherry Turkle's thesis that Virtual Worlds are merely a simulation of real-life social action (Jakobsson 2006; Turkle 1995). Wertheim states that 'cyberspace is not merely a store of information, but primarily a space of 'social interaction and communication' (Wertheim 1999: 232). For this reason, Virtual Worlds offer a completely new field of research when it comes to studying culture, religion and especially ritual and their dynamic processes.

In this essay, I present a case study of a wedding ritual and explore its impact on ritual theory. Until now, the research area of so-called 'Virtual Worlds' has mostly been excluded, sometimes even banned from scholarly attention. As a consequence, there have hardly been any studies covering this field of research with the exception of a few surveys carried out by US scientists (Taylor 2006). But even including these, the religious or ritualistic significance of Virtual Worlds has yet to be explored. This essay is divided into three sections: First of all, an exemplary case study of an Online-Wedding in *Second Life* will be presented, then the question to what extent changes or inventions in the processes of performance, interaction and communication are caused by the change of media will be discussed. In the end, the focus will be laid on the question of efficacy: do people ascribe efficacy to the rituals performed in *Second Life* and if so, how?

Second Life and Online-Weddings: A Case Study

From the very beginning, one phenomenon has been very popular within *Second Life*: the so-called 'Online-Weddings'. The possibility of getting married online exists in other games too, such as 'Diablo II' or 'World of Warcraft'. At users' request and to the surprise of the game developers an additional tool had to be implemented — for example wedding places or animation poses — so that the users have the option of getting married within the game.

In *Second Life* there are a lot of residents who offer their land and their service as wedding planners. The wedding coordinators own private land or islands on which different wedding locations are built. Each bridal couple chooses its favourite location for the event. If the privileged setting does not yet exist, it can be built. A host of settings has thus been generated, ranging from big castles, beach bays, rune stone settings, big or small romantic churches to fairy tale scenarios Cinderella-style. As in real life, the whole setting as well as the equipment for the avatar such as flowers, decorations, the wedding dress, jewellery, hair-style and make-up depend on the price the bridal couple is willing to pay. When it comes to a *Second Life* wedding, the same economic factors as in real life have to be considered. This matches with the fact that most interviewed wedding couples — in relation to other expenses in *Second Life* — spent a lot of money and time on planning and arranging.

Three elements seem to make up *Second Life* weddings:

> after the arrival of the guests, the 'handing over' of the bride and the opening words from the 'reverend', who is mostly the wedding designer himself — but may also be an extra 'reverend' for the ceremony who is permanently employed in case the wedding design company consists of more people — the ceremony begins with the questioning of the couple whether they are willing to love each other, be honest and be there for the partner and vice versa (Radde-Antweiler 2007).

The composition and structure mostly includes the marriage sermon, (*i*) the wedding vows, (*ii*) the exchange of rings and (*iii*) a personal statement from bride and groom about their love and commitment to each other.

In the research project 'Online-Weddings' the methods of *Virtual Ethnography* from Christine Hine (Hine 2001), a mixture between different qualitative methods, are used, all of which acknowledge the guideline of the 'Code of Ethics'[9]: There is the 'online participant observation'. This alteration of classical ethnography refers to the observation and filming of different religious events by means of research avatar created by me, expert interviews with the provider of religious services and also with the religious actor, and last but not the least the analysis of the used religious commandments for processes of reception and transformation. Because of the multimedia-based character of the research object, such a multi-method approach seeks to ensure an intensive reflection of the research design. The research project provides furthermore an additional interview space in order to adapt the interview-situation to the virtual space and to ensure adequate data collection.

The case study concentrates on the wedding ceremony of the female-looking avatar L.L.[10] and the male-looking avatar R.D. The wedding took place in a park with ocean view on the land owned by the wedding planner on 19 September, 2006.

For the wedding ceremony, an open pavilion containing an altar is built in white and pink. The pavilion is decorated with flowers and candles. Several benches in the same colours as the pavilion

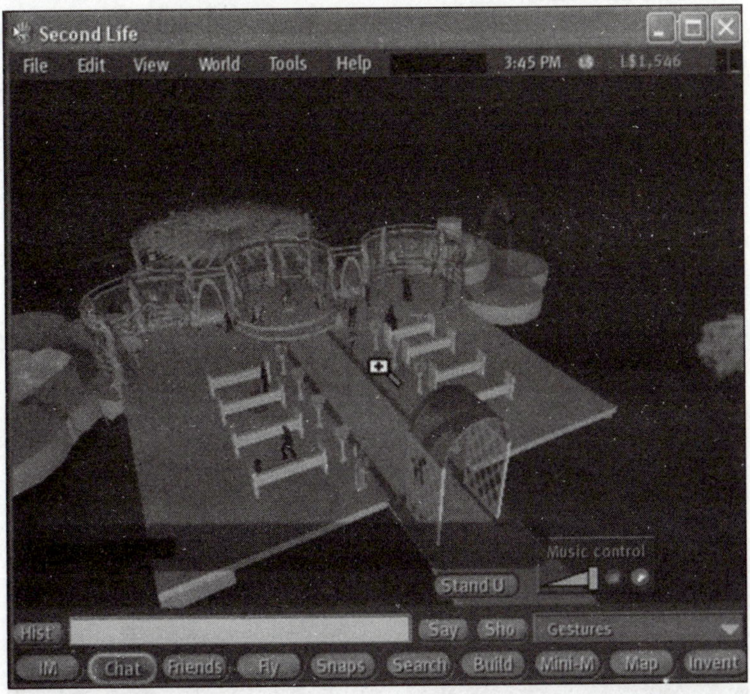

Figure 2: *Second Life*-Wedding of L.L. & R.D. on 19 September 2006: The Setting.

are provided for the guests. A nice arch is placed at the aisle entry. The bridal couple is given the possibility to animate their avatar so that they could enter solemnly. After their arrival, the sixteen gossiping guests split up and take a seat either on the bride's or on the groom's side. Thereafter, the groom, his three grooms-men and the 'chaplain' E.Z. arrive and take their positions in front of the alter located at a height. Half an hour later, the bride L.L. arrives by teleporting[11] with her three bridesmaids and her best friend J.C. Checking the flexible dress, veil, hairstyle — an action not so needless because of the fact, that sometimes because of the teleporting an avatar can 'lose' his or her clothes and appear naked somewhere else — B.M. a male-looking, avatar escorts the bride to the altar, where all position themselves in the given animation poses. E.Z., with a female-looking avatar, frames the beginning of the ceremony with the words 'Ladies and gentlemen, we are about to begin'. After the handing over of the bride by her best friend J.C., opening words about the meaning of relationships, love and commitment follow:

Figure 3: *Second Life*-Wedding of L.L. & R.D. on 19 September 2006: Opening Words.

E.Z.: [...] ths is the time you have chosen to become husband and wife. We are here, not only to show your commitment to each other, but also to wish you both every happiness in your future life together.
E.Z.: As your love has grown into a deep bond of love, strength and security, may your marriage forever fill your hearts and souls.
E.Z.: As you know, a love so true and strong is rare in our world, and when it is found, a connection that will cross oceans, a love that will bring together two lives to be as one.
E.Z.: it should be not overlooked, but embraced.
E.Z.: Within its framework of commitment and loyalty, marriage enables the establishment of a home, where through trust, patience and respect,
E.Z.: the love and affection which you have for each other may develop into a deep and lasting relationship.
E.Z.: Despite the stresses inevitable in any life it is hoped that your love, your respect for each other and your trust and understanding of each other will increase your contentment and heighten your joy in living.

Figure 4: *Second Life*-Wedding of L.L. & R.D. on 19 September 2006: The Questioning.

E.Z.: Everyday you live, learn how to receive love with as much understanding as you give it. Find things within yourself, then you can share them with each other.
E.Z.: Do not fear this love. Have an open heart and a sincere mind. Be truly interested in each other's happiness.
E.Z.: Be constant and consistent in your love. From this comes security and strength. All that we love deeply becomes a part of us on this day of your marriage. Commit yourselves fully and freely to each other.
[...]
E.Z.: I am to remind you of the serious and binding nature of the relationship you are now about to enter.

Then the questions addressed to groom and bride follow.

E.Z.: R., do you take L. to be your lawful wife, will you love her, honor and keep her in sickness and in health and forsaking all others keep only unto her from this day forward?
R.D.: I will
[...]
E.Z.: L. will you take R. to be your lawful husband, will you love him, honor and keep him in sickness and in health and forsaking all others keep only unto him from this day forward?
L.L.: I will.

The next element of the ritual deals with the meaning of the ring.

E.Z.: The ring is an ancient symbol used to seal a solemn promise. These wedding rings [...] the perfect circles of love will serve as symbols of your unending love and faithfulness and remind you of the vows you are making today.

After that, the exchange of the rings follows.

E.Z.: R., repeat after me ..... with this ring I thee wed.
R.D.: with this ring, I thee wed.
E.Z.: L., repeat after me ..... with this ring, I thee wed.
L.L.: with this ring, I thee wed

Figure 5: *Second Life*-Wedding of L.L. & R.D. on 19 September 2006: The Rings.

Finally, E.Z. pronounces them to be a married couple by the words 'E.Z:: By the authority vested in me, according to the laws of Second Life [sic!], I now pronounce you to be husband and wife.' and closes the ceremony with the following sentence: 'E.Z.: Now that the ceremony is over and the experience of living day by day is about to begin, go and meet it gladly.'

Last but not the least, the groom kisses the bride and draws applause from the guests. The wedding couple is congratulated by chaplain E.Z. and after that, the guests move from the pavilion to the reception area, the place where the wedding party takes place.

Figure 6: *Second Life*-Wedding of L.L. & R.D. on 19 September 2006: End.

Processes of Ritual Transfer

Yet are these weddings 'really' rituals and, if so, what are the structural differences from an Offline-Wedding? As Dawson and Cowan suggest, the Web is 'changing the face of religion worldwide' (Dawson and Cowan 2004: 1). Hence the way a ritual is conceived and practised also has changed with the development of new technologies: 'technical innovations on the Net are likely to encourage the development of new forms of ritual' (Kinney 1995: 763). Transfer processes of 'offline-rituals' into an online environment and the consequences for the form and practice can be analysed with the concept of 'Transfer of Ritual' (Langer et al. 2006). This concept implies that 'when a ritual is transferred, i.e., when one or more of its context aspects changes, changes in one or more of its internal dimensions can be expected.' (ibid.: 2) The term 'context aspects' classifies the aspects of a context which are related to each other and to the ritual, for example, media or geographical, political, social or religious contexts. If these aspects are changing, a modification of the internal dimensions of the ritual can be assumed. 'As "ritual dimensions", we define the specific structure and — depending on the prevailing perspective — the mode of action, such as script, performance, aesthetics, innovation, intention, reflexivity, interaction, communication, function, meaning, and so on.' (Radde-Antweiler 2006: 5)

In this context, the ritual cannot be regarded in an essentialist way. Rather, its contextual location must be taken into account. In most former ritual theories rituals are regarded as unchangeable, repetitive processes pursuing a fixed intention and based on a certain framing and as only performed within a community or group. In contrast to that, rituals are considered as a polythetic class, where these ritual dimensions can be understood as a set of attributes that may feature in various rituals but do not necessarily need to occur in every ritual.[12]

As a result of the drastic media change, online-weddings represent a typical example of transfer processes which can be analysed by means of this concept. Within this concept, the question arises as to what extent modifications or inventions in the processes of performance, interaction and communication can be caused by the change of media being observed in the religious practice. With respect to this case study, the crucial change lies in the contextual aspect 'media'. This affects different 'internal dimensions'. In the context of performance, a reduction occurs in both cases. The ritual action of the involved avatars is restricted to predetermined animation poses. Due to the limited technical possibilities only a few action modes can be chosen, like 'bridal walking to the altar', 'standing in front of the altar', 'kneeling down', 'wedding kiss', 'sitting down on chairs', 'applause after the wedding' et cetera. After the guests have taken their seats and after the bridal couple and the reverend have arrived, the scene becomes relatively static. Individual gestures and actions are rare. This is why essential performed gestures such as the 'sit down of the reverend and the bridal couple' or the 'wedding kiss' gain importance and underline the framing plots. In the presented case, audio elements such as music, songs, prayers and so forth, are missing. The emphasis is put on visual elements like the arrangement of the whole wedding setting like the pavilion or the altar. Due to the fact that the communication focuses on written words via chat and instant messaging — a form of real-time communication between two or more people conveyed via computers — the words chosen by the reverend and by the bridal couple become more important. The ritual activities themselves primarily consist of written communication instead of ritual action.[13]

Another major technological element affects the number of invited guests and thus the ritual choreography: due to technical limitations only a restricted number of participants can be invited. If too many avatars are at the same place at the same time, the system software causes technical problems such as a so-called 'time lag', which means that the user's graphic representation becomes slower. Some wedding planners even use this mishap for consumption advertisements:

> *LAG* the dread of every Bride in SL [Second Life]! How embarrassing will it be when you drift off course because you're so lagged you think you are still walking down the aisle when in fact you have walked over half of your guests on accident! Not at Wedding Belle's! We've developed a remedy to wedding day lag! No more cumbersome balls to stand on while someone else *drags* you down the aisle, no more 'floating' on an unanimated pose ball; no more hitching and straying off course by trying to walk on your own. Simply Glide down the aisle on our Custom Made Bridal Party Gliders and actually 'Walk' down the aisle, serene and smiling at your guests and your Beloved awaiting you at the altar. Even hold Daddy's arm as he escorts you to the altar.[14]

But even if there are only a restricted number of people attending the ceremony the system can still crash and the bride, the groom or even the reverend can disappear for a while during the ceremony. In such a case, participants like the chaplain or the bridal couple have to adjust spontaneously to such a 'ritual mistake'. Great changes also take place in the so-called internal dimensions, for example, the ascribed meaning. The following conclusions were drawn from the interviews and observed weddings. I would like to propose three reasons for getting married online: In contrast to real life, it is very easy to get married in *Second Life*. One does not have to face the challenge of geographical distance or specific laws in one's country. This is the reason why a lot of weddings between — in real-life — homosexuals can be observed in *Second Life*. Another criterion seems to be related to the wide range of choices users have. The residents can fulfil all their dreams: marrying in a huge castle, look like a princess, et cetera. The fact that 'you can do whatever you ever want to do' as opposed to the limited possibilities in real life — due to financial or appearance limitations — seems to be the decisive criterion to marry within *Second Life*. Especially couples who already got married in real life state that the scope for improvisation is the reason why they want to get married in *Second Life*, too. The aspect of 'playing the princess' raises the question of the role of aesthetics within this ritual performance. Beauty plays a great role in Virtual Worlds, even though some of the figures and designs still lack the capacity of creating a 'real-life' appeal. In general, aesthetics become more and more the criterion for rituals and even for their efficacy. This also applies to *Second Life* and most interviews conducted with bridal couples and especially with the brides confirmed the increased role of aesthetics. For example, a short, overweight female in her mid-forties can become a tall twenty-something beauty with the body of a supermodel. She also has the choice as to whether she wants to be a man or a woman; or she can choose a skin colour that is different from her own. Overweight, physically challenged or old avatars are the rare exception in such Virtual Worlds. Especially in the context of weddings you can find 'the most beautiful' women with the 'prettiest' dresses getting married in the 'most magnificent' landscape and so on.

Another type of motivation deals with weddings as an explicit signal for the unity of the couple. This sounds similar to real world, but one has to consider the fact that in a world like *Second Life* the users have the possibility to meet, come together, communicate, flirt and so on with thousands of other users. These relationships are usually quite short-termed and emotionally superficial. Sometimes even the groups constituted within *Second Life* survive only for a short period. From this, the question arises if rituals in Virtual Worlds, in which change and instability are the norm and common in daily life, should present a certain continuity? In the analysis of rituals on personal homepages (Radde-Antweiler 2006) the most interesting fact that was discovered was the invariance, the explicitly individualised design of rituals, for instance new forms of traditional rituals, one time performances, and so forth. In Virtual Worlds, completely different settings and other types of rituals, the so-called *'rites de passage'*, with repetitive and strict structure and traditional form can be found. According to my observation, innovative forms of rituals are relatively rare. Virtual weddings strongly remind one of traditional offline weddings. Surprisingly, they usually lack any creative elements in spite of all the technical possibilities. The question arises as to whether this is due to the fact that the recognition of the ritual as a ritual is stressed? Rituals and their different elements have to be recognised by their performers and therefore depend on the parties concerned. The German historian of religion Burkhard Gladigow stresses in the context of ritual elements that:

> Ritual elements are defined as those that can either be repeated within the same rituals or are also 'recognisable' in other rituals. [...] Typical ritual sequences are defined by the fact that they link a 'clear' number of separate ritual elements with another and that this constellation can appear in different complex rituals, and that they must also be 'recognisable' and 'identifiable'. (Gladigow 2004: 59f).[15]

In a highly fluent and creative 'new world' such a recognition or identification seemingly has to be ensured by using traditional ritual elements.

The Question of Ritual Efficacy

Online-Rituals do not lack controversy, neither from the participants' nor the offline observers' points of view. A major objection against the legitimacy of Online-Rituals as rituals has to do with the fact that 'outside' and even within *Second Life* such rituals are questioned because of the classification of being, just virtual' without any relevance to the real life. If the attribute 'virtual' is understood vis-à-vis the allegedly 'real', Online-Weddings could be classified as 'un-real' rituals. The problems of defining 'reality' and 'virtuality' and their relation to each other is a popular and endless topic in the field of media theory. Concerning rituals and especially Online-Weddings this discussion is often simultaneously linked — by the participants and the opponents — to the question of efficacy. What does efficacy actually mean? In contrast to the mere 'effect' — a result that comes right after the ritual and is by the participants, the observer and so on causally determinedly linked with the ritual itself — the concept 'efficacy' is understood as

> a perspectively ascribed quality that results from the establishment of one or more of its effects. This ascription relates (at least one of)

> these established effects to intentions, expectations and/or perceived functions of the ritual. Hence, to speak of efficacy is to make a statement about certain effects relative to the interests of some agent refers only to some effects — whether they are actual effects or only imagined. (Quack/Többelmann forthc.)

Thus the efficacy of a ritual depends to a large extent on the adscription by different parties involved, both participants and observers. Their definition renders the ritual along a scale between the poles 'effective' and 'ineffective' or 'failure'. The analysis of efficacy can always cover certain aspects of efficacy due to the fact that a ritual might have a variety of effects on various layers and on various social agents.

The essay will now focus on three different aspects of efficacy and their relevance in the field of Online-Weddings.

In most observed weddings the physical location where the wedding 'takes place' is clearly marked as a wedding site equipped with specific wedding decorations. Examples for such decorations — the so-called 'means of efficacy,[16] in German 'Wirkungsmittel' — are an altar for the reverend, the reverend her- or himself, bridesmaids, guests, wedding gown, festive clothing and so on. Additionally, specific supplementary animation programs have to be integrated. These animate the avatar of a person to perform a specific gesture or procedure such as the position 'holding hands' in front of the altar or while performing the rite of the wedding kiss. Particular standardised gestures and activities such as the wedding blessing or kiss can be observed, too.

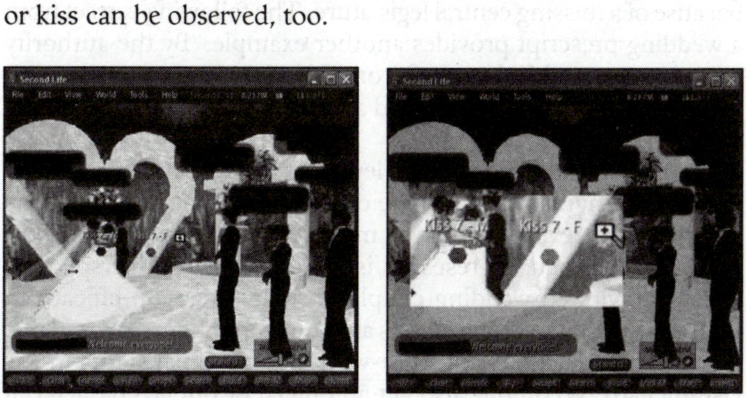

Figure 7: *Second Life*-Wedding of S.R. & R.T. on 18 September 2006: Animation Poses 'Kissing'.

The exchange of the rings is usually mentioned and plays an important role in the ritual as a performative speech act (Austin [2]1979). But due to technical limitations rings cannot be exchanged in the Virtual World. Instead, the procedure is replaced by written words. Thus the actual ritual consists of only words instead of action, or in other words the performative speech act takes place without the performance.

The notion of the wedding's efficacy is another important issue that requires visualisation. In general, there are different active actors taking part in the wedding ritual: the bride's male attendant leads the bride to the respective location. The bridal couple itself performs the ritual by making the vows. The reverend or the chaplain dominates the scene and pronounces the ritual as fulfilled. Yet, the authority is not his own but bestowed by an entity beyond himself, often of transcendent origin. In this case, it depends on the wedding and on the reverend on which authority he refers to. In most of the weddings I observed, the reverend referred to 'God' in general. Depending on the specific religious background of the wedding couple he might also refer to the High Goddess, the Holy Trinity and so on.

In the presented wedding of L.L. and R.D., the wedding chaplain pronounced them as husband and wife by referring to the laws of *Second Life*: 'E.Z: By the authority vested in me, according to the laws of Second LIfe [sic!], I now pronounce you to be husband and wife.'

Interestingly there aren't such universal laws within Second Life because of a missing central legislature. The following extract from a wedding prescript provides another example. 'By the authority vested in me as a Minister in Second Life, I now pronounce you to be husband and wife. What God and Love has joined here today, let no man set assunder.'[17]

Another topic concerns the level of efficacy. At this point we have to distinguish between the cosmological, the social and the psychological level. Due to the material and the methodological approach the focus of research is laid on the social perspective. Most interviewed wedding couple attribute a certain efficacy to Online-Weddings. Visible effects and transformations, for example, are the entry of the changed in-world matrimonial status in the visiting card. Weddings also get an official or public character, if the partners decide to record the name of their respective partner in the in-world-profile, like visit cards providing information about the avatar's activity, first life, et cetera.

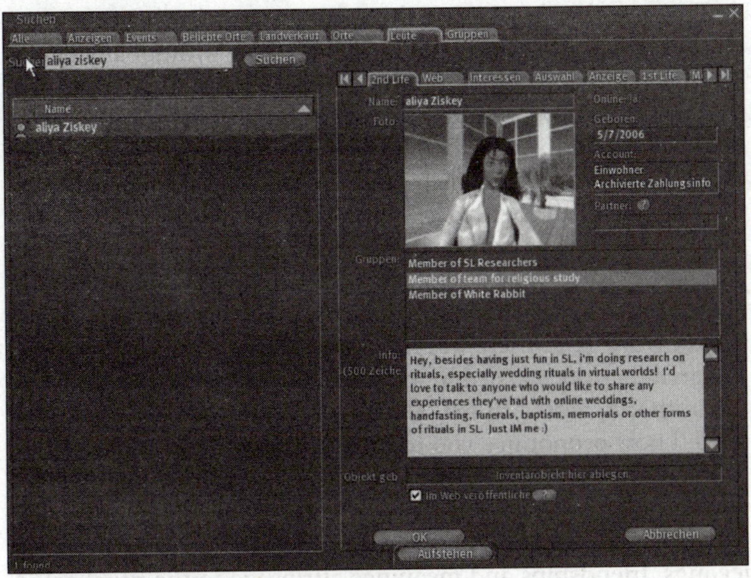

Figure 8: Notecard of the Research Avatar of the author.[18]

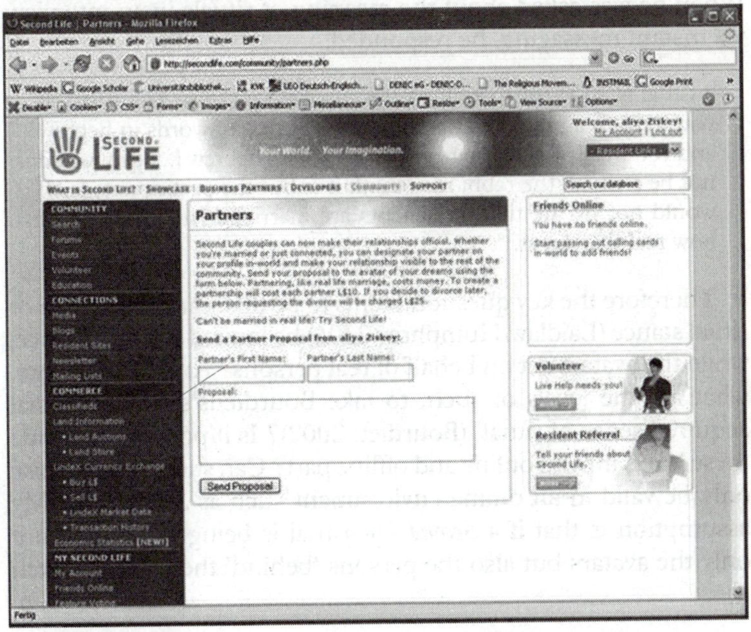

Figure 9: Homepage of *Second Life* with the 'Partner proposal'.

The question is whether there are any ascribed processes of efficacy which exist only within *Second Life* — without any effects on the first, the 'real life'? In this context, it is almost impossible to give a generally applicable answer because everything depends on the bridal couple and their intention and therefore also on their ascription of efficacy, which is also temporarily changeable. In the example of the S.B. & R.'s wedding, the following restriction is made — 'This is just a virtual wedding.' 'J.M. shouts: R., do you take S. to be your virtual wife. R.T.: I do.' And vice versa. So the efficacy in this case is only ascribed to virtual space. In the wedding of J. & E. there was no such restriction and the reverend declared them as married in the same way as in first-life: 'E.Z.: By the authority vested in me, according to the laws of Second Iife [sic!], I now pronounce you to be husband and wife.'

In contrast to that reduction to 'only a virtual wedding', a lot of wedding couples and wedding planners stress the interconnection between their online and offline lives, or their First and *Second Life* feelings, friendships and meanings attributed to the ritual act. A real-life Anglican reverend from the United Kingdom who acts as reverend in *Second Life*, underlines such processes of ascription. When he was asked about the meaning of rituals in an interview via instant messaging, he responded:

> a ritual is an event that all parties involved perceive as a ritual. If you went to a rabbi and had him say a bunch of words in hebrew and you were raised french and new [sic!] no hebrew [...] this would not be a ritual. the rabbi may think it is but the partisipants [sic!] would not by the time my clients are marriend [sic!] they know how real this day is.[19]

Therefore the key question seems to be this: can ritual sense or ritual stance (Laidlaw/Humphrey 2006) be limited to virtual space, while the avatars act on behalf of real persons? And furthermore, what are the levels of such, to take Bourdieus's words, 'social acquired sense of ritual' (Bourdieu 2002)? Is it possible to divide these levels into an online and offline part? Can such a ritual sense only be valid in an online environment such as *Second Life*? My assumption is that if a *Second Life* ritual is being performed not only the avatars but also the persons 'behind' them are involved and have therefore a ritual stance online and offline. For a lot of bridal couples who have already married in real life and who repeat their wedding ceremony in *Second Life*, the second wedding was as important as the real-life wedding. For instance, a bridal couple renewed their wedding vows in *Second Life* after they had already been married for eighteen years in real life. When they were asked about their motivation for a second wedding ceremony they replied:

> S.A.: first 1 [one = wedding] was at jp [Japan] no friends just us and family […] this 1 [one wedding] i have a gown a wedding like i dreamed about but couldnt afford in rl [real life] and good friends to celebrate with.
> A.Z.: is there a difference for you between wedding IRL / ISL [in Real Life / in Second Life]?
> S.A.: this 1 [one = wedding] I have a gown a wedding like I dreamed about but couldnt afford in rl [Real Life] and good friends to celebrate with.[20]

It comes as a surprise that the couple hardly saw any difference between virtual and real life and that the participation of good friends and the online community meant so much to them. But there are also other couples who get to know each other in *Second Life*, get married in the Virtual World and after a while get to know each other in real life and finally also get married in first life.

However, it is obvious that both online-efficacy itself and the rituals stir up controversies. There have been heated debates about the role of rituals in *Second Life*. The main question is whether rituals should be allowed at all in three-dimensional environments. One of the consequences was the formation of so-called 'wedding crasher groups'. In interviews with members of the so called 'wedding crasher groups', nearly all participants stressed the aspect of 'game' in an opposition to 'rituals'. Since *Second Life* is classified as a game, 'serious rituals' cannot be tolerated. But interestingly the Online-Wedding itself is doubted as a ritual as such by both parties — even the wedding crashers define them as 'serious rituals'. However, another group considers *Second Life* as an online environment in which all kinds of cultural activities and rituals can take place.

'T.O.: there are two camps here [...] most of the people I meet are resolved to the fact this is really not a game but an online culture
T.O.: I find the second camp to be made of newer 'players' those who still think this is a game
T.O.: and I find less folks who find it to be a game
[...]
T.O.: If reverend T.O. is running the wedding it is just as real as any commitment ceremony you eill [will] ever engaged in
[...]
T.O.: I just surveyed [sic!] the dance club I am in [...] no one said it is a game [...] it has games in it but as one of my friends just said [...] games dont [sic!] make you cry'[21]

The mentioned second camp doesn't acknowledge cultural activities and rituals in Virtual Worlds as serious action. As a consequence, the ritual efficacy and the ritual itself are doubted as well.

The question that emerges from this is this: do people doubt the efficacy of online rituals or do they doubt the efficacy of online environments in general? Or, in other words, are the social and cultural meaningfulness and the influence of online environments questioned as such? This is certainly something to be explored in further research.

Conclusion

This essay introduces Online-Weddings as a new and highly relevant field for ritual studies. After presenting a case study, the paper deals with processes of ritual transfer and changes occurring through these processes. Major changes primarily affect the role and emphasis of aesthetics with the focus on visual elements. Concerning the function of online-weddings, the most interesting observation presents the aspect of stability. In contrast to results from the analysis of homepages in the World Wide Web, the residents prefer online rituals very similar to offline-rituals in Virtual Worlds. Thereby the presented examples made clear that virtual wedding ceremonies are in general very traditional in their style and procedures. Besides the fact that a ritual has to be recognised as a ritual by the participants, as Gladigow stresses, for instance[22], the question raises whether rituals in Virtual Worlds in which change and instability are the norm and common in daily life rituals should pursue a certain continuity. In this context further research is required to explore this assumption.

The last part of this essay dealt with the question of efficacy in the field of Online-Weddings. The analysis showed that rituals in an online environment such as *Second Life* are often mistrusted. Depending on the classification of *Second Life* itself — as a game or as an online culture — rituals can either have an effect or not. Depending on the different aspects of efficacy different processes of ascription have been shown. Whether ritual efficacy is restricted only to Virtual Worlds without any influence or ritual stance on first or real life can be considered as one of the key questions. To sum up one can say that nowadays rituals play an important role both in real life and in Virtual Worlds. Hughes-Freeland's assumption that '(t)here is a strong evidence for the claim that ritual cannot be subsumed or reproduced through media representations' (Hughes-Freeland 2006: 613) becomes highly problematic and has to be challenged. A lot of participants consider the performance of rituals in an environment such as *Second Life* as normal and as an enlargement of the possibilities of 'real' life. Yet, there are a lot of critics within and outside of *Second Life* who doubt, do not accept and even try to avoid these rituals — a not so unfamiliar procedure within First Life.

◈

Notes

1. See http://secondlife.com/ (accessed 18 November 2006).
2. Examples for the beginning of ritual space online presents the Inanna-Tempel on http://www.inanna.de/inanna_tempel2.html (accessed 18 November 2006) or the replication of the Redemptoris Mater Chapel on the Vatican Website, See http://www.vatican.va/redemptoris_mater/index_en.htm. (accessed 18 November 2006).
3. For the characterisation of synchronous and asynchronous forms of interaction, see Jacobs (2007).
4. Avatar is a Sanskrit word, which in Hindu mythology means 'the descent of a deity to earth in a *visible form* [...] Computing has borrowed this term to denote the *visible form* (*representation*) of a character, controlled either by a human or a software agent. [...] Avatars are essential part of the embodiment and immersion of humans

in 3D virtual worlds, as their visible dimensions scale to the other visual forms in the virtual world. They span from simple images to photorealistic 3D […]' See Duridanov and Simoff (2008).

5. Other examples for Virtual Worlds are *Active Worlds* and *The Palace* — both in use since 1995 and *There* since 1998.
6. The actual numbers amount to 10,000 on 60,000. The current numbers related to residents logged in during the previous 7, 14, 30 or 60 days along with the economical data can be found on the official website http://secondlife.com/ (accessed 18 November 2006).
7. Thereby the German community with over 16,000 residents represents the biggest European community (numbers from December 2007).
8. According to http://secondlife.com/whatis/faq.php (accessed 18 November 2006). Because of the regularised and age-restricted access, only persons over the age of eighteen can create an account for Second Life. In the middle of 2006 Linden Lab developed 'Teen Second Life', a Virtual World very similar to Second Life for Teens in the age group of thirteen to eighteen.
9. See 'Code of Ethics': http://www.ucm.es/info/isa/about/isa_code_of_ethics.htm.
10. Applying the Code of Ethics all interviewed persons are anonymised by abbreviation.
11. 'Teleporting' represents the usual way of getting around in Second Life: it '(m)oves the agent directly to a location as quickly as possible.' See http://wiki.secondlife.com/wiki/Teleport (accessed 29 November 2007).
12. See for example Snoek: 'A class is polythetic if and only if (A) each member of the class has a large but unspecified number of a set of characteristics occurring in the class as a whole, (B) each of those characteristics is possessed by a large number of those members, and (if fully polythetic) (C) no one of those characteristics is possessed by every member of the class.' (Snoek 2006: 4f)
13. Also the exchange of rings for example as a missing plot has not been discussed or thematised. See below.
14. Notecard retrieved from 'Wedding Belle's at Cameo Island' on 26 July 2006.
15. Translation of Gladigow 2004: 59f: 'Rituelle Elemente seien dadurch definiert, daß sie entweder innerhalb desselben Rituals wiederholt werden können, oder daß sie, erkennbar' auch in anderen Ritualen vorkommen. (…) Typische Ritualsequenzen seien dadurch definiert, daß sie eine 'überschaubare' Zahl diskreter ritueller Elemente miteinander verbinden und daß diese Konstellationen in unterschiedlichen komplexen Ritualen vorkommen können, daß sie also 'erkennbar' und 'identifizierbar' sein müssen.'

16. For the theoretical approach, see Quack and Töbelmann (forthc.).
17. Wedding Prescript 'Wedding T.H. & L.G.', Notecard retrieved on 1.7.2006.
18. On the site http://secondlife.com/community/partners.php (accessed 18 November 2006) one can fill in a proposal form that officially codifies a virtual matrimony. This form is published in one's profile in-world.
19. Interview conducted by the author on 12.09.2006.
20. Ibid, 25.09.2006.
21. Ibid, 24.07.2006.
22. See Gladigow (2004: 59f).

References

Austin, J.L.[2] 1979. *Zur Theorie der Sprechakte*. Stuttgart: Reclam.

Bourdieu, P. 2002. *The Logic of Practice*. Stanford: Stanford University Press.

Dawson, L.L. and Cowan, D.E. 2004. 'Introduction', In *Religion Online: Finding Faith on the Internet*. New York, London: Routledge.

Duridanov, L. Simoff, S. 2008. '"Inner listening" as a Basic Principle for Developing Immersive Virtual Worlds', in: K. Radde-Antweiler (ed.) *Being Virtually Real? Virtual Worlds from a Cultural Studies' Perspective* (*Online — Heidelberg Journal of Religions on the Internet* 3): pp. 290–315. Available http://www.ub.uni-heidelberg.de/archiv/8299 (accessed 18 November 2006).

Gladigow, B. 2004. 'Sequenzierung von Riten und die Ordnung der Rituale', in M. Stausberg (ed.) *Zoroastrian Rituals in Context*, pp. 57–76. Leiden, Boston: Brill.

Grimes, R.L. 2000. *Deeply into the Bone: Re-inventing Rites of Passage*. Berkeley: University of California Press.

Helland, Ch. 2000. 'Online-Religion/Religion-Online and Virtual Communitas' in: J.K. Hadden and D.E., Cowan (eds) *Religion on the Internet: Research Prospects and Promises*, (*Religion and Social Order* Vol. 8), pp. 205–23. Amsterdam: JAI.

Hine, Christine. 2001. *Virtual Ethnography*. London: Sage.

Hughes-Freeland, F. 2006. 'Media', in J. Kreinath, J. Snoek, M. Stausberg (eds) *Theorizing Rituals, Vol. 1. Issues, Topics, Approaches, Concepts*, pp. 595–614. Leiden: Brill.

Jacobs, St. 2007. 'Virtually Sacred: The Performance of Asynchronous Cyber-Rituals in Online Spaces', in *Journal of Computer-Mediated Communication* 12(3).

Jakobsson, M. 2006. *Virtual Worlds and Social Interaction Design.* Available http://www.diva-portal.org/diva/getDocument?urn_nbn_se_umu_diva-750-2__fulltext.pdf (accessed 25 January 2007).

Kinney, J. 1995. 'Net Worth? Religion, Cyberspace and the Future', *Futures* 27 (7): 763–76.

Laidlaw, J., Humphrey, C. 2006. 'Action' in J. Kreinath, J. Snoek, M. Stausberg (eds) *Theorizing Rituals: Issues, Topics, Approaches, Concepts,* pp. 265–83. Brill: Leiden.

Langer, R., Lüddecken, D., Radde, K., Snoek, Jan 2006. 'Transfer of Ritual', in *Journal of Ritual Study* 20 (1): 1–10.

Mayer-Schönberger, V., Crowley, J. 2005. *Napster's Second Life? — The Regulatory Challenges of Virtual Worlds.* Faculty Research Working Papers Series RWP05–052, 6f. Available http://www.law.northwestern.edu/lawreview/v100/n4/1775/LR100n4Schonberger&Crowley.pdf. (accessed 18 January 2006).

Quandt, Th., Wimmer, J., Wolling, J. 2008. *Die Computerspieler. Studien zur Nutzung von Computer- und Videogames.* Wiesbaden: VS-Verlag.

Quack, J., Töbelmann, P. (forthc.) *The Efficacy of Rituals.*

Radde-Antweiler, K. 2006. 'Rituals Online. Transferring and Designing Rituals', in K. Radde-Antweiler (ed.). *Online — Heidelberg Journal of Religions on the Internet* 2.1. Available http://www.ub.uni-heidelberg.de/archiv/5823 (accessed 18 October 2006).

———. 2007. 'Cyber-Rituals in Virtual Worlds. Wedding-Online in Second Life', in *Masaryk University Journal of Law and Technology,* 1(2).

Snoek, J. 2006. 'Defining 'Rituals'', in: Kreinath J., Snoek J., Stausberg M. (eds) *Theorizing Rituals Vol. 1. Issues, Topics, Approaches, Concepts.* Leiden: Brill.

Taylor, T.L. 2006. *Play between Worlds: Exploring Online Game Culture.* Cambridge, Massachusetts: MIT.

Turkle, S. 1995. *Life on the Screen: Identity in the Age of the Internet.* New York: Simon & Schuster.

Wertheim, Margaret. 1999. *The Pearly Gates of Cyberspace: A History of Space from Dante to the Internet.* New York: W.W. Norton & Co.

Referred Websites

Inanna. Domainholder: Robert Valerius.
http://www.inanna.de (accessed 18 November 2006).

Redemptoris Mater Chapel of John Paul II. http://www.vatican.va/redemptoris_mater/index_en.htm (accessed 18 November 2006).

Second Life. Domainholder: Linden Lab. http://secondlife.com/ (accessed 18 November 2006).
Teen Second Life. Domainholder: Linden Lab. http://teen.secondlife.com/ (accessed 18 November 2006).
There. Domainholder: There, Inc. http://www.there.com/ (accessed 18 November 2006).
Wiki Second Life. Domainholder: ALLINDOMAINS, LLC. http://wiki.secondlife.com/wiki/Teleport (accessed 29 November 2007).

16

Gender, Generation and the Public Sphere

Islamic Values and Literary Response[1]

Susanne Enderwitz

To an outsider looking at Egypt the last stronghold of Muslim traditionalism in the middle of the last century, the country seemed to be inexorably on its way to modernisation and secularisation which had begun half, or almost a century earlier, manifesting itself most clearly in the abolition of the segregation of the sexes. In 1899 and 1900, the Egyptian lawyer Qāsim Amīn had published two pioneering works, *Taḥrīr al-mar'a* (The Liberation of Women) and *al-Mar'a al-ğadīda* (The New Woman) which met with strong but also fruitless opposition. While the conservative leaders of the religious al-Azhar University clung to what they considered an undebatable Islamic tradition, the wind was blowing in a different direction, as the debate around the Egyptian nation in the dusk of the Ottoman Empire came along with issues of modernity, secularism and gender. In 1923, the Egyptian feminist Hudā Šaʻrāwī publicly took off her veil after returning from a women's conference in Rome, and her Egyptian Feminist Union undertook the task of preparing women to claim their rights through education and extensive social work among the poorer classes. By the time Šaʻrāwī died in 1947, other women's organisations had begun to eclipse the Egyptian Feminist Union by providing a platform that addressed the more complex political and professional needs of this new generation of women. The revolution of 1952 put an end to colonial rule and marked the beginning of the secularist Nasserism and embraced this new middle-class agenda and used it as a source of national and international support (Hatem 2005: 68).

The turning point came after Egypt's military defeat against Israel in 1967, followed by Nasser's premature death in 1970, and as a result of Prime Minister Anwar as-Sadat's economic 'opening' policy towards the West (*infitāḥ*), which seemed to be going hand-in-hand with societal disintegration (*inḥilāl*). Sadat, who lived in constant fear of the Nasserist 'Left' threatening to overthrow his regime, favoured the religious and heavily-persecuted opposition of the Nasser era, the Muslim brothers.[2] However, the more he proceeded on his way to open the country to foreign capital, the more the neo-traditionalists turned against him. 'Islam is the solution' (*al-Islām huwa al-ḥall*) became the slogan of the 1970s and after, fuelled by the fears of the professional classes that the liberation of the market would turn against them and their future aspirations. The opposition against Sadat became visible first in an anti-Western impulse which cherished Islamic values against Western indulgences; in the course of this the use of the 'Islamic dress' (*ziyy islāmī* — for both sexes) became popular.

The 'Islamic dress', with regard to the complex female dress code, oscillated between ritual and fashion. As a ritual, it denoted more than mere modesty of its bearer. Rather, it created something like a 'sacred sphere' as it demanded respect for the integrity of the person. It was attributed to the Islamic tradition, attached itself to a normative code and indicated a segregation of the sexes in public. The 'Islamic dress' became a demonstration against the national bourgeoisie and especially against the *nouveaux riches*, as the veiled woman came to represent a well-ordered community which rested on solidarity and values as opposed to the anarchic and libertine order of the capitalist dog-eats-dog society. As we shall see, this movement did not really mean to go back to the roots; at least, it did not mean the roots of the harem system which had disappeared with the decline of the Ottoman Empire. Rather, it fostered the idea of a gendered division of labour (including the labour-market) within an 'Islamic' modernity. Taking up the veil became a commitment to Islamic values which began with a *rite de passage* including several phases like a declaration of intent, the studying of the Koran and the successive covering of parts of the body (hair, shoulders, legs, hands and face). Interviews with young women have shown that there are several stages during which the woman felt 'not yet' mature enough to wear the complete veil.[3] However, the covering was — and is — highly ambiguous:

on the one hand it indicated the priority of values like marriage, motherhood and family, but on the other it also smoothed the way to a public society generally dominated by males.

Although Egypt was the first, it was neither the sole nor the most determined Arab country in which the Islamic movement took hold. For an insider, the process of modernisation and secularisation in Egypt and elsewhere had always been restricted to the urban elite, and while it was supported by the middle classes in times of prosperity, it was rejected by them in times of crisis, as was again the case under Sadat. Despite an increase in women's labour-force, the role models of the initial feminist movement in Egypt were steadily losing ground. Women from the Islamic past began to replace the 'famous women' of the West, and by the 1990s Islamic role models had the public opinion almost to themselves (Booth 2001: 59).

For an outsider this was an open contradiction as the trend manifested itself as being diametrically opposed to Western concepts of women's emancipation. After all, the new Islamism went — and still goes — even beyond traditional Islam in preaching (and condemning) the ritual impurity (*'awra*) of women. *'Awra*, literally 'nakedness', 'weak point' or 'flaw', relates to women and men alike, but while men's *'awra* is restricted to the genitals, women's *'awra* is greater: it comprises the upper part of the body as well and can extend to the whole body including hair, hands and mouth, even the voice. The basic assumption is the same as in traditional Islam. In the public sphere a woman's *'awra* serves as a cause for discord (*fitna*) among men, either in attracting attention or giving rise to violence or both (Ammann 2004: 85–86).[4]

Not surprisingly, neither the feminists nor the modern and secular state in Egypt and elsewhere adopted these arguments. Instead, they encouraged women to freely enter the public sphere unveiled. However, at a closer look it was obvious that the modernising attempts of the state boiled down to an invitation to enter the half-public working places in the factories, offices, schools, hospitals or media. Modernisation does not automatically lead to emancipation (McLeod 1991: 12), and regardless of its half-hearted attempts to improve the legal situation of women, the state never strengthened the enforcement of the laws. On the contrary, in the 1970s–'80s, the state continuously reduced women's rights, first in order to appease the Islamists and then to counter them (Hatem 1997: 4).

Paradoxically, even the vacillation in the discussion on the so-called 'Jihan's Law' (named after Sadat's wife) which aimed to improve the status of divorced women bears witness to the deterioration of the situation of women. When Sadat tried to enact the reforms in an authoritarian manner, he had to face not only religious but also Leftist and secular opposition. In the end 'Jihan's Law' was struck down on procedural grounds in 1985 (Bier 2005: 265). Therefore, it may be safely said that 'patriarchy successfully clung to its own privileges and continued to dominate in the private sphere' (Badran 1993: 44). Correspondingly, outside the family women were — and are — still vulnerable with regard to their reputation and freedom from bodily harm (McLeod 1991: 83).

Seen from this perspective, Islamist organisations and ideology had more to offer than the state, as they were closer to reality, particularly for ambitious young women from families of modest standing. For these families, the veiling served as proof of the young woman's earnest interest in acquiring the fundamentals of religious ethics and technical skills in order to fulfil her duties as a future mother and working woman. The organisations provided cheap (Islamic) clothing for the benefit of students who could not compete with the expensive clothes of their rich fellow-students. They also provided taxi services which helped the women avoid uncomfortable and embarrassing situations in overcrowded buses. They distributed learning material which helped the women to pass university examinations, and set up religious groups which served as an ideal place for a preliminary search for suitable marriage partners.[5] As Fadwa El Guindi wrote in the beginning of the 1980s: 'Therefore, a woman in public has a choice between being secular, modern, feminine and frustratingly passive (hence very vulnerable), or becoming a *mitdayyinan* [sic] (religious), hence formidable, untouchable and silently threatening' (El Guindi 1981: 481).

In the long run, i.e., between the 1970s and today, young women found it increasingly convenient to attach themselves to the Islamist call to the veil, as secularists offered them neither equality with their male colleagues nor protection from male abuse. This is all the more so as veiling is seen not as re-veiling, but as new veiling (McLeod 1991: 14). The new veiling, which in itself has turned into a kind of multi-coloured fashion (*ibid.*: 105), has no precedence in the Islamic past. Instead of restricting women to the closed circle of the family, it seems to have paved the way to an entrance into the public sphere (*ibid.*: 3). In the last few years, there has been a vigorous discussion around this point. Does the veiling, including its links to the other realms of religious, social and political life, provide and offer an opportunity for the emancipation of women or not? As social scientists tend to pose this question from the outside, I have chosen to present three answers from the inside. Formulated by writers of literature, they are subjective to their chosen medium (autobiography, autobiographical novel, novel), representative of certain — and different — strands of society, and unique or original for their documentary value. The authors are all female, but they differ in every other respect: one is an Egyptian Islamist, one a Palestinian feminist and the last a Lebanese expatriate living in France.

Gender and Public Sphere — An Islamist Apology

'The young men of the Institute (of Islamic Studies) look at me with an eye that is all astonishment. As though I were from another star that fell by accident on the Institute [...] My clothes are very short, my hair descending, hanging down wild behind my back [...] All stare at this strange creature [...] Me' (Malti-Douglas 2001: 18).[6] This is, in 1960 and in her eighteenth year, the starting point of a *rite de passage* in the life of the Egyptian Karīmān Ḥamza, as recorded in her autobiography *Riḥlatī min al-sufūr ilā al-ḥijāb* (My Journey from Unveiling to Veiling) which appeared, for the first time, in 1981. Born in 1942 a family of good standing and secular outlook, living in a reasonably bourgeois suburb of Cairo, Karīmān the daughter of a professor of journalism at Cairo University received an excellent education, married at sixteen and had children, obtained a university degree and became one of the most popular TV-announcers and anchorwomen in Egypt as well as a prolific author (Malti-Douglas 2001: 15–16).

Spiritual journeys, like Karīmān Ḥamza's, are not uncommon in Islamic literature, the most famous being Abū Ḥāmid al-Ghazālī's *al-Munqidh min al-Ḍalāl* (Deliverance from Error) from the eleventh century. Karīmān's closest contemporary, perhaps, is another Egyptian spiritual autobiography, Muṣṭafā Maḥmūd's *Riḥlatī min al-shakk ilā al-īmān* (My Journey from Doubt to Belief) which was to appear ten years later, in 1991. There is, however, a difference between the two titles which seems gender-specific and far from accidental. Both titles express the idea of a journey, but the journeys themselves are incomparable with each other. 'Muṣṭafā Maḥmūd moves from doubt to belief, Karīmān Ḥamza, from unveiling to veiling. He draws the reader to the mental aspects of the journey, she, to the vestimentary' (Malti-Douglas 2001: 16). For a spiritual autobiography, Karīmān Ḥamza's text is amazingly deeply concerned with the body.

Karīmān Ḥamza's depiction of the body as defined by and for men is an unusual and striking feature in the work of a Muslim woman. She rejects what her mother stands for, i.e., the exposure of the Western body (hair, breasts, make-up). Instead, she stands for the exposure of the covered Islamic body. As she becomes increasingly conscious of male dissatisfaction with her Western appearance, she finally accepts and adopts a complete veiling of her body and head. 'Once the corporeal change is effected, the fashion-conscious narrator does not shy away from describing her appearance, taking special pains to inform her readers that the new clothing is not only colour coordinated but also extremely elegant and modest' (Malti-Douglas 2001: 56). This consciousness corresponds exactly to Karīmān's real career, the journey from the initial invisibility of an average Westernised young student to the full visibility of a unique re-born Muslim TV-star. In fact, Karīmān Ḥamza was not the first woman who profited by her decision to embody 'Islamic' values. Zaynab al-Ghazālī (b. 1917), the famous Muslim sister,[7] laid claim to be exempted from obedience in marriage and child-rearing along with her claim to dedicate her life to the propagation of Islam.

Gender and the Generations — A Feminist Critique

'You whore! ... I drink your blood!' (Khalīfa 1990: 134), a young man shouts at his sister in the novel *Bāb al-sāḥa* (The Courtyard's Gate) of the Palestinian writer Saḥar Khalīfa, who was born in Nablus in 1941. Her arranged marriage at the age of eighteen ended in divorce, and her career has since taken her to the United States of America, where she completed a doctorate in American Studies, and back to the Westbank, where she established a Women's Resource Center (Harlow 2002: 13). Her fifth novel, published in 1990, marks a shift from a political to a more feminist viewpoint which she has maintained ever since. The novel, whose plot is set in the heart of Nablus in the late 1980s, picks up another kind of transformation than the one mentioned above. Its starting point is not so much the Islamist trend itself but the disintegration of tradition. Khalīfa's novel deals with the hardships of young women brought about by the premature transfer of authority from the generation of the fathers to the generation of the sons.

In the course of the Israeli occupation of the Westbank and Gaza from 1967 onwards, but increasingly during the Intifada, thousands of young men, particularly from the lower strata of Palestinian society were exposed to beatings, detention and arrest by the armed forces. When the young men were released from jail, the beatings were framed — by themselves as well as by their families and Palestinian society as a whole — as *rites de passage* that became central in the making of an adult, gendered (male) self with critical consequences for political consciousness and agency (Peteet 2000: 105). The scar, a mark intented to cause humiliation, was transformed into one of honour, manhood and moral superiority. 'But bodies do more than represent; torture and beatings are ordeals one undergoes as sacrifices for the struggle' (ibid.: 109). In effect, a decline of traditional authority in an otherwise traditional society took place. Instead of the generation of the fathers, the *shabāb*, the bands of stone-throwing boys and young men took the lead. The result was social imbalance. While mothers rose in esteem, young wives and sisters began to complain that their husbands and brothers returned from interrogation and detention with a new authoritarianism expressed in attempts to reduce their mobility, pressure to wear a veil and an increase in domestic violence (ibid.: 120).

These are the problems which Saḥar Khalīfa addresses when she narrates the stories of four women as their lives intersect in a Nabulsian brothel whose own local history recapitulates the significant pressures on the social order in which it is situated.

> 'The personal and social trajectories of these women cross in that forbidden terrain when the young men, the *shabāb*, of the Intifada must seek refuge in the same house from the Israeli patrols who

endeavor to regain control of the neighborhood and its byways from the demonstrating and resisting inhabitants' (Harlow 2002: 124–125).

In an unsentimental, lucid and courageous way which renders this novel somewhat unique among contemporary Palestinian literature, the author breaks national taboos when she has her characters struggle about the preponderance of the national cause, the laws of national and family honour, the superiority of the male fighters, the stigmatising of women as collaborators, the *shabāb*'s taking the law into their own hands, and the like. The new leadership of the young men, who combine the religious tradition of their fathers with their own nationalist fervour and revolutionary zeal, only adds to the disintegration of Palestinian society in general and the marginalisation of the women in particular.

Gender and Gender — An Experiment in Identity

'I would like to be both man and woman in my writing', said Hudā Barakāt, author of (*Ḥajar al-ḍaḥk*) (The Stone of Laughter) in an interview (Aghacy 1998: 192). Barakāt, born in Lebanon in 1952, comes from a liberal Christian family. In 1974, she graduated with a degree in French Literature, left for Paris a year later, but returned to Lebanon after the civil war broke out. There, she worked as a journalist, teacher and translator, as well as being an active member in a number of organisations. In 1989, she moved to Paris, where she lives as a writer and journalist, publishing in Arabic and French.

The Lebanese Civil War (1975–1990) brought about a whole range of novels, whose authors were mainly women.[8] Barakāt is one among them but, unlike her colleagues, she does not write from an autobiographic, female perspective at the margins of the war. Instead, her main character, Khalīl, is an ambiguous, androgynous, homoerotical figure, who rejects the war situation as one 'where gender identity is rigidly overdetermined' with a focus on male violence, 'where participation in the community through fighting is the basic touchstone of masculine identity, and where dedication to an ethnic group is measured by one's willingness to sacrifice oneself in battle' (Fayad 2002: 163). In this male-dominated and violence-ridden atmosphere, Khalīl retreats into a feminine, apolitical, uninvolved existence, keeping the male self in abeyance. He cooks and knits, cleans his room, and remains generally indoors, basking in a private domestic world where emotions and feelings remain the locus of existence and moral value, thus enjoying the freedom of marginalisation (Aghacy 1998: 187). Seen from the author's as well as her hero's perspective, the public sphere in Lebanon during the civil war is nothing to be sought after, not even for a man. But this is not the end of the story, as gender roles turn out to be stronger than individual strategies of escape.

Again, we witness a *rite de passage*, as becomes clear from the last and — with only four pages — shortest section of the novel. In these very last pages of the book, the hitherto omniscient author explicitly reveals being female, as she has to concede that her hero has slipped out of her hands and has chosen to re-enter the public sphere as a man. Throughout the novel, she has enveloped, overpowered and taken possession of Khalīl, constantly referring to him as 'poor Khalīl' (Aghacy 1998: 197). Now, at the very end, he revises his self-sacrifice and turns into the caricature of a man with a moustache, a leatherjacket and sunglasses, who starts his new life with the rape of a young woman, then proceeds to participate in the smuggling of weapons and melts into the body of war. In the last sentences of the novel, Barakāt 'exscribes' this creation of hers, Khalīl, after he has refused to respond to her calling his name. 'Her separation from him marks his entrance into the community, while she has chosen to stay outside it, and through that separation to be able to continue to write' (Fayad 2002: 178).

I have discussed here three literary texts with three *rites de passage*, none of which is precedented in the Islamic or Arabic tradition as they all stem from crises peculiar to the twentieth century. The first *rite de passage* is due to the decision of a young woman who passes through a process of religious rebirth, the second concerns a generation of young men who re-evaluate humiliation into a sign of masculinisation, and the third — the most fictional — presents an androgynous figure who sheds his skin in order to adapt to the notions of manliness of his compatriots. Yet, the three texts give only one answer to the initial question of whether the public sphere is male. It is male, in today's Cairo as well as in the occupied territories and war-ridden Lebanon. But the authors differ in assessment and outlook. Hudā Barakāt and Saḥar Khalīfa depict a development from the good to the bad or from bad to worse. Barakāt, who keeps the greatest distance from the parties involved in her story, whether Muslim Christian, or other (Fayad 2000: 173), comes to the conclusion that androgyny is unattainable and that the gap between the masculine and feminine worlds is unbridgeable (Aghacy 1998: 200). There is only one escape, 'the woman who writes', who trespasses her household circle by writing, an opportunity which was brought about by the breakdown of Lebanon's identity as an independent patriarchal polity (Cooke 1988: 12). Khalīfa shares this opinion with respect to the Palestinian situation, but she is less optimistic when it comes to the power of the argument. Her main male character, the *shabāb*-fighter Ḥuṣām, shrinks back from a revision of his firm political beliefs (Klemm 1993: 17). On the other hand, Khalīfa the citizen has always been active alongside her writing, in doing social work for women. Karīmān Ḥamza is far from considerations of this kind, as she firmly maintains that obeyance to God's commands will bring about a perfect society, but it is significant that she does not take notice of any other woman in the public sphere, be it Muslim or otherwise. She seems totally unaware of the fact that she made her career only on the condition that she would remain a female exception in a male universe, and it is this ambiguous, narcissistic and exhibitionist personality that is most striking in her account. To me it seems that there is no Islamic short-cut for women to enter the public sphere by way of observing the ritual of veiling, as the ritual of the veil is no mere artefact that has become a fashion, a form devoid of content and meaning, but is still a living performance and a strong means of keeping women away from full participation in the public sphere.

◈

Notes

1. For a general outline of the private vs. public sphere in Islam, see Ammann (2004); the contemporary Egyptian case of gender division is thoroughly discussed in McLeod (1991) and Zuhur (1992).

2. In 1928, the school-teacher Ḥasan al-Bannā founded the Muslim Brothers (*Iḫwān al-muslimūn*) which was soon to turn into the strongest opposition against the secularist forces in the Egyptian society. Although the *Brothers* were prosecuted and banned several times in the course of the decades, they turned out to be a success 16:15 story in the Arab world. Today, most — if not all — Islamists in one way or the other trace themselves back to the Muslim Brothers.
3. This is a notion which can also currently be observed on a whole range of websites and forums.
4. See also Stowasser (1993: 17–20); Malti-Douglas (2001: 37–39).
5. The first empirical study at Cairo University was conducted by El Guindi and published in 1981. For a comparison between the ideology of the state and the Islamists see Booth (2001: 67); Slyomovics (1995: 8–13); Stowasser (1993: 3, 6).
6. I have had to rely on the (extensive) quotations in Malti-Douglas' text as I was unable to get a copy of the original Arabic text.
7. Although Ḥasan al-Bannā invited Zaynab al-Ghazālī to merge her organisation with his, she refused as she wished to retain autonomy. However, she founded an organisation under the name *Jamā'at al-sayyidāt al-muslimāt* (Muslim Women's Association) which cooperated with the Muslim Brothers. After Hassan al-Bannā's assassination in 1949 until the early 1990s, she played a pivotal role in recognising and expanding the Muslim Brotherhood and its female counterpart.
8. Still the best and best-available research on this subject is the work of Cooke (1988), who coined the term the 'Beirut Decentrists' for the Lebanese women writers of that time.

References

Aghacy, S. 1998. 'Hoda Barakat's *The Stone of Laughter*: Androgyny or Polarization?', *Journal of Arabic Literature*, 29: 185–201.

Ammann, L. 2004. 'Privatsphäre und Öffentlichkeit in der muslimischen Zivilisation', in N. Göle and L. Ammann (eds) *Islam in Sicht. Der Auftritt von Muslimen im öffentlichen Raum*, pp. 69–117. Bielefeld: transcript.

Badran, M. 1993. 'Independent Women: More than a Century of Feminism in Egypt', in J.E. Tucker (ed.) *Arab Women: Old Boundaries, New Frontiers*, pp. 129–48. Bloomington: Indiana University Press.

Barakāt, H. 1990. *Ḥajar al-ḍaḥk*. London.

———. 1995. *The Stone of Laughter: A Novel*, transl. S. Bennett. Brooklyn, N.Y.: Interlink Books.

Bier, L. 2005. 'Law: Modern Family Law, 1800–Present, Egypt', in S. Joseph et al. (eds.) *Encyclopedia of Women & Islamic Cultures (EWIC)*, vol. II, 463–65. Leiden/Boston: Brill.

Booth, M. 2001. 'Infamous Women and Famous Wombs: Biography, Gender, and Islamist Concepts of Community in Contemporary Egypt', in M.A. Fay (ed.) *Auto/Biography and the Construction of Identity and Community in the Middle East*, pp. 51–70. New York: Palgrave.

Cooke, M. 1988. *War's Other Voices: Women Writers on the Lebanese Civil War*. Cambridge: Cambridge University Press 1988 (Berkeley: University of California Press 1996).

El Guindi, F. 1981. 'Veiling Infitah with Muslim Ethic: Egypt's Contemporary Islamic Movement', *Social Problems*, 28: 465–85.

Fayad, M. 2002. 'Strategic Androgyny: Passing as Masculine in Barakat's *Stone of* Laughter', in L.S. Majaj, P.W. Sunderman, T. Saliba (eds) *Intersections: Gender, Nation, and Community in Arab Women's Novels*, pp. 162–79. Syracuse: Syracuse University Press.

Hatem, M. 1997. 'Diskurse über Gender und politische Liberalisierung in Ägypten', *INAMO*, 9: 4–9.

Ḥamza, K. 1986. *Riḥlatī min al-sufkr il al-ḥijāb*. (Cairo 1981) Beirut: Dār al-fatḥ li l-ṭibā'a wa l-nashr.

Harlow, B. 2002. 'Partitions and Precedents: Sahar Khalifeh and Palestinian Political Geography', in L.S. Majaj, P.W. Sunderman and T. Saliba (eds) *Intersections: Gender, Nation, and Community in Arab Women's Novels*. pp. 113–31. Syracuse: Syracuse University Press.

Hatem, M.F. 2005. 'Egypt', in S. Joseph et al. (eds), *Encyclopedia of Women & Islamic Cultures* (EWIC), vol. II, 66–69. Leiden/Boston: Brill.

Khalīfa, S. 1990. *Bāb al-sāḥa*. Beirut: Dār al-ādāb.

———. 1994. *Das Tor*, transl. R. Karachouli, Zürich: Unionsverlag.

Klemm, Verena. 1993. 'Saḥar Ḥalīfas *Bāb as-Sāḥa*. Eine feministische Kritik der Intifada'. *Die Welt des Islams* N.S. 33: 1–22.

MacLeod, A.E. 1991. *Accommodating Protest: Working Women, the New Veiling, and Change in Cairo*. New York: Columbia University Press.

Malti-Douglas, F. 2001. *Medicines of the Soul: Female Bodies and Sacred Geographies in a Transnational Islam*. Berkeley et al.: University of California Press.

Peteet, J. 2000. 'Male Gender and Rituals of Resistance in the Palestinian Intifada: A Cultural Politics of Violence', in M. Ghoussoub and E. Sinclair-Webb (eds) *Imagined Masculinities: Male Identity and Culture in the Modern Middle East*, pp. 103–26. London: Saqi Books.

Slyomovics, S. 1995. '"Hassiba Ben Bouali, If You Could See Our Algeria": Women and Public Sphere in Algeria', *Middle East Report*, No. 192: Algeria: Islam, the State and Politics of Eradication (Jan.–Feb. 1995): 8–13.

Stowasser, B.F. 1993. 'Women's Issues in Modern Islamic Thought', in J.E. Tucker (ed.) *Arab Women: Old Boundaries, New Frontiers*, pp. 3–28. Bloomington: Indiana University Press.

Zuhur, Sh. 1992. *Revealing Reveiling: Islamist Gender Ideology in Contemporary Egypt*. Albany: State University of New York Press.

17

On the Representation of Presence
The Narrative of Devnārāyaṇ as a Multimedia Performance[1]

Aditya Malik

'What he (the lover-devotee) said'
As grass, as plant, as worm, as tree,
As many a wild beast;
As bird, as snake, as stone, as man,
As devil, and as demons;
As unbending celestial, as sage, and as god:
In a hurry,
Having taken birth upon birth, in ever different crowds,
Having grown so tired —
I came home, today,
Seeing
The golden feet in the very substance of our Lord!

Written in the ninth or tenth century by the Tamil devotional poet Manikkavacakar in the so-called *akam* style of composition, this poem has been translated from the original Tamil by the anthropologist Saskia Kersenboom in her book *Word, Sound, Image: The Life of the Tamil Text* (1995: 71). As a style of poetry, *akam* signifies an inner world of emotion and love, 'of intense longing and vulnerable yearning, an opening up until borders of the Ego melt and merge with the divine' (Kersenboom 1995: 70). In her commentary on the poem, Kersenboom points out that in the context of *bhakti* (Sanskrit: 'share, partake, enjoy, experience, feel') or devotion this poem expresses:

> The love between god and man (that) is consummated in the moment of grace (Tamil: *arul*). This experience redescribes — in

> fact, reshapes — reality [...]. This type of appropriation is deeply and openly devotional. It is believed to be two-sided: god appropriates man, and man appropriates god; god becomes man and man becomes god. This is not the recovery of 'meaning', but a recovery of 'Being'. (Kersenboom 1995: 71).

While we could spend considerable time debating the *meaning* of 'meaning' and of 'Being', I would like to draw attention to Kersenboom's purpose in making this distinction between the 'recovery of meaning and the recovery of Being'. This distinction implies a contrast between two kinds of textual activity — one, the activity of analytical, written textuality that scholars engage in, and the other, the spoken, performative textuality of what she calls the Tamil text:

> While the nature of the Western text is static, an object of analytical abstraction, and takes the form of a document, the Tamil text is organic in nature, a process of synthetic absorption, living a reality of performance. The application of both differs as well: while the document adds to a database that eventually will produce the ultimate interpretation a truth, the performance offers a becoming, an embodiment of life, here and now. These extremes are substantiated in their material representations. (Kersenboom 1995: 16).

While the Tamil text is rooted in ritual and performance that are played out in the multiple dimensions of space and time and of presence, the analytical activity of scholarship involves reducing these multiple levels to the single linear dimension of thought. While it is the job of the ritual specialist to 'render the text into meaningful action', it seems to be the job of the scholar 'to reduce meaningful action into text and to sever its umbilical cord to presence [...].' (Kersenboom 1995: 226). But if, as scholars, we seriously intend to go beyond the objectification of that which we 'study' — whether it is ritual or other forms of life — then we need to engage in a cross-cultural hermeneutics that allows the interpretative and representational modes of the cultures we seek to understand to critically impact our own interpretative and representational horizons.

In this essay I will extend the application of some of the considerations that Kersenboom raises with respect to the 'Tamil text' to my research on the Rajasthani narrative tradition of Devnārāyaṇ.

The question that arises here, and one that is also addressed by Kersenboom in her work on the 'Tamil text', concerns the scholarly representation of ritual performance in the context of Devnārāyaṇ's narrative. How does scholarship deal with the purpose of such a ritual, which is the elicitation or evocation of *presence*? Does, for example, the linear, static text of scholarship that is meaningful only in the context of analysis and interpretation, provide an adequate means of representation for a ritual performance that manifests an essentially ephemeral presence arising out of an oral-aural situation embedded in sensory experience? If the linear, written word is an inadequate mode of representing the ritual performance of the narrative of Devnārāyaṇ, what other possibilities offer themselves?

By providing a brief description of the ritual performance of the narrative, I will show that it is embedded in the simultaneous use of spoken and sung words, visual signs, bodily movement, musical instrumentation and audience participation. Furthermore, it will become clear that the spoken or sung word and visual sign, and, in fact, the entire performance are meaningful only in the context of manifesting and participating in divine presence.[2]

The oral narrative of Devnārāyaṇ, which has frequently been classified as an 'epic' is one of the most well-known folk narratives in Rajasthan.[3] The narrative is composed of two main parts. These are recognised by singers as being distinct halves, and are called Bagaravat or Bagaṛāvat Bhārat and Shri Devnārāyaṇ Kathā. The first half deals, as its title suggests, with the Bagaṛāvats or the Twenty-Four Brothers who are the ancestors of Devnārāyaṇ. The second half, as is also clear from its title, deals with Shri Devnārāyaṇ. While both halves of the narrative extol the heroic deeds of the Bagaṛāvats and Devnārāyaṇ, they also articulate different sets of values. Above all, this is apparent in the sources of sacred power that each give prominence to. In the first half, sacred power flows from the devotional, self-sacrificial deeds of the twenty-four brothers. In the second half, it issues directly from the divine acts of Devnārāyaṇ, an *avatāra* of Bhagavan. The narrative as well as Devnārāyaṇ's religious cult covers a large area extending over most of Rajasthan and Malwa, the north-western region of Madhya Pradesh.[4]

While observing and participating in performances of the narrative, I was confronted with a number of questions at the outset. Most immediate amongst these were: How is it recited or performed? Who are the performers? How is the oral recitation structured? What is the relationship between verbal narrative and visual narrative? Why is the narrative performed — what is its purpose?

I will begin this section with a brief description of the performance[5], before moving on to an analysis of the ritual performance within the framework of terms and categories used by singers and audience, and in particular, also the participatory category of 'presence'.

The narrative of Devnārāyaṇ is usually performed in the context of a *jāgraṇ,* 'awakening', vigil or 'night-wake'.[6] The purpose of a *jāgraṇ,* quite simply, is to evoke or manifest the *prakāsh* (Rajasthani: presence, radiance, appearance or splendour) of the deity Devnārāyaṇ, in whose presence performers and audience alike dwell and participate. The performance itself is described as *'paṛ vā̃cno'* ('speaking or reading the paṛ') implying the use of an elaborately structured 8 × 1.50 metre painted scroll, on which characters and scenes of the narrative are depicted. The literal meaning of the word *paṛ* is simply 'cloth'. As a ritual object, however, it is a *'calato devaro'* or *'calato mandir'*, i.e., a 'moveable' or 'moving' shrine or temple.[7] This notion of a 'portable' shrine provides a contrast to the 'fixed' or 'immovable' shrines or temples of Devnārāyaṇ in which the deity together with his two attendants Kala and Gora Bheru, and his four brothers[8] or his ancestors[9] are worshipped in the form of aniconic bricks (*ī̃th*). These forms of mobile and immobile worship are reminiscent of the concepts of the *'sthāvara'* and *'jaṅgama'* of Virashaivism. Here *'sthāvara'* represents the established, immovable and *'jaṅgama'* the moving or moveable:

> sthavara is that which stands, a piece of property, a thing inanimate. Jangama is moving, moveable, anything given to going and coming. Especially in Virashaiva religion, a Jangama is a religious man who has renounced world and home, moving from village to village, representing god to the devoted, a god incarnate. Sthavara could mean any static symbol or idea of god, a temple, or a linga worshipped in a temple. Thus the two words carry a contrast between two opposed conceptions of god and of worship. (Ramanujan 1973: 20f.).

In contrast to the Virashaiva tradition, in the case of Devnārāyaṇ it is the scroll, and the brick(s) in the temple that respectively embody Devnārāyaṇ. The emphasis here is therefore on the deity who is manifest in both places rather than in the person of the Bhopa, i.e., the singer or the priest. Moreover, it is interesting that the status of the Bhopas are reversed to that of the *jaṅgama* and *sthāvara*. Whereas in the Virashaiva tradition it is the mobile jangama who has renounced the world to incorporate god, and to move from place to place, in the Devnārāyaṇ tradition it is the *bhekdhārī* Bhopa or the Bhopa who tends the shrines and temples, who has renounced the world and taken a vow of celibacy. The *paṛdhārī* Bhopa or the itinerant Bhopa who performs in front of the *paṛ*, is, on the other hand, also called the *ghardhari* or householder Bhopa.

Performances take place in three distinct locations: (*i*) the home of a devotee, (*ii*) in front of a Devnārāyaṇ, or Savāī Bhoj temple,[10] and (*iii*) in front of the community meeting place (*hathai*). Performances can take place any time of the year except for the period called '*caumāsa*' (rainy season). During this time Devnārāyaṇ (and other Hindu deities) are supposed to be asleep. Performances begin on the eleventh day of the bright half of the month of Karttika which falls in October-November. During the '*caumāsa*' period the *paṛ* which is a central element in performances, is not unrolled. Narratives and songs may be sung, but in the so-called seated posture (*baiṭho gāṇo*) without the use of the *paṛ* and other dance techniques operative during 'regular' performances. There is thus a restricted use of the scroll and narrative during the deities' 'sleeping period'.

Once the scroll is unfolded and stood up, the space marked by it is made sacred. As a 'portable' temple, the centre of the scroll contains a life-size figure of Devnārāyaṇ, seated together with his four brothers in his royal court (*darbār*). A makeshift altar is set up in front of his image. Incense sticks are burnt, and offerings of grain and money are made. Each time an offering from a member of the audience is made the Bhopa or his co-singer blows a conch (*shaṅkh*) and proclaims the devotee's name and the quantity and item offered by him or her. The performance is interrupted here. Besides such interruptions, there are other pauses, during which the singers are offered tea or tobacco and are asked to be seated.

Such pauses can be relatively frequent so that out of a total time of about nine hours, six are spent in narrating and performing the story.

The singers wear a particular costume (*bāgā*) and use a stringed instrument called '*bīṇ*', or '*jantar*'. This double gourd instrument is worn by the main singer who plays on it while singing the narrative and pointing to corresponding sections of the scroll. His partner carries an oil lamp which illuminates the scroll during the performance that involves a series of movements back and forth along the length of the scroll, and between the two singers. The main singer may also undertake a series of pirouette-like steps at specific moments during the recitation. There is a great deal of interaction between singers and audience. Audience members often comment on the episode concerned or the singers' performance itself. The singers are also apt to comment on the audience's degree of attentiveness and so on. Audience members may also claim to know more than the singer who must claim and reclaim his authority as a 'specialist' by successfully answering 'critical' questions.[11] At times during pauses members of the audience may also entertain the audience by performing a few lines themselves.

The performance, besides being participatory and interactive, involves the use of different media: verbal, visual, musical and kinaesthetic. The sequence of a performance can be summarised in the following points:

i) Purificatory rites.
ii) Setting up the *paṛ*.
iii) Wearing of the costume by the Bhopa or singer.
iv) A *sevā* (service) for consecrating the *paṛ*.
v) Invocation of different deities.
vi) Spoken and sung narration of the story.
vii) Donations during frequent intervals.
viii) An *ārtī* (worship, praise) for deities and characters on the *paṛ*.
ix) A *sevā* at the end of the performance when the *paṛ* is rolled up again.[12]

However, beyond the external descriptions given above, what exactly are the scroll, the story and the performance in terms of meanings provided by the narrative tradition itself? Similarly, in this context, who are the singers and what is it that they are wearing? Further, what is the significance of bricks in the worship of Devnārāyaṇ? The following short narrative tells us about the creation of the scroll, of 'bricks', and the 'science of singing'. This brief account belongs to the last sections of the narrative when Devnārāyaṇ is about to depart to Baikunth[13] after having completed his 'mission' on Earth:

> Now about the science of singing (gāṇo bidyā).[14] It's like this. The day Bhagavān went to Indrasan — [when] he returned after 11 years [had passed][15] — after that, on that day Devnārāyaṇ's wife [Rāṇī Pīpalde], she said: 'Māhārāj, you've departed to Indrāsan. What about me? What's going to happen to me?' So, Devnārāyaṇ said: 'Rāṇī Pīpalde, now in my temples — the worship (pūjā) will be for you, the name will be mine.' So, in all the big temples there are, Rāṇī Pīpalde is worshipped in [the form of] bricks (ī̃ṭh).[16] Now when we go into a temple we say, 'Oh, ī̃ṭha kā Shyām.'[17] So, we make Devnārāyaṇ Shyām, and, for Rāṇī Pīpalde there is the worship of bricks. We say: 'Let's go to Demālī's devarā'.[18] After going inside the temple, the worship is done to bricks. So, the worship (pūjā) is Rāṇī Pīpalde's, and the name is Dev's. So, Bhagavān gave that promise to Rāṇī Pīpalde: 'Go, the worship is [for] you. The world will worship you.' [But Rāṇī Pīpalde said:]
>
> 'Well, Māhārāj, I'm alone. I don't feel good like this.' [So,] he created Bilā and Bili, two children [for her].[19] Even then, Rāṇī Pīpalde said: 'I won't let you go now!' So, when Devnārāyaṇ departed he wore a bāgā.[20] So, Rāṇī Pīpalde caught hold of the bāgā — of the cloth: 'I won't let you go!' Darbār[21] gave a jerk. So, Bhagavān sat down in the celestial chariot (*biyān*). And, from that (baga) a long piece of cloth was made. On that [piece of cloth], by Bhagavān's command — Bhagavān thought: 'I'm going to Indrāsan — what sign will the world have?' — on its own — because of Devnārāyaṇ — on that cloth 'mūrtīs'[22] appeared — a map (*naksho*) was created. So, on that day [on] the cloth of that 'bāgā', the 'paṛ' originated. And, these Pandits called Joshi in Bhilwara, the design was appropriated by them. At no other place is there Dev's map (*naksho*). [People] can of course make false images, but the real thing is over there. The real thing is not available anywhere else but in Bhilwara. Some say Brahmin or Pandit — only they do the writing of the paṛ.[23] Only they have the old plan (*naksho*) of the paṛ. And, from that day onwards there has been a paṛ — and it came to belong to Bhopas. And, the Bhāṭ's[24] bai[25] — by looking at it — everyone by looking

at the Bhāṭ's — Nārad Bhāṭ's[26] bais began the song. From then on the song originated, and the recitation of Bhagavān's story began. There you are sir! (Malik 2005: 39)

Although the row of bricks in shrines and temples are usually considered to be a manifestation of Devnārāyaṇ, the narrative above also connects them specifically to Devnārāyaṇ's wife, Rāṇī Pīpalde. Similarly, the creation of the *paṛ* is also indirectly caused by Rāṇī Pīpalde who holds onto Devnārāyaṇ's knee-long coat. In addition to this, two other important constituents of worship in shrines are related to Devnārāyaṇ's first two wives (Rāṇī Pīpalde being his third wife): the seat, throne or *pāt* to his wife Cā̃vtī, the daughter of a Dait (Sanskrit. *daitya*); and, the flame, light or *jot* to his wife Nāgkanyā, the daughter of a Serpent (Nāga) king.[27] Furthermore, in this account we find that two potent signs of continuity are being given shape: the one hard and indelible (brick), the other soft and fragile (cloth).[28] The story also expresses a notion of continuity in a very literal sense: the cloth of Devnārāyaṇ's coat is extended to accommodate the size and dimensions of a *paṛ*. Each individual *paṛ* is thus at least figuratively, if not literally, speaking for devotees, an extension of that first length of cloth.[29] Thus, similar to the case of the verbal narrative being transmitted from generation to generation after Devnārāyaṇ's bard and genealogist, Chochu Bhāṭ's recording of the events he had witnessed, the visual narrative in the appearance of the *paṛ* too is an 'unbroken' roll of sacred image and cloth. It is 'complete' in its form by being connected to Devnārāyaṇ's apparel. Moreover, the appearance of *mūrtis* on the scroll also substantiates the idea that it is a concrete manifestation of divine presence. Thus the *paṛ* is, in terms of the above story, an enduring replica of the past in the present. Not only this, it is also, like components of a Bhopa's costume, a recreation of Devnārāyaṇ's regal body constituted through items of his dress.

The creation of the *paṛ* and individual elements of a Bhopa's costume, as well as forms of worship in shrines, is not limited to Devnārāyaṇ's immediate self, but to the social extensions of it in the form of marriage bonds and kin-relationships. For example, the costume worn by Bhopas is composed of signs or emblems of the god and his wives: the coat (*bāgā*) and turban (*sāphā*) represent the god himself; the wrap of thin cloth worn around the coat represents Pīpalde; the ornament attached to the front of the turban, Devnārāyaṇ's first wife, Nāgkanyā; the peacock feather pointer used for referring to the *paṛ*, his second wife Cā̃vtī. This feature of the god's signs is also repeated in the items occurring in the shrines mentioned above. While the name (of temples) is the god's, the bricks, seat, and flame are signs of his wives. Moreover, the *bīn/jantar* played by Bhopas is considered identical to the one played by Chochu Bhāṭ. Finally, as another story shows, Bhopas themselves are the direct descendants of Devnārāyaṇ's son, Bilā.[30] Almost each and every important facet of the worship is therefore defined in terms of the god or through an extension of his own self in the person of his wives, children, or genealogist. By identifying these different features with the god, or his wives, children and genealogist, his devotees not only keep his memory alive, they also participate in the recreation and reconstruction of the god's 'extended' self as expressed through these different relationships.

Does the performance of the narrative of Devnārāyaṇ as it has been described above both in terms of its sequence and the narrative retold here, therefore, represent a coherent 'system' of ideas, or, indeed of communication? And, if it does, is there a specific framework in which the arrangement of terms and components can be placed? Are there distinct and articulate notions of what constitutes a text and what constitutes a ritual performance at play here? In other words, do the singers and devotees make use of meta-level concepts to describe the narrative and its performance?

The first term that provides us with a correspondence to 'performance' is *paṛ vā̃cno*. The external description of song, narrative, dance, pointing to the *paṛ*, audience participation, et cetera, is — for singers and devotees alike — simply called 'speaking or reading the *paṛ*'. The performance is not — as one might expect from a textually oriented perspective — described as 'narrating or telling Devnārāyaṇ's story'. The focus here is not on the 'text' as such, but on the scroll, which is an icon of the deity, and of the text. However, the scroll is not self-explanatory: it needs to be 'read', i.e., it needs to be 'decoded' and rendered meaningful by a specialist, namely the singer.[31] Each performance involves a deconstruction of the entirety of images on the *paṛ*, and a simultaneous reconstruction of its meaning. The meaning of the images becomes distinct or emerges through the juxtaposition of spoken and sung narrative together with visual images located on the *paṛ*.[32] The *paṛ*, therefore, is not read like a picture-book. It is read through a narrative which manifests on account of its own recitation. Only with the sung word do the images become meaningful.

Further, the Bhopa does not decode the images on the *paṛ* according to his own interpretation like an art historian may; he is bound by the interpretation of the images encoded in the narrative. The *paṛ*, according to the definition provided by the term '*paṛ vā̃cno*', is not, therefore, simply an illustration of verbal, narrative content. It is that which gets revealed through the interpretative framework provided by the narration. It would appear then that the imagery and iconicity of the *paṛ* is much more central to a performance than is the narration itself, since the ritual performance is about eliciting the presence of Devnārāyaṇ which is primarily located in his image. This iconic emphasis can also be traced in sentences such as '*paṛā̃ kā lekh*', meaning 'writing of the *paṛ*', that the singer whom I worked with, Shri Hukāmarām Bhopa, used in order to prove the existence and authenticity of specific passages and episodes from the narrative. The *paṛ* was 'proof' of the oral text, and not *vice versa*. Visual imagery and iconicity are thus considered primary to verbal expression. But without verbal expression, the meaning(s) of the images do not reveal themselves.

The 'images' on the *paṛ* are 'icons' in a special sense of the term.[33] They are not icons in the sense of being traditionally-conceived visual representations of religious themes, they are the iconic or *visual presence* of characters and scenes from the narrative. Even to claim that these images are strongly denotative in the sense of being icons, would, therefore, be to fall short of their meaning.[34] A term often used by singers when pointing to deities, persons, and animals on the *paṛ*, is that they are '*birājmān*', i.e., they are 'present', 'seated' or 'manifest'. The images of deities, persons, or animals et cetera, therefore, *are* those deities, persons and animals. There is no distance created between word, symbol and thing. This correlation is also evident in the case of the metaphor of 'written text' or 'script' (*lekh*). It is not as though the *paṛ* is simply a picture-book spread out to accompany the narration. The *paṛ* and its imagery is a concrete expression of the presence of the content of that imagery. This is particularly evident in the case of Devnārāyaṇ, himself, who is seated on his 'python throne' in the centre of the *paṛ*. The presence of Devnārāyaṇ in the two dimensional image is as real as the presence of a deity in *mūrtīs* in Hindu temples. The presence of Devnārāyaṇ and other deities or persons on the *paṛ* is crucially important because the performance is focussed on manifesting Devnārāyaṇ's *prakāsh* (presence, radiance, splendour). The activity of 'speaking or reading the *paṛ*' which involves not only the narration of the text, but also dancing, musical instrumentation et cetera, occurs within the larger, more fundamental context of 'presencing' Devnārāyaṇ. This key term indicates that the entire performance 'presences' Devnārāyaṇ, and makes his presence 'experienceable'. Unlike scholarly analysis, the narration does not stop at revealing or decoding the meaning of the *paṛ*. The decoding continues further than the semantic and cultural meanings into the domain of experiencing 'presence' (*prakāsh*). The culturally specific sense of both 'speaking or reading' (*vā̃cno*) and 'the written' (*lekh*) in terms of visual images of the *paṛ* extends into the realm of *presencing* the divine.[35]

Moreover, the narrative 'text' itself is not distinct from Devnārāyaṇ: it is an embodiment of the deity; it *is* divine presence rather than being a story *about* divinity, in the same way the scroll is not simply a representation of that which is depicted upon it. Knowledge exists and is created in the present moment of the performance — in the 'speaking' of the 'scroll'. Knowledge is not about compilation, building up information, stacking data, or even about 'discovery'.[36] While the narrative follows a linear structure, its telling is non-linear: it can be told from anywhere, creating reversals of time. Past and present exist simultaneously on the scroll, as do physical locations. It is a map of place, but also of time.

The narrative activity of telling the story of Devnārāyaṇ is, on several levels, as I have shown, about eliciting and establishing divine presence. To return to the distinction that Kersenboom draws between 'the recovery of meaning and recovery of Being'[37] it is evident that the ritual performance of the narrative of Devnārāyaṇ is about the recovery of divine presence or Being. This 'recovery of Being' is embedded in the different media that are involved in the performance of the narrative: the expression of spoken and sung words, visual signs, dance, costumes, musical instrumentation and audience participation.[38]

◈

Notes

1. This essay is based, in part, on sections from chapters two and three of my book on the narrative tradition of Devnārāyaṇ (Malik 2005). Parts of it have been revised in the context of the conference 'Change and Stability of Rituals' in New Delhi, October 2006.
2. There is no doubting the fact that performances are held for a number of reasons, such as the fulfilment of individual vows or during religious festivals. However, the binding feature of all performances beyond individual or group motivations is the celebration of the deity's presence. Without this, the fulfilment of vows and other religious observances do not make sense.
3. Together with the epic narratives of Pabuji, Gugaji, Tejaji, Ramdevji, Gopi Cand and Bharthari, it belongs to a rich and significant corpus of oral narratives current in Rajasthan today. See Binford (1976), Blackburn et al. (1989), Gold (1992), Lapoint (1978), Smith (1991).
4. Blackburn classifies the narrative under the category of so-called 'martial epics' in India that emphasise 'group solidarity' and are 'concerned with power, social obligation, and social unity; they turn on themes of revenge, regaining lost land, or restoring lost rights [...]. Martial epics celebrate external — often military or political — conflict and a warrior ethic.' (1989: 5)
5. Since my intention here is to provide an understanding of the 'concept' of performance, I do not describe the performance itself in great detail. The main features are summarised below. A complete documentation of a single night's performance would, as Thiel-Horstmann's study mentioned later shows, entail a monograph in itself. For details on the performance situation of Devnārāyaṇ, see further Miller (1980 and 1994).
6. Thiel-Horstmann (1985) provides a complete documentation of the *jāgraṇ* in the context of worship conducted by the north-Indian Bhakti sect, the Dadupanth. In the preface she notes that the *jāgraṇ* is temporally speaking, the most extended form of worship that occurs in front of the community. During the course of a *jāgraṇ* a number of texts are either sung or declaimed. The purpose of these texts is to 'awaken' the devotee, and to motivate him or her to be free of *saṃsāra*. She also notes that the documentation in published form denies the reader many other components of the night-wake (ibid.: 10). Again, the implication here is that the texts are embedded in a larger aesthetic, 'performative' situation, in which their meaning unfolds, thereby motivating singers and listeners.
7. Smith (1991: 8) refers to the scroll of Pabuji as a 'portable temple'.
8. In most cases Devnārāyaṇ is shown with his brother Bhūnājī, and also sometimes with his mother Sāḍu Mātā.

9. In particular his father Sāvāī Bhoj.
10. As mentioned above, Sāvāī Bhoj is Devnārāyaṇ's father. He is the leader of the twenty-four Bagaṛāvat brothers.
11. This is not unlike a situation scholars or other 'specialists' face.
12. See Mair (1988: 102), and Miller (1994).
13. Lord Vishnu's celestial dwelling place.
14. Bidyā can also be translated as knowledge.
15. Devnārāyaṇ is considered to be no more than 11-years-old when he accomplishes his task on earth. His four elder brothers are also understood to be only a few years older than this.
16. The self-referential interrelationship between visual narrative, verbal narrative, and religious cult is potently expressed in the fact that the image of the bricks is represented on the *paṛ* as well. The verbal narrative and the *paṛ* both refer to this manifestation of Devnārāyaṇ's power, while at the same time themselves being the result of that same power.
17. 'Krishna of Bricks'.
18. The shrine of Demālī is considered to be Devnārāyaṇ's first place of worship. It was established prior to his departure to Baikuṇṭh. The first priest to perform service (*sevā*) here was his son Bilā.
19. A son and a daughter. Whereas Devnārāyaṇ's daughter Bili recognises and acknowledges his divinity, his son is rebellious to the point of going through a great deal of physical suffering before assenting to his father's authority.
20. A knee-length outer garment worn by men. Bhopas wear this regularly during performances of the narrative. This item of their costume is supposed to represent Devnārāyaṇ. See below, for more details on other features of their costume.
21. 'King' or 'Royal Court'. Devnārāyaṇ is often referred to in this way, suggesting his royal character.
22. *Mūrti*s are strictly speaking not 'images' of a deity, they are a concrete manifestation of a deity and its divine power.
23. In reality, *paṛ* painters are not Brahmins, but derive their name from a lineage of artisans of craftsmen (*shilpi*) called Joshi.
24. The reference here is to the Bagaṛāvats' genealogist, Chochu Bhāṭ, who witnessed all the events of their lives, as well as that of Devnārāyaṇ's.
25. The book of records kept by a genealogist. (Hindi: *bahi*).
26. Chochu Bhāṭ is frequently referred to as *nāradā bhāṭ* implying his trickster-like qualities. The name also reflects an affinity between Devnārāyaṇ and Chochu Bhāṭ, and their *purānic* counterparts, Nārāyaṇa and Nārada.
27. The significance of Devnārāyaṇ's marriage to Rāṇī Pīpalde, and to his other two wives in the narrative is discussed in more detail in chapter seven of my book (Malik 2005).

28. These two forms of representation also allude to the different ways in which Devnārāyaṇ is conceived: formless and untainted (*nirākār, niranjan*), on the one hand, and, a regal deity (*darbār, ṭhākur*) with all the attributes of a king, on the other.
29. Although cloth as a material is more susceptible to decay than brick or stone, it is still a strong constituent of rituals and metaphors of connectedness and continuity. This is evident in rituals of tying fabrics together (as in marriage ceremonies in India); in the use of threads in initiation rites; in the wide-spread understanding of textile and fabric as being family heirlooms and, therefore, a source of wealth; or, for that matter, in the usage of terms related to weave, thread, fabric etc., to describe the *interwovenness* of society. On the cultural, economic, and political significance of cloth, see, for example, Weiner and Schneider (1989).
30. ibid.
31. Similarly Smith (1991: 17) writing on the related 'picture story-telling' tradition of Pabuji points out that '[...] the use of the phrase "reading the *paṛ*" is a valuable indication of the way in which bhopos conceptualize their work. They do not speak of "singing an epic"; they refer not to singing or narrative but to performance, and their term for performance invokes the cloth-painting. [...] We approach Pabuji through his *paṛ*, and we approach the *paṛ* through the bhopos "reading" of it'.
32. For an analysis of the *paṛ*, see also the work of Jain (1998), Singh (1995) and Smith (1991).
33. Icon can normally refer to a picture, reflection or likeness (Hebrew: *tselem*, Greek: *eikon*, Latin: *imago*). In the Judeo-Christian theistic tradition icon does not refer to the material picture itself, but to 'an abstract, general, spiritual "likeness"...' (Mitchell 1986: 31).
34. Miles (1985: 34) distinguishes between religious images that are either iconic, representational, impressionistic, or abstract. According to her, of these four types, iconic images are 'most denotative [...] that is, organized according to traditional depiction whose every detail [...] may be "read" by the worshipper in terms of a particular content of scriptural or historic significance. [...] The interpreter of images, like the interpreter of texts, must determine the denotation of the image as a preliminary step to suggesting the spectrum of meanings it was likely to have had for the different members of its historical community.'
35. It is interesting to note that the notion of 'speaking/reading' and 'writing' should relate to visual images in a predominantly oral tradition. The orality of the narrative, does not allow for a notion of

reading and writing connected to the written word, i.e., to the symbolic manifestation of language in script. It is, of course, surprising that concepts of reading and writing at all emerge in such a context. The occurrence of such terms could also be attributed to the fact that we are not dealing here with a primary oral culture, but with one that exists in relationship to written culture.

36. Hermeneutics, particularly in the context of nineteenth and twentieth century orientalist discourse, Kersenboom suggests, proved to have a hidden agenda. It was not, as Ricoeur postulates, 'to reproduce an interconnection, a structured totality by drawing support from a category of signs which have been fixed by writing, or by any other process of inscription equivalent to writing'. (Kersenboom 1995: 5). The scholarly drive toward textualisation and fixity, was, in fact, motivated by an implicit agenda: '[...] phenomena were not studied in order to detect their individual coherence and autonomy, but rather for the sake of something hidden, behind them: a *universal-validity-of-interpretation-upon-which-all-certainty-in-history-rests*.'
37. In her critique of the hermeneutical position outlined in the above note, Kersenboom points out: 'This cascade of concepts was bewilderingly strange to Tamil experts [...] interconnectedness, comparison, structured totality, fixation [...] produced constructs that had no physical shape or presence [...] The agenda of Tamil experts was a straightforward one: their language, and *eo ipso* their literature, were of divine origin, of divine substance and directed at a divine aim.' (ibid.) Furthermore, if there is going to be a departure from this agenda of modernity to arrive at a '*universal-validity-of-interpretation-upon-which-all-certainty-in-history-rests*', then there is a necessity also to break away from modernity's 'media of representation'. (Kersenboom 1995: 234). In this context, an interactive CD-ROM 'may therefore be considered a representation of human knowledge that is "post-modern" in the contrastive sense of the term: organic, flexible and concretely practical, communicative and playing with the categories of time and space. (ibid.: 235). An interactive CD-ROM while still perhaps being disconnected from 'primary' 'presence' has the dimension of sight, sound, movement and interaction. In the case of the narrative performance of Devnārāyaṇ, it would involve a multitude of media in the same way the performance of the narrative is a multi-media event.
38. I have being developing the representational possibilities offered by a DVD-ROM suggesting that this may provide a non-linear, multi-media modality that simulates the multi-medial qualities of the ritual performance of the narrative of Devnārāyaṇ. The interactive DVD-ROM on Devnārāyaṇ is currently under preparation with

collaboration of the Cultural Informatics Lab. at the Indira Gandhi National Centre for the Arts (New Delhi).

References

Binford, M.R. 1976. 'Mixing in the Color of Ram of Ranuja', in B.L. Smith (ed.) *Hinduism: New Essays in the History of Religions,* pp. 120–42. Leiden: E.J. Brill.

Blackburn, S.H., Claus P.J., Flueckiger J.B., and Wadley S.B. (eds) 1989. *Oral Epics in India.* Berkeley: University of California Press.

Gold, A.G. 1992. *A Carnival of Parting*: The Tales of King Bharthari and King Gopi Chand as Sung and Told by Madhu Natisar Nath of Ghatyali, Rajastan. Berkeley: University of California Press.

Jain, J. (ed.) 1998. *Picture Showmen: Insights into the Narrative Tradition in Indian Art.* Mumbai: Marg Publications.

Kersenboom, S. 1995. *Word, Sound, Image: The Life of the Tamil Text.* Oxford: Berg Publishers.

Lapoint, E.C. 1978. 'The Epic of Guga: A North Indian Oral Tradition', in S. Vatuk (ed.) *American Studies in the Anthropology of India,* pp. 281–308. Delhi: Manohar Publishers.

Mair, V. 1988. *Painting and Performance*: Chinese Picture Recitation and its Indian Genesis. Honolulu: University of Hawaii Press.

Miles M.R 1985. *Image as Insight*: Visual Understanding in Western Christianity and Secular Culture. Boston: Beacon Press.

Malik, A. 2005. *Nectar Gaze and Poison Breath: An Analysis and Translation of the Rajasthani Oral Narrative of Devnārāyaṇ.* New York: Oxford University Press.

Miller, J.C. 1980. 'Current Investigations in the Genre of Rajasthani *Paṛ* Painting Recitations', in W.M. Callewaert (ed.) *Early Hindi Devotional Literature in Current Research,* pp. 116–25. New Delhi: Impex India.

———. 1994. *'The Twenty-four Brothers and Lord Devnarayan: The Story and Performance of a Folk Epic of Rajasthan'*, Ph.D. thesis, University of Pennsylvania.

Mitchell, W.J.T. 1986. *Iconology: Image, Text, Ideology*, Chicago: Chicago University Press.

Ramanujan, A.K. 1973. *Speaking of Siva.* Harmondsworth: Penguin Books.

Singh, K. 1995. 'The Painted Epic: Narrative in the Rajasthani Phad', in B.N. Goswamy (ed.) *Indian Painting*: Essays in Honour of Karl J. Khandavala. New Delhi: Lalit Kala Akademi.

Smith, J.D. 1991. *The Epic of Pabuji*: A Study, Transcription and Translation. Cambridge: Cambridge University Press.

Thiel-Horstmann, M. 1985. *Nächtliches Wachen*: eine Form indischen Gottersdienstes. Bonn: Indica-et-Tibetica-Verlag.
Weiner, A.B. and Schneider J. (eds). 1989. *Cloth and Human Experience.* Washington: Smithsonian Institution Press.

About the Editors

Christiane Brosius heads a research project entitled 'Agency and Territorial Rituals in India' (Collaborative Research Centre 'The Dynamics of Rituals', Heidelberg). She is co-founder of Tasveer Ghar/House of Pictures: A Digital Network of South Asian Popular Visual Culture (www.tasveerghar.net). With a background in Cultural and Social Anthropology, Art History and Art Education, and having studied in Frankfurt, Oxford and London, Brosius worked on and published about the cultural historian Aby Warburg (Hamburg, Germany) in her Master's Thesis (1999). For her book *Empowering Visions: A Study on Videos and the Politics of Cultural Nationalism in India* (London: Anthem Press 2005), Brosius explored the iconography, rhetoric and production context of video propaganda and political rituals of the Hindu Right (especially late 1980s to 1990s). Her latest book will be out in 2009, entitled *India's Middle Class: New Forms of Urban Leisure, Consumption and Prosperity* (New Delhi: Routledge), with case studies about real estate advertising and urbanisation, religious leisure parks, heritage tourism and rituals, themed weddings, lifestyle specialists and magazines. Additional research interests are urban anthropology, diaspora studies and ritual performance.

Ute Hüsken is Professor of Sanskrit at the University of Oslo (Norway). She was educated as an Indian and Tibetan Studies scholar and as a Cultural Anthropologist. Since 2005 Hüsken is the head of the project, 'Initiation, Priestly Ordination, Temple Festivals, and Ritual Traditions in the South Indian Temple City of Kancipuram.' Until June 2007 she was member of the executive committee of the Collaborative Research Centre 'The Dynamics of Ritual', Heidelberg University. Since 2008 she is co-chair of the steering committee of the Ritual Studies Group of the American Academy of Religion. Hüsken has published several articles and edited volumes on ritual. She is the editor of *When Rituals Go Wrong: Mistakes, Failure, and the Dynamics of Ritual* (Brill 2007) and co-editor of *Words and Deeds: Hindu and Buddhist Rituals in South*

Asia (Harrassowitz 2005). Her book-with-DVD, *Viṣṇu's Children: Prenatal Life-cycle Rituals in South India* (Harrassowitz) was published in 2009. Currently, she is writing a book on the acquisition of ritual competence in Hindu traditions.

Notes on Contributors

Anindita Chakrabarti works in the area of Sociology of Religion and Social Movements. She received her doctoral degree from the Department of Sociology, University of Delhi in 2007 and is currently the Assistant Professor of Sociology at the Department of Humanities and Social Sciences, Indian Institute of Technology, Kanpur, India. Her publications include 'Assertive Religious Identities, the Secular Nation-State and the Question of Pluralism: The Case of the Tablighi Jamaat' in *Assertive Religious Identities: India and Europe*, edited by Satish Saberwal and Mushirul Hasan, 2006, New Delhi: Manohar and 'Judicious Succession and Judicial Religion: Internal Conflict and Legal Dispute in a Religious Reform Movement in India' in *Permutations of Order: Religion and Law as Contested Sovereignties*, edited by Thomas G. Kirsch and Bertram Turner, 2009, London: Ashgate. She was a Visiting Research Scholar at the University of California, Berkeley in 2005. Her current research project is on a nineteenth century Islamic movement in Bengal.

Angelos Chaniotis, formerly Professor of Ancient History at the Heidelberg University (1998–2006) and associate speaker of the Collaborative Research Centre 'The Dynamics of Rituals' (2002–2006), is currently Senior Research Fellow for Classics at All Souls College at the University of Oxford. In 2010 he will be joining the Institute for Advanced Study in Princeton as Professor of Ancient History. His research focuses on the social and cultural history of the Hellenistic World and the Roman East, Greek religion and Greek epigraphy. His books include *Historie und Historiker in den griechischen Inschriften* (1988), *Die Verträge zwischen kretischen Poleis in der hellenistischen Zeit* (1996) and *War in the Hellenistic World: A Social and Cultural History* (2005). He currently directs the project 'The Social and Cultural Construction of Emotions: the Greek Paradigm' (Advanced Investigator Grant of the European Research Council, 2009–2013).

Fletcher DuBois, Full Professor in the departments of Educational Foundations and Integrated Studies in Teaching, Technology and Inquiry at National-Louis University, Chicago and guest researcher at the Medical Psychology department of Heidelberg University Clinic and member of Collaborative Research Centre 'The Dynamics of Rituals', is currently coordinating a project involving both universities in promoting critical media literacy in research, teaching and learning. He has written on the biographical method, museum pedagogy, catharsis and most recently on image and ritual. He is also a professional singer and songwriter.

Susanne Enderwitz, Prof. Dr., graduated in Islamic Studies and Religious Studies from the Free University of Berlin, in Alexandria, Paris and Jerusalem. From 1984–1989 she was assistant and from 1991–1998 assistant professor at the Institute of Islamic Studies at the Free University of Berlin. Since 2002, she is professor for Arab and Islamic Studies at Heidelberg University. She has authored numerous publications on women, Islam and veiling. Other focuses of her research are medieval and modern Arabic literature, classical and modern religious literature, medieval and modern Arabic history.

Fabrizio M. Ferrari was educated in Indology at the Ca' Foscari University of Venice (Italy) and received his Ph.D. from SOAS (University of London) in 2005. He taught South Asian religions and Religious Studies at SOAS and from 2007 is lecturer in Religious Studies at the University of Chester. He specialised in the study of South Asian popular Hinduism and folklore and has published on Bengali religions, with particular reference to village disease goddesses and healing rituals. His first book is on the Bauls of Bengal (*Oltre il confine, dove la terra è rossa. Canti d'amore e d'estasi dei baul del Bengala*, Milan: Ariele, 2001) while his second one discusses the *gajan* festival of Bengal (*Guilty Males and Proud Females: Negotiating Genders in a Bengali Festival,* Kolkata: Seagull, forthcoming 2010). He is finalising the first monograph in English on Italian anthropologist and historian of religion Ernesto de Martino (*Ernesto de Martino on Religion: The Crisis and the Presence*, London & Oackville: Equinox, forthcoming 2011) and is editing the forthcoming volume *Health and Religious Rituals in South Asia:*

Disease, Possession and Healing (Routledge). He researches into subaltern studies, ritual theory and folklore studies.

Sudhir Kakar, psychoanalyst and novelist, has been Lecturer at Harvard University, Research Fellow at Harvard Business School, Professor of Organisational Behaviour at Indian Institute of Management, Ahmedabad and Head of Department of Humanities and Social Sciences at Indian Institute of Technology, Delhi. He has been a Senior Fellow at the Centre for Study of World Religions at Harvard as also a visiting professor at the universities of Chicago (1989–92), McGill, Melbourne, Hawaii and Vienna. He was a Fellow at the Institutes of Advanced Study, Princeton and Berlin, Watumull Distinguished Scholar, Fellow of the National Academy of Psychology and has been the recipient of Bhabha, Nehru and ICSSR National Fellowships in India. Currently, he is Adjunct Professor of Leadership at INSEAD in Fontainbleau, France and lives in Goa. Kakar's fifteen books of non-fiction and four of fiction include *The Inner World* (in its 16th printing since its first publication in 1978), *Shamans, Mystics and Doctors, Tales of Love, Sex and Danger, Intimate Relations, The Analyst and the Mystic, The Colors of Violence, Culture and Psyche,* (with K. Kakar) *The Indians: Portrait of a People* and (with Wendy Doniger) a new translation of the *Kamasutra* for Oxford World Classics. He is also the author of the novels *The Ascetic of Desire, Ecstasy* and *Mira and The Mahatma.* His latest book is *Mad and Divine: Spirit and Psyche in the Modern World.* His books have been translated into twenty-one languages around the world.

Saskia Kersenboom is Associate Professor of Theatre Studies at Amsterdam University, The Netherlands. Indology and Theatre Studies at Utrecht University resulted in her Ph.D *Nityasumangali* on the Devadasi Temple Dancers in South India (1984). The investigation of oral tradition, performance and problems of representation led her to the exploration of multimedia to complement academic publishing. Her monograph *Word, Sound, Image:The Life of the Tamil Text* with an interactive CD set a landmark in multimedia documentation as early as 1995. Other than her academic work, she pursues an artistic career as a teacher, dancer and choreographer based on her apprenticeship in South Indian music and dance since 1975. This aspect of her work is accessible at Paramparai Foundation (www.paramparai.eu)

Robert Langer, member of the Collaborative Research Centre 'The Dynamics of Rituals' and academic associate of one of its subprojects at the Heidelberg University's Department of Languages and Cultures of the Near East (Islamic/Ottoman Studies), studied Oriental Studies and Cultural Anthropology at Heidelberg (M.A. in 2000), Damascus, Ankara and Istanbul. He was member of an 'Emmy-Noether Research Group' (2000–2002, DFG) on Zoroastrian rituals at the Institute for Religious Studies, Heidelberg University, where in 2002 he completed his Ph.D.-dissertation on the interaction of Muslim and Zoroastrian shrine worship in Iran, which was awarded as 'Cultural Research of the Year 2002', Ministry of Culture, Iran (Ph.D. in 2004). His fields of research are Anthropology, Geography and History of Religion, especially of the 'Muslim World'. After working in Iran with contemporary Zoroastrians, he is now conducting fieldwork with Alevi and Yezidi groups in Turkey, Armenia and West-European Countries ('diaspora'). He lectured at the University of Berne and is currently teaching at Heidelberg University.

Aditya Malik has a Ph.D. in Indian Religions and a *Habilitation* (professorial degree) in Modern Indian Studies from the Heidelberg University. He has done extensive field research on pilgrimage, oral narratives and ritual performance in Rajasthan and Uttarakhand, publishing several edited books and monographs and numerous articles in these areas of research including two volumes on the oral narrative of Devnarayan from Rajasthan (*Nectar Gaze and Poison Breath: An Analysis and Translation of the Rajasthani Oral Narrative of Devnarayan*, OUP, New York, 2005, and *Shri Devnarayan Katha: An Oral Narrative of Marwar*, D.K. Printworld, New Delhi 2003). He is currently preparing a monograph and a series of articles on narratives and rituals of divine embodiment, and alternative legal and healing practices in the Central Himalayas as well as a literary and historical study of a medieval Sanskrit poetical work from Rajasthan. He has held fellowships of the German Research Council and the Israel Academy of Sciences and has been the Resident Representative of the South Asia Institute of the Heidelberg University in India. He is a UNESCO International Consultant and founding member of the newly established New Zealand South Asia Centre. Aditya Malik is currently Associate Professor/Reader in Indian Religions in the School of Social and Political Sciences at the University of Canterbury, New Zealand.

Frank Neubert is currently 'Oberassistent' at the Institute for the Study of Religions, University of Lucerne. He has been a member of the Collaborative Research Programme on 'The Dynamics of Ritual', Heidelberg, 2005–2008. His research interests concern the history of South Asian religions (especially modern history and Western forms of Hinduism and Buddhism), the sociology of religions as well as studies in modern Western religious discourses. He has recently published a book on the International Society for Krishna Consciousness (*Krishnabewusstsein*, Remid, 2009).

Tulsi Patel, Professor of Sociology, teaches at the Department of Sociology, Delhi School of Economics, University of Delhi. Her research interests include gender and society, anthropology of reproduction and childbirth knowledge systems, medical sociology, sociology of the kinship and family and old age. She has authored, *Fertility Behaviour: Population and Society in a Rajasthan Village* (OUP, 1994), and edited *The Family in India: Structure and Practice* (Sage, 2005) and *Sex Selective Abortion in India: Gender, Society and New Reproductive Technologies* (Sage, 2007). She has published several articles in national and international journals and is on the editorial board of scholarly journals. After being the Convenor of the Indian Sociological Society's Research Committee 19 on Age and Social Structure for six years, she is presently the convenor of its Research Committee 12 on Population, Health and Society. She was awarded the Rotating Chair: India Studies which she occupied at Heidelberg University for a semester in 2005–06. She was the coordinator of the Higher Education Link Programme with the Department of Sociology, University of Manchester, UK (1999–2004), and was also an honorary Research Associate there from 2001–04, besides being a Commonwealth Fellow at London School of Economics and Shastri Fellow at McGill University, Canada.

Karin Polit is a research fellow in the Collaborative Research Centre 'The Ritual of Dynamics' since 2005. After studying Anthropology, in Germany and Australia, she conducted research in Indonesia, the Netherlands and Northern India. Her main interests lie in the fields of Performance Studies, Medical Anthropology and the Anthropology of Youth. For her Ph.D. thesis, she has done extensive research amongst low-caste village women in the Indian part of the central Himalayas . Since then she has worked with traditional medical practitioners in India and ritual specialists involved in ritual healing as well as with traditional and new ritual performers of Garhwal and Uttaranchal. She is currently writing a book on divine performances of northern India and has started a research project on youth, education and health.

Kerstin Radde-Antweiler is an assistant professor at the Institute for the Scientific Study of Religions at the University of Bremen, Germany. She received her diploma in Protestant theology at the Heidelberg University and finished her doctoral dissertation, *Ritual Design on the Internet: Reception and Invention of Magical Rituals of New Wiccan Groups,* while she was a member of the Ritual Dynamics Collaborative Research Centre at the Heidelberg University. She has conducted research on wedding rituals in *Second Life* and edited a special issue on virtual-world research for *Online–Heidelberg Journal of Religions*.

William S. Sax was born in Washington State and educated in Seattle, Madison, Benaras and Chicago, where he completed his Ph.D. in Anthropology in 1987. He taught and conducted research at Harvard University for two years as a Harvard Academy Fellow, and after that fulfilled a lifelong dream by moving to Christchurch, New Zealand where he taught Religious Studies for eleven years. In 2000 he became head of the Department of Ethnology (Social Anthropology) at the South Asia Institute in Heidelberg. He has written extensively on ritual, performance, gender and pilgrimage. His current work focuses on ritual healing, stress and industrialisation, and 'folk psychology' in Hindi-speaking areas of North India.

Barbara Schuler is Associate Director at the Center for Buddhist Studies, Asia-Africa-Institute of the University of Hamburg. She studied Indology (classical and modern), with a focus on Tamil, Indian History of Religion and Social Anthropology at the universities of Heidelberg (South Asia Institute) and Hamburg, at Madurai and Chennai, as well as at the Hebrew University of Jerusalem, and was awarded a Ph.D. by the University of Hamburg. Since 1997 she has frequently taught Tamil language and culture at the Department for Indian and Tibetan Studies at Hamburg University. She has mainly worked on classical and modern

Tamil literature. Her recent research focuses on ritual and text in local south Indian traditions, particularly on their interaction. She also engages in visual anthropology. Her recent publications are *Of Death and Birth: Icakkiyamman, a Tamil Goddess, in Ritual and Story*. Wiesbaden: Harrassowitz (Ethno-Indology 8) and a Film on DVD, *Of Death and Birth: A Ritual of the Velalas in Palavur,* India. Wiesbaden: Harrassowitz.

Udo Simon read history, Islamic studies, anthropology and general linguistics at Mannheim and Heidelberg. After completing M.A., he was a member of a research unit working on language processing in social context. He received his Ph.D. with a dissertation on medieval Arabic rhetorical theory. After working as a musician and in publishing, he taught at the Department of Languages and Cultures of the Near East in Heidelberg. Before doing research within the framework of the Collaborative Research Centre 'The Dynamics of Ritual' he worked as a visiting professor of linguistics and communication studies at the Faculty of Social and Cultural Studies at the University of Applied Sciences Darmstadt. His chief concerns are Arabic studies, Islam, the sociology of religion, and migration studies.

K.K.A. Venkatachari, born in 1930, lives in Chennai (India). He received his *Kalakshepan* (traditional training) under his father K.K. Appan Tirumani Swamy and Karpangadu Venkatachariar Swamy, and studied Vyakarana Siromani at the Ubhaya Vedanta Vardini in Sriperumbudur. For five years he also studied Tamil with Sri V.M. Gopalakrishnamachariar, the commentator on the Kamba Ramayana. He received his Ph.D. at Utrecht University, the Netherlands, under Jan Gonda and Kamil Zwelebil in 1975. He was repeatedly invited as visiting professor at Harvard University and the University of California at Berkeley, and is the founder (and was a long-time director) of the Ananthacharya Indological Research Institute (post graduate centre), Mumbai.

Rolf Verres is Medical Director of the Institute of Medical Psychology, Centre for Psychosocial Medicine, University Hospital of Heidelberg. Since 2002 he has been working as head of the project 'Ritual Dynamics, Salutogenesis, and Use and Abuse of Psychoactive Substances' as part of the Collaborative

Research Centre 'Dynamics of Ritual' in Heidelberg. His main research interests are: use and abuse of psychoactive substances in relation to ritual studies, subjective theories of illness, psycho-oncology, spiritual care, health psycholology and music therapy. He has co-edited the volumes *Rituale erneuern* (Renewing Rituals, Psychosozial-Verlag, 2006) and *'Therapie mit psychoaktiven Substanzen: Praxis und Kritik der Psychotherapie mit LSD, Psilocybin und MDMA* (Therapy with psychoactive substances: approaches to, and critique of psychotherapy with LSD, Psilocybin and MDMA, Huber-Verlag, 2008).

Jan Weinhold studied psychology at the Humboldt University of Berlin. Since 2002 he has been working as a research psychologist within the RISA-study (Ritual Dynamics, Salutogenesis, and Use and Abuse of Psychoactive Substances) as part of the Collaborative Research Centre 'Dynamics of Ritual' Heidelberg. His research interests cover the use of psychoactive substances in relation to ritual studies, drug-abuse prevention, cross-cultural psychology, altered states of consciousness, and systemic psychotherapy. His Ph.D. project ('Controlled use of illicit psychoactive substances within therapeutic professions') deals with functions, settings, and meanings of physicians', psychologists' and psychotherapists' use of illicit drugs. He has published articles in the field of ritual studies and drug-use, intercultural dream research, and has co-edited the volumes *Rituale in Bewegung* (Rituals on the Move, LIT-Verlag, 2006) and *'Therapie mit psychoaktiven Substanzen: Praxis und Kritik der Psychotherapie mit LSD, Psilocybin und MDMA* (Therapy with Psychoactive Substances: Approaches to, and Critique of Psychotherapy with LSD, Psilocybin and MDMA, Huber-Verlag, 2008).

INDEX

agency, concepts of ix
AIDS-ammā 11, 144–45, 159–61, 163–64, 168; creation of 160. *See also* smallpox goddess; Śītalā
AK Party (*Adalet ve Kalkınma Partisi*) 95
alaṅkāra tīpārātaṉai 178, 180, meaning of 193n20
Alevi(s) 10–11, 88, 90, 102; anti-Sunni 112; cultural performances of 98; in the diaspora 101–02, 116n10; European 109, 113; German 103; identity of 116; internet sites of 112; Kurdish 90, 104; media stations run by 112; *Muharrem* fast and 107; organisation *CEM Vakfi* 111–13; organisation in Germany 11, 104; religious identity 109; religious practice 97–98; from Turkey 95, 107, 109
Alevism or Yezidism 90–94, 96; essence of 99–100; modern 111, 114–15; revival of 108
'Alî, veneration of 89–90, 92
alternative modernity 43–46; treatment 243
animal slaughtering 132–33, 180, 224, 225. *See also* sacrifice
Appadurai, A. 300–01, 304–06, 308; and Breckenridge 300, 304–06
Arati as ritual 244
artificial goddess, worship of 163
avatar 331–48, 351–52n4
Avrupa Alevi Birlikleri Konfederasyonu 113
Balaji temple 244–46, 250n7
al-Bannā, Ḥasan 366n2, 366n7
Barākāt, Hudā 363–65
barat or *jaan* 275, 277
Barbers (Ampaṭṭars) 173–74, 181, 184–87, 196n51; ritual of 182–83
bath, of goddess 179; of gods 62, 296; with milk 296; and myth 153; public 134. *See also* purity
beauty industry 284
Bektashi order by Hacı Bektaş 100, 103, 111
bhagats (healers) 246–47
bhaktipherī 9, 10, 55–58, 63, 65, 69, 70
bhūmipūjan 58, 60–61, 63–64, 71
Bhopa, 373–78; costume of 376, 379, 381n20
Boddy, Janice 236
Bourdieu 19, 242, 248, 249, 312, 318, 327, 348; *habitus* of 312; practice theory by 19, 248–49, 327
Brahmanic temple priests 15
Brahmotsava festival 324
Burhdeva play 42, 43
burning torch 191

cāmar as *mūrti* 168n21
Caldwell, Sarah 207
cāmiyāṭi 176, 178, 185, 191
Carrier-Group (German: 'Trägergruppe') of ritual 102–04
caste 9, 16, 30–31, 37, 44, 60, 67, 108, 156, 274; and kinship 49,

51, 52; context of 66; *dede* 91, 108; of priests performs death rituals 294
Celvakanapati, T.S. 320
cemevis 93–94, 112–13; modern 104. *See also* Alevis
cem-rituals 91–94, 102–04, 111, 113, 115; by adding Qur'ân recitations 104; ceremony of 110; in Europe 93, 107, 115; performances of 93–94
Christian ritual, element of 106–07
cinna melam, small band of *devadasis* 311, 320–23
cleanliness 83–84, 105, 127–30, 132–35; al-Qaraḍāwī on 134; in Turkish Culture 118–19n22; Harun Yahya and 134–35. *See also* bath, purity.
community of practice, of Alevi 115; concepts of 117n14; virtual 11, 92–94, 114
Complementary and Alternative Medicine (CAM) 236–37
Confirmation and First Communion 257–61; Joan G. Miller on 262
'confirmation' ritual in Germany 254
cult foundations and emotion 226–29
culture industry and Indian wedding 280–88. *See also* online wedding

Dadaji's wife Tai's birthday 60
Dalit 20
dance, ritual 30, 37–38, 40–41, 46, 59, 94, 104, 109–10, 176, 240, 309; and costumes 46; of deity 178; groups 110, 113; at night 40; possession 191; and songs 41
daris 37; as Narad, or Burhdeva 38–39, 41
darkhast 244, 246; *parhez* 244
darśana 53–54
darshanic gaze 17
dedelik 106, 108
dedes 91, 93, 96, 102, 104, 106–11, 115
Deity Worship Research Group 81
demon 63, 192n12, 240, 243. *See also pēy*
devadasi/devadāsī 174–75, 312, 320–27, dance 320; as *nityasumangali* 322, 390
devil, in obsessions, whispering of 129–30
Devnārāyaṇ 21, 370–73, 375–79; oral narrative of 379, 383n37; shrines or temples of 372
devotional songs 61, 72n7; Svadhyaya 53, 59
devotionalism (*bhakti*) 295
dharma 145, 153, 164, 318, 327
dīkṣā 65
Dikshitar, Muttusvami 320
Dikshitar, Ramasvami 320
'Dimensions of ritual' as concept by Jan G. Platvoet 105
Dissociative Identity Disorder (DID) 239, 240, 249n1. *See also* spirit possession
Dissociative Identity Phenomena (DIP) 239. *See also* spirit possession
domestic rituals 5, 294–95, 306n3; twenty-four life-cycle rituals (*saṃskāra/sanskār*) 5, 67, 108, 272, 294
Douglas, Mary 70, 203
dowry 271, 273–74, 279, 290n3. *See also kanya daan*
drummers 37–38, 178
Durkheim, Émile 2, 280

ekādaśī 56
emotions, and funerary rituals 220–23; of hatred 224; language of 217; in rituals 212–15; rituals to manipulate 212–15; and tensions 215–20

Fadwa El Guindi 359
'father rituals' 205. *See also* mother rituals
female deity (*devi*) 37, 146–47
female infanticide 277
fertility/reproduction 165, 176, 179–81, 186, 192n11, 271, 325, 327
fire walking (*tīmīti*) 182–83
flowerbed 177–84, 187, 190, 193n23
'folk Islam' in Ankara 96; Turkish 101
folk, healers of Bengal 145, 155, 157–59
folk performance of arts (*karakam*) 182
food 38–39, 56–57, 65–66, 70; for gods (*naibedya/naivetiyam*) 157, 296–97
formality 1, 7, 19, 22
Frazer, James George 2
funerary ceremony 222–23

Gauḍīya Vaiṣṇava, practices 84; religious tradition 79
gender and the generations 361–63; in identity 363–65; and public sphere 360–61
Germany, non-German immigration to 139–40n20
ghar-jamai, practice of 274
al-Ghazālī 128–29; on excessive cleaning 129–30; precepts of 129; on visiting bathhouse 129
ghost 242–47, 249. *See also* spirit possession
ghulûw traditions 89
gift 272, 288; virgin daughter as 272, 275; and Marcel Mauss 275, 290n5. *See also kanya daan*
goddess, iconography of 147, 182; maternal names of 146, 152
Goffman, Irving 3–5
Grimes, Ronald 3, 4, 253, 258, 330; on memories 13
group weddings 287
guilt, definition of 228
gurukkal 319, 322

help-seekers 243–44
'heretic' 99, 104
heritage 8–9, 11, 32, 35; intangible cultural, 34; ritual as cultural 8, 9, 32, 99
Herzig, Thomas as Tamāl Kṛṣna Goswami 77–79, 86n5. *See also* International Society for Krishna Consciousness (ISKCON)
heterodox Islam 88–89, 92, 100, 101, 111
honours (*mariyātai*) 223, 297–300
http://www.secondlife.com 331
humanities as text-focussed 18
hypergamy 273–76, 277, 280

Ibn Qayyim al-Jawziyya, Ḥanbalī jurist 127, 130
Ibn Rushd 130–31
Icakki temples 194n26
Icakkiyammaṉ, Tamil goddess 172–73, 175, 183, 185–86, 189; worship of 191n2, 26, 194n34; riot at Maṇṭaikāṭu temple of 194n26. *See also koṭai*
ikhlāṣ 128
ikhtilāf 128, 130
'images' on *paṛ* 376–79
'imagined community' of Benedict Anderson 32

Imams, role of 89; twelve 104, 109
Indian Folk Theatre Festival 43; music 45
International Society for Krishna Consciousness (ISKCON) 10, 76–84, 85n1, 391, in America 76, 77; history of 76–77; members of 83; religious practices of 77–78; Satsvarūpa Dāsa Goswami on 80; Vrindavan to establish temple of 82
Islamisation of ritual script and *decorum* 104

jāgraṇ 372; Thiel-Horstmann on 380n6
jajmān 61, 62, 63, 73n20
Jakh *devtas* 37, 40
James, William 206–07
janmāṣṭamī 58–59
'Jihan's Law' 359

kaḷḷi 174, 175; milkweed 192n11
Kallimachos 212
kanya daan 272, 274, 275–76, 287, 288–89; and female foeticide 277–80; Levi-Strauss on 277; Marcel Mauss on 275; as '*manya*' 276
Karīmān Ḥamza's 360–61, 365
karma 5, 51, 52, 63, 69; fruits of 51, 63, 68; theory of 68–69
Khalīfa, Saḥar 361–62
Kizilbaş, 90, 114, 119n24
Koṭai, meaning of 191n3; festival 172–73, 175, 191n3; rituals 172–78, 181–86, 188, 189, 196n47; story of 174–76, 184
Kumaratantra 324–25
Kumaratantra Skandotsavavidhi 325
Kurdish Workers Party' in Turkey as PKK (*Partiyê Kârkerân-ê Kordestân*) 90

Lakṣmīdevī 295
language, logic of 248; as medium 18–19; Talal Asad on 328
left-and right-hand communities, rituals of 194n35
Lewin, Kurt 256
'life over death' 320
lokasaṃgraha 52, 72n5

Manikkavacakar 323; *akam* and 369
marapu- 'Prose of World' 311–12, 314, 315, 318–21
'marijuana cigarette' 254–55
Markali 323
marriage 272; as symbolic act 289; ceremonies 16
Mauss, Marcel 275, 290n5
marutal 312–18
material culture 98; and aesthetisation 104
Mevlevî Sufism 112
Mevlevîlik 112
middle class 273, 278–79, 281, 283–85, 290n2; rituals of *phera* and *kanya daan* in 280, 288; wedding among 286–87
modernisation 9, 21, 22, 356–58
monotheism 124, 128
'mother rituals' 205. *See also* 'father rituals'
motivational psychology 253–54, 256, 258
Mukund, K. 299, 302–04
Museumisation 3
Muslims, in diaspora 107, 113; Germany diaspora and purity concepts 131–36; heritage 124–31; 'sects' 99; Sunni environment in Turkish 107; in Western societies 131–32; woman 56, 134, 361
Mustafa Kemal (Atatürk) 103, 104

Nāṭārs 173–74, 176, 185–86, 187; ritual of 181. *See also* Vēḷāḷas' ritual; as Shanar 194n36
nagasvara, players 311–12, 320, 321–25
nagasvaram 'sound of snake' 311–12, 320, 321–25; art of 320
naimitta 324
Naimittikarcana — festival ritual 324–25
Narad performances 41–42
Narasiṃha 295
nātasvaram 178–79
Nityaracana 321–24
nityasumangali 322, 390. *See also devadasis/devadāsīs*

ocakzade, non-practising 108, 110
ocakzade-dedes to conduct rituals 108
offerings 157–58, 163, 275, 322, 373
Oktar, Adnan 134
online, *murti darshan* 17 23n3. *See also* rituals 17, 330–31, 343, 350; religion 331
Ottoman–Iranian dualism 100
otuvar singer 322, 323
Öztürk, Nuri, Turkish theologian 134

Palani, T.C. 320
Pandanus odoratissimus 178–79, 182
'Patterned Dissociative Identity' (PDI) 239–41, 249–50n2
performances ix, xi, 4, 8, 12, 18, 29–34, 319–20, 371, 373, 380n2; as cultural truths 34; *Jakh*'s procession and Narad's 37–41; *paṛ vačno* 377–78; Richard Schechner on 326; ritual traditions 30, 33–34
periya melam, or, 'big band' 311, 320
peshi, practice of 244–49
pēy and *pūtam* 192n12
picture storytelling' tradition 382n31
pigs, taboo on 138n4
Pillai, T. Natarajasundara, *nagasvaram* player 311, 326
play, acts of 41–43
possession rituals 241–42, 243–47; and body-mind System 242–48; Cardeña on 238; Klass's categorisation of 239–40; 249–50n2; Krippner on 238; 239–40; Pakaslahti on 243–45 247;
prasād/prasādam 69, 70, 80–81, 158, 164, 298, 322
prayer as ritual act 125–28, 130
priests 15, 37, 215–16, 219, 220–21 303; fees (*dakṣinā*) 294
public rituals. *See* temple rituals
pūjārī 179. *See also* priests
punya 275, 289
purification and *dynamisation* 126
purity, Ahmad Reidegeld on 135; as norm 132
puruṣārtha 52, 72n4

Qāsim Amīn 356

rāmnavamī 58–59
raga etukulakambhoji 325
Rajput *jatis* 37
Ramanujan, A.K. 313; context-sensitive logic 314
Rapaport, Roy 203
re-Islamisation of Turkey 91
religious images 382n34
rituals ix; Barbara Myerhoff on 29; bedtime 206–08; calendar 58–64; commitment 249; concept of 22; definition of 4–6; depth 188, 193–94n22, 32; design to social order 184–87; difference 312–14; as discursive *topos* 79, 106, 110; as dynamic ix–x, xi, 1, 124, 172, 253, 260,

262; efficacy 342–48; and emotions 13–14; government-affiliated temple 174, 183–84; as human action 1; Jack Goody on 6; of *kanya daan* 16, 274, 279, 289; online 331; patterns 6–7, 15, 161, 164; performative traditions 43; of possession 14; practice of South India 294; purity 124–25, 127, 129, 135, 218, 228, 319; S.J. Tambiah on dynamic aspect of 71; singing 38, 40, 59, 91, 101, 158, 176 193–94n32; social dynamics of ix, x; structural dynamics x–xi; transfer x; understanding of 2; William Robertson Smith on 29
ritual shares 296–301; as 'luxury goods' 304, 305; as property 304–06; Simon Harrison on 305; in Varadarāja Temple 301–04
ritual transfer x, 11–12, 112, 340–44, 350; concept of 95, 340; in e-rituals 340; between Turkey and Germany 99–101. *See also* 'transfer of ritual'

sacrifice 5, 16, 40, 52, 61, 62, 64, 73n18, 91, 108, 162, 184, 189, 210–13, 217, 218, 275
śakti 154, 163, 164
Śītalā, in Bengali villages 157, 163; cult of, 11, 144–45, 164; as 'humoral' and 'theurgic' 164; meaning of 146–47, 152–53; presence of 146, 153–55; ritual of 154–59; as 'smallpox goddess' 145–52; as theophany of disease 164
Śītalā-pūjā 145, 154, 156, 158–59, 163, 165, 168n26; beliefs of 162–63; as euphemistic name 152; generally representation of 167n10
sacred, laws 212, 215–18, 226, 230; listening 53, 55; regulation 212, 214, 216, 218–20, 226–29, sacrifice 275. *See also* offerings
salvation, B.K. Mukherjea on 73n18
samadhi-sthal 246, 247
sandhi 322
sangha of listeners 53–55
saṃskāra/sanskār 5, 57, 64–69, 294; illustration of 68; concept of 68–69; meanings of 73n15
Santoshi Ma goddess 11
'*satsangī*' 49, 71n1
Schechner, Richard 3
'science of singing' 375
Second Life 17, 20 330–33; Jakobsson's qualitative survey on 333; and online-weddings 20, 333–40, 344–46, 350, 351
Self Determination theory 263
self-containment 180, 183
semah dance 94, 104, 109. *See also* dance, ritual
Shankland, David 117n15
'shares' (*paṅku*) 300
Shiism, tradition of 100
sin: *See* guilt, definition of
'smallpox goddess' 11, 144, 145–52, 154, 159–60. *See also* Śītalā
smallpox myth of 152–54, 159, 163
Smith, William Robertson 2, 29
smoking, marijuana 254, 255, 257, purifying 178
'source' ritual 173
'spirit possession' 14, 236–37 237–41; and rituals of Body-mind System 241–42; rituals 243–47
Śrīla Prabhupāda's teachings 76–84
stage performance 44; costumes of 45; modern stage performances 46; performance in villages 43–45

Stratonikeia, singing of hymns in 213
Sufism 112, 132
sunna 130
Sunni Islam 101, 103, 128, 131; ritual elements of 107
superstition 43, 202–03
svadharma 318
Svadhyaya 9, 50–53; anti-ritualism of 69–70; *bhaktipherī* 55; chants *Isa Upanishad* 53; and food taboo 66–67; *gṛhasthāśram* 51; John D. Kelly on 70; on *karma* 52; *lokasaṃgraha* 52; Louis Dumont on 50; Martha Kaplan on 70; *mokṣ* 51; N.R. Seth and 55; origin myth 50–51; Pandurang Shastri Athavale 50–52; Patrick Olivelle on 66; ritual of *bhūmipūjan* 60–64; rituals of sacred congregation 71; Video Kendra 'sermon centres' 53–54; *Yajña* 5, 52, 72n5, 52
Svadhayī 50, 57–58; through *bhaktipherī* 55–58; celebrations of 59

Tambiah, Stanley 3
Tamil language 316, 393; *Col atikaram* 314, 315; *Tolkappiyam* 314–15, 318, 320, 326
tantriks 247
Taylor, Charles 265
'teleporting' 336, 352n11
temple rituals 295–96, 299; material expression of 297, 304; South Indian 19, 300–01
Tevaram 323, 325
tīrtakārar 298
Tilakam, P. 321–22
timeless other 3
tradition 12–13, 19, 312, 315, 317, 326; D.R. Purohit on 41; Devnārāyaṇ 373; illusion of 29; Islamic 356–57, 362, 364; oral 319–20; picture storytelling 382n31; as theatrical 37, 41, 43; Virashaiva 373
'traditional performer' 19
'transfer of ritual' ix, 97, 105–13, 114, 173–74; concept of 95; ritual from Turkey to Germany 95. *See also* ritual transfer
triadic sign system, C.S. Peirce on 314, 317
trikāl sandhyā, reciting 65
Turkish *Alevi–Bektaşi Federasyonu* 113; to German 104; 'spiritual language' 105; values 105
Turkishness, culture of 97
'Türk-Islam Synthesis' 104
Turko-Islamic mysticism 112
Turner, Victor 3, 15, 317
'Twice born' 53, 72n8

umma 124–25, 130
upanayana 49–50, 86n8
Upanishads 72n9
Uttarakhand 9, 30–31, 35–36, as *Dev Bhumi* 30; heritage industry of 33–35

Vaiṣṇava 76, 78, 79, 81–85; festivals of 81–82
Vaiṣṇavism, transfer to West 76, 77, 82, 84–85
van Gennep, Arnold 2
variolation 143–45, 155–56, 167n17
variolators 145, 155–56, 158; vs folk healers 159
Vaṭakalai sect 296
veiling 20–21, 359–61; ritual of 365
Vēḷāḷas 173, 175–76, 189–90; forms 192n4; ritual 177–81, 188;

self-containedness of ritual of 196n53, 54
villuppāṭṭu (bow-song) 173–74, 176; text 174, 175–76, 178, 181, 184, 186, 187, 192n11, 195n49
'Virasat' heritage festival 43
Virtual Worlds 20, 330–31, 332–33, 343, 350–51
virtualisation of ritual 110, 116
Viṣṇu called Varadarāja 295
voluntary initiation (*dīkṣā*) 49

washing 125, 128, 130–31, 134–35, 205, 227; god 298. *See also* bath, of god; ritual 128, 203
wedding ritual 20, 272–74, 276, 281; cuisine/dishes at 281–83, 287; designer garments for 280, 281, 283, 287; designer jewellery 283; films on 285; location 281; services of 282–83
woman, emancipation 358, 360; exclusion of 228; rights and duties of 21; ritual impurity (*'awra*) of 358
worship 370; acts of 41–43; AIDS-goddess 144, 159; *bhakti* 54; concept of 17; of Devanārāyaṇ 375–76; of 'disease goddesses/spirits' 167n16. *See also* Śītalā; in ISKCON 81; to Kṛṣṇa 80; of Śītala 145, 159, 161; of smallpox goddess 11; and Svadhyaya 50; temple 78; through tilling 71; Zoroastrian shrine 391